THE THEOLOGICALLY FORMED HEART

The Theologically Formed Heart

Essays in Honor of David J. Gouwens

edited by
**Warner M. Bailey,
Lee C. Barrett III,**
and **James O. Duke**

with a foreword by
D. Newell Williams

◂PICKWICK *Publications* • Eugene, Oregon

THE THEOLOGICALLY FORMED HEART
Essays in Honor of David J. Gouwens

Copyright © 2014 Wipf and Stock Publishers. All rights reserved. Except for brief quotations in critical publications or reviews, no part of this book may be reproduced in any manner without prior written permission from the publisher. Write: Permissions, Wipf and Stock Publishers, 199 W. 8th Ave., Suite 3, Eugene, OR 97401.

Pickwick Publications
An Imprint of Wipf and Stock Publishers

199 W. 8th Ave., Suite 3
Eugene, OR 97401
www.wipfandstock.com

ISBN 13: 978-1-62564-191-5

Cataloging-in-Publication data:

The theologically formed heart : essays in honor of David J. Gouwens / edited by Warner M. Bailey, Lee C. Barrett III, and James O. Duke.

xvi + 282 p. ; 23 cm. —Includes bibliographical references.

ISBN 13: 978-1-62564-191-5

1. Theology. 2. Reformed Church. 3. Kierkegaard, Søren, 1813–1855. 4. Gouwens, David Jay. I. Title.

BT28 T451 2014

Manufactured in the U.S.A.   09/11/2014

All Scriptural texts, except as where noted, are reprinted from the Common Bible New Revised Standard Version Bible, copyright 1989. Division of Christian Education of the National Council of the Churches of Christ in the United States of America. Used by permission. All rights reserved.

Contents

List of Contributors and Editors • vii
Acknowledgments • xi
Foreword by D. Newell Williams • xiii

Theological Reflections

1 Passionate Doctrine: David Gouwens and the Role of Subjectivity in the "Yale School" • 3
   —*Lee C. Barrett III*

2 Reflections on Religious Pluralism: Disciples Re-imagining Mission 1941–1973 • 24
   —*Don A. Pittman*

3 "The Church Militant": A. Maude Royden and the Quest for Women's Equality in the Inter-War Years • 47
   —*Susan J. White*

4 The Best Friend of Jesus: A Model for Pastoral Leadership in the Gospel of John • 72
   —*Nancy Claire Pittman*

5 Self-Made Eunuchs as Model Disciples: Matthew 19:12 in Narrative and Historical Context • 89
   —*Jennifer Sylvan Alexander*

Reformed Theology in Service to the Church

6 Theological Education in a Secular Age: Challenges and Possibilities • 117
   —*Nancy J. Ramsay*

7 The Aesthetics of Persuasion: Rhetoric in Calvin's *The Golden Book of the True Christian Life* • 140
   —*Warner M. Bailey*

8 Hearts Kindled: Reformed Theology and *Glory to God: The Presbyterian Hymnal* • 163
 —*Michael Waschevski*

9 Learning to Live with and Love Our Neighbors: Setting Genesis 2 and John 21 in Conversation • 178
 —*Stephen W. Plunkett*

10 World-Filling Word: The *extra Calvinisticum* and Interfaith Dialogue • 194
 —*Cynthia L. Rigby*

11 Robert Elliott Speer, Some Transatlantic and Ecumenical Considerations • 211
 —*Kenneth Cracknell*

Studies in Søren Kierkegaard

12 Kierkegaard on Anxiety and Original Sin • 231
 —*C. Stephen Evans*

13 At the Foot of the Altar: Kierkegaard's Communion Discourses as the Resting Point of His Authorship • 241
 —*Sylvia Walsh Perkins*

14 Kierkegaard for *This* World: Thinking with Kierkegaard about the Desire for Security as a Sickness unto Death • 264
 —*Paul Martens*

Publications of David J. Gouwens • 279

Contributors and Editors

Jennifer Sylvan Alexander is a doctoral student in the Graduate Department of Religion at Vanderbilt University. Her dissertation centers on Matthew 19:12.

Warner M. Bailey is Director of Presbyterian Studies at Brite Divinity School, Texas Christian University, following retirement as senior minister of Ridglea Presbyterian Church of Fort Worth, Texas. He is the author of *The Self-Shaming God Who Reconciles, A Pastoral Approach to Abandonment within the Christian Canon*.

Lee C. Barrett, III is the Henry and Mary Stager Professor of Theology at Lancaster Theological Seminary. He is the author of *Kierkegaard* in the *Pillars of Theology* series and *Eros and Self-Emptying: The Intersections of Augustine and Kierkegaard*. He has written numerous essays on Kierkegaard and nineteenth-century theology, and has co-edited two volumes concerning Kierkegaard and biblical interpretation.

Kenneth Cracknell was Distinguished Visiting Professor of Theology at Brite Divinity School from 1996–2006. He has written many books and articles including *Justice, Courtesy and Love: Missionaries and Theologians Encountering World Religions 1846–1914* and *In Good and Generous Faith: Christians and Religious Pluralism*.

James O. Duke is the I. Wylie and Elizabeth M. Briscoe Professor of History of Christianity and History of Christian Thought at Brite Divinity School. His books and articles, including the introductory textbook *How To Think Theologically*, have focused on theological method, hermeneutics, and ecumenical dialogue.

C. Stephen Evans is University Professor of Philosophy and Humanities at Baylor University. He has published more than 15 single-authored books, and the most recent ones are *God and Moral Obligation* and *Natural Signs and Knowledge of God*.

Paul Martens is an Associate Professor of Religion (Christian Ethics) at Baylor University. He has published *The Heterodox Yoder* and numerous articles on various themes in Christian ethics, especially the thought of Søren Kierkegaard.

Don A. Pittman is the William Tabbernee Professor of the History of Religions, Emeritus, at Phillips Theological Seminary. His notable publications include *Ministry and Theology in Global Perspective: Contemporary Challenges for the Church* and *Toward a Modern Chinese Buddhism: Taixu's Reforms*.

Nancy Claire Pittman is Vice President for Academic Affairs and Dean and Associate Professor of the Practice of Ministry at Phillips Theological Seminary. Ordained by the Christian Church (Disciples of Christ) in the Southwest, she has served as a minister in several churches across Texas or Oklahoma and preached or lectured in numerous congregations and regional and national events.

Stephen W. Plunkett was pastor of St. Andrew Presbyterian Church, Denton, Texas (1989–2014). He is the author of *This We Believe: Eight Truths Presbyterians Affirm*, and an article on conversion in *The Encyclopedia of Protestantism*.

Nancy J. Ramsay serves as Professor of Pastoral Theology and Pastoral Care at Brite Divinity School. Her publications give particular attention to critically engaging therapeutic resources, intimate violence, emerging paradigms in pastoral theology and care, and resisting oppressive responses to forms of difference such as gender, race, class, and sexuality.

Cynthia L. Rigby is the W. C. Brown Professor of Theology at Austin Presbyterian Theological Seminary and an ordained minister in the Presbyterian Church (USA). She is the co-editor of *Blessed One: Protestant Perspectives on Mary* and the author of *The Promotion of Social Righteousness*. She blogs regularly for the religion section of the *Dallas Morning News* and is currently completing a book on grace.

Sylvia Walsh Perkins is a Scholar in Residence at Stetson University and has been an adjunct professor and visiting associate professor in philosophy at Stetson since 1989. She has written extensively on Søren Kierkegaard including *Kierkegaard: Thinking Christianly in an Existential Mode*. She has served twice as president of the Søren Kierkegaard Society in the United States.

Michael Waschevski is Associate Pastor at First Presbyterian Church of Fort Worth, Texas and member of the Presbyterian Committee on Congregational Song, which has produced *Glory to God: The Presbyterian Hymnal (2013)*. He has published in *Presbyterians Today* and *The Presbyterian Outlook*.

Susan J. White is Harold L. and Alberta H. Lunger Professor Emerita of Spiritual Resources and Disciplines, Brite Divinity School. She is the author of *A History of Women in Christian Worship* and (with Kenneth Cracknell) *An Introduction to World Methodism*. She resides in Norwich, Vermont.

D. Newell Williams is President and Professor of Modern and American Church History of Brite Divinity School. He is co-editor of *The Stone-Campbell Movement: A Global History* and *The Encyclopedia of the Stone-Campbell Movement* and author of *Barton Stone: A Spiritual Biography*. He has written widely on the history of the Christian Church (Disciples of Christ).

Acknowledgments

The editors express their deep gratitude to the individuals and congregations who have made generous gifts to support the publication of this work.

Congregations

- First Presbyterian Church, Fort Worth, Texas
- Ridglea Presbyterian Church Foundation, Fort Worth, Texas
- St. Andrew Presbyterian Church, Ruth Anderson Committee, Denton, Texas

Individuals

- The Reverend Dr. Lucia Kremzar
- The Reverend Dr. Joretta L. Marshall
- The Reverend Warren and Katherine Moody
- The Reverend Betty Youngman

Foreword

—D. Newell Williams

The Theologically Formed Heart invites the reader to consider the role of theology in the formation of virtues and passions and, conversely, the role of virtues and passions in understanding Scripture and theology and living a Christian life. It is offered in appreciation of the teaching, scholarship, and service to church and world of Professor of Theology David J. Gouwens.

Professor Gouwens joined the faculty of Brite Divinity School at Texas Christian University in 1983. He arrived at Brite with a newly minted Ph.D. from Yale University (1982). He had previously completed a B.A. at Hope College, Holland, Michigan, and both the M.Div. (1973) and S.T.M. (1974) at Yale Divinity School. While at Yale he had served as a Teaching Assistant in the Divinity School and as Visiting Lecturer at Hope College and in the Residential Colleges of Yale College.

Professor Gouwens soon became known at Brite as an excellent classroom teacher and as a valued and trusted conversation partner and advisor. He was Brite's nominee for a teaching award in 1989 and again in 1990. He later received Brite's highest teaching awards: The Louise Clark Brittan Endowed Memorial Faculty Excellence Award (1998); The Brite Divinity School Distinguished Teaching Award (1998) and later its successor, The Brite Divinity School Award for Distinguished Achievement as a Creative Teacher and Scholar (2009); and the Catherine Saylor Hill Endowed Faculty Excellence Award (2001 and, again, in 2010).

Meanwhile, he was busy revising his Ph.D. dissertation into a book that was published as *Kierkegaard's Dialectic of the Imagination* (1989). This book was followed by *Kierkegaard as Religious Thinker* (1996). In addition, he contributed numerous journal articles and chapters in books on aspects of Kierkegaard's theological contributions. He also co-edited with Lee C. Barrett, *The Paul L. Holmer Papers*, in three volumes (2012), based on research in the posthumous Holmer papers housed in the Yale

University Special Collections. A long-term research interest in aesthetics in the Reformed tradition has borne fruit in published articles and reviews and a manuscript currently in progress. Throughout his authorship, Professor Gouwen's distinctive contribution to theology has been the wedding of the rigor and clarity of analytic philosophy (particularly Wittgenstein), with Kierkegaard's attention to Christian pathos in order to illumine the central motifs of the Reformed tradition.

Professor Gouwens's service to church and world has included both the academy and the church. Active in The Søren Kierkegaard Society since 1989, he has held every office in this scholarly organization and has given leadership to numerous sessions at both the national and regional levels of the American Academy of Religion. His service to the church has focused on the Presbyterian Church (U.S.A.), in which he was ordained in 1986. He has been active in Grace Presbytery and has frequently taught in Presbyterian congregations, as well as congregations of the Christian Church (Disciples of Christ) and The United Methodist Church. With his wife, the Reverend Sharon Iverson Gouwens, an ordained minister in the Christian Church (Disciples of Christ), he frequently co-officiates at Holy Communion at the 8:00 a.m. Sunday worship service of First Presbyterian Church, Fort Worth.

Within Brite Divinity School, Professor Gouwens has given leadership to numerous faculty committees and served from 2002–2005 as Interim Dean. Although, when it comes to administration, Professor Gouwens, in the memorable phrase of his Brite colleague and friend Kenneth Cracknell, "was not to the manor born," he served as dean at the request of his faculty colleagues and the Brite Board of Trustees. And, although it was always teaching and writing, and not administration, that added a spring to his step, he fulfilled the office of dean with distinction, bringing to that assignment the same qualities of integrity, genuine interest in the other, fairness, and love for the theological enterprise that have marked his teaching, scholarship, and larger service to church and world.

The essays in this volume are organized in three sections, corresponding with aspects of Professor Gouwens's professional life, starting with the most general and moving to the most particular. James O. Duke, Brite's I. Wylie and Elizabeth M. Briscoe Professor of History of Christianity and History of Christian Thought, edited the first section titled, Theological Reflections. This section includes an essay examining the "Yale School" of theology and David Gouwens's distinctive response to issues raised by that school—a response that is reflected in the title of this volume: *The Theologically Formed Heart*. Other essays in this section explore the relationship of particular theological reflections to issues of practice, ranging from Christian mission in a religiously pluralistic world, to the equality of women and men in the church, to the character of ecclesial life and leadership, and to models of discipleship.

The second section was edited by Warner M. Bailey, Presbyterian minister, scholar, and Director of Presbyterian Studies at Brite. This section recognizes Professor Gouwens's use of Reformed theology in service to the church. While Professor Gouwens's publications have focused on the Lutheran Søren Kierkegaard, he has regularly taught a course in Reformed Theology. Moreover, his service to the church has been primarily, though not exclusively, in the Presbyterian Church (U.S.A.). The authors of these essays, with the exception of Kenneth Cracknel, who is a British Methodist, are leaders in the Presbyterian Church (U.S.A.) from both theological education and congregational ministries. The essays examine challenges and possibilities for theological education in a secular age, Calvin's use of rhetoric to influence the heart, the function of music in the Reformed tradition to teach theology and kindle the heart, and how the radical good news of God's love for the world empowers believers to live with and love their neighbors. Also addressed, in two separate essays, are efforts to come to terms with religious pluralism by leaders in the Reformed tradition. The first is a constructive contribution, drawing upon Calvin, by contemporary Reformed theologian Cynthia L. Rigby. The second is an historical study of theology and political dynamics in the Presbyterian Church that influenced the theology of religions of early twentieth-century Presbyterian missionary leader Robert Elliott Speer.

The third section, titled, Studies in Søren Kierkegaard, was edited by Professor Gouwens's fellow Kierkegaard scholar and co-editor of *The Paul L. Holmer Papers* Lee C. Barrett, Henry and Mary Stager Professor of Theology at Lancaster Theological Seminary. These essays address Kierkegaard on Original Sin, the place of the Communion Discourses in the Kierkegaard corpus, and the implications for life in *this* world found in Kierkegaard's understanding of the desire for security as a "sickness unto death." Individually, and as whole, they advance the Kierkegaard scholarship to which Professor Gouwens has made such distinguished contributions.

Not long ago two prospective Master of Divinity students visited Brite. They attended a class in the morning, our Tuesday chapel service, the community conversation that follows, and a class with Professor Gouwens that afternoon. In between, they spoke with students and other members of the faculty, and staff. Ending their day at Brite in my office, they told me that they were visiting several theological schools and were trying to identify the distinctive quality of each of the schools they were visiting. Based on their experiences of the day, it seemed to them that Brite was a place where theology and life in this world, in particular, Christian life and ministry, are integrated. They asked if I recognized Brite in what they were describing. I replied that I thought that if they asked that question of the faculty as a whole we would answer, "That is exactly what we are seeking to do." And, though I did not say so to these two prospective students, I thought to myself that this distinctive character of Brite Divinity School which they had discerned has been nurtured and matured in large measure through the teaching, research, and service to church world of Professor of Theology David J. Gouwens.

Theological Reflections

1

Passionate Doctrine

David Gouwens and the Role of Subjectivity in the "Yale School"

—Lee C. Barrett III

The publication in 1984 of *The Nature of Doctrine* by George Lindbeck, a Yale theologian who had previously been known mostly for his participation in Lutheran/Catholic ecumenical conversations and for his encyclopedic knowledge of medieval scholasticism, heralded the advent of an innovative and controversial approach to theological reflection.[1] Taking a cue from the slim volume's subtitle, this novel way of doing theology was promptly labeled "postliberal." Observers of the theological scene immediately detected parallels with the work of Hans Frei, Lindbeck's colleague, from the 1970's. Similarities were even discerned with the so-called "canonical" approach to biblical studies pioneered by Brevard Childs, and with the reflections on scriptural authority by David Kelsey. In some ways, Paul Holmer's work in philosophical theology also seemed to dovetail with important features of Lindbeck's book. Because Lindbeck, Frei, Childs, Kelsey, and Holmer all taught at Yale, soon the religious studies world was referring to a "Yale School" of theology. While interpretations of its significance varied, the one common assessment in the early literature about the Yale School was that this alleged movement was intent upon preserving the central theological convictions of the historic Christian tradition. The scholars commonly associated with the movement all sought to protect Christian teachings from over-assimilation to contemporary ideologies and cultural sensibilities. As

---

1. Lindbeck, *The Nature of Doctrine*.

such, this seemingly novel postliberalism actually appeared to be an extension of many of the concerns of the neo-orthodoxy of the mid-twentieth century. The obvious difference from neo-orthodoxy was that these Yale theologians had been somewhat chastened by the perspectivalism and constructivism associated with the intellectual orientation that was already being dubbed "postmodern." Some commentators applauded these new theological developments as the antidote to the erosion of Christianity's identity, while others decried it as a resurgence of a retrograde theological tribalism. I shall argue that this allegedly cohesive movement was never monolithic, and, in fact, had significant internal tensions, paradoxes, and conundrums. I will also argue that the expositions of Kierkegaard by David Gouwens, who studied under the progenitors of the movement, point to a way to resolve these tensions and integrate the trajectories of Frei and Lindbeck on the one hand, and Holmer on the other.

In popular perception, the alleged "Yale School" enjoyed a meteoric career. On the positive side, it was seen as one of the progenitors of a wider "postliberal" mood in theology that included such disparate phenomena as Radical Orthodoxy in Britain and the liturgical turn in much of American neo-evangelicalism.[2] By the 1990's analyses and even histories of this Yale School were being penned, sometimes laudatory, but often excoriating the movement for being fideistic, confessionally authoritarian, and hopelessly sectarian. Cautiously sympathetic but critical responses appeared by more conservative and evangelical authors, such as Alister McGrath and Nancy Murphy, who celebrated the putative movement's fidelity to historic Christianity, but feared its ostensibly weak commitment to the objective reference of Christian language.[3] In spite of the initial furor, by the 2000's retrospective obituaries of the Yale School were being composed by scholars like Paul DeHart.[4] Far from being the most exciting theological development since neo-orthodoxy, postliberalism was being described as a passing fad that had dissipated its energies and fragmented into divergent theological trends.

Assessing the evolution of the so-called Yale School has been complicated by the lack of agreement concerning what exactly it was or continues to be. Some things, however, were clear. Whatever it was, it was clearly nonfoundationalist. Lindbeck, Frei, and Holmer all rejected the claim that Christian convictions are grounded in a set of self-evident and universally plausible principles or in a generic and self-authenticating religious dimension of

---

2. See Pecknold, *Transforming Postliberal Theology*.

3. See Murphy, *Beyond Liberalism and Fundamentalism*; see also McGrath, *Understanding Doctrine*.

4. See DeHart, *The Trial of the Witnesses*.

experience. What counts as human rationality is always culturally constructed, and experience comes always already interpreted. The convictions of religious traditions cannot be based upon some primordial, unmediated, raw data provided by reason or experience. Religious teachings cannot be understood by situating them in a metaphysical analysis of the universe or in a phenomenological description of the religious dimension of human experience. Secondly, Lindbeck, Frei, and Holmer eschewed classic apologetics, denying that there is any framework logically prior to Christian belief, in terms of which Christian convictions must be understood and defended. Thirdly, all of them attended to the particularities of Christianity, rather than construing the faith as an instantiation of religion-in-general. Finally, Frei, Lindbeck, and Holmer all emphasized the Bible as the source of the stories, narratives, and concepts by which Christians construe God and their own lives, and resisted efforts to reduce the "meaning" of Scripture to its moral message, or its propositional content, or its capacity to evoke a depth experience, or its symbolization of truths about the cosmos or human nature.

In spite of these commonalities, Frei, Lindbeck, and Holmer were never of a unitary mind. Against the narrative of postliberalism as a monolithic movement, I am proposing that the "Yale School," if there ever was such a thing, was not a common set of theological affirmations, nor was it a cohesive theological method. Rather, the Yale School was (and is) unified by a concern for a common set of problems and a common set of deep-seated worries about Christianity. Tension always existed between the approaches of its most prominent exponents and even within the works of individual authors. Prominent among the common concerns that united them was a desire to highlight the uniqueness of Christianity, rather than allowing it to be treated as one more variation on the theme of generic human spirituality. Another was a fear that the Bible was no longer being read over against the norms of the prevailing culture, nor as a bearer of good news from beyond the aspirations and values of that culture. It was suspected that the Bible was not being heard as a word from a transcendent source. Closely allied with this was a desire to stabilize the meaning of Scripture and hear it as unified message of hope rather than as a concatenation of religious opinions, experiences, and practices from diverse ancient sources. This concern was symptomatic of an anxiety that the Bible was no longer being construed according to the liturgical and confessional heritage of the church, and therefore its meaning was at the mercy of the vagaries and whims of the academy and popular culture. The Yale theologians fretted that the Bible could become the wax nose that Luther feared, susceptible to being twisted into any shape the contemporary reader chose, if it were left at the mercy of the imperative to be culturally relevant and plausible. In short, these New Haven postliberals shared a concern that the uniqueness, self-identity, coherence, and meaningfulness of the Christian message had become obscured.

The main rift in the group arose out of the tension between Frei and Lindbeck's deep and pervasive suspicion of the "subjective" turn in theology, and Holmer's commitment to clarifying Christian passions and dispositions. Both Frei and Lindbeck feared that structuring Christian beliefs according to the drama of the individual's spiritual development would reduce theology to anthropology, or at least trigger its degeneration into a projection of human needs. Both Frei and Lindbeck sought to foreground the triumph and sovereignty of God's grace enacted in the Incarnation, and worried that undue attention to human subjectivity would imply some meritorious value to that experience, and therefore lead to Pelagianism. Holmer, however, tended to identify the distinctiveness of Christianity with the distinctiveness of the emotions, passions, dispositions, and attitudes that constitute the Christian life. Consequently, Holmer's main goal was to illumine the nature of Christian pathos, a project which involved a resistance to the reduction of the faith to any textual or historical objectivities. To Frei at least this concentration on Christian pathos did look suspiciously like a sophisticated variant of the subjective turn. Holmer's flamboyant enthusiasm for Kierkegaard, often regarded in theological circles as a notorious champion of subjectivity, did not sit well with Lindbeck and Frei's Barthian sensibilities. Anyone who praised an author who had famously claimed that "truth is subjectivity" would necessarily be suspect in the eyes of the Barth-leaning Yale mainstream. Frei once quipped that Kierkegaard was the most dangerous Pelagian of all time, because he was the most seductive.[5] Kierkegaard, Frei alleged, had turned anxiety, despair and guilt into meritorious works, and thereby had valorized the self-absorbed angst of modern individualists. Given Holmer's attention to emotions and passions, it was inevitable that he, too, would be tarred with the brush of Pelagianism. It was Holmer's attention to the passional qualities of the Christian that made him the odd man out in New Haven's theological scene in the late twentieth century. It was this suspicion of any constitutive role for subjectivity in theology, a suspicion that was identified as a hallmark of the Yale School, which led to the marginalization of Holmer in accounts of the so-called movement's evolution and obscured the extent of his positive impact on his colleagues. It may also have contributed to the actual distancing of his colleagues from Holmer.

---

5. Author's conversation with Frei, November, 1982.

When the Yale School is defined as a shared set of worries rather than as a shared set of conclusions or a shared method, Holmer's role in it, and his attention to subjectivity, can be seen as significant. He cannot be dismissed as a peripheral character, lurking in theological corridors and flirting with the anthropological reduction of theology. Nevertheless, this approach to the so-called Yale School will also show that Holmer's response to these worries was indeed very different from that of Frei and Lindbeck. In terms of the popular construal of the Yale School, there may be very good reasons for continuing to regard him as a maverick. But however different he may have been, Holmer's perspective drew attention to internal problems in the approach of Frei and Lindbeck, exposing subtle fissures in their own work concerning the relation of the objective grammar of Christianity to the self-involving enactment of the faith. Both Frei and Lindbeck said puzzling things about the relationship of objectivity and subjectivity in the living of the Christian life. Unfortunately Holmer's elusive and nuanced essays often made it difficult to see how exactly he connected subjectivity and objectivity, or how he avoided Frei's accusation that he was making the meaning of the Christian faith dependent on a prior analysis of human subjectivity.

In different ways, both Frei and Lindbeck sought to stabilize the meaning of biblical texts and to preserve the uniqueness of Christianity, particularly the centrality of the Incarnation and the priority of grace, by appealing to allegedly "objective" features of the Bible or the Christian tradition. Holmer, I will suggest, was just as concerned with stabilizing the meaning of Christian convictions, just as intent upon preserving the uniqueness of Christianity, and just as devoted to the theme of Incarnation and grace. However, he shifted the locus of the meaning of Christian teachings away from textual objectivities and resituated it in the passions of the faithful Christian. As a result, exactly what the objective referential force of the doctrines contributed to their meaning became a bit unclear. I will argue that David Gouwens's work, relying upon Kierkegaard, pointed to a promising way beyond these conundrums.[6] Gouwens showed how Kierkegaard's authorship attempted to do justice both to the "what" of the teaching and the "how" of the subjective appropriation. Kierkegaard's attention to Christian pathos could resolve some of the quandaries that Frei and Lindbeck's work generated, and also could exonerate Holmer's approach from the accusation of reducing theology to anthropology.

First, let us consider the "objectivist" pole of the tension in the Yale School. To illustrate the strategy of grounding the meaning of Christianity

---

6. Gouwens, *Kierkegaard as Religious Thinker*; Gouwens, "Kierkegaard's Understanding of Doctrine."

in some sort of objective feature of the Bible or the tradition, let us examine the writings of Hans Frei, whose seminal work was actually published a decade before Lindbeck's. In *The Eclipse of Biblical Narrative* of 1974, Frei claimed that modernity's typical ways of reading Scripture either identified the meaning of Scripture with its historical reference, the truth of which could in principle be either verified or falsified, or with a concept, be it moral, metaphysical or experiential, that the text symbolized in a pictorial form.[7] Fundamentalists and progressive new questers for the historical Jesus alike pursued the first form of hermeneutic reductionism, while less positivistically inclined liberals opted for some version of the second. Over against these strategies, Frei argued that the entire biblical canon is unified by a narrative structure, or, more precisely, by two intertwined narrative patterns. The first narrative is the overarching story of God's dealings with the people of Israel and the church, and through them with all of humanity. The second is the less stylized, more history-like and particularized account of Jesus' life, especially the sequence of events surrounding his passion and resurrection. Frei concentrated on these formal properties of the text partly because he had learned from the New Critics like Cleanth Brooks and William Wimsatt that the meaning of a literary work cannot be controlled by its author but is resident in the text itself. Accordingly, he rejected the identification of scriptural meaning with the intentionalities of its human authors, their inner experiences, or with the experiences of the original readers of the texts. Rather, Frei regarded the texts as an aesthetic object, analogous to a painting, unified by given rhetorical structures and dynamics. A literary text is like a verbal icon, and its meaning is established by its internal, objectively given properties. These dynamics and structures, discernible to any sensitive and skilled reader of literature, suggest that the Bible should be read as a history-like realistic narrative. According to Frei, this history-like realistic narrative was a unique genre in the ancient world, utterly different from the more prevalent genres of saga, folk tales, and myth. To support this claim Frei appealed to the work of Erich Auerbach, the great literary theorist who had emphasized the unprecedented realistic features of Biblical narrative.[8] Of course, Frei quickly added the qualification that these literary theories were not the real ground of the interpretation of scripture, for that ground can only be the Holy Spirit. Nevertheless, he did employ these interpretive theories as adequate descriptions of the way that the Holy Spirit guides the church's reading of the Bible. In his actual expository practice the formalism

---

7. Frei, *The Eclipse of Biblical Narrative*.
8. See Auerbach, *Mimesis*.

of the New Critics was very much implicit in the way that Frei read the story of Jesus.

To justify concentrating on the passion/resurrection stories, rather than on the imagery about Jesus, or the parables of Jesus, or the mythic resonances between Jesus and other savior figures, or the similarities between Jesus' sayings and various wisdom traditions, Frei appealed to the reflections of the philosophers Gilbert Ryle and P. F. Strawson on personal identity.[9] These British philosophers argued that personal identity is constituted by a publically observable pattern of intentional action. For Frei, this insight helpfully illumined the way that the gospel narratives function. Accordingly, Frei concluded that in order to understand the gospel portrayal of Jesus, the reader must focus on Jesus' pattern of behavior as he pursued his purposes and responded to social circumstances.[10] For Frei that identity-establishing pattern of behavior becomes most evident during the events of Passion Week. Consequently, the fulcrum of the biblical narrative is the very detailed recounting of Jesus' actions and responses to situations from his entry into Jerusalem to his crucifixion. Although Frei claimed that the story of Jesus should generate its own principles of appropriate reading, in his actual practice he relied on a very particular philosophical anthropology to determine which features of the story of Jesus are important.

What is significant here is that Frei grounded the unity and meaning of the canon in allegedly objective features of the biblical texts. Frei asserted that the interpretive procedures applied to Scripture must be governed by the unique features of Scripture itself, in the way that the idiosyncratic properties of a block of marble determine the selection of the type of chisel that will be employed to sculpt it. Ordinary people familiar with the ordinary practice of reading a story should be able to discern these objective narrative features and grasp the meaning of the text. The more probing analyses of scholars should simply be more sophisticated and nuanced applications of these ordinary reading strategies. As we have seen, Frei justified this general interpretive practice by appealing to a theory of realistic narrative as a distinctive literary genre, and supported the concentration on the story of Passion Week by appealing to a theory of personal identity as intentional action. In spite of his protestations that biblical hermeneutics should not be subservient to a general hermeneutic theory and should be determined purely by the shape of Scripture itself, Frei's reliance upon theory-based methods of reading to uncover the objective features of the Bible seemed

---

9. Frei, *The Identity of Jesus Christ*, 36–44, 92.
10. Ibid., 36–96.

to mimic the very hermeneutic foundationalism that he decried. Perhaps he was not so very different from interpreters like Ricouer and Gadamer, both of whom he had criticized for distorting Scripture by subjecting it to an analysis based on overly formal and allegedly universal interpretive principles. Frei wrote as if all right-thinking people, sensitive to literary dynamics, should see that the biblical text is indeed narratively structured, functions realistically, and most centrally portrays the identity of a very particular intentional agent, Jesus Christ. All competent readers, therefore, should agree that theories of realistic narrative and enacted personal identity should inform the interpretive strategies to be applied to the biblical texts. Ironically, a general literary theory and a general philosophical anthropology ended up supporting the entire project that was supposed to liberate the Bible from its foundationalist captivity.

Later in his career Frei recognized the existence of this incongruity. In his essay "The 'Literal Reading' of Biblical Narrative in the Christian Tradition: Will It Stretch or Will It Break?" he distanced himself from his earlier appeals to the putative objective properties of the biblical text, and tempered his reliance upon the New Critics.[11] In that crucial essay Frei proposed that what counts as the obviously "normal" way to read Scripture is determined not by the inherent features of the text, but by the interpretive conventions of a community of readers who put the text to certain purposes. In a way, Frei was inching closer to the literary critical viewpoint of the later Stanley Fish, who asserted that validity in interpretation is a function of a community's consensus about what counts as the normal way to read a particular type of text. But even in this essay Frei was still appealing to something objective to stabilize textual meaning, only now it was the objectively given practices of a tradition of reading. Presumably the use of Scripture in the liturgies, creeds, and devotional practices of the churches, rather than the Bible's internal narrative structures, would now furnish the "normal" meaning of a biblical text. These practices are just as public, just as objective, and just as authoritative as were the literary features of the verbal icon, to which Frei had earlier appealed. In spite of his hermeneutic shift, Frei still wrote as if something objective could clarify and stabilize the Bible's meaning, and thereby protect it from aberrant readings.

George Lindbeck's work exhibited a parallel concern to root the meaning of Christian discourse in publically accessible objective givens. In 1974 Lindbeck's lecture series at Gonzaga University revealed the rudiments of a new understanding of the nature of religious doctrines. His musings were motivated by the problems with cross-confessional communication that he

---

11. See Frei, "The 'Literal Reading' of Biblical Narrative in the Christian Tradition."

had experienced in his own ecumenical activities. His innovative way of thinking about doctrines relied on a theory of religion that proposed that religions function as linguistic systems that shape communal ways of thinking, feeling, and acting. The roots of this view were to be found in the writings of Clifford Geertz and Peter Berger, both of whom compared a religion to a culture that inculcates certain sensibilities, values, and practices into individuals. The cultural system stipulates the proper ways of doing things according to generally accepted and usually implicit principles, much in the same way that a language stipulates the proper way to combine sounds and marks on paper into intelligible communications. Inspired by Ludwig Wittgenstein's remarks about language games, Lindbeck construed the doctrines of religious communities as efforts to articulate the implicit depth grammar, the basic rules, governing the way of life of a group of believers. Just as all languages are particular, so also are all religions particular, including Christianity. Christians are socialized into the distinctively Christian way of life by internalizing the unique "grammar" of an ecclesial community. Consequently, a church's regulated way of life must be sharply differentiated from the values and behavior of secularized western culture, and its grammar must not be confused with the grammar of the environing society.

Lindbeck distinguished his view of doctrines from popular alternative understandings.[12] According to Lindbeck, doctrines are not primarily assertions making truth claims about the universe. They do not refer ostensively to supernatural states of affairs, as if some specific "fact" out there corresponded to every doctrinal sentence. Lindbeck described the misleading characterization of doctrines as factual assertions as being the "cognitive propositional" approach, and lamented that it was typical of fundamentalists and many Protestant and Catholic scholastics. Lindbeck also insisted that doctrines are not evocative expressions of the spiritual experience of religious individuals or their communities. This misunderstanding of doctrine he dubbed the "emotive-expressive" view, and identified it with many post-Enlightenment progressive theologians. It was to provide an alternative to these unhelpful construals of doctrine that Lindbeck proposed his own "cultural linguistic" theory.[13] For him, doctrines are rules, and as such are just as publically describable as are the rules of a language. Their meaning is not to be identified with the unknowable objects to which they seem to refer, nor is it hidden in the depths of the individual's interiority. Rather, the meaning of a doctrine is evident in the way of life of the community that employs it, and that way of life is amenable to objective description.

12. Lindbeck, *The Nature of Doctrine*, 16.
13. Ibid., 32–41.

However, certain ambiguities haunted Lindbeck's appeal to the objectivity of doctrine as the grammar of the Christian community. One fissure in his work appeared in regard to the issue of who should count as a competent language speaker whose practice should be taken as an instantiation of the implicit grammar of Christianity. This was a serious problem, because Lindbeck's notion of grammar required that there be a loose transcultural and transhistorical consensus of the faithful displayed throughout time and space. For him, the grammar of Christianity is an abstraction from the actual linguistic practice of Christians as they pray, worship, exhort, etc. But which ones of the communities that claim to be bodies of faithful Christians should actually be included in the consensus? Should non-Trinitarian Christians, such as "Oneness" Pentecostals, be regarded as competent language users? If they are, it would be difficult to treat the doctrine of the Trinity as an example of the depth grammar of Christianity as a whole. Should non-Chalcedonian Christians, such as the Monophysites and Nestorians of the East, be counted as members of this linguistic family? Should Mormons and Quakers be included? Whether these groups are included or excluded, criteria would need to be specified in order to justify the decision.

Another ambiguity became evident concerning the way that doctrines come to have particular meanings. Lindbeck seemed to say conflicting things about the relation of the doctrinal rules to Christian practices and passions. On the one hand, Lindbeck spoke of doctrines as a formal property of Christian language, existing objectively in spite of the variations and fluctuations in communal use.[14] In these contexts it seemed that doctrinal rules have meaning in themselves quite apart from any particular employment in the passional life of faith. Lindbeck often treated doctrines as having some sort of specificity, significance, and self-identity independent of their particular applications to the motley circumstances of human life. For instance, he suggested that doctrinal rules are related to the actual employment of Christian concepts in particular circumstances as form is related to matter. The doctrine, the self-identical formal principle, is conceptually distinguishable from the varying matter which it governs. That matter is the concrete emotions, experiences, actions, and purposes that constitute the actual living of the Christian life.

On the other hand, Lindbeck was aware that rules do not apply themselves. Every time that a rule is applied to a novel situation an act of imagination is involved. Consequently, the way that a rule is followed at least partially constitutes its meaning. Lindbeck alluded to the example of Christological doctrine as an example of the way in which a rule could take

14. Ibid., 32–41.

on very different meanings depending on the way in which it is followed.[15] In the life of a Byzantine Christian as he adored the Pantocrator the Chalcedonian formula meant one thing, but in the life of Dietrich Bonhoeffer as he cared for his fellow prisoners it meant something entirely different. This type of consideration sometimes led Lindbeck to admit that the meanings of doctrines depend on the practices of a community as that community attempts to live according to those doctrines. Accordingly, Lindbeck in some contexts emphasized skill in the application of rules, asserting that to learn Christian doctrine is to "interiorize a set of skills by practice and training."[16] He even suggested that, if Christian doctrine is likened to a map, the map only acquires meaning when it is used in the appropriate way, for the appropriate purpose.[17] The map by itself is not sufficient to determine what would count as the correct following of its cartographic marks. In order for geographic intelligibility to be achieved, there must be a shared practice of applying the map. By analogy, there must be a shared practice of living out Christian doctrine, including a doctrine's implications for what an individual should do and what an individual should feel.

However, Lindbeck failed to give an account of what should count as skill in the application of Christian rules. He did not articulate any shared habits of application that would give a doctrinal rule genuine specificity. When discussing the self-identity of Christianity, he generally appealed to the doctrinal formulae in the abstract, as if doctrines had meaning apart from their instantiations in human lives. In spite of his protestations that skill and practice are necessary for the significant use of a doctrine, Lindbeck's basic tendency was to reify doctrines as objectivities that have meaning above and beyond the messiness of human actions and passions.

Frei and Lindbecks's propensity to rely upon certain putatively "objectively" understandable features of Christianity to establish its unique identity was very alien to the thought of Paul Holmer, who represented a different trajectory at Yale. It is significant that most of the recent analyses and histories of the Yale School only mention Holmer in passing. Usually he is merely credited with inspiring Frei and Lindbeck to take the writings of Ludwig Wittgenstein seriously, and perhaps with motivating his colleagues to appropriate aspects of J. L. Austin's theory of performative utterances and Gilbert Ryle's critique of dualistic theories of the self. To many analysts of the Yale School, Holmer was a shadowy figure hovering in the background, a kind of *éminence gris*, or perhaps a maverick provocateur. To

---

15. Ibid., 82–83.
16. Ibid., 36.
17. Ibid., 51–52.

most historians of theology Holmer was at best a sort of John the Baptist character, a forerunner who alerted his colleagues to the theological potential of certain aspects of Anglo-American linguistic philosophy, and then, his mission accomplished, he faded from the picture.

Holmer's early work, however, was more than a methodological prolegomena to the flowering of the Yale School. He shared and even anticipated many of Lindbeck and Frei's worries and concerns. Like them, he sought to liberate Christianity from its cultural captivity, struggled to present the faith as a coherent whole with a saving message, and also strove to rescue it from absolute indeterminacy of meaning. But Holmer's substantive response to these issues was different from that of Frei and Lindbeck, and far more radical. Here Holmer's appropriation of Kierkegaard did indeed make all the difference in the world.

Holmer found the entire project of trying to stabilize the meaning of Scripture by appealing to objective features of the text or of the ecclesial tradition to be both futile and pernicious. The project is futile because objective knowledge is always an approximation to truth, for it is always tentative, always debatable, and always revisable.[18] New data may be discovered, new features of the text may be noticed, new perspectives may be adopted, and new methods of interpretations may be employed. Allegedly objective construals of the unity, uniqueness, and basic essence of any phenomenon, including the Bible, are always colored by the interests and concerns of the interpreter. Consequently, any appeal to a supposed "objective" interpretation is a chimera.

But even more damningly, the mood of the objective interpretive enterprise is all wrong, and actually militates against the cultivation of authentic Christian faith.[19] The quest for an objective grounding of an interpretation is actually a yearning for certainty and closure. The attainment of any such certainty or closure would rule out the risk, decision, self-concern, and commitment that the faith requires. Accepting an interpretation because its accuracy has been objectively established would merely be an exercise in prudential self-interest. If a viewpoint were known to be indubitably true, adopting it might be nothing more than an individual's adaptation to the way things obviously are. The motivations for this adoption might be a simple desire to survive and avoid unpleasantness. For example, if it could be proven that damnation awaits those who flout God's will, the decision to obey God might only be a function of a self-oriented desire to avoid eternal

---

18. Holmer, *On Kierkegaard and the Truth*, 79–108.
19. Ibid., *Truth*, 109–57.

misery. Moreover, objective certainty about any Christian teaching, such as God's providence, could easily degenerate into complacency. Such a smug attitude would have nothing to do with the passionate commitment to the cultivation of sincere love for God and neighbor that genuine Christian faith requires. For Holmer (who followed Kierkegaard on this matter) faith requires passion, passion requires risk, and risk requires objective uncertainty.

Holmer's observations about Kierkegaard's discussion of Christian faith point to a very different way of determining the nature and self-identity of Christianity. In the final analysis it is not the objective features of the biblical text or of the ecclesial tradition that are decisive, but rather the interests and concerns of the reader. In other words, the unity and meaning of the canon and of the Christian tradition are functions of the virtues and passions that the reader brings to bear upon the biblical texts and the history of the church. What is needed for a genuinely canonical reading of the Bible is a hunger for righteousness, a disquietude with one's own moral and spiritual failings, a disillusionment with worldly success and pleasures, and a longing to grow in faith, hope, and love. As the reader's character is formed by these passions, the Bible takes on a new coloration, and certain readings become more natural than others. Loving, hopeful, and faithful people will notice certain textual details, privilege certain textual dynamics, and become sensitive to certain recurrent themes. The problem, according to Holmer, is not in our inadequate grasp of the text's narrative structure, or in our faulty understanding of the church's magisterial tradition, or in our deficient grasp of the grammatical rules of the faith, but in ourselves. Readers of Scripture and participants in the Christian tradition will discern the uniqueness, cohesion, and self-identity of the Christian message if they have developed the requisite passions and virtues. Hermeneutical and doctrinal issues are ultimately affairs of the heart.

Holmer's work, however, also suffered an ambiguity, but it was different from the tensions that were evident in the corpus of Frei and Lindbeck. Holmer often wrote as if he assumed that Christian language refers to states of affairs that exist beyond the subjectivity of the believer, but he was often vague about the nature of that objective reference. Frequently he was accused of being a non-cognitivist who reduced the meaning of Christian doctrines to exhortations to cultivate certain passions and dispositions.[20] For example, belief in the Creator might be nothing more than the adoption of a stance of delight about the existence of this world. At the very least, Holmer stressed the necessity of nurturing the appropriate Christian form of subjectivity so intensely that the positive value of affirming the objective

---

20. McGrath, *Understanding Doctrines*.

existence of the referents of Christian doctrines was not entirely clear. To be accurate, Holmer repeatedly distanced himself from all philosophers and theologians who reduced talk about God to nothing more than talk about human passions and dispositions, but the difference between Holmer and someone like D. Z. Phillips remained obscure to many readers.

David Gouwens outlined a way to move beyond this impasse and to synthesize the positive concerns and insights of Lindbeck and Frei with those of Holmer. Gouwens did so in an unobtrusive way that did not attract the attention in constructive theological circles that it deserved. Gouwens limned the contours of this integrative vision that did justice both to the objective teachings of Christianity and to the necessity of subjective appropriation through his exposition of the writings of Kierkegaard. According to Gouwens, Kierkegaard, like Lindbeck and Frei, adamantly resisted the assimilation of Christianity into alien cultural categories. He decried the effort to translate the doctrinal content of the Christian faith into other conceptualities that were purported to be their functional equivalents, conceptualities that were lauded as being more relevant and intelligible to contemporary society.[21] Gouwens proposed that Kierkegaard's resistance to the program of reconceiving Christianity in Hegelian or Romantic terms prefigured the Yale post-liberals' objections to Tillich's program of correlating Christian symbols with human questions unearthed by a foundational ontology, and to Bultmann's project of translating the language of the New Testament into the language of existentialism.[22] Kierkegaard agreed with the post-liberals that the basic task of theology is not to render Christianity understandable and palatable to modern sensibilities, but rather is to illumine the unique contours of the faith.

Gouwens notes that Kierkegaard's authorial practice assumed the dogmatic presuppositions of Christianity, and worked from them to their implications for understanding human existence. Kierkegaard should not be regarded as an instance of the type of theology that Frei described as the attempt to correlate Christian concepts with the meaning structures of the environing culture. In other words, Kierkegaard was not a precursor of Tillich.[23] Nor should Kierkegaard be regarded as an example of the type of theology that, according to Frei, employs an independent account of the dynamics of authentic selfhood to reconceptualize the faith. Contrary to many popular interpretations, Kierkegaard was not a prefiguration of Bultmann. For Kierkegaard, doctrines are not expressions of Christian

---

21. Gouwens, *Kierkegaard as Religious Thinker*, 11.
22. Ibid., 12.
23. Ibid., 73.

self-consciousness, not pictorial representations of metaphysical truths, and not mythic pictures that must be translated into pure concepts. Clearly, in Gouwens's view, Kierkegaard's work should definitely not be situated in Lindbeck's "experiential-expressive" category.

Far from advocating for the foundational status of an analysis of human subjectivity, Kierkegaard scathingly critiqued authors like Magister Adler who confused the subjective and the objective dimensions of faith, at the expense of the objective pole. Kierkegaard regarded doctrines as rules governing the Christian stage of existence.[24] In his authorial practice Kierkegaard treated doctrines as descriptions of the grammatical rules implicit in Christian discourse, much as Lindbeck would later do. More precisely, according to Gouwens, Kierkegaard's writings present doctrines as articulations in a second-order language of the proper use of the concepts that constitute the first-order language of faith. Those ordinary concepts of the faith, like "grace," "sin," etc., are authoritatively given and exhibit a certain coherence among themselves that the rules describe. Kierkegaard was different from Lindbeck in that he recognized that even the articulated doctrinal rules only acquire meaning when they are used in the appropriate contexts with the appropriate passions. Not even a doctrinal formula is intelligible until it is put to some use in structuring human actions and passions. But this "subjectivity" qualification did not entail a denigration of doctrines as the regulative principles of the Christian life. Because Kierkegaard did see the faith as structured by doctrinal convictions, Kierkegaard should at least partially be located in the type of theology that Frei characterized as the practical discipline of Christian self-description. As such Kierkegaard's approach resists understanding Christianity in terms of the general criteria of meaning current in the environing culture (such as the popular Hegelianism of his day) and emphasized the unique meaning of Christian concepts. Consequently, Gouwens's analysis would suggest that Kierkegaard and the later Barth shared many common concerns. Gouwens concludes that Kierkegaard, like the Yale post-liberals, exhibited many of the characteristics of Lindbeck's "cultural-linguistic" approach to theology.[25] The subjectivity that typifies genuine Christianity is made possible only through the attempt to live according to the doctrines that regulate the Christian life. Christian passion and Christian experience are shaped by authoritative Christian concepts that logically precede the subjectivity.

However, Gouwens further argues that Kierkegaard was by no means a mere foreshadowing of Frei and Lindbeck; the Dane's concern for Christian

---

24. Ibid., 79.
25. Gouwens, "Kierkegaard's Understanding of Doctrine," 21.

subjectivity did distinguish him from the theological project of the most two celebrated exponents of the Yale School. Holmer was entirely right in emphasizing the centrality of the passions and virtues in Kierkegaard's writings. According to Kierkegaard Christianity intrinsically involves particular passions, attitudes and dispositions, and these features of subjectivity help constitute Christianity's unity and identity.[26] The subjective mood of a doctrine is just as crucial to its meaning as is the correctness of its articulation in theological language. Kierkegaard critiqued any form of orthodoxy that ignored the subjectivity of the believer and reduced Christian faith to cognitive assent to propositions.[27] Doctrines are not purely propositional assertions, for they only acquire meaning in the context of human experience. Instead of focusing on the "what" of faith, the given doctrinal content, Kierkegaard concentrated on the "how" of faith, the way in which the Christian faith must be appropriated.[28] Following Holmer's pioneering work, Gouwens proposes that Kierkegaard's main concern was not with the logic of belief, the way in which doctrines hang together, but in the logic of coming to belief. Kierkegaard saw his task as the encouragement and provocation of modern people to cultivate the capabilities that can allow them to understand the gospel. Doctrines are intended to be realized in existence; they sketch the contours of an existential task. Without understanding the possibility for a new kind of passional life that a doctrine presents, its meaning evaporates.

At this point Gouwens's treatment of Kierkegaard becomes quite subtle and nuanced. On the one hand, Kierkegaard did not want to interpret Christian convictions in purely experiential terms, even though he focused on subjectivity. As we have seen, Kierkegaard did not want to reduce the objective moment to the subjective moment. The logic of coming to belief should not determine the logic of belief. On the other hand, the objective doctrines only have meaning when they are used in the proper context of passionate concern for the quality of one's own life. Consequently, the issue for Kierkegaard becomes: if Christianity requires both a "what" and a "how," how are the two related?

Gouwens concludes that Kierkegaard addresses this issue by carefully showing how doctrinal language must function in order to acquire meaning.[29] Kierkegaard insisted that the right passional context is necessary for grasping any existential communication, and doctrines are the

---

26. Gouwens, *Kierkegaard as Religious Thinker*, 16–20.
27. Ibid., 144.
28. Ibid., 142.
29. Gouwens, "Kierkegaard's Understanding of Doctrine," 17–21.

quintessential example of existential communications. Meaning and truth are not properties of the doctrines in themselves, treated in abstraction from their existential employment. Rather, the doctrines become meaningful and true only when they are used properly in the lives of Christians.[30] It is passionate Christians who refer truly to God with the language of faith as shaped by the doctrines, not the doctrines considered in isolation. According to this functional view of doctrinal language, the activity of using doctrines to shape individuals' lives is a necessary condition for establishing their meaning. The proper context of human passion and interest must be present in order for the doctrines to refer meaningfully to "objective" realities. It is for this reason that Kierkegaard devoted his authorship to clarifying the passional context of their use. Without that context, the doctrines become indeterminate and infinitely malleable. Taken in the abstract, the biblical narratives can be read and abused in an almost infinite number of ways. If doctrines are likened to a picture, their meaning is dependent upon how one uses that picture. Gouwens implies that Kierkegaard, by taking this approach, was resisting the twin themes that doctrines are objective grammatical rules that exist independently of their employment, as was sometimes suggested by Lindbeck, or that they are objective narrative structures of the biblical text , as was sometimes implied by Frei. Kierkegaard consistently anticipated the other, more recessive dimension of Lindbeck and Frei's thought that suggested that doctrines only become meaningful when they are put to specific passional uses.

Gouwens shows that doctrines acquire meaning in the Christian's passional life in a few different ways. Some doctrines foster the subjective qualifications that are needed as prerequisites for even beginning to understand the Christian faith.[31] For example, the doctrine of original sin, properly understood, suggests that a pervasive discontent with one's own character is necessary for understanding the doctrine of grace through Jesus Christ. The doctrine of original sin should be used to encourage the practice of self-examination that leads to a more profound sense of guilt than is possible in the ethical sphere. Without that relentlessly critical self-concern, or at least the ability to imagine it, teachings about justification by grace and the forgiveness of sins would be meaningless.

But the appropriate forms of subjectivity are much more than the necessary conditions for beginning to grasp the meaning of the objective teachings of Christianity. Full-blown Christian subjectivity is also shaped by those teachings. Doctrines should be used to give birth to the new emotions

---

30. Ibid., 20.
31. Ibid.," 19.

and passions that constitute the Christian life. For example, appropriating the concept "justification by grace" involves growth in a sense of gratitude, humility, and relief. Such growth cannot occur without the shaping force of the doctrine. The gratitude, humility, and relief that are central to Christianity do not just naturally well up in people. Similarly, genuinely living according to the doctrine of the imitation of Christ produces a hope and a certainty about God's ultimate benevolence. That unique hope and certainty, unlike anything that the world can offer, can arise only as the central doctrines of Christianity are lived out. Taken as a composite, Christian doctrines sketch out the contours of a new subjectivity characterized by faith, hope, and love, and encourage that subjectivity as the doctrines are used to shape a life.

But Kierkegaard's attention to the subjectivity-shaping force of doctrines is only half of the story. Gouwens makes it clear that for Kierkegaard Christian doctrines do more than function to form a unique type of pathos. By explicating Kierkegaard on this point, Gouwens clarifies some of the obscurities in the writings of Holmer about Kierkegaard. Gouwens insists that, for Kierkegaard, persons do make objective and referential truth claims when they employ doctrinal language.[32] A doctrine is not a mere expression of one's attitude toward the world or an exhortation to cultivate a certain set of emotions and passions. For example, Gouwens notes that Kierkegaard uses the language of atonement in a realist fashion. Kierkegaard talks about Christ's saving work *extra nos* as being independent of and logically prior to any individual's subjective response of faith in Christ. Kierkegaard assumes the validity of the Chalcedonian definition of Christ's identity as a summation of the narrative of salvation that has truth quite apart from anyone's belief in it. For Kierkegaard, the story of Jesus as the unique and unsubstitutable savior who embodies divine love does refer to the actual relation of God to humanity. Christ's life, death, and resurrection are the logical and actual basis of Christian existence. In Kierkegaard's writings, faith is a response to an external historical event. Christians do believe that there really was an incarnation and that there really was a satisfaction for sin.[33] Redemption is not something that takes place solely within the believer, as a kind of profound insight or spiritual transformation. Gouwens asserts that Kierkegaard did not interpret the significance of Christ purely in terms of the impact of Christ on the experience of the believer. Unlike common interpretations of Schleiermacher, Kierkegaard did not describe salvation as nothing more than as new mode of experience, as the communication of Jesus' God consciousness. Nor did Kierkegaard declare Jesus

---

32. Gouwens, *Kierkegaard as Religious Thinker*, 20, 146.
33. Ibid., 142–45.

to be the divine savior simply because Jesus inspires the power of New Being, as Tillich would later claim. Rather, Gouwens argues, for Kierkegaard Christology precedes soteriology. Salvation is not the apotheosis of human subjectivity, but rather is the incarnation of God in the human world. While the passional virtues are the necessary subjective means for apprehending Christ, this mode of pathos is not the ground for affirmations about Christ.

Kierkegaard's way of relating the referential force of Christian doctrines to the role of pathos in the constitution of the meaning of those doctrines was to insist that the appropriate passions are a necessary condition for using those doctrines referringly. There is no univocal sense of "refer," and no one-size-fits-all way to refer to objective realities. Not all statements refer to the world in the same context-neutral way. Different sorts of referring require different sorts of conditions in order for the act of referring to be intelligible. Christians do refer to God, but the meaning of that reference only becomes clear in the appropriate passional contexts. When Christians say "I believe in God" they are indeed affirming that God exists beyond their consciousness, but what it means to say "I believe in God" only becomes manifest in the contexts of praising God, thanking God, etc. The "what" (the doctrine used referringly) is the logical ground and presupposition of the "how" (the proper pathos) but the "how" is a necessary condition for establishing the meaning of the "what." In other words, without the passion-laden activities of praising and thanking we would not know what the concept "God" refers to. It is this subtle dialectic of the "what" and the "how" that Lindbeck and Frei sometimes obscured, often contrary to their better intentions, by appealing to a "what" that seemed to be understandable somewhat independently of the "how." Moreover, it was the importance of this referring use of doctrines that Holmer sometimes neglected to clarify, even though he affirmed it.

Gouwens notes that in Kierkegaard's writings this dialectic of objective reference and subjective conditions for meaningfulness parallels a rather different dialectic, the dialectic of grace and faith. Here a substantive doctrinal difference between Kierkegaard and Barth concerning soteriology becomes evident, a difference that sheds light on Frei's suspicion of Kierkegaard.[34] Gouwens observes that for Kierkegaard Christ's saving work, although it is objective, does not become efficacious for any given individual until that individual develops the pathos of faith. Coming to have faith is decisive for the actual salvation of any particular individual. In Kierkegaard's work this conviction is evident in his insistence that despair over sin is a prerequisite for truly appropriating concepts like grace, justification, and atonement.

34. Ibid., 149–50.

Such a view is very different from the theological objectivism of Barth, who rejected the position that the experiential moment of faith is part of what salvation involves. However, Kierkegaard's soteriological orientation does not necessarily follow from his practice of relating objectivity and subjectivity. The fact that objective reference is dependent upon certain subjective conditions does not entail that salvation is dependent upon its reception. But the conflation of soteriology with a theory of meaning may account for Frei's enduring distrust of Kierkegaard. More significantly, it may also account for Lindbeck and Frei's repeated retreats from the notion that the meaning of a doctrine is intrinsically tied to the context of its use, including the context of passions and dispositions.

Gouwens's main contention is that Kierkegaard combined a concern for orthodox doctrines and a concern for passionate existence.[35] He tried to do justice both to the object of faith and to the subjective qualifications of the believer. Doctrines define the object of faith so that the individual can relate to God in faith, and faith is necessary for talk about God, the object of faith, to be meaningful. Although the doctrines state publicly the main convictions and principles of the Christian life, their meaning is only fully grasped as the individual passionately appropriates them.[36] In effect, Gouwens's exposition of Kierkegaard shows how the seemingly countervailing themes of the objectivity of doctrines and subjectivity as a necessary condition for the meaningfulness of doctrines can be harmonized. The tendency of Frei and Lindbeck to reify doctrine could be resisted, and the perception that Holmer reduced doctrine to its subjectivity-shaping role could be dispelled. In Gouwens's work on Kierkegaard the theme of doctrines as the grammar of the faith and the theme of Christianity as a set of passions and practices are synthesized. Both of the major trajectories in the Yale School are taken into account. Ultimately, it is the passionate and skilled living out of the doctrinal grammar that establishes the self-identity and uniqueness of the Christian faith. The coherence and continuity of Christianity is not rooted in anything that can be cognized in a purely "objective" manner, but is grounded in the coherence and continuity of the passions and virtues that constitute the Christian life.

---

35. Ibid., 12–23.

36. For an example of how Calvin manages the dialectic between passion and doctrine see the essay by Warner Bailey in this volume [editors' note].

Bibliography

Auerbach, Erich. *Mimesis: The Representation of Reality in Western Literature*. Princeton: Princeton University Press, 1953.
DeHart, Paul. *The Trial of the Witnesses: The Rise and Decline of Postliberal Theology*. Malden, MA: Blackwell, 2006.
Frei, Hans. *The Eclipse of Biblical Narrative: A Study in Eighteenth and Nineteenth Century Hermeneutics*. New Haven: Yale University Press, 1974.
———. *The Identity of Jesus Christ: The Hermeneutic Basis of Dogmatic Theology*. Philadelphia: Fortress, 1975.
———. "The 'Literal Reading' of Biblical Narrative in the Christian Tradition: Will It Stretch or Will It Break?" In *The Bible and the Narrative Tradition,* edited by Frank McConnell, 36–77. Oxford: Oxford University Press, 1986.
———. *Types of Modern Theology*. New Haven: Yale University Press, 1992.
Gouwens, David. *Kierkegaard as Religious Thinker*. Cambridge: Cambridge University Press, 1996.
———. "Kierkegaard's Understanding of Doctrine." *Modern Theology* 5 (1988) 13–22.
Higton, Mike. *Christ, Providence, and History*. New York: T. & T. Clark, 2004.
Holmer, Paul. *The Grammar of Faith*. San Francisco: Harper & Row, 1978.
———. *On Kierkegaard and the Truth*. Edited by David J. Gouwens and Lee C. Barrett. Eugene, OR: Cascade, 2012.
Lindbeck, George. *The Nature of Doctrine: Religion and Theology in a Postliberal Age*. Philadelphia: Westminster, 1984.
McGrath, Alister. *Understanding Doctrine*. Grand Rapids: Zondervan, 1990.
Michener, Ronald. *Postliberal Theology: A Guide for the Perplexed*. New York: T. & T. Clark, 2013.
Murphy, Nancey. *Beyond Liberalism and Fundamentalism: How Modern and Postmodern Philosophy Set the Theological Agenda*. Harrisburg, PA: Trinity, 1996.
Pecknold, C. C. *Transforming Postliberal Theology: George Lindbeck, Pragmatism and Scripture*. New York: T. & T. Clark, 2005.

2

Reflections on Religious Pluralism
Disciples Re-imagining Mission 1941–1973

—Don A. Pittman

In honor of David J. Gouwens
Professor of Theology. Conversation Partner. Friend.

As David J. Bosch has observed, most American Protestants in the twentieth century, through the 1950s, shared an expectation for the complete evangelization of the world that was more "futurist rather than eschatological."[1] In fact, the hope that this great task could actually be accomplished within a single generation had been championed at the World Missionary Conference in Edinburgh in 1910, at the peak of Western missionary enthusiasm for foreign missions. The contagious confidence of the Methodist layman and leader in the Student Volunteer Movement (SVM) who chaired the conference, John R. Mott (1865–1955) was grounded in his buoyant sense of a contemporary *kairos*, a uniquely opportune moment for transforming the world provided by the converging energies and accomplishments of an ancient faith and a modern science. Wrote Mott:

> The hand of God in opening door after door among the nations of mankind, in unlocking the secrets of nature and in bringing to light invention after invention, is beckoning the Church of our day to larger achievements . . . .It seems entirely possible to fill the earth with the knowledge of Christ before the present

---
1. Bosch, *Transforming Mission*, 338.

generation passes away . . . . Ours is an age of unparalleled opportunity. 'Providence and revelation combine to call the Church afresh to go in and take possession of the world for Christ . . . . Now steam and electricity have brought the world together. The Church of God is in the ascendant. She has well within her control the power, the wealth, and the learning of the world. She is like a strong army in the presence of the foe . . . . The victory may not be easy, but it is sure.'[2]

While the brutality of World War I (1914–1918) soon shattered that optimism in the Protestant churches of Europe, it was not until the 1960s, as Bosch claims, that the churches of North America saw "the last, even if convulsive, attempts at reasserting the philosophy of Western programs proffering a panacea for the world's ills."[3] Indeed, throughout the years of World War II (1941–1945) and at least a decade beyond, there appeared to be a broad consensus among Protestant leaders in the U. S., including leaders of the Disciples of Christ, that the "decisive hour" for Christian mission work was at hand, even if delayed by the exigencies of war.[4]

To be specific, it was the common expectation of a great many in the churches that the ancient religious "superstitions" of Africa, Asia, and the Middle East would very soon fall by the wayside of history. This would occur, on the one hand, many imagined, as a result of advances in modern science, technology, and education that would create a modern global mono-culture, shaped by Western Christianity and favorable to its growth. On the other hand, it would occur in relation to the implementation of ecumenical Protestant plans for global evangelism, to which, as Bosch observes, they often referred in devotional literature and hymnody with provocative military terms such as "crusades," and "crusaders;" "conquests" and "Christian soldiers;" "marching orders" and "advancing armies," etc.[5] In a 1941

---

2. Bosch, *Transforming Mission*, quoting Mott, *The Evangelization of the World*, 338. The quotation included within the block quotation is cited by Bosch as "*The Student Volunteer* and Calvin W. Mateer." Readers should note that while using inclusive language to construct this essay, I have not tried to reconstruct the non-inclusive language employed by others.

3. Bosch, *Transforming Mission*, 338.

4. In view of my aim to describe elements of the practical theological dialogue within the life of the Protestant communion known now as the Christian Church (Disciples of Christ) I shall stipulate that, in addition to official members of the denomination, all ecumenical leaders whose written work appears in the denomination's magazine, *World Call*, and cited here may be considered "Disciples leaders" because of their assumed intention to contribute to the denominational dialogue and the decision of the editors to include their voices.

5. Bosch, *Transforming Mission*, 338.

World Call essay, "A Decisive Hour of Christian Missions," Iowa pastor Harold Roberts asserted, "Strife is in all the earth. Fear and suspicion cast their awful pall upon life. Hate, poisoned brew of diabolical witches, corrupts the health of mankind. Fanatical devotion to nationalism . . . is everywhere. A new order of paganism is on the march in the earth . . . . Can one—in his right mind—insist that this is 'the decisive hour of Christian missions?' The picture does not overwhelm me. Man's extremity is God's opportunity . . . The time is now! This is the decisive hour!"[6]

Most Christians acknowledged that on one point, at least, Mott was undoubtedly correct: the evangelization of the whole world would not be an easy matter. Much prayerful consideration and hard work would be needed by denominational leaders to determine how the Disciples of Christ could most effectively communicate the Christian witness in word and deed in an increasingly pluralistic, religiously competitive, and war-torn world. However, first, they failed to anticipate fully how well many ancient indigenous religions would be able to adapt and flourish within modern urban societies. Second, they did not anticipate how polarized and fractured their own Protestant "brotherhood" would soon become in their efforts to address a whole range of practical theological issues related to mission outreach both at home and abroad, issues about which they could not agree—from restorationism to racism, restructure to relationships with union and 'younger' churches. And, third, by the time of the IMC Jerusalem conference in 1928, and most certainly by the 1932 publication of the study, *Re-Thinking Missions: A Laymen's Inquiry After One Hundred Years*, edited by William Ernest Hocking and offering support for theological pluralism, members of the denomination began to face new and unexpected theological challenges, as many Disciples found themselves, uncomfortably, on the opposite sides of a "conservative/ liberal divide" from family and friends, clergy and colleagues.[7] This development of difference, which James Duke identifies with an "era of Disciples theological liberalism," extends, he says, from approximately 1910 to 1950.[8] Interconnected with other forms of liberalization rooted in the "fundamentalist/modernist" split at the turn of the century, the theological commentary on these developments by the missionary historian, Stephen C. Neill, makes his own orientation rather clear. He writes, with reference to the appearance of a "very different gospel:"

> In those years of rapid missionary expansion, *a very different Gospel* had been growing up and taking hold of the minds of a

---

6. Roberts, "A Decisive Hour of Christian Missions," 13–14.
7. See Hocking, *Re-Thinking Missions*.
8. Duke, "Liberalism," 473–76.

great many Christians, especially in America. The liberal was not by any means so sure that Jesus Christ was the last word of God to man. He was repelled by the exclusive claim to salvation through Christ alone. He tended to take a much more favorable view of the other religions than his more conservative colleagues, and to look forward to some kind of synthesis of religions rather than to the disappearance of any of them. The real enemy is secularism. Adherents of all the great religions should stand together in defense of the spiritual reality of man's life. There should be no hostility between them, the spirit of proselytism being replaced by the willingness to learn from one another.[9]

Toward Interreligious Understanding and Mission Re-imagining

In a 2009 essay, I explored one of those sensitive issues that characteristically distinguishes theological conservative from liberal, i.e., different perspectives on religious pluralism, limiting the scope of the study to clippings from the denomination's international monthly magazine *World Call* published in the years between World War I and II (1919–1940) with special attention to the two world missionary conferences sponsored by the International Missionary Council (IMC) in the period under review: Jerusalem (1928) and Tambaram, near Madras (1938).[10] I argued that, in relation to the Disciples' gradual transition from a moderately conservative, evangelical communion toward a more progressive, mainline Protestant communion with liberationist alignments, one can, indeed, find a range of materials published in *World Call* which provided readers greater access to the diversity of Christian voices that both defended as well as challenged the traditional "replacement model" of theological exclusivism, thereby enriching the church's theological conversations on the reality and vitality of other faiths.[11] Nevertheless, I acknowledged that the publication of any particular

9. Neill, *A History of Christian Missions*, 454.

10. See Pittman, "Clippings from *World Call*: Disciples Perspectives on Religious Pluralism, 1919–1940," 57–76; Pittman, "Clippings from *World Call*: Disciples on Racism, 1941–1973," 65–91; and Pittman and Williams, "Interpretations of Mission and Evangelism: The Continuing Debate on Strategy in Overseas Ministries in the Christian Church (Disciples of Christ)" 206–47. Kenneth Cracknell's examination of this era in this volume from a Presbyterian perspective is a companion to this essay [editors' note].

11. For a study of the development "from missions to mission," see Toulouse, *Joined in Discipleship*, 189–217.

essay in *World Call* provides insufficient evidence to judge its ultimate influence within the denomination. That acknowledgement is equally applicable with regard to the findings in this 2014 essay.

I will extend here my earlier study on religious pluralism by asking what kind of practical theological reasoning concerning interfaith issues did members of the Disciples of Christ see modeled by their leaders in their denominational magazine, *World Call*, during the middle years of the twentieth century, 1941–1973, i.e., from the year in which the U.S. became directly involved in World War II to the date when the magazine ceased publication, succeeded by *The Disciple* in January 1974. The thesis I shall argue is that during that thirty-two year period, the Disciples' ongoing conversations on religious pluralism may be said to have coalesced around answers to two controversial but important questions: first, in view of the Jews' confrontation with radical evil in the "Shoah," (the Holocaust, the genocidal "annihilation") how did Disciples leaders respond with instruction concerning Jewish-Christian relations? And, second, in view of the increasingly plural societies in which virtually all Christians have lived during the last century, what did Disciples leaders say in the limited period under review about engaging non-Christian neighbors in interreligious dialogue and cooperative work on important eco-justice issues?

The Shoah and the Church

In February 1939, more than two years before the United States formally entered World War II, the Board of Trustees of the United Christian Missionary Society (UCMS) declared anti-Semitism and racial animosities to be "foreign to the teaching of Jesus and repugnant to his spirit."[12] The formal resolution adopted by the board read in part:

> Anti-Semitism has raised its frightful head in Europe and there are increasing evidences that this sinister spirit is being deliberately fostered and propagated by organized groups in our own beloved land, some of whom presume to speak in the name of the Christian church. As Christians we utterly repudiate any such doctrine. . . . We therefore urge all our brethren to regard persons of all races and colors as sons and daughters of God, differing in color, in customs and outlook, but of one brotherhood in God's love and grace, and to oppose by all means at the command of Christians every effort to fan the flames of racial hatreds against Jews, Negroes, Orientals and other racial,

---

12. Crain, "Social Trends," 24.

national and religious groups. We urge instead that there be demonstrated toward all peoples that spirit of love and brotherhood which Jesus Christ exemplified in his life and teaching.[13]

Supportive of the board's action, a strong case linking the future of Christianity to that of Judaism appeared in a January 1941 essay by Robert A. Ashworth, editorial secretary of the National Conference of Christians and Jews (NCCJ). One of the first interreligious leaders to use the term "Judeo-Christian tradition," Ashworth remarked in *World Call*, "Long before Hitler, there was anti-Semitism. The history of Christianity—the religion of love—is stained throughout with the blotches placed upon it by the oppression and torture of the Jews. And this in spite of the fact that without the foundation laid by the Jews there would have been no Christianity.... Now is the time for Christian clergy and laity to operate, and to cut out anti-Jewish hate as a surgeon removes cancer tissue. It is the common enemy of Christian and Jew."[14]

Reporting on various ecumenical conferences in the late 1930s and 1940s, the editors of *World Call* repeatedly warned that anti-Semitism was anti-Christianity, and that Christians in the United States should not repeat the tragic mistake of German Christians "who failed to speak forth their condemnation clearly and unequivocally when this evil first raised its head."[15] Indeed, the editors of the magazine asserted that Disciples of Christ churches should take extra steps to ensure that children are protected from expressions of the hateful and dehumanizing agenda of anti-Semitism.[16] As the director of the Christian Institute for American Democracy, William C. Kernan argued in a parallel way, "Anti-Semitism is not only a crime against Jews. It is a crime against the human race.... Its goal is to make man lose his sense of God-likeness and dignity.... Nazism is not out to destroy the Jew. It is out to destroy humanity, *beginning with the Jew*."[17] Indeed, Kernan stated forcefully in another *World Call* essay, "We should let no opportunity pass to make known to our Congressmen, our editors, our neighbors, how strongly we feel about this matter. We should not be happy in a society that permits the persecution of Jews, the suppression of the press, the confinement of religion within the four walls of the church from which it dare not come out except at the risk of persecution. Yet there are people who want

---

13. Ibid.
14. Ashworth, "Danger to Christianity," 19.
15. Editorial, "Intolerance in National Debate," 3.
16. Editorial, "Anti-Semitism and the Churches," 3.
17. Kernan, "A Crime against Humanity," 19.

that and who would welcome it. We are not those people."[18] In tracing the "Logic of Race Hatred," Kernan concluded, "Hatred is Nazism's motivating power.... Hate demands ever more and more victims. It is insatiable. The Nazis called it up out of the darkness as a demon for persecuting the Jews. This was their first crime. They did not intend that it should be their last. Hate is now strong in them. It needs new meat to feed on."[19]

In an October 1942 essay, "The Church Looks at Race," George Walker Buckner, Jr., the editor of *World Call*, and also, from 1941 to 1961, the executive director of the Council on Christian Unity, highlighted the mutual respect, interdependence, and dignity of origin as children of the one God, which are as much in focus in Christian theological reflection and practices of care as they are absent in the dark, Nazi vision of the world. Writes Buckner:

> A first and basic assumption is the fact that all men are the children of God, and thus brothers and sisters to one another. As members of the family of God, all men, regardless of race, are to be accorded the respect to which such dignity of origin entitles them. No man looked upon as a son of God can be regarded cheaply; nor are his rights to be satisfied with ease. But when this Christian conception of the dignity of human life is absent ... [any] man is to be looked upon as a cheap person—one whose rights you do not have to respect and whom you may use and exploit to your advantage without regard for his person... . The only possible solution of the race question is that of cooperation. This is the Christian solution. Its proposal is one which recognizes the interdependence of all peoples and races. This interdependence is both economic and spiritual.... [And] there is no nation which affords greater opportunity for the working out within its own life of the principles of interracial cooperation than the United States of America.[20]

Improving Jewish-Christian relations and overcoming racial prejudice were, undoubtedly, matters of significance for the Disciples of Christ, as reflected by the large number of essays and reports dedicated to the subjects in *World Call* from the 1930s on. However, the denomination's critical conversations took on a more explicitly theological character only with the 1960s and the constructive resolutions of Vatican II, 1962–1965. That

18. Kernan, "Christians and Future Society," 19.
19. Kernan, "The Logic of Race Hatred," 17.
20. Buckner, "The Church Looks at Race," 3. See also Conning, "Why I am Not an Anti-Semite," 10–11.

is, through the war years and more, the issues most under discussion with regard to Judaism remained essentially ethical ones related to our churches' opposition to the Nazi's immoral practices of racial discrimination, their denial of basic human rights and democratic freedoms, and, ultimately, their implementation of the Führer's "final solution." Church leaders and members found it necessary to acknowledge not only that the unbelievably horrific genocide undertaken by the Nazis actually happened on the scale reported, but also that it was facilitated in part by the passive complicity of a great many Christians. Perhaps even more significant, church members had to face the fact that the Nazi's crimes all had to be interpreted against the background of nearly two thousand years of the church's irresponsible and hateful "teaching of contempt" for Jews and Judaism. Accordingly, news of a rise of Anti-Semitism within the U.S., even as the war in Europe neared its end, was extremely disturbing to the staff of *World Call*, which responded with redoubled efforts to educate their readers about the evils of such injustices. Buckner—under appointment as Special Representative of the American Committee of the World Council of Churches(WCC)—reported to what he had seen and heard on his WCC fact-finding tour in Europe in the summer and fall of 1945. The extent of the human suffering, he testified, was truly staggering: Six million Jews killed or eliminated in the persecution. According to Nazi admissions at Nuremberg, 4 million of these were killed outright and an additional 2 million died under the pressure of mass removals and similar travails. Much of Europe was reduced to ruins. An estimated death toll in all war related action ultimately approached fifty million human beings.[21]

Eventually, the ethical discourse on Anti-Semitism and Jewish-Christian relations took on the character of a more fully developed theological conversation with the remarkable pronouncements (or, more accurately, "four constitutions," "nine decrees," and "three declarations") debated and approved by the Second Vatican Council. Convened by Pope John XXIII and adjourned by his successor, Pope Paul VI, Vatican II met in Rome for four lengthy sessions during the years 1962–1965. In the presence of invited observers representing the Disciples of Christ and other Protestant denominations, the Council considered a number of important documents relevant to a theology of religions, interreligious relations, and the church's mission in the modern world, such as *Nostra Aetate, Declaration On the Relation of the Church to Non-Christian Religions*, 1965; *Lumen Gentium, Dogmatic Constitution On the Church*, 1964; and *Ad Gentes, Decree On the Mission Activity of the Church*, 1965. The practical theological shifts approved at

---

21. Buckner, "Notes on Anti-Semitism in Europe," 6.

Theological Reflections

Vatican II came as a breath of fresh air for Roman Catholics and Protestants alike, as the Council declared all races to have a common religious origin and single final end, with assurance that God's providence, goodness, and plan of salvation extend to all persons, a significant distance from the doctrine of "limited atonement," so central to the theological teachings of John Calvin (1509–1564) and the Reformed tradition (cf. Wis 8:1; Acts 14:7; Rom 2:6–7; 1 Timothy 2:4). The opening lines of the introduction to *Nostra Aetate*, in language influenced by existentialism, traces human unity to common questions about life and death:

> In this age when the human race is daily becoming more closely united and ties between different peoples are becoming stronger, the Church considers more closely her own relation to non-Christian religions. Since it is her task to foster unity and love among men, and indeed among nations, she first considers in this declaration what men have in common and what draws them into fellowship together. . . . From his different religions, man seeks the answer to the riddles and problems of human existence; these exercise him What is man? What is the meaning and purpose of life? What are goodness and sin? What is the origin and purpose of suffering? Which is the way to attain true happiness? What is death, judgment and reward after death? What, lastly, is that ultimate and indescribable mystery, embracing the whole of our, which is our existence, which is both our origin and our end.[22]

An important section of *Nostra Aetate* on Jewish-Christian relations continues:

> The Jews have not, for the most part, accepted the gospel; some indeed have opposed its diffusion (cf. Rom 11:28). Even so, according to the Apostle Paul, the Jews still remain very dear to God, for the sake of their fathers, since he does not repent of the gifts he makes or the calls he issues (cf. Rom 11:28–9). . . . Even if the Jewish authorities, together with their followers, urged the death of Christ (cf. John 19:6) what was done to him in his passion cannot be blamed on all Jews living at that time indiscriminately, or on the Jews of today. Although the Church is the new People of God, the Jews should not be presented as rejected by God or accursed, as though this followed from Scripture.[23]

---

22. Quoted in Hick and Hebblethwaite, *Christianity and Other Religions: Selected Readings*, 83–84.

23. Ibid.

Only two years later, in September 1967, Paul G. Barker, New York Region Director of the National Conference of Christians and Jews (NCCJ) published a provocative article in *World Call* on the subject of "Changes in Relationships between Christians and Jews," released as a supplement to world outreach study materials already prepared on "Christ and the Faiths of Men." Encouraging consideration of relevant New Testament texts—such as Rom 11:1 ("I ask, then, has God rejected his people? By no means!"); Rom 11:29 ("for the gifts and the calling of God are irrevocable"); and Eph 2:15 ("He has abolished the law with its commandments and ordinances, that he might create in himself one new humanity;) etc.—Barker also called for special attention to the recently published "Guidelines for Catholic-Jewish Relations," from the U.S. Catholic Bishops' Commission for Ecumenical and Interreligious Affairs, which followed the Vatican II pronouncements.

Barker describes in his important essay the historical development of the relationship between Christians and Jews in three distinct stages. The initial period, he suggests, was from the time of Jesus and his disciples to the earliest church leaders, when Christianity was considered but one of the many distinct sects of Judaism (e.g., the Pharisees, Essenes, Zealots).

The second period Barker identifies with "the doctrine of replacement." This period, he says, covers the great expanse of time from the reign of Constantine in the early 4th century until the end of World War II. During this period, Christians understood their primary missional duty to be involved with the personal conversion and baptism of all non-Christians and the maintenance of a Christian social order, believing confidently that Christianity in time would become the universal religion and provide the fundamental ideology for governments everywhere. Wrote Barker:

> The methods and techniques that were used throughout the history of the church to carry out this commitment resound with the greatest acts of man's inhumanity to man. Wherever Christianity spread, forced conversions were the order of the day. The Inquisition of the Counter-Reformation period, especially in Spain, speaks tragically of the replacement doctrine. The most tragic result of this doctrine was that for almost 1,800 years Christianity and Judaism stopped communicating in any meaningful way. Most Christians sincerely believe, because they have never been told differently, that when Christianity arrived, Judaism somehow spiritually died, and that no thought, no development and no creativity ever existed again within that faith.[24]

---

24. Barker, "Changes in Relationships between Christians and Jews," 13. All subsequent quotations from Barker are from this three-page source. On Vatican II, see also Blakemore, "A Protestant Looks at Vatican Council," 24–25.

To be sure, one of the most disturbing strands in the long history of Western civilization are accounts of Christian mistreatment and violence toward the Jews. In many times and places, Christians have appeared all too ready to spend their energies and material resources on converting Jews, at whatever cost, prohibiting the development of more reasoned and reasonable relationships of mutuality and dialogue. Observes Barker:

> More important than the social manifestation of anti-Semitism to the maintenance of the breach between Christian and Jew has been the religious fervor for conversion of the Jew to Christianity. This one element has been the single most effective bar prohibiting the development of meaningful Jewish-Christian dialogue. As long as Christians maintain that they, and only they, have the facility for supplying the religious meaning to life and all other religious manifestations are inferior, no possibility exists for anything other than hostility.[25]

The third period, which Barker claims is just now beginning in our own lifetime, is to be identified with what he terms, "The Doctrine of Parallel Covenants." In other words, he says:

> The first covenant, that with Israel, maintains its validity to the end, side-by-side with the new covenant, or the new Israel that is the church. The main difference in the current period in Jewish-Christian relations, at least as manifest by proclamations of the Roman Catholic hierarchy and the Protestant establishment through the World Council and National Council of Churches, is that conversion is no longer the basis, either theologically or socially, for Jewish-Christian relations. In fact, proselytization must be consciously avoided, so that mutual trust may grow between the groups. This does not in any way renounce the missionary nature of Christianity, but it recognizes the validity and the vibrancy of Judaism as a meaningful religion for those who adhere to it. As yet, this period in Jewish-Christian relations is still tenuous and insecure. No one has had enough experience in either of the groups to know all the answers to the problems that inevitably arise. But, at a minimum, a new day has dawned for Christianity and Judaism and both will grow.[26]

Responding to the new day for Jewish-Christian relations, Rabbi Marc H. Tanenbaum, Director of Interreligious Affairs for the American Jewish Committee, asserted: "Now Christians are seeking out Jews for dialogue. If

25. Barker, "Changes in Relationships between Christians and Jews," 14.
26. Ibid.

these exchanges are to have any real effect, the first priority is to overcome the incredible, abysmal, mutual ignorance we have about each other." In addition, claimed Dore Schary, Chairman of the Anti-Defamation League, B'nai B'rith, in order to address such ignorance, "there needs to be a clear and more widespread recognition of the Jewish roots of the Christian church. The victim of the crucifixion," he commented, "was Jewish; those who wept were Jewish; and those who first carried the Christian message were also Jewish." In view of such Jewish statements, ecumenical Protestant delegates at the Third Assembly of the World Council of Churches, meeting in New Delhi, India, in 1961, approved a resolution which stated: "In Christian teaching the historic events which led to the crucifixion should not be so presented as to fasten upon the Jewish people of today the responsibilities which belong to our corporate humanity and not to one race or community."[27]

The documents excerpted here from *World Call* published in the 1960s demonstrate the intention of denominational leaders in the period to work toward better understanding and improved relationships between Christians and Jews. "Supersessionism," the Christian doctrine according to which Judaism was completely superseded or replaced in the economy of God's salvation by the new covenant in Jesus Christ, was being increasingly rejected by Disciples. At the same time, however, it was certain that Christians and Jews did not yet know one another sufficiently well, trust one another adequately, or have a vital sense of belonging to one another. Simply stated, no one doubted that there was a great deal of dialogical and relational work yet to be accomplished.

Disciples and Interfaith Dialogue

Delegates at the 1928 IMC conference in Jerusalem adopted a statement more appreciative of the continuity between Christianity and other religious traditions than could have ever been contemplated at Edinburgh.[28] In fact, they affirmed that the salvation, or healing, encountered most fully in Christ is also to be found even where Christ is not acknowledged. The report stated:

> To non-Christians also we make our call. We rejoice to think that just because in Jesus Christ the light that lighteth every man

27. These remarks are taken from a regular column in *World Call* titled "Quote . . . Unquote," in *World Call* 49, no. 8 (September 1967) 14.

28. Cracknell, in an essay in this volume, presents evidence of this discussion as early as the 1910 WMC among American Presbyterians.

shone forth in its full splendor, we find rays of that same light where He is unknown or even is rejected. We welcome every noble quality in non-Christian persons or systems as further proof that the Father, who sent His Son into the world, has nowhere left Himself without witness.

Thus, merely to give illustration, and making no attempt to estimate the spiritual value of other religions to their adherents, we recognize as part of the one Truth that sense of the Majesty of God and the consequent reverence in worship, which are conspicuous in Islam; the deep sympathy for the world's sorrow and unselfish search for the way of escape, which are at the heart of Buddhism; the desire for contact with Ultimate Reality conceived as spiritual, which is prominent in Hinduism; the belief in a moral order of the universe and consequent insistence of moral conduct, which are inculcated by Confucianism; the disinterested pursuit of truth and of human welfare which are often found in those who stand for secular civilization but do not accept Christ as their Lord and Savior.[29]

With regard to the question as to whether a non-Christian religion could, in any sense, be grounded in an actual encounter with the divine and could contribute positively, even if only imperfectly or partially, to the salvation, or "healing," that we can come to know fully in Jesus Christ, many readers of *World Call* in the period under review would have immediately rejected the possibility, emphasizing rather the "once and for all" character of the atoning life, death, and resurrection of Jesus Christ and denying any real point of contact between Christianity and other faiths. Accordingly, for them, humanity's spiritual options may be expresssed in starkly simple terms: "Chaos or Christianity." Indeed, the church is "the only world community upon which peace may be built."[30]

However, while the representatives at the 1910 Edinburgh conference were largely committed to a form of theological exclusivism and had a strong interest in global evangelism, it also became clear, when it came to their attitudes towards the non-Christian religions, there was, in fact, a diversity of opinion about the extent to which one could speak of the activity of God's Spirit outside the bounds of the church. Some pointed out that according to

---

29. "The Christian Message," quoted in DuBose, *Classics of Christian Mission*, 336.

30. Sly, "The Work Is Life," 26. At the time of writing, Sly was an executive secretary in the department of financial resources of the UCMS. In quotations from and titles of the historical sources cited in this essay, I have chosen to retain the original language of the historical documents, rather than to attempt the complicated alterations necessary to correct all non-gender-inclusive terms.

the author of Luke-Acts, "God shows no partiality," but accepts in every nation "anyone who fears him and does what is right" (Acts 10:34–35); a God who in past generations "allowed all the nations to follow *their* own ways; yet has never left himself without a witness in doing good (Acts 14:16–17); a God who, though worshipped as unknown by the people of Athens, is "the God who made the world and everything in it (Acts 17:24);" the God who determined when and where all nations would live throughout the whole world, "so that they would search for God and perhaps grope for and find him—though indeed God is not far from each one of us" (Acts 17:27); a God who "desires everyone to be saved and to come to the knowledge of the truth" (1 Tim. 2:4).

In 1960, an essay appeared in *World Call* titled, "Challenge of the Other Religions," by Harry B. Partin, a Disciples minister and scholar serving in Geneva with the World Council of Churches—under the auspices of the Disciples' Council on Christian Unity. Recognizing that the United States would soon be the most religiously diverse society on earth, the Disciples charged Partin to "investigate the current revival of non-Christian religions, the meaning for Christians, and the relevance of the Christian gospel for non-Christian faiths."[31] Partin emphasized in his essay that, as a result of the remarkable wisdom and courage displayed by early Disciples missionaries, and those from other Protestant denominations, the stage of "church planting" overseas had generally been accomplished, and, in most places, schools and seminaries had been educating their own local leaders for some time. Yet, most Christians in the West had anticipated that the old indigenous religions, in various cultural contexts around the world, would quickly begin to lose their attractiveness in the 20th century, especially in light of the growth of ecumenical Christianity, and advances in modern science, democracy, and education.

However, according to Partin, we have discovered that "there is new life in the old religions!"[32] First, new forms of modern nationalist movements throughout Asia have thrived in the post-World War II period in connection with creative recoveries of ancient religio-cultural traditions. In fact, as the countries of Asia have become independent, they have recovered to some extent the value of their own religious and cultural heritages. [They] are seeking to face the problems of modern life," writes Partin, "on the basis of a revival and reinterpretation of the traditional religions, [and] many are

---

31. Editorial "Illinois Minister Takes Ecumenical Post," 2.
32. Partin, "Challenge of the Other Religions," 16.

finding more satisfaction and help in the religions than we ever thought possible."[33]

Partin proceeds then to highlight a second interesting dimension of this resurgent spirituality that calls church members to recognize their changed situation: mission efforts are no longer merely "from the West to the rest," but "from the rest to the West." After describing briefly the missionary-minded efforts of important Buddhist and Hindu teachers both within their own Asian countries, as well as in North America and Europe, Partin comments, "Compassion for men of other religions does not require us to accept the other religions as adequate expressions of the love and truth of God. Neither does it mean that we should cease to witness to the love and truth of God we know in Jesus Christ. Respect and compassion for other men does demand of us," he concludes, "that we seek earnestly to understand the other religions and to see the best in them as well as the worst."[34] Partin called for members of Disciples churches to engage in "deep and sustained thinking" about these matters so as to remain both faithful to the God of justice and love whom we have come to know in Jesus Christ and honest, open, effective communicators in our relationships with our neighbors who believe that they too have been touched by the holy.[35]

West Virginia pastor Dwight E. Stevenson argued that the primary reason for the lack of interest in and support for global mission is the unfortunate association of Christian missionaries with Western colonialism, neo-colonialism, and imperialism. In his 1942 article, "Let Christian Missions Continue!" Stevenson wrote, "Unaware of the changing temper in the missionary movement itself, most Americans tend to think of missions in the light of its goals and techniques of 50 and 100 years ago. They see it as a kind of religious imperialism, bent upon spiritual exploitation, an arrogant encroachment upon cultures older than our own, religions older and culturally more suited to their devotees."[36] In fact, however, claims Stevenson, modern missionaries understand themselves to be *invited guests* and *partners in ministry*; "*guardians of the best in cultures that are now disturbed and threatened by political and industrial upheavals;*" and *agents of peace and reconciliation.*"[37]

---

33. Ibid.
34. Ibid.
35. Ibid.
36. Stevenson, "Let Christian Missions Continue!" 11.
37. See, "Disciples Are Preparing to Launch 'Crusade for a Christian World,'" *World Call* 28, no. 5 (May 1946) 18–20; "This Is the Year!" *World Call* 31, no.10 (November 1949) 25–32; and "Looking at the Crusade," *World Call* 33, no.3 (March 1951) 5.

Aware that many evangelical Disciples had remained convinced that the non-Christian religions of the world had their source in either futile human attempts at self-justification or satanic trickery, Jack Finegan, a professor of religious education at Iowa State University, recommended in a 1944 essay a less rigid and negative approach:

> To be sure, it is no longer possible to maintain the naïve earlier theory that, while God gave us the Christian religion the other religions were created by the devil. The study of comparative religions shows us earnest longings after God and genuine truths about God in all the great religions. But certainly all people should have a chance to share the best . . . . We believe that Jesus Christ is the truth. We believe that in him is the very best in all the world, that in him is something universal to which there is an answering chord in the hearts of men wherever he becomes known.[38]

Historically, Christians have boldly claimed that their self-emptying spirituality of altruistic love, in which one saves one's life by losing it, offers a stark contrast to the non-Christian religious traditions of the world which have characteristically taught forms of self-concerned religiosity with little sustained attention to ethical issues related to and compassionate care for one's neighbors.[39] Such was the final position taken, among others, by John A. MacKay, the distinguished president of Princeton Theological Seminary and chair of the IMC, who, following a trip through East Asia in 1950, concluded that the region's older religions, whether indigenous or not, such as Buddhism, Confucianism, and Shinto, were unquestionably moribund and had "nothing to give for such a revolutionary period as ours."[40]

While Disciples with conservative theological orientations continued to emphasize the absolute discontinuity between Christianity and all other religious traditions, those with more progressive theological orientations were more open to the notion that God is always at work for good in the lives of all human beings whom God has created and loves unconditionally, more open to the idea that in so far as they attend to the leading of the Holy Spirit and the dictates of conscience, their salvation remains a possibility with God. Accordingly, individuals committed to non-Christian religions can serve as dialogue partners and co-workers with Christians on important eco-justice issues of common concern, this being especially the

---

38. See Finegan, "Why Do You Believe in Missions," 11.
39. Ibid.
40. Editorial, "Opportunity in East Asia," 6.

case when those non-Christian partners are associated with modern reform movements within their larger religious communities.

For example, even before the end of World War II, there were progressive Disciples leaders who recognized that there were different forms of Mahayana Buddhism in East Asia, including those Chinese forms in harmony with the teachings of the highly educated, social-activist master, the Venerable Taixu (1890–1947) who had asked to discuss his ideas for transmitting Buddhism to the West with the Disciples' missionary-scholar, Clarence H. Hamilton.[41] Similarly, there were Disciples missionaries in Japan who recognized that the militarized form of Shinto represented an aberration from the classical or "pure" form. In fact, wrote W. H. Erskine, we may come to recognize certain forms of these religions that may serve as a "schoolmaster" to Christ, "preparing to receive the Word made flesh:"

> Shintoists still have many loyal followers who have not bowed to the military rulers at the expense of religious liberty. They believe that there is truth and righteousness in the idealism of their national thoughts and historical personalities. Japanese Christians, who confess their faith in Jesus as the Christ (known by the thousands) feel that they must keep their feet on the historical background while they reach forth to the heights of spiritual idealism. Such souls would use their Old Testament [i.e., pure, classical Shinto] as the *schoolmaster to lead them to the Christ*. They are the Christians who take the writer of Hebrews at face value when he says that the "God who at sundry times and in divers manners has spoken unto men through prophets has in these days spoken unto us by his son."[42]

In the late 1950s, the Disciples sought to become more self-conscious with regard to their approach to mission. After wide circulation in Disciples congregations for reflection and critical review over a four-year period, (1955–1959) the important document, "Strategy of World Mission," was ultimately approved to provide clarity with regard to its principles, purposes, and procedures in global mission. The extended debate on the strategy statement did not resolve all of the theological differences and tensions within the church, to be sure, as the missionary-scholar, Joseph M. Smith has pointed out.[43] Nevertheless, according to Robert A. Thomas, who served for a number of years as president of the Division of Overseas Ministries (DOM) the

---

41. See Pittman, *Toward a Modern Chinese Buddhism*, 115–117.

42. Erskine, "Shintoism," 25. Emphasis mine.

43. Smith, "A Strategy of World Missions," 26. See also on this point, Pittman and Williams, "Interpretations of Mission and Evangelism," 206–47.

church did commit itself in the early 1970s to four new "directions" in mission. In fact, in 1973, the final year of the period under review here, Thomas summarized the four directions in his booklet, *Where In the World Are We Going? The Overseas Ministry of the Christian Church (Disciples of Christ)* i.e., more ecumenism; evangelism for wholeness; local control; short-term service.[44] All four were grounded in an affirmation of the universality of God's presence and work in the world and of our relation to one another as teachers and learners. As one writer put it:

> Every man has to be met and respected in full awareness that God has "passed this way before." Most serious and careful account has to be taken of every man's cultural as well as religious background and traditions with the expectation that some evidences of the work of God whom we know in Jesus Christ may be found there. Every culture as well as every man will be presumed capable, at least *in potentia*, of teaching us something of the things of God. Every Christian will therefore witness with intent to learn as well as to teach. "The expansion of the Christian Church" will be an exercise in modest appreciation and gratitude, not a manifestation of racial, cultural, or institutional triumphalism.[45]

Also in 1973, then president of the Council on Christian Unity of the Christian Church (Disciples of Christ) George G. Beazley—following his participation in the "Salvation Today," conference in Bangkok, Thailand, sponsored by the Commission on World Mission and Evangelism of the WCC—struggled to articulate in a *World Call* essay, "The 'Hidden Christ' and Commitment," an acceptable form of theological inclusivism. Beazley writes that he is quite aware that Christians have always believed that God has not left himself without witness in any culture; that the Apostle Paul is represented as having made this point about the "hidden Christ" in his sermon at Athens (Acts 17:16–33); and that he treats this question at some length in 1 Corinthians and Romans, while the prologue to John (John 1:1–18) speaks of the Logos or Word which became flesh and Jesus Christ as "the true light that enlightens everyone." It is these passages which have provided the primary points of contact for most Christian missionary endeavors and have prompted our commitment to dialogue with persons of other faiths and ideologies.

---

44. Thomas, *Where In the World Are We Going?* 43–51.

45. Drummond, "Reflections on Overseas Christian Mission," in Thomas, *Where in the World Are We Going?* 42.

Yet, many are aware that Christian converts around the globe are often cut off not only from their families, but also from the entire culture of which they are a part, if they espouse a faith which has come in Western forms from another part of the world. As a convert from India expressed his concern to Beazley: "Can't we retain word and sacrament and yet not demand this [ritual] break through so radical a symbol as baptism? If we can't, is there any hope of our converting a vast Hindu or Buddhist majority, when this view is so woven into a national and cultural existence that Christianity seems like a foreign import from a part of the world that once conquered and exploited us?"[46] The critical conversation is about how much freedom exists for the indigenization and contextualization of the gospel in another culture? The appropriate attitude for beginning such a critical conversation on Christ and culture was captured effectively by an unnamed American missionary to the Philippines, widely known, claims Joseph M. Smith, for "his identification with the life and aspirations of the Filipino people," who once said: "I did not come here to change these people. I came here to change. Until I understand their culture and enter into their point of view, I cannot tell what belongs to my culture and what belongs to the gospel."[47]

Following the WCC conference in Bangkok, the editor of *World Call*, James L. Merrell, wrote of the need to act in accord with what we know about the mind of Christ. And, most fundamentally, what we know is what we have learned from the cross of Christ: we are loved! Writes Merrell: "[It] impels us to start walking joyously even if the path leads to sacrifice. It compels us to engage in spoken witness and to enter into dialogue with all those, of one faith or another, of one conviction or another, who are also loved by God. In spite of differences, the other must never be regarded as an enemy, but, through Jesus Christ, as a brother or sister through whom God wants to enrich us."[48]

As Disciples have discovered through the practice of interreligious dialogue, Christians must be willing in the process both to give and to receive, to talk and to listen, i.e., to offer opportunities for the development of meaningful relationships in the hope of reciprocal responses. In fact, in a 1973 *World Call* essay titled "Giving and Receiving," Robert S. Bates, the Disciples' secretary for East Asia and the Pacific at the time, notes, "Since we believe that the Holy Spirit moves where it wills, and is, therefore, not restricted to the church, we should expect that God will bear us gifts through

---

46. Beazley, "The 'Hidden Christ' and Commitment," 18–19. This section represents a close paraphrase of the original text.

47. Smith, "The Philippines After Twenty Years," 15.

48. Editorial, "A Message About Salvation," 17.

Hindus, Buddhists, Muslims, Jews, and Marxists as well—for these, too, are his children, fellows with us on this planet."⁴⁹ Beazley, Smith, and Bates provide no easy answers about how to become one with the mind of God, but each one calls for greater Christian sensitivity in dialogical engagement on the broadest scale possible, considering all related issues of Christ and culture, for "the whole future of the Christian faith," Beazley declared, "may depend on all of us finding the right solution."⁵⁰

Fellowships of dissatisfaction, islands of creative good

Not all Disciples, of course, have been convinced that interfaith activities are important. For example, in 1950, according to a report by the Religious News Service, Charles Clayton Morrison, the retired editor of the *Christian Century*, told more than 3,000 persons attending a Reformation Day service: "The Protestant faith is being watered down today by an organized propaganda [campaign] under the guise of interfaith 'good will' and 'brotherhood' . . . . False tolerance . . . has lulled Protestants to sleep" in the face of grave perils to religious liberty and separation of church and state."⁵¹ Yet as Vern Rossman asserted, when serving the UCMS as Director of Church and Community, the religious tradition most likely to survive into the human future will be the one that can give individuals and communities a lasting sense of their meaning and significance, as it relates them to the movements of history. In fact, Rossman remarked, "The religion that survives will be the one that pours itself out for the salvation of . . . [all] . . . physically, mentally and spiritually . . . [that will] out-love, out-give, out-suffer all other faiths . . . If the church does not become such a force [in history], God will raise up men and movements that will. . . . [God] will not be defeated by our unfaithfulness.⁵²

Not long after the end of World War II, in a *World Call* essay, "There Must Be Understanding," W.W. Waymack, a member of the U. S. Atomic Energy Commission, remarked: "We are not at the end, but a mere step beyond the beginning of the Atomic Age."⁵³ In other words, we are but one pace beyond the first great nuclear weapon of mass destruction which will provide the template for ever more powerful and destructive bombs in

49. Bates, "Giving and Receiving," 25.
50. Beazley, "The 'Hidden Christ' and Commitment," 18–19.
51. Morrison, quoted in a Religious News Service (RNS) report and printed in *World Call*, 32, no. 1 (1950) 2.
52. Rossman, "Christ and the Faiths of Men in the City," 13.
53. Waymack, "There Must Be Understanding," 10.

the future. As Waymack writes: "Not in a sylvan Eden, but in a complex, intimately interrelated . . . society of billions, there has suddenly appeared . . . a new 'Tree of Knowledge.' It is a new challenge to human intelligence and vision and yes, goodness, which tests us as to whether we can rise to it or whether we cannot."[54]

Buckner identifies the ultimate test as that of discerning the mind of Christ; recognizing his way of thinking, his way of looking at life, his way of being in the world, for us. Sharing the concerns of Jesus, remarks Buckner, the church becomes *"a fellowship of dissatisfaction,"* "a fellowship of those who rebel against all that is but should not be."[55]

Having served as a missionary in China at a time of great disorder, Lewis S. C. Smythe tried to focus our conversation on how we can start "making the new world better." Our churches have to begin thinking of themselves, he comments, as *"islands of creative good,"*[56] borrowing terminology from Henry Nelson Wieman. They must become, for Smythe, centers for study, critical thinking, and communication on a global scale. In all cases expanding our ministries, in all directions, our lives transformed by the God who calls us into dialogue with one another, and to work for the healing of all that is not as it should be, for the reconciliation of all that is not well. In that context, the body of Christ on earth can begin re-imagining its mission and re-imagining the world.

Bibliography

Ashworth, Robert A. "Danger to Christianity: Anti-Semitism Prepares Way for Anti-Christian Attack." *World Call* 23, no. 1 (January 1941) 19.
Barker, Paul G. "Changes in Relationships between Christians and Jews." *World Call* 49, no. 8 (September 1967) 13.
Bates, Robert S. "Giving and Receiving." *World Call* 55, no. 1 (January 1973) 25.
Beazley, George G., Jr. "The 'Hidden Christ' and Commitment." *World Call* 55, no. 5 (May 1973) 18–19.
Blakemore, W. Barnett. "A Protestant Looks at Vatican Council." *World Call* 48, no. 5 (May 1966) 24–25.
Bosch, David J. *Transforming Mission: Paradigm Shifts in Theology of Missions*; Maryknoll: Orbis Books, 1981.
Buckner, George Walker Jr. "The Church Looks at Race." *World Call* 24, no. 9 (October 1942) 18–19.
———. "Let the Church Be the Church." *World Call* 24, no. 2 (February 1942) 20–21.
———. "Notes on Anti-Semitism in Europe." *World Call* 28, no. 2 (February 1946) 6.

---

54. Waymack, "There Must be Understanding," 7.
55. Buckner, "Let the Church Be the Church," 13.
56. Smythe, "Making the New World Better," 16.

"The Christian Message." Chapter 13 in *The Christian Life and Message in Relation to the non-Christian Systems of Thought and Life*. The Jerusalem Meeting of the International Missionary Council, March 24–April 28, vol. 1. Quoted in Francis M. DuBose, *Classics of Christian Mission*. Nashville: Broadman, 1979.

Conning, John Stuart. "Why I am Not an Anti-Semite." *World Call* 25, no. 3 (March 1943) 10–11.

Crain, James A. "Social Trends." *World Call* 21, no. 4 (April 1939) 24.

Duke, James O. "Liberalism." In *The Encyclopedia of the Stone-Campbell Movement*, edited by Douglas A. Foster, et al., 473–76. Grand Rapids: Eerdmans, 2012.

Drummond, Richard H. "Reflections on Overseas Christian Mission," *Occasional Bulletin of Missionary Research Library*, 23, no. 2 (February 10, 1972) 5.

Editorial. "Anti-Semitism and the Churches." *World Call* 27, no. 4 (April 1945) 3.

———. "Illinois Minister Takes Ecumenical Post." *World Call* 39, no. 2 (February 1957) 2.

———. "Intolerance in National Debate." *World Call* 23, no. 10 (November 1941) 3.

———. "A Message About Salvation." *World Call* 55, no. 5 (May 1973) 17.

———. "Opportunity in East Asia." *World Call* 32, no. 5 (May 1950) 6.

Erskine, W. H. "Shintoism." *World Call* 25, no. 9 (October 1943) 25.

Finegan, Jack. "Why Do You Believe in Missions." *World Call* 26, no. 8 (September 1944) 11.

Hick, John and Brian Hebblethwaite. *Christianity and Other Religions: Selected Readings*. Philadelphia: Fortress, 1980.

Kernan, William C. "Christians and Future Society." *World Call* 24, no. 2 (February 1942) 19.

———. "The Logic of Race Hatred." *World Call* 24, no. 10 (November 1942) 17.

———. "A Crime against Humanity." *World Call* 26, no. 3 (March 1944) 19.

Merrell, James L. "Living in Dialogue." *World Call* 55, no. 7 (July–August 1973) 31 and 45.

Mott, John R. *The Evangelization of the World in this Generation*. New York: Student Volunteer Movement for Foreign Missions, 1900.

Neill, Stephen. *A History of Christian Missions*. New York: Penguin, 1964.

Partin, Harry B. "Challenge of the Other Religions." *World Call* 42, no. 11 (December 1960) 16.

Pittman, Don A. "Clippings from *World Call*: Disciples Perspectives on Religious Pluralism, 1919–1940." In *A Passion for Christian Unity: Essays in Honor of William Tabbernee*, edited by John M. Imbler, 57–76. St. Louis: Chalice Press, 2009.

———. "Clippings from *World Call*: Disciples on Racism, 1941–1973." *Encounter* 73, no.1 (2012) 65–91.

———. *Toward a Modern Chinese Buddhism: Taixu's Reforms*. Honolulu: University of Hawaii Press, 2001.

Pittman, Don A., and Paul Williams. "Interpretations of Mission and Evangelism: The Continuing Debate on Strategy in Overseas Ministries in the Christian Church (Disciples of Christ)." In *Interpreting Disciples: Practical Theology in the Disciples of Christ*, edited by Dale Richesin and Larry Bouchard, 206–47. Fort Worth: Texas Christian University Press, 1987.

Roberts, Harold. "A Decisive Hour of Christian Missions." *World Call* 23, no. 6 (June 1941) 13–14.

Rossman, Vern. "Christ and the Faiths of Men in the City." *World Call* 49, no. 6 (June 1967) 11–13.

Sly, Virgil A. "The Work Is Life." *World Call* 23, no. 9 (October 1941) 26.

Smith, Joseph M. "The Philippines After Twenty Years: Birth in the Land of Morning," *World Call* 17, no. 5 (May 1963) 15.

———. "A Strategy of World Missions: The Theory and Practice of Mission as Seen in the Present World Mission Enterprise of the Disciples of Christ." Th.D. dissertation, Union Theological Seminary, 1961.

Smythe, Lewis S. C. "Making the New World Better," *World Call* 28, no. 3 (March 1946) 15–16.

Stevenson, Dwight D. "Let Christian Missions Continue!" *World Call* 24, no. 1 (January 1942) 11.

Thomas, Robert A., *Where In the World Are We Going? The Overseas Ministry of the Christian Church (Disciples of Christ)*. St. Louis: Christian Board of Publication, 1973.

Toulouse, Mark G. *Joined in Discipleship: The Shaping of Contemporary Disciples Identity*. Revised and expanded edition. St. Louis: Chalice, 1997.

Waymack, W. W. "There Must Be Understanding." *World Call* 29, no. 7 (July/August 1947) 7–10.

3

"The Church Militant"

A. Maude Royden and the Quest for Women's Equality in the Inter-War Years

—Susan J. White

On the same day that the most-welcome invitation to contribute to this volume arrived in my mailbox, the General Synod of the Church of England was meeting in session to consider the matter of the ordination of women to the episcopate. Having decided 20 years before to admit women to the presbyteral ministry,[1] albeit with certain 'conscience clauses' designed to appease those who could or would not accept the change in polity, the three Houses of Synod—Bishops, Clergy and Laity—were ready to take the final step toward the full inclusion of women in the leadership of the Church. On the night of November 21st, 2012 the three bodies were scheduled to vote separately on a motion to admit women to the episcopate. In order for women to become bishops, a two-thirds majority of each of the three houses would have to vote in the affirmative on the motion. Confidence was running high throughout the afternoon debates that full equality for women in the Church of England was finally about to be achieved.

At 6:17pm GMT the results were announced. The vote in the House of Bishops was 44 to 3 in favor (with 2 Bishops abstaining); in the House of Clergy it was 148 to 45. The vote in the House of Laity, however, was 132 to 74 in favor. In the House of Laity the motion had failed to achieve the two-thirds majority by 6 votes.

1. The Synod approved the ordination of women to the presbyterate in 1992 and the first ordinations were held two years later in 1994. (Women were ordained to the "permanent Diaconate" in 1987.)

The journey toward this vote to admit women to the most senior of the three apostolic ministries in the Church of England has been a long and uneven one. One hundred years before in 1913, with the Great War on the near horizon and the Women's Suffrage Movement gaining momentum, the Convocations of Canterbury and York were beginning to consider the matter of women's proper role in church life in a serious way for the first time.[2] Among those most responsible for raising the issue and ensuring that it remained a part of the Church's ongoing conversation was an Anglican laywoman of strong convictions, wide-ranging talents, deep theological insight, and considerable political savvy. Although Agnes Maude Royden (1876–1956) would not live to see women regularly ordained within her denomination,[3] and is little-remembered today, through her writing, lecturing, preaching and social action, she helped to lay the foundations for an expanded role for women in both Church and political life.[4]

As timely a subject as the theological arguments marshaled in support of women's full inclusion in the ordained ministries of the Church may be in itself, it also seems a fitting addition to a volume intended to honor David J. Gouwens. At Brite Divinity School, Texas Christian University, many generations of women gained a thorough theological grounding for ministry under his guidance. But David's presence on the faculty was particularly important to large numbers of women students who came to Brite having been barred from training for the ministry in their own denominations. In David they found a generous welcome and steady encouragement, and were able to put both their calling and their intellectual and pastoral gifts to the test. All of these women students can count Maude Royden as a sister-in-arms.

---

2. These provincial Convocations of clergy had been in existence as the canonical legislative bodies of the Church of England since the beginning of the 15th century, each with an Upper House (Bishops) and a Lower House (Clergy). In 1919 the Church Assembly (Powers) Act established the Church Assembly by adding a House of Laity to the two standing Convocations, and in 1970 the name of this body was changed to The General Synod.

3. She did, however, live to see Li Tim-Oi (1907–1992) ordained to the priesthood in Hong Kong in 1944, as an emergency measure in response to the acute pastoral needs of Anglican Christians in China after the Japanese invasion. Although Li resigned her license (but not her orders) after the war, in 1971 she was recognized as a priest in her diocese. See also below at n. 82.

4. The only full-length work devoted to Royden is Fletcher's biography, *Maude Royden: A Life*. Royden merits mention in Oldfield, *Women Against the Iron Fist*, 52–64; Alberti, *Beyond Suffrage*, 17 and 42; Ceadel, *Pacifism in Britain*, Jones, *Sexual Politics*, and Heeney, *The Women's Movement*.

The Nineteenth Century Foundations for Women's Ministry

When Maude Royden was born in 1876 an enormous change had been taking place in the nature of the ordained ministry in the Church of England. During the course of Victoria's long reign, that change that had been accelerating and could be clearly seen in the emergence of a new kind of Anglican clergyman. Even in the four short decades between Jane Austen's Edward Ferrars,[5] who like many younger sons of gentlemen and minor nobles 'entered the Church' as a way of respectably making a living without having unduly to exert themselves, and Charlotte Bronte's St. John Rivers, the zealous and dedicated missionary-cleric in *Jane Eyre*, there is already a world of difference. The transformation of the ordained ministry from the desultory occupation of the well-bred amateur to something more recognizable as a learned profession has been dealt with at length elsewhere.[6] Suffice it to say here that the increased availability of theological education and training and the expansion of professional literature and other resources were accompanied by higher expectations of competence in preaching, the leadership of worship, and pastoral care.[7] This change was such that by the late-19th century the notion that the average parson was simply a 'gentleman' with a particular set of social and economic loyalties had begun to disintegrate.[8]

In many ways, Church of England laymen were the beneficiaries of this new understanding of the clergy, and from the 1860's onwards there was an expansion of their role in both public worship and parochial Church governance. But it was a different story for their wives, sisters and daughters. Although women were by far the majority of Victorian churchgoers, they were barred from most public religious activities including reading the lessons, taking up the offering, serving at Communion, becoming choristers, and (with exceptions) participating in any of the various Councils of the Church.[9] And of course they were most clearly and emphatically forbidden

---

5. See Collins, *Jane Austen and the Clergy*.

6. For more on this topic see, for example, Russell, *Clerical Profession* and Heeney, *A Different Kind of Gentleman*.

7. Most of the Church of England's theological colleges were founded in this period before the Great War, e.g. St John's (1863) Lincoln (1874) Wycliffe Hall (1877) Westcott House (1881) Ripon (1897) Mirfield (1903) and smaller diocesan institutions such as the Schola Archiepiscopi at Bishopsthorne (1892). To these were added lay training colleges such as the Church of England Sunday School Institute at Blackheath (1843).

8. Heeney, *The Women's Movement*, 77–78.

9. Owen Chadwick, *The Victorian Church, Part 2*, 222–23.

to preach or preside at services, or they would have been forbidden had they had the temerity to make such a request.

But to say that women were merely passive consumers of male religious experience during this period would be to mistake the case. With the Industrial Revolution, and the burgeoning middle-class that was its immediate consequence, women's horizons and options had begun to widen considerably. Leisure-time had also become an increasingly-available commodity. As a result, women were able to put their surplus energies and gifts to use in the ecclesiastical sphere, and especially through the wide array of women's para-professional service organizations that flourished in this period. The Mothers' Union (founded in 1896) the Girls' Friendly Society (1874) the Women's Help Society (1889) the Women's Committee of the Church of England Temperance Society (1863) The Ladies' Association of the Society for the Propagation of the Gospel (1866) and the various smaller mission societies and 'sisterhoods' gave women scope for pastoral care and teaching, including Sunday School teaching, parish visiting and service to the sick and destitute.[10] It is in this work that the foundations for the quest for women's admission to the ordained ministry can be found. Women whose activity had previously centered on home and family (and then mainly under the direction of fathers and husbands) gained not only a deeper knowledge of the inner workings of ecclesiastical institutions, but also began to take their place in the public sphere.

Symbolic of the increasing sense that women's pastoral and spiritual work had a status within the Church was the restoration of the Order of Deaconesses. In 1861, Elizabeth Ferard (1825–1993) was 'commissioned' a Deaconess by Bishop A.C. Tait of London, who noted the ancient biblical precedent in the ministry of Phoebe (Romans 16:11) as his authority.[11]

---

10. We can see, however, the ways in which this organized women's work was still under the direct control of the clergy in a letter to the Editor of *The Spectator* in 1903, which describes the aims of the Women's Help Society: "The object of the Women's Help Society is to establish and maintain homes or clubs for the poorest classes of women and girls in all parishes *where the clergyman so desires*." (emphasis added) Basil Leverett, "The Women's Help Society: An Appeal," in *The Spectator*, 14 March 1903. And for a more cynical view of the domestic fallout from women's widening social concern we have the example of Charles Dickens' Mrs. Jellyby in *Bleak House*, for whom the African missions involved "the devotion of all my energies, such as they are," leaving her own family to fend for themselves.

11. The immediate precedent was the Kaiserswerth Institution, founded in 1836 in order to train Deaconesses for the German Lutheran churches. This was followed by the restoration of the Order of Deaconesses among Wesleyan Methodists, the Church of Scotland, and the Church of Sweden. Encouraged by Bishop Tait, Ferard visited Kaiserwerth prior to her commissioning. See Blackmore, "The Beginning of Women's Ministry."

(The social needs of London being what they were in this period, the Order's London origins are not surprising.) But the Order did not flourish, and even at its height in the 1920s there were only 300 Church of England Deaconesses. The clear identification of the Order of Deaconesses with the upper classes ("A Deaconess should be socially a gentlewomen of education and some means."[12]) and the expectation that the Deaconess would live a celibate life were probably discouragements to many otherwise capable and gifted women. Perhaps more importantly, the church could never decide whether the Order was an ordained ministry or not (or, in the rarefied world of Anglican argumentation, was it simply an 'order' or was it a 'holy order?') and it was not a ministry widely recognized and valued within the Church.

Many of those who were reluctant to accept the Order of Deaconess were convinced that it represented a very slippery slope; namely, that women who entered the diaconate might also be motivated to seek license to preach and ordination to the presbyterate. Even among the staunchest supporters of the Order there were those who took pains to state emphatically that it was never intended as a stepping-stone to the priesthood. In 1914, the Warden of the Deaconess Institution in Rochester and Southwark insisted that "deaconesses in the Anglican Communion and body do not regard their Order as any way whatever a step in the direction of the priesthood."[13] This regularly-reiterated position necessitated, of course, making a distinction between the male and female forms of the diaconate, the former a transitional ministry and the latter a permanent office or order.[14]

But not everyone was convinced that such a distinction between the male and female diaconate could or should be made, and they were quick to point out the range of theological, biblical, historical, and practical difficulties that arose out of making it. Certainly those who sought admission for women into all the forms ordained ministry saw the re-establishment of a vigorous Order of Deaconesses as healthy first-step. Between the first commissioning of a Deaconess in the Church of England in 1861 and the rather ambiguous and sometimes contradictory statements of the Convocations, Assemblies and Conferences that considered the matter in the 1920s and 1930s,[15] many found in the Order of Deaconesses real encouragement for

12. Gilmore, "Deaconesses: Their Qualifications and Status," 2.

13. Rev. J. H. Browne, "Letter to the Editor" in *The Guardian*, 30 July 1914.

14. In 1920 the Lambeth Conference finally made its position clear: "The Order of Deaconesses is for women the one Order of Ministry which has the stamp of Apostolic approval, and is for women the only order of ministry which we can recommend that our branch of the catholic church should recognize and use." Floor Debate, 29 July, *Lambeth Conference* 1920, 92.

15. Three Resolutions from the 1920 Lambeth Conference made its position on

their work. Certainly Maude Royden was one who viewed the restoration of the diaconate for women as both a theological and a practical foundation for her quest for a gender-inclusive Anglican ministry.

Women's Suffrage: Groundwork for the Work for Women's Ordination

But the first goal for those seeking equality for women was the vote, and it was in this struggle for enfranchisement that Maude Royden initially made her mark. During her time as a student at Oxford (1896–1899) and afterwards as a worker in the Victoria Women's Settlement House in her native Liverpool, she became a strong proponent of votes for women. She was the first chairman of the Church League for Women's Suffrage, founded in 1909, the aim of which was "to secure for women the Parliamentary vote as it is or may be granted to men; to use the power thus obtained to establish equality of rights and opportunities between the sexes; and to promote social and industrial well-being of the community."[16]

It would be sexual politics in one form or another, and in both Church and society, that would occupy all of Maude Royden's working life.[17]

Much in Royden's background, and many of her natural talents and inclinations, had prepared her for this work. She was the youngest of eight children, raised in an upper middle-class family in Liverpool. From her father, a gregarious and prosperous ship-builder, she had inherited a forceful

---

Deaconesses rather clearer:

Canon 47: The time has come when, in the interests of the Church at large and in particular of the development of the Ministry of Women, the Diaconate of Women should be restored formally and canonically, and should be recognised throughout the Anglican Communion.

Canon 48: The Order of Deaconesses is for women the one and only Order of the Ministry which has the stamp of Apostolic approval, and is for women the only Order of the Ministry which we can recommend that our Branch of the Catholic Church should recognise and use.

Canon 49: The office of a Deaconess is primarily a ministry of succour, bodily and spiritual, especially to women, and should follow the lines of the primitive rather than of the modern Diaconate of men. It should be understood that the Deaconess dedicates herself to a lifelong service, but that no vow or implied promise of celibacy should be required as necessary for admission to the Order. Nevertheless, Deaconesses who desire to do so may legitimately pledge themselves, either as members of a Community, or as individuals, to a celibate life.

16. *Church Militant*, March 1918. The Church League for Women's Suffrage existed from 1909 to 1919 (when votes for women were granted by Parliament).

17. Not only did she see women vote in Parliamentary elections, in 1922 she received at least four requests to stand for Parliament herself.

personality and an interest in and commitment to public service. Thomas Royden, who entered politics and was serving in Parliament when Maude was in her early adolescence,[18] was known as an honest man and a fair-minded employer. And that same sense of fairness ruled at home as well. Royden recalls her parents making no distinction in their expectations of their sons and their daughters, and those who were intellectually-inclined equally received a first-rate education.[19] It was a family of strong-willed, articulate people, and Maude clearly had the temperament to hold her own among them.

She was, however, also born with a physical disability: two dislocated hips, which took some time to diagnose and treat. She always described herself as being 'lame,' and in times of stress she could tire easily and was sometimes in considerable discomfort. But her condition seems to have given her a warmer and more lively sympathy for the frail and dispossessed than many of those from backgrounds similar to hers could muster. Indeed, she confided to a friend that "she was rather glad to be lame, since otherwise she would have succumbed to temptation, to be idle and frivolous, 'a regular society girl.'"[20] In her later years, walking became routinely painful and difficult, and her usually buoyant spirit sometimes succumbed to periods of severe despondency.

But for most of her working life she was both tireless and fearless, and her early efforts toward gaining the franchise for women honed her skills in writing, public speaking[21] and organizing, skills that would be invaluable in the fight for women's ordination. Although she was a leader within many local and national Suffrage organizations, the one dearest to her heart was the Church League for Women's Suffrage (CLWS) which had as an explicit aspect of its mission to "draw out the deep religious significance of the women's movement."[22] So the two causes, full equality for women in the matter of the vote and full equality for women in the matter of admission to Holy Orders, were inextricably linked in Royden's mind from very early on in her career.

---

18. Thomas Royden also served as Mayor of Liverpool and received a baronetcy in 1905.

19. Fletcher, *Maude Royden: A Life*, 12.

20. Ibid., 44.

21. By 1912 she was giving well over 250 speeches a year and ran 'Speakers classes' for National Union of Women's Suffrage Societies (NUWSS) and the London Society for Women's Suffrage (LSWS).

22. Claude Hinscliff to Archbishop Randall Davidson, 3 May 1912. Cited in Heeney, *Women's Movement*, 105.

Under Royden's direction, the CLWS communicated the aims and principles of the women's movement to a wide audience. In 1917, it staged a number of conferences, the first of which was a primer on the women's movement from a Christian perspective, and in the lead-up to the Parliamentary debate on the franchise for women it implemented a targeted lobbying campaign. Church services and religious meetings not only gave people theological and Biblical foundations for the feminist cause, but also raised a considerable amount of money. And through regularly-published newsletters, members were kept apprised of the progress of suffrage at home and abroad. While skilled in the practicalities of community organizing, Royden always had one eye on the broader philosophical underpinnings on which her defense of votes for women rested and which she promulgated in monographs and journal articles. She also brought to her suffrage efforts a more 'global' vision than many of her fellow workers. When she took up the editorship of the National Union of Women's Suffrage Societies (NUWSS) journal *Common Cause* in 1912,[23] her first headline was "Women's Suffrage: The Cause for All Humanity!"[24]

Royden poured considerable energy into the NUWSS, which had been founded in 1897 and was intended to gather under one umbrella-organization all the various Suffrage groups in Great Britain. But as the years went by, internal conflicts arose over both tactical and philosophical issues, and fissures began to appear in the movement. In 1902 the Women's Social and Political Union (the organizational home for the 'Suffragettes') broke away from the NUWSS, wishing to pursue more militant action. Royden and the CLWS stood firmly against the tactics of the more aggressive wings of the Suffrage Movement, although some members acknowledged that without the violence on both sides (that is, without both the harsh treatment of the women hunger-strikers and the destructive behavior of the Suffragette mobs) the urgency of the situation might not have been brought home to Parliament so forcefully. The outbreak of the 1914–18 War resulted in another serious fracture of the movement. Royden had always been naturally inclined toward pacifism,[25] and she found she could not remain in close

---

23. *Common Cause* was published between 1912 and 1917. Royden gave up the editorship in 1915.

24. At this time, the NUWSS was locked in conflict with the more militant Women's Social and Political Union, which had begun to use violent methods in their quest for equal rights for women.

25. She was an early member of the Women's International League for Peace and Reconciliation, and in 1914 became the secretary for the Fellowship of Reconciliation. This pacifism lasted throughout her life. Ceadel in *Pacifism in Britain 1914–1945* has pointed out: "Indeed what was perhaps the most sanguine pacifist initiative of the entire twentieth century occurred in February 1932: the attempt by a trio of leading Christian

collaboration with her compatriots who actively and enthusiastically supported the war effort.

But despite these tensions and disagreements over practical and theoretical details, Royden pressed on in the cause of Women's Suffrage from a Christian perspective. Indeed, the CLWS was the primary force through which churchwomen worked for the vote; by 1914 it had a membership of over 5000. And finally in 1918, one hundred years after Jeremy Bentham had called for universal suffrage in *A Plan for Parliamentary Reform* (1818) all women over 30 who met minimum property requirements were given the franchise. Ten years later in 1928 it was extended to all women over 21. But Royden was never one to rest on her laurels. Wherever and whenever women were exploited, treated unequally, or denied opportunities because of their gender, Royden was ready to speak out.

A Call to Preach

During much of the period during which Royden was working on gaining the vote for women, she was also deeply involved with work on behalf of equality for women within the structures of the Church of England. Armed with an impressive toolkit of skills and strategies, "by 1917 she was in the forefront of a struggle to make some claims for women in the Church of England."[26] The first of these 'claims' was that women should have a right to representation in the Councils of the Church.[27] With the battle for the franchise essentially won, Royden felt that the spiritual equality of women had been widely acknowledged in political life and that "it becomes ludicrous [for us] to accept a position of subordination [in the Church]."[28] She had always viewed the women's movement as deeply and essentially Christian, and as a result she argued not so much from a position that it was a woman's 'right' to active participation in Church government, or to be admitted to the priesthood, but rather that women's full inclusion would make the Church more completely itself. She urged: "Today if we feel that women should be welcomed into the ministry, into all the ministries of the Church

---

pacifists to form a Peace Army of unarmed passive resisters to intercede between the combats in the world's military confrontations, starting with the one in Manchuria. The prime mover of this scheme was one of the inter-war period's best-known woman pacifists, Dr Maude Royden, a former suffragist who . . . had devoted herself to the cause of peace."

26. Fletcher, *Maude Royden*, 137.

27. When the system of Parochial Church Councils was established in 1897, women were allowed to vote but not to stand for office.

28. Royden, "History of Antiquarianism" in *LCM Leaflet 1* (1917).

of the future, it is not only or chiefly because we think it is our right. It is because we are deeply convinced that our very idea of God in impoverished unless the idealism of all humanity, the spiritual experiences of both sexes, all classes and all races, are brought into the ministry of Christ."[29]

The essential equality of women before God made their equality in the Church a self-evident necessity.

At the same time Royden was also coming to terms with her own call to preach. Now 'coming to terms' implies she experienced a deep internal struggle to reconcile her sense of ministerial identity with the canonical limitations imposed on her as a woman by the Church. But there is very little evidence in her writing of such a struggle. She seems to have had no doubt that God had given her the gifts and graces of a preacher (and by extension of a priest) and that the task before her was simply to find a way to exercise her calling. She was a child of the Church of England, and was deeply attached to it. ("I am an Anglican and the Church is very dear to me."[30]) But she had no difficulty in declaring the Church to be wholly wrong in the matter of women and the ministry. And although she would initially seek permission from ecclesiastical authorities to preach, she seemed to have little reluctance to defy them when they refused to grant it.

Maude Royden always marked the beginning of her public ministry as the Sunday in 1917 when for the first time she read the lesson at St. Botolph's Church, London, where her dear friend—and later her husband—Hudson Shaw (1859–1944) was rector. She feared a public protest, but none came, and she reports being more nervous on that occasion than on any other in her long career in public speaking. Shaw's sermon that day began with the words: "Today for the first time in this historic church you have heard a woman's voice proclaiming the glad tidings of Christ's gospel. Some of you may have objected to the innovation. If so, I think you should call yourselves Jews rather than Christians."[31]

Shaw was always one of her greatest supporters. As proposals for a wider inclusion of women in the Church's liturgical and political life wound their way at a snail's pace through the Convocations and Councils of the Church, he periodically petitioned the Bishop to grant Royden permission to preach from his pulpit. The answer was always 'no.'

In 1919 Shaw again applied to the Bishop, asking that he grant Royden leave to conduct the Three Hours Service on Good Friday. But even though an ecclesiastical consensus was growing that women should be allowed to

29. Royden, *Consider the Days*, 25.
30. Royden to the Executive Council of the City Temple, 1 July 1917.
31. Picton-Turbervill, *Life is Good*, 132–33.

speak at 'non-statutory services' (which would have covered this occasion) the Bishop again refused. Royden did conduct the service, but in the parish hall rather than in the church itself. But the absurdity of the situation did not escape her. "I said exactly the same things to exactly the same people . . . as if we had been in church," she wrote, "but the fact that we were *not* in church apparently made all the difference."[32] The exercise of Shaw continuously asking the Bishop for permission for Royden to preach in his church, and the Bishop refusing, was carried out routinely in these years, even after the 1920 Lambeth Conference finally affirmed a woman's right to preach at non-statutory services at the discretion of the Rector.

But when the Bishop continued to refuse to give Royden leave to preach,[33] matters finally came to a head. In 1923 Hudson Shaw went in person to see the Bishop to press the matter of her preaching the Three Hours Service that year. The result was less than satisfactory. Royden writes: "[The Bishop] admitted that the rector had a right to invite me to his pulpit for a non-statutory service. He admitted that the Three Hours Service was a non-statutory service. He admitted that the Lambeth Conference had affirmed the right of women to preach in church. But no woman could take the Three Hours Service because it was *a specially sacred service*. [emphasis hers]"[34]

Shaw was furious and, and perhaps for the first time in his clerical career, he was determined to defy his Bishop's orders. Royden remembers him returning from their meeting saying that in his ordination vows he had promised to obey only the Bishop's "godly admonitions and godly judgments: [but] this is not godly at all!"[35] And so the service was held in the church on 30 March 1923 with Royden in the pulpit, and the building was crowded to overflowing. Although Royden and Shaw received a number of letters threatening a public protest, none came. But from then onwards, Royden reports, Shaw "became something of an outcast in the diocese, and was shouted down when he tried to speak in the diocesan conference."[36]

But if her own beloved denomination was reluctant to avail itself of Royden's homiletical gifts, other communities of faith were more welcoming. She had spoken in Nonconformist chapels for many years, especially

32. Royden, *The Three-fold Cord*, 59.

33. Indeed a challenge was made in the London Diocesan Conference, both to Shaw's stance on women preachers and the Lambeth Conference's positive approach. The conference passed a motion to the effect that: "It is generally inexpedient and contrary to the interests of the Church that women should publicly minister in consecrated buildings." See Heeney, *Woman's Movement*, 91.

34. Royden, *The Three-fold Cord*, 59–60.

35. Ibid.

36. Ibid., 61.

in those which had supported her suffrage work. But it was an invitation to preach at London's famous City Temple in March 1917 that would mark a change in direction.[37] The Temple soon became Royden's pulpit. As assistant pastor to Joseph Fort Newton (1876–1950) Royden now had a wide scope for her abilities, an intellectually-stimulating community, and huge audiences that no other British churchwoman could boast. From 1917 to 1920, she exercised a full range of ministries, both pastoral and liturgical, at the City Temple. Then in 1920 she and Anglican priest-theologian Percy Dearmer (1867–1936)[38] founded the Fellowship Guild, and they established The Guildhouse as an ecumenical worship and cultural center in a converted chapel in Eccleston Square, within walking distance of Victoria Station. Assisted by composer Martin Shaw (1875–1958)[39] she preached Sunday evening sermons at The Guildhouse on issues such as unemployment, peace and marriage. People, and especially young people, came from all over the city, the country and the world to hear "the really famous Maude Royden."[40]

We get some sense of the excitement of those days from a contemporary observer. "Each Sunday evening," she says, "we went to hear Maude Royden, who in our opinion was one of London's best preachers . . . We had to go early to get a seat."[41] "Miss Royden was a scholarly speaker, but in her aftermeetings when she left the pulpit and answered questions ranging from British foreign policy to advice for the lovelorn, she captivated her audience with her radiant good humour. She was very impressive, too, in her blue gown and blue cap."[42]

Royden did not intend The Guildhouse to be either a schismatic church or a sect ("I will not start a new Church," she told a friend[43]) and she never held services there at the same time as normal Sunday morning church services. Nor did she offer the Eucharist.[44] But at the same time she

---

37. The City Temple, founded sometime in the 1640s and the oldest Nonconformist church in the City of London, was always known for great preaching, an ecumenical spirit and lively theological debate. Perhaps its most famous preacher was Leslie Weatherhead, a Methodist of international reputation.

38. See for more on Dearmer, see Gray, *Percy Dearmer: A Parson's Pilgrimage*.

39. See for autobiographical material, Shaw, *Up to Now*.

40. *Sydney Daily Guardian*, June 3, 1928.

41. McClung, *Nellie McClung: The Complete Autobiography*, 78.

42. Ibid., 43.

43. Fletcher, *Maude Royden*, 209.

44. When she was minister at the City Temple Royden had baptized three children. But that action would have its consequences. "She was appointed a council member of William Temple's Life and Liberty movement. In October 1917, the council was to meet at Cuddesdon Theological College. At first, the principal refused to admit Royden to the college because of the baptisms; he compromised by insisting she sleep in nearby

knew that a model for a more equal church must be available: "People who desire any great reform must create a fellowship in which to work for it."[45]

Although Royden preached on a wide variety of topics, from pacifism to prostitution, as well as on general principles of Christian thought, she and Dearmer had founded The Guildhouse specifically to advance the ordination of women in the Church of England.[46] And in this cause it made a substantial impact. As one journalist wrote:

"All who still maintain that the Ministry should be rigidly closed to women should, if and when in London, worship at The Guildhouse. If they do, they are almost certain to be convinced of the error of their ways."[47]

And there was some actual progress being made. The 1920 Lambeth Conference's declaration about women's preaching at non-statutory services was one encouraging step; another was the organizational plan for the reformation of church governance in 1919. When the General Assembly of the Church of England met for the first time in 1920, 40 of the 357 members the House of Laity were women. One of these was Maude Royden.

Opposition to the Ordination of Women

But for the Church at large, the admission of women to Holy Orders was a different matter. In their essentials, the conventional arguments used against the ordination of women have changed little in the century since Royden began making her case. Many are arguments from particular interpretations of Scripture: that woman was created after (and subordinate to) man in Genesis, that her disobedience was the proximate cause of the Fall, that Jesus chose only male disciples, that God is always spoken of as male and that Jesus took on human nature as a male in the Incarnation, that Paul's image of man as the head of the woman just as Christ is the head of the Church is critical to understanding Church government, that the submissiveness of Mary the Mother of God is the model for female behavior, and so on. (These were, of course, the same grounds on which many Church of England people opposed women's education, women's right to hold property independent

---

Oxford. In protest, she resigned from the council." Street, "A Life Spent Battling for Women," *Church Times*, 2 November 2006.

45. "The Church of England and the Free Church: Miss Royden at the City Temple," in *The Coming Day* (March 1920) 112–14.

46. Other women preachers barred from taking the pulpit in Church of England churches also presided at The Guildhouse on occasion. One of these was Evelyn Underhill (1875–1941) the Anglo-Catholic scholar and writer. See Cropper, *Evelyn Underhill*, 130.

47. "As Others See Us," in *Guildhouse Monthly* 1, No. 6 (June 1927) 164.

of their husbands, women's entry into the professions, and their ability to vote and to hold elected office.[48]) Other arguments were grounded upon that rather amorphous thing called "tradition," the uninterrupted history of male priesthood since the time of the Apostles.

But Royden was convinced that there was something more going on in the minds and hearts of opponents to women's ministry in general and women's ordination more specifically. The deepest roots of the Church's position on admitting women to the ordained ministry, she believed, did not lie in interpretations of Scripture, nor in the tradition of male authority, nor even in a more general sense of a woman's spiritual or mental unfitness; rather it rested in the notion that having a woman in the pulpit or at the altar would "result in the desecration of the Church." Thoroughly steeped in post-Freudian analysis of gender-relations, Royden was persuaded that it was the fear of women's sexuality, combined with the ancient "blood taboo," that fueled much of the hostility which surrounded questions of women's equality in the Church. This explained to some extent the "singularly noxious quality" of the opposition to women preachers that, according to Royden, "exceeded anything I met with in the fight for the vote."[49]

In this interpretation of her opponents' motivations she agreed wholeheartedly with another proponent of women's ministry, Dr. Letitia Fairchild, a noted woman physician,[50] who testified before the 1920 Lambeth Conference in the debate on the matter of women and ministry. Fairchild's particular interest on that occasion was in marshalling scientific evidence to debunk the conventional medical grounds for barring women from professional ministry: that is, women's physical weakness and more particularly the debility caused by menstruation. "Neither preaching nor serving [at the altar] is a harder task physically than district visiting or Sunday School teaching" (both of which were generally deemed appropriate tasks for women). Like Royden, Fairchild argued that the root cause of the prohibition on women's sacramental service a belief in their "ceremonial uncleanness."[51]

But these arguments were not persuasive to the opponents of women's ordination. And woven throughout the debates in Lambeth session on women and ministry in 1920 are ideas about women's sexuality as a barrier to ordination. The attitudes of the bishops at Lambeth toward women in

---

48. "Anti-suffragist Mr. H. W. Hill . . . opined that 'the monstrous regiment of women in politics would be bad enough but the monstrous regiment of priestesses would be a thousandfold worse.'" Heneey, *Women's Movement*, 108.

49. Royden Papers, cited in Heeney, *Woman's Movement*, 125.

50. Fairchild was medical director of the Royal Air Force during the 1914–18 War.

51. Fairchild, "Women and Lay Ministries," 61–70.

positions of leadership can also be seen in the Committee Report on "Industrial Problems," which contains the following statement:

> Women have the power of moving men. By effective speech on religious truths and experiences, strong emotions are called into play. On strong emotions possible perils wait. And, especially in a generation which seems sometimes even contemptuously and recklessly to brush aside what a very few years ago were regarded as wise and indeed necessary restraints, the Church must be above suspicion. . . . Again, there is a deep wisdom in the words of the New Testament which say of a faithful Christian woman "she shall be saved through her child-bearing."[52]

Despite some positive progress on the matter of Deaconesses, overall the 1920 Lambeth Conference gave slight encouragement to those seeking admission to Holy Orders for women. Arguments from Scripture and tradition dominated the discussions, with little in the way of theological reasoning. The tone, moreover, was to sensitive women like Royden, deeply offensive: "Human nature, being what it is, the Christian Church . . . must exercise unsleeping vigilance that in its regulations for worship in the congregation there lurk no occasion for evil or even for suspicion of evil; no occasion for confusion or strife; nothing which falls below the purest and strictest ideal of peace and seemliness and order."

Bishop H. Hensley Henson (1863–1947) would later describe desire of women to extend their reach beyond the domestic sphere "the most menacing evil of our time." "The world wants desperately," he wrote, "not female priests and bishops, but Christian wives and mothers."[53] And another Lambeth participant, the admittedly eccentric William Cecil, Bishop of Exeter, was even less ambiguous about his concerns: "the religious instinct and the sexual instinct are too close to be allowed to come into close contact," he argued. A commentator on Bishop Cecil's remarks observed that "It was an acknowledgement that religion per se could be sexually exciting for churchmen so women must not be too religiously interactive with churchmen in case they aroused male 'sexual instinct.'"[54]

Over and over again, it was claimed that it was inappropriate for women to minister in a "consecrated building," with the clear implication that their presence in a position of ministerial leadership would render the space profaned.

52. *Lambeth Conference Papers 1920*, (cxl) 158–59.
53. Henson, "The Most Menacing Evil of our Time," in *Newcastle Daily Chronicle*, 24 March 1928.
54. Rose, *Freedom From Sanctified Sexism*, 129.

The League of the Church Militant

Royden and others believed that the only way to fight against this kind of virulent sexism was increased militancy, and the CLWS was her chosen vehicle. "The CLWS ought to be really 'militant,' ought it not?" Royden wrote to a friend. But she recognized that this might seem to be in contradiction to her previous stance. "It seems strange to me, who fought against militancy years ago, when it took the form of physical violence, to have to urge the League now to a more energetic spiritual warfare."[55] In 1918, with the vote for women finally won, the CLWS was renamed the League of the Church Militant (LCM). As one foreign newspaper article described it: "The League for [sic] the Church Militant gave top priority to equality of opportunity for the sexes in the Anglican Church ministry, becoming one of the most radical feminist groups in Anglicanism. There was no hesitation in putting delicate subjects such as male attitudes to female sexuality before the bishops."[56]

The CLWS journal *Common Cause* was renamed *Woman's Leader*, a new newsletter *Church Militant* carried news of the progress of the cause, both at home and abroad, and the newborn LCM redoubled its efforts toward making certain that women's ordination was at the top of the agenda of the various Councils and Convocations of the Church.

On the Saturday that the 1920 Lambeth Conference was set to debate the *Women in Ministry* report, Royden and the LCM organized a rally in Trafalgar Square. Royden addressed the thousands of participants before the march to the rally-point began, urging them to stand firm in their convictions. Singing "Onward Christian Soldiers," the marchers followed banners of women saints and waved palm branches. At Nelson's Column both Royden and Dr. Fairchild gave addresses, and the marchers prayed that the Lambeth bishops would affirm the ministry of women. The bishops' affirmation on the matter of Deaconesses and lay ministries at non-statutory services was seen as answer to those prayers.

In the decade between the 1920 and 1930 Lambeth Conferences, the LCM pressed the issue of the ordination of women, employing the same means by which the CLWS had successfully pressed the issue of the franchise: conferences, journal articles, letters to the editors of national newspapers, lectures, and lobbying the members of Church Councils.[57] At one public meeting in 1928 it was reported that: "Church House was besieged

---

55. Maude Royden to Miss Corben, 23 January 1919. Cited in Fletcher, 188.

56. *Brisbane Courier*, June 11, 1928.

57. "Wear the familiar badge—the Cross and circle—to show what you stand for. It is the same badge we wore in the old days . . . and a tremendous link just now when we have such strong opposition." *Church Militant* (March 1920) 19.

. . . by enormous crowds eager to hear the debate on women and the Priesthood arranged by the League of the Church Militant. Some time before the doors opened a queue of people consisting mainly of women stretched halfway down Great Smith Street and hundreds had to be turned away . . . those who were lucky enough to get in spent a lively evening."[58]

In all of these efforts Maude Royden was the leading light. She traveled widely, taking the cause of women's ordination to all parts of the Anglican Communion. And she continued to write and preach, described by most commentators as "England's most famous woman preacher." She was also under intense scrutiny by those who found her activities radical and alarming. The English Church Union, which was vigorous in its opposition to the ordination of women, investigated Royden for her pro-ordination activities.[59]

But the principal goal, for both Royden and the LCM, was to prepare for the Lambeth Conference in 1930 in which a second report on women and the ministry would be debated.[60] But because of the lack of clarity in the mission of the LCM, and because it had been so closely associated with the Suffrage cause, it was disbanded just prior to the 1930 Conference. In its place were formed two organizations whose sole and unambiguous aim was the realization of women's ordination in the Church of England. The Anglican Group for the Ordination of Women to the Historic Ministry of the Church (AGOW) held its first annual meeting in 1933. The Society for the Equal Ministry of Women (SEMWI) was a parallel interdenominational group with a more militant agenda. Both groups affirmed very similar resolutions with regard to Lambeth:

> Resolution: That this Council reaffirms its conviction that the full ministry of religion should be open to both sexes, and further, it urges upon the Archbishops and Bishops of the Established Church of England the importance of dealing with this matter at the forthcoming Lambeth Conference.[61]

But indeed Lambeth 1930 actually took a step backwards in the matter of women's ordination. Reversing its thinking from the previous Conference on the matter of Deaconesses, the Conference declared that deaconesses

---

58. *The Guardian*, 12 June 1919.

59. Jones, 100.

60. There were a number of Conference and Convocation reports on the matter of women's ordination during this period: "The Ministry of Women: A Report by a Committee appointed by the Archbishop of Canterbury" (1919) "Women and Priesthood" (1929); "The Ministry of Women: A Report of the Archbishops' Commission" (1935).

61. *The Church Militant*, January 1928.

were not female deacons, but laywomen. According to this decision (which was not changed until 1968) the Order of Deaconesses was not a Holy Order, but an order *sui generis*, "supplementary and complementary" to the three historic orders of bishop, priest and deacon.[62]

In the matter of women's ordination to the other orders of ministry the Lambeth bishops were even less encouraging. While the Bishops admitted that more theological work needed to be done (which would not be difficult since virtually no theological work had been done previously) they said that the ordination of women was essentially impossible. They would not allow themselves, they declared, to be swayed by feminist pressure groups, which were erroneously determined "to secure for women both equality of opportunity and similarity of function with men in every department of life." According to the report, "a majority of the sub-committee believes that there are theological principles which constitute an insuperable obstacle to the admission of women to the Priesthood, apart from all considerations of expediency." But what those principles were, the Bishops were not able to articulate.

Clearly the tide had turned, and what progress had been made in the inter-war years toward the acceptance of the possibility of women's ordination was quickly being reversed. A Commission appointed in 1931 by the Convocations of Canterbury and York on the admission of women to the priesthood made the following remarkable statement:

> We maintain that the ministration of women will tend to produce a lowering of the spiritual tone of Christian worship, such as is not produced by the ministrations of men before congregations largely or exclusively female. It is a tribute to the quality of Christian womanhood that it is possible to make this statement; but it would appear to be a simple matter of fact that in the thoughts and desires of that sex the natural is more easily made subordinate to the supernatural, the carnal to the spiritual, than is the case with men, and that the ministrations of a male priesthood do not normally arouse that side of female nature which should be quiescent during the times of the adoration of almighty God. We believe, on the other hand, that it would be impossible for the male members of the average Anglican congregation to be present at a service at which a woman ministered without becoming unduly conscious of her sex.[63]

---

62. Resolution 4.2.19.

63. Report of the Convocation of Canterbury and York Commission on Women and the Ministry (1931).

As one writer in the LCM journal put it: "The attitude of the Church in refusing to ordain women priests and the very general practice of individual Churches with regard to lay offices, tend to perpetuate the shocking ideas of ceremonial uncleanness and the inferiority of women."[64]

After the 1930 Lambeth Conference, the fight for women's equality in the Church suffered a severe blow when Royden experienced something akin to a nervous breakdown. When she recovered, which took nearly a year, she went back to the United States where she addressed large audiences once or twice a day and gave interviews for the radio and newspapers in between. In the lead-up to the War, she was active in peace and anti-Fascist activities (she had been deeply influenced by Mohandas K. Gandhi).[65] When she was at home her house was full of people seeking her advice and counsel. In 1919 she had adopted a war orphan, and she devoted what little extra time she had to being a mother to her child and a support to her friends.

She never said as much, but the Lambeth bishops and the attitudes of the Church on the matter of the ordination on women had clearly defeated her. Other forms of sexual politics were calling her: marriage equality, prostitution, the plight of poor women, and the persecution of women overseas. The Church that she loved had let her down. And about her own vocation to the priesthood she finally says: "I no longer wish for it. I wish intensely that it may be possible for others, but for me it can never be. I am much lamer now than I used to be, and doubt if it would be possible for me to celebrate Holy Communion."[66]

She says that she might continue in the struggle were it not that she was growing old, and that she found it "more and more difficult to accept what the Church of England demands." For Royden, the quest for an inclusive Anglican ministry was essentially over.

Royden's Theological Principles

Maude Royden is by no stretch of the imagination a "systematic theologian." She is doing theology in the trenches, and one must ferret out her theological principles and method from various kinds of her writing: sermons, addresses, manifestos, journal articles, and autobiographical work. She is a

---

64. Pollard, "Equality, Moral and Spiritual," 41.

65. Although finally she recognized that the need to address the threat presented by Hitler was incompatible with the pacifist cause, and she resigned from the Peace Pledge Union.

66. Maude Royden to Ursula Roberts (18 December 1935). More important, she adds, "I am too far away from 'orthodoxy' to make public profession of the 39 Articles."

public theologian, she is an ecclesial theologian, and as such many of the nuances of Christian doctrine are of little interest to her. For Royden, theology is always in the service of human well-being, and she paints her theology in broad pastoral strokes. As one commentator put it, "The Gospel she preaches is a leaf torn from her own experience."[67]

If one thing is abundantly clear, however, it is that the effort to secure admission for women to the various Orders of ministry is holy work, and that it is grounded in the radical equality of men and women before God. Royden sees in Christ's teaching no suggestion of any distinction in the spiritual ideals, the spheres, or the potential of men and women, and the Church (which is the Body of Christ) has no authority for imposing such a distinction now. Not only is there no special teaching for women as apart from men; if Christian baptism is baptism "into Christ," then all the baptized partake of the universality of Christ: "Every human being is, in a sense, an Incarnation, for there is the Spirit of God in the human heart."[68]

But the particulars of that Incarnation always mattered to Royden. In her view, the inherent equality between women and men did not ever mean equivalence.[69] "After all, it does matter in what kind of body your spirit is enshrined," Royden declared.[70] She believed that women had a distinctive perspective to bring, not only to ministry but to the whole theological enterprise. The particularity of gender carries with it "a certain point of view which will enable women to give to the world not only in practical service but in theology—in the world's idea of God himself—some fresh understanding, some new light."[71] She is clear that our understanding of God is incomplete until women bring "their particular spiritual genius." Likewise, the tragedy in the loss of women's ministry is not primarily for women themselves, but rather for the Church. The fullness of the ministry of Christ, embracing both male and female, is truncated when only men are allowed to exercise it.

All those to whom gifts have been given have, by definition, a "call." Just as it was not a matter of women's 'rights,' neither was it a matter of women's 'wishes:'

---

67. *Methodist Review* 105 (September 1922) 755.

68. Royden, *Consider the Days*, 93. She often quotes Galatians 3:38 as authority for her work.

69. Jesus "gave to both men and women the same teaching, but He enforced it by applying it to their different lives." Royden, "Women's Service to Theology" in *Women at the Crossroads*, 84.

70. Ibid., 79.

71. Ibid.

> It is not a question of whether we want women to be priests or prophets. It is simply a question of whether God has given them the gift, whether he calls them. It is not a question of whether women might not occupy themselves more usefully in other directions, whether the physical strain of such work is not too great, and so on. The question is, has God called them to *this* vocation? If so, the choice of no other vocation, however much more desirable, or expedient in the world's eyes, will serve as an excuse for neglecting that to which God has called them.[72]

It is always clear in Royden's thought that the traditions and canons of the Church are subordinate to the will of God. In support of this view, she points to the emphasis on vocation that is embodied in the Ordination rites for deacons and priests as found in the Book of Common Prayer. "It is never suggested there that it is the Church which gives the vocation, nor is it suggested that the Church, therefore, has the right to withhold it."[73]

Prevailing attitudes in the Church about female uncleanness and impurity were particularly odious to Royden, because she believed that God intended the relationship between men and women to be "sane . . . wholesome . . . and sweet," and without any taint of subjugation or baseness.[74] She was convinced that the world was at a crossroads "one going to destruction and the other to a new humanity."[75] This "new humanity" would be marked not only by gender equality, but by a spirit of tolerance and of openness to the will of God.

At the same time, Royden recognized that the movement of the Spirit, while often unpredictable, could also be thwarted. "Those who contend that we are accusing the Church of error of nineteen hundred years," she wrote of the opposition to ordination for women, "do not understand how slowly the spirit of Christ manifests itself in the world and against what hard conditions it has to make its way."[76] And it is always the work of the Christian

---

72. Royden, "The Ministry in the Church of To-morrow," in *Church Militant Supplement* (Number 9, October 1924) cl.

73. Ibid., cli. Royden here is operating like a proper liturgical theologian, presuming that an argument *from* the liturgy is a valid theological move.

74. Royden moved a resolution in the House of Laity in the 1923 and 1925 Convocation discussion of removing 'obey' from the woman's marriage vows for the service in the "deposited" Prayer Book 1928 (see Jones, 41). The LCM journal *The Church Militant* announced with some jubilation in 1928 that the Church of Scotland Provincial Synod had altered the vows in the marriage service from "love and obey" to "love and cherish" by a vote of 19 to 14. "Monthly Notes," *The Church Militant*, July 1928, 36.

75. "Maude Royden has Tolerant Views on Life," in *Winnepeg Tribune*, 28 April 1922.

76. *Church Militant* Supplement 25, cxci.

believer to "translate the world's values into the value of life." But women, however, have a special calling in this regard, in that they "instinctively seize upon" that notion, and because of this "have in their hands, if they will use it, the power that will change the world."[77]

But above all, Royden's theology was a theology of the love of God. This was a subject that she returns to again and again, and on which all other theological argument ultimately rests. Whether at a wedding, where she never failed to preach on "the position of Love in the world,"[78] or in her regular sermons at the City Temple or The Guildhouse, or in reflecting on her own love relationships, Royden is clear and consistent that all true love is a sacrament of Divine Love: absorbing, passionate, generous. All such love unites the soul to God.

Royden's Legacy

When the whole history of the progress of women in the Church comes to be written, Maude Royden should certainly receive a prominent place. At the very least, she holds a number of ecclesiastical "firsts": she was the first woman—perhaps with the exception of Hilda of Whitby in the 7th century—to preach in an English cathedral (Liverpool) and in 1931 was the first woman to be awarded an honorary Doctor of Divinity degree.[79] She was among the first group of women to hold a seat in the national Church Assembly. And in an age when many educated Britons were fleeing the Church, Royden was an example of (and for) the astute and intellectually-curious Christian woman, with a deep involvement in both ecclesiastical and state politics. In all of these activities, Royden was called upon to be physically, emotionally, and mentally resilient, and to stand up against controversy and censure both at home and on her worldwide preaching tours.

In the era between the two world wars, the need for someone to speak to "the soul that was drifting" cannot be overestimated, And Royden did this with exceptional skill. In more than twenty books and hundreds of articles,[80]

---

77. Royden, "Women's Service to Theology," 98.

78. *Oshkosh [WI] Daily Northwestern*, 7 September 1920, 12. "Miss Royden, who it will be remembered preached at Geneva during the women's congress, was in cassock and biretta." (Royden had preached from "Calvin's pulpit" in the Geneva Cathedral at the 8th Congress of the International Woman Suffrage Alliance, June 1920.)

79. The second D.D. for a woman would be awarded 7 years later to Evelyn Underhill. "I think Maude Royden and I will be the only female D.D.s," Underhill wrote at the time, "a pretty pass I must say!" Cropper, *Evelyn Underhill*, 208.

80. Royden's books include: *Downward Paths* (1916); *The Making of Women* (1917); *Women and the Sovereign State* (1917); *Women at the World's Crossroads* (1922);

she touched people where they lived, and confronted without flinching their deepest concerns, political, sexual, social, religious. Observers spoke of her ability to address not only to the seeking mind, but to the seeking heart as well: "[S]he is preaching Christ as a Power in human life—a power that can change the habits of a lifetime, that can heal the tissues of a poisoned body, that can give a steady course to the soul that is drifting without aim."[81]

For that alone, her place in ecclesiastical history should be assured.

But in terms of the primary concern of her life as a Christian leader, the admission of women to Holy Orders, her legacy is less than clear. Her own sense of vocation to the priesthood was certainly never realized. She wrote in 1946 to Li Tim-Oi (when Li "resigned her orders") "perhaps may I express a special sympathy with you, because I myself have felt the call to the priesthood and been refused."[82] As many women have had to do, in every generation, Royden managed to exercise a holy and vital ministry in spite of the rejection of her call by the Church that she loved. But it was always a source of deep sadness for her and for those who depended on her ministrations and leadership.

And her success as a catalyst for women's admission to Holy Orders in the Church as a whole is also ambiguous. There was a point early in her career when success in the matter of women's ordination seemed inevitable. In 1922, one observer spoke for many when he opined: "Maude Royden's name is safe among the pioneers. She has broken through one of the thorniest and most rigid barriers: that which, ever since Protestantism existed as an ecclesiastical establishment, closed the priesthood against women. She has, it is true, not yet won her formal admission to the hierarchy; she may, in her own person, never achieve that ultimate symbolic stage . . . but for all that, the barrier is down, the rest is only a matter of time. The woman bishop belongs to the near future."[83]

Of course, as we have seen, in Church of England terms that future was neither realized in her lifetime nor has it yet to be fully realized. What one writer has called "sanctified sexism" has been revealed to be far more persistent than Royden could have predicted. Some questions that she wrestled with in the inter-war years seem archaic in the extreme in today's church

---

Political Christianity (1922); *The Hour and the Church* (1922); *Prayer as a Force* (1923); *Sex and Common Sense* (1922); *The Church and Woman* (1923); *Christ Triumphant* (1924); *The Friendship of God* (1924); *Life's Little Pitfalls* (1925); *I Believe in God* (1927); *Beauty in Religion* (1928); *Problem of Palestine* (1939); *Women's Partnership in the New World* (1941); *Consider the Days* (1942); *A Threefold Cord* (1947).

81. *Methodist Review* 105 (September 1922) 756.
82. Cited in Fletcher, *Maude Royden*, 281.
83. "Women of Today and Tomorrow," in *Westminster Gazette* (March 1922).

(for example, should women receive Communion after men as an indication of their subordination?). Others, such as whether women should have authority over men in the Church, are still being vigorously debated today.

But those women, among whom are numbered many of David Gouwens's female students at Brite Divinity School, who wish a grounding for their own call to the ordained ministry would do well to take a closer look at the life and work of Agnes Maude Royden. Her advice to those who worked with her in the cause of women's equality in the Church still rings with authority:

> When you stand up to preach, every weakness, every cowardice, every fault and every sin strive to get in between you and the things you are to say, so that your prayer can only be that God will not let you stand between the thing you have to say and the people to whom it is to be said. Let us realize the greatness of the tradition from which some find it so hard to go forward . . . Let there be in our hearts a great conviction, for assuredly we are right.[84]

As a model of practical ability in the politics of Church and state, of clear and persuasive pastoral, biblical, and theological reasoning, and of a life lived in humble service to clear sense of her own clerical vocation, she will be a most amiable and supportive companion on their journey.

Bibliography

Alberti, Johanna. *Beyond Suffrage: Feminists in War and Peace, 1914–1928*. London: Palgrave Macmillan, 1989.
Blackmore, Henrietta (ed.). *The Beginning of Women's Ministry: The Revival of the Deaconess in the 19th Century Church of England*. In The Church of England Record Society 14, Suffolk: Boydell and Brewer, 2007.
Ceadel, Martin. *Pacifism in Britain, 1914–1945: The Defining of Faith*. Oxford: Clarendon, 1980.
Chadwick, Owen. *The Victorian Church*. Edinburgh: A. C. Black, 1970.
Collins, Irene. *Jane Austen and the Clergy*. London: Bloomsbury Academic, 2002.
Cropper, Margaret. *Evelyn Underhill*. London: Longmans Green, 1958.
Fairchild, Letitia, "Women and Lay Ministries" *Lambeth Conference Papers 1920*, (cxxxvi) 61–70.
Falby, Allison. "Maude Royden's Sacramental Theology of Sex and Love." *Anglican Theological Review*, 79 (2010) 124–43.
Fletcher, Sheila. *Maude Royden: A Life*. Oxford: Basil Blackwell, 1989.

---

84. Maude Royden, Address before the march on the occasion of the 1920 Lambeth Conference. Cited in Fletcher, *Maude Royden*, 191.

Gilmore, Isabella, "Deaconesses: Their Qualifications and Status," *Pan-Anglican Papers* (1908) 2–9.
Gray, Donald. *Percy Dearmer: A Parson's Pilgrimage*. Norwich: Canterbury, 2000.
Heeney, Brian. *A Different Kind of Gentleman*. New Haven: Yale, 1976.
———. *The Women's Movement in the Church of England*. Oxford: Oxford University Press, 1988.
Jones, Timothy Willem. *Sexual Politics in the Church of England, 1857–1957*. Oxford: Oxford University Press, 2013.
McClung, Nellie L. *Nellie McClung: The Complete Autobiography*. Peterborough, ON: Broadview, 2003.
Oldfield, Sybil. *Women Against the Iron Fist: Alternatives to Militarism 1900–1989*. Oxford: Basil Blackwell, 1989.
Picton-Turbervill, Edith. *Life is Good*. London: Frederick Muller, 1939.
Pollard, Joyce. "Equality, Moral and Spiritual." *Church Militant* (July 1928) 39–42.
Rose, Mavis. *Freedom From Sanctified Sexism: Women Transforming the Church*. MacGregor, Queensland: Allira, 1996.
Royden, A. Maude. *Consider the Days*. New York: Woman's Press, 1942.
———. "The Future of the Women's Movement." In *The Making of Women: Oxford Essays in Feminism*, edited by Victor Gollancz, 128–46. London: George, Allen and Unwin, 1917.
———. *The Three-fold Cord*. London: Victor Gollancz, 1947.
———. *Women and the Sovereign State*. London: Headley Brothers, 1917.
———. "Women's Service to Theology." In *Women at the World's Crossroads*, 75–101. New York: Woman's Press, 1923.
Russell, Anthony. *Clerical Profession*. London: SPCK, 1980.
Shaw, Martin. *Up to Now*. Oxford: Oxford University Press, 1929.

4

The Best Friend of Jesus

A Model for Pastoral Leadership in the Gospel of John

—Nancy Claire Pittman

To my very good friend, David Gouwens, who was first a trusted teacher to me, embodying what it means to be a best friend of Jesus and serving as a model of that friendship throughout my own life and ministry.

In 1979 Raymond Brown, Catholic priest and biblical scholar, published his seminal work on Johannine ecclesiology, *The Community of the Beloved Disciple: The Life, Loves, and Hates of an Individual Church in New Testament Times*.[1] In it he argued that a reconstruction of the history of the community in which the Fourth Gospel and the Johannine epistles was produced can be detected in a sequential reading of these texts. He was building on the earlier work of Louis Martyn who argued that this gospel can be read on two levels, i.e., the level of the unfolding story of Jesus and his disciples itself, and the level of the community in which the gospel was actually produced and read some fifty to sixty years later.[2] Brown was well aware that his theory about the development of the Johannine community was speculative; nonetheless, as Adele Reinhartz notes, Martyn's and Brown's work have become "virtually axiomatic in New Testament studies."[3] At the same time, she, among other biblical scholars, has challenged many of the

---

1. Brown, *The Community of the Beloved Disciple*.
2. Martyn, *History and Theology in the Fourth Gospel*.
3. Reinhartz, *Befriending the Beloved Disciple*, 37.

details of their telling of the story of the Johannine community.⁴ One claim, however, remains largely unassailed: the Fourth Gospel and the subsequent Johannine epistles were written in a time of considerable social change and conflict outside and within the community that produced these writings. As Brown himself wrote, "If the Johannine eagle soared above the earth, it did so with talons bared for the fight; and the last writings that were left us show the eaglets tearing at each other for the possession of the nest."⁵

This observation has remained with me as I have pastored congregations, taught students who were preparing for ordained ministry, and assumed the deanship of a denominational seminary. In all of these capacities I have worked with dedicated followers of Jesus who have dealt with the sweeping changes that have taken place in North American culture in the last thirty years. Too frequently churches, denominations, and seminaries have responded to these changes with anxious bewilderment, a kind of "circle the wagons" mentality in which like-minded people converse among themselves without regard to those who are outside their groupings, reaffirmation of non-negotiable theological commitments, and heart-rending internal conflict, often over these theological commitments and the responses to the external change that they represent.

These responses are similar to the ways in which the Johannine community reacted to their own changing circumstances which the Brown hypothesis makes clear. As both a biblical scholar and a practical theologian, I am interested in the similarities of aspects of the situation of 21st century mainline churches to that of the 1st and 2nd century Johannine community. Further, I am wondering what we can learn from that ancient community's implied understandings of ecclesiology and leadership that might help us negotiate the change and conflict occurring in our own time. How might we respond to threats inside and outside our own churches in ways more faithful to our vocation as followers of Jesus and less reactive to our own fear and angst over cultural, social and communal factors beyond our control? In this article, I begin to offer some responses to these musings by focusing specifically on John 15:12–17, Jesus' command to his disciples to love one another as friends, and its restatement in 1 John 4:7–12.

---

4. For a review of the scholarly critiques of the two-level hypothesis, see ibid., 39–40.
5. Brown, *The Community of the Beloved Disciple*, 24.

Theological Reflections

Friends, Lovers and the Ecclesial Community in the Gospel of John and 1 John

> John 15:12–17
>
> 12'This is my commandment, that you love one another as I have loved you. 13No one has greater love than this, to lay down one's life for one's friends. 14You are my friends if you do what I command you. 15I do not call you servants any longer, because the servant does not know what the master is doing; but I have called you friends, because I have made known to you everything that I have heard from my Father. 16You did not choose me but I chose you. And I appointed you to go and bear fruit, fruit that will last, so that the Father will give you whatever you ask him in my name. 17I am giving you these commands so that you may love one another.'[6]

> 1 John 4:7–12
>
> 7 Beloved, let us love one another, because love is from God; everyone who loves is born of God and knows God. 8Whoever does not love does not know God, for God is love. 9God's love was revealed among us in this way: God sent his only Son into the world so that we might live through him. 10In this is love, not that we loved God but that he loved us and sent his Son to be the atoning sacrifice for our sins. 11Beloved, since God loved us so much, we also ought to love one another. 12No one has ever seen God; if we love one another, God lives in us, and his love is perfected in us.

These two passages reflect the constant iteration of the commandment to love one another that characterizes the Johannine writings. However, although the message remains consistent, the socio-historical circumstances of the communities that first read them were in flux as they developed a distinctive Christology, quarreled with their fellow Jewish religionists, and eventually resorted to infighting among themselves. In this section I review the salient features of the social-historical contexts of the gospel and the epistles, before turning to implications for ecclesial life and leadership in early 21st century North America.

The text from the gospel, John 15:12–17, appears in the approximate middle of the Farewell Meal and Discourse scene, John 13:1—17:26. Within

---

6. All biblical quotations are NRSV unless otherwise noted.

this Johannine version of Jesus' last evening with his disciples, John, according to Jo-Ann A. Brant, "provides the uplifting speech that ancient readers expected to hear before a hero departed to death."[7] Here he is giving instructions to his followers about their future life together once he departs from them through the cross. He is also offering comfort and reassurance through the promise of the gift of the Paraclete and through ongoing relationships with the Father and with one another. It is within the web of these internal relationships that the Johannine Jesus sets the direction for the quite unknown prospects of this group. In other words, this complex of interconnections among Jesus and God, "the Father," his disciples, and the Paraclete is the key for understanding the future of this community. As Jesus says, "On that day you will know that I am in my Father, and you in me, and I in you." (15:20) In fact, we should note that aside from a few vague words about the world hating the disciples (e.g., 15:18; 17:14) little is said about both the explicit future of the disciples and their interactions with the external world. This is in stark contrast to the more frank warnings of the last speeches of the synoptic Jesus who speaks openly of coming tribulation and disaster.

The instructions and words of encouragement of the Johannine Jesus reverberate some sixty years later within the community that produced and read this gospel, that ecclesiological level I mentioned in the introduction to this article.[8] Still living within the Jewish cultural and religious sphere of the first century, the community was in the midst of conflict with fellow groups of Jews over synagogue participation and Jewish identity.[9] Even if we reject the aspect of the Martyn two-level hypothesis regarding a definite expulsion from the synagogue of Jews confessing Jesus as Messiah by Jews not making that claim, we can still detect at least in dim outline the social and historical circumstances of the late first-century Johannine community. Reinhartz summarizes the situation like this: 1) by the time this gospel was written there was an already institutional separation between those Jews who confessed Jesus as Messiah and those who did not—regardless of which group separated from the other group first; and 2) the two groups continued to have social contact with each other that was likely fraught with some tension.[10] Reinhartz also suggests that though we may not be able to identify or describe the exact historical situation of the first readers of this gospel,

---

7. Brant, *John*, 209.

8. Reinhartz calls this level an "ecclesiological tale;" *Befriending the Beloved Disciple*, 37.

9. See O'Day, "The Gospel of John," 504–6.

10. Reinhartz, *Befriending the Beloved Disciple*, 52–53

we can see that "the Gospel . . . declares its continued relevance to the lives of its readers."[11]

Conflict among close communities was not the only contextual problem Johannine Christians had to address. In fact, that conflict between Johannine Jews and traditional Jews associated with the synagogues of Judea and the diaspora was most likely exacerbated by the changes that were occurring throughout the Greco-Roman world. Both communities, for example, had to deal with the Roman defeat of the Judean uprising in 66–70 C.E., the destruction of the Temple in Jerusalem, and the resulting devastation of Jewish culture, religion and national life. As Rome consolidated its empirical power throughout the remainder of the first century, vassal peoples had to learn to deal with peculiarly Roman institutions, religious expressions, and its concomitant cultural social and cultural hegemony over the Mediterranean world. Rome's legions swallowed up local societies and governments; its bureaucrats followed behind to count, organize, and annex land, its produce, and its people. Such rapid change throughout the Middle East and Asia Minor would surely have marked the communities that struggled to face it.[12]

By the time the first epistle of John was produced, according to the Brown hypothesis, the community that had gathered around the teaching of the beloved disciple had turned away from conflict with explicitly Jewish communities and towards conflict with one another. As members of this Johannine community began to interpret the traditions that had been delivered to them, they began to disagree and their unity began to shatter.[13] Of course, that unity was always a bit tenuous; in John 6 disciples who are offended by Jesus' words about his body and flesh are turning away (6:66). Here again, the content of this conflict had to do with the identity of Jesus, a reexamination of the Christological controversy that a decade or two earlier had propelled the separation of a Johannine Jewish community from a more orthodox Jewish community.[14] In 1 John we see argumentation against those "who went out from us" (2:19) and espoused some kind of idea of a Jesus who was not fully human.[15] The language against these intra-communal opponents is as heated in the Johannine epistles as the language against the

---

11. Ibid., 51.

12. See Carter, *The Roman Empire and the New Testament*, for a concise description of the Roman Empire and its effects on early Christian communities.

13. Brown, *The Community of the Beloved Disciple*, 97, 106. See also Van der Watt, *An Introduction to the Johannine Gospel and Letters*, 20–21.

14. See Black, "The First, Second, and Third Letters of John," 367 for a discussion of dating the epistles in relationship to the Gospel of John.

15. Pittman, "The Epistolary Tradition," 271.

extra-communal opponents in the Fourth Gospel. In the gospel, the adversaries are "the Jews," who are children of the devil (10:44). In 1 John they are called "antichrists," (2:18) liars (1:4) and "children of the devil," (3:10).

In the midst of such alienation from those who disagree and the accompanying name-calling in the communities who produced the gospel and the epistles, themes of love and friendship become even more significant. In the gospel the Johannine Jesus speaks to his followers of their need to hold on to one another in the Final Discourse. In this context the two terms *agapein*, the verb "to love," and *philos*, "friend," are, if not exactly synonymous, coterminous. In his Anchor Bible commentary, Brown says, "The noun in 13:15 that we have translated as 'those he loves' is *philos*, 'friend,' a cognate of the frequent Johannine verb *philein*, 'to love.' The English word 'friend' does not capture sufficiently this relationship of love (for we have lost the feeling that 'friend' is related to the Anglo-Saxon verb *freōn*, 'to love')."[16] The Greek, of course, preserves the connection in such a way that we can treat the two concepts as so close in the Johannine context as to be inseparable.

The more important issue is what meanings they convey. The commandment to love is, of course, a restatement and extension of the commandments to love both one's neighbor (Lev 19:18) and the alien (Lev 19:34; Deut 10:19) found in Torah. However, in the gospel setting the commandment takes on a particular Christological twist.[17] In the Greco-Roman world love was not primarily a matter of an internal state or feeling, but continual external expressions of attachment to some group, be it biological family, ethnic grouping, or a fictive kin group, i.e., a "surrogate family" which could "serve many of the same functions as a biological family."[18] Further, say Bruce Malina and Richard Rohrbaugh, "to love one another here is more than general group attachment. It takes on the dimensions of interpersonal attachment, of loyalty, and of the value of reliability revealed in practical actions . . . . This bond of mutual loyalty is the social, externally manifested, emotionally rooted behavior of commitment and solidarity."[19] In the Fourth Gospel this attachment and loyalty is not only rooted in the presence and activity of Jesus, it is made possible through him and his relationship with God. And when Jesus repeats a common philosophical adage of his day about loving one's friends enough to lay down one's life for them (15:13) it is also loaded with Christological content because Jesus actually

---

16. Brown, *The Gospel according to John XIII-XXI*, 664. See also Johnson, "Making Connections," 159.

17. Koester, *Symbolism in the Fourth Gospel*, 267.

18. Malina and Rohrbaugh, *Social-Science Commentary on the Gospel of John*, 89.

19. Ibid., 228; see also 86–88.

acts it out in his crucifixion. In Gail O'Day's words, "His life is an incarnation of this teaching."[20] And it is a call to his followers to love one another to the same extent.

Friendship, in this context, is thus another expression of mutual attachment and fidelity articulated by the love commandment. Although the word "friendship" and the concept it represents are rare in the writings of the Hebrew Bible, it is fully developed in ancient Greek philosophy and subsequent Greco-Roman literature and cultural documents.[21] Here friendship has hierarchical and egalitarian dimensions as well as political and personal connotations, all of which have some bearing on interpreting John 15:12–17.[22]

First, there were friendships in the ancient world that were based on the exchange system that characterized patron-client relationships.[23] A client would be at the disposal of a patron, defending his honor and working for his good; the patron, in exchange, would perform favors and offer protection for the client. As a case in point, Malina and Rohrbaugh point to John 19:12: "From then on Pilate tried to release him, but the Jews cried out, 'If you release this man, you are no friend of the emperor.'" If Pilate were to release Jesus, he would show disloyalty to his patron, Caesar, and thereby abrogate their friendship.[24] Being a friend of Caesar in Roman society corresponds to the phrase repeated when Bill Clinton was president of the United States: "She is a friend of Bill."

In this same way, the disciples were called friends of Jesus. In the Gospel of John, even in the text we are considering in which Jesus says that they are no longer servants (or slaves) but friends, his followers are still not his social, political or, in this case, theological equals. After all, he is *commanding* them to do something—not exactly the action that characterizes a request between mutual friends. Here we clearly see that they are his clients; and thus clients of the God who sent Jesus as a mediator, or broker, between them and God.[25] The language of friendship, suggests Zeba A. Crook, is

---

20. O'Day, "Jesus as Friend in the Gospel of John," 150.

21. See Koester, *Symbolism in the Fourth Gospel*, 267. See also Schnackenburg, *The Gospel According to St. John*, 109, in which it is noted that while "friendship" may not appear frequently in the Hebrew Bible, values and practices related to friendship are certainly present.

22. For a discussion of the conventions of friendship in the Greco-Roman world, see Fitzgerald, *Greco-Roman Perspectives on Friendship*.

23. See Crook, "Fictive-friendship and the Fourth Gospel."

24. Malina and Rohrbaugh, *Social-Science Commentary on the Gospel of John*, 267; see also 117–19.

25. Ibid., *John*, 116. See also Crook, "Fictive-friendship and the Fourth Gospel," 7.

used in this situation "to mask unequal but elite relationships and thus to diminish the shame associated with relationships of dependence."[26]

This is not the state of affairs, however, among the disciples themselves. While they are connected with one another through their affiliation with Jesus, he calls them to turn toward one another as well in complete love and affiliation and to be friends with one another, to treat one another as family in a fictive-kinship relationship. In this call the Gospel is drawing upon the myriad *topoi* for friendship that are found throughout Greco-Roman culture. Luke Timothy Johnson summarizes them this way: "Friends are one soul (*mia psychē*). The friend is another self (*ho philos allos autos*). Friends are in harmony (*homonia*) and have the same opinion (*gnō mē*). Friendship is fellowship (*phila koinōnia*) and 'life together' (*symbios*). Therefore, friends are 'partners' *koinōnoi*) hold all things in common (*tois philois panta koina*) and 'being of one accord' (*epi to auto*). Like brothers in a family, friends are in a relationship of equality and reciprocity (*phiotēs isotēs*)."[27]

These characteristics mark the bonds of friendship into which Jesus is calling his disciples. Further, this friendship, especially during the Hellenistic period, included frankness of speech in which friends, both those of the hierarchical sense described above and in the egalitarian sense I am discussing now, were urged to speak honestly and openly to one another. True friends, the philosophers explained, eschew flattery, avoid insincerity, and tell the whole truth even if it is unpopular or painful.[28] So Jesus says "I have called you friends, because I have made known to you everything that I have heard from my Father." (15:15) In the same way, his followers are to speak fully and frankly to one another.

One other word can be said about friendship in the Hellenistic context and Johannine setting. The political dimensions of friendship are obvious when we think about friendship as a code word for a patron-client relationship. The patronage system that characterized the Greco-Roman world determined the economic station and political status of everyone in any given society; the obligations and responsibilities that are set up in these relationships, which were passed down from generation to generation, offered a measure of stability and order throughout the Roman Empire, even in times of civil unrest. And collecting patrons situated above any given family opened access to more resources and power.[29] When Jesus speaks of

26. Crook, "Fictive-friendship and the Fourth Gospel," 5.

27. Johnson, "Making Connections," 160.

28. O'Day, "Jesus as Friend in the Gospel of John," 152–53; see also Koester, *Symbolism in the Fourth Gospel*, 267.

29. Malina and Rohrbaugh, *Social-Science Commentary on the Gospel of John*, 117–19.

another patron other than the political authorities of the region and Caesar, i.e., God, he is setting up an alternative patronage system and inviting his own followers into that system. Furthermore, Jesus in the scene of the trial with Pilate (John 18:28—19:16) challenges Roman hegemonic claims to truth and power. This had economic and political ramifications as once dependable relationships are severed; mutual obligations are revoked; and responsibilities to the group faithful to Jesus are placed in the center of social life.[30]

What may not be so clear is that there are political dimensions within the egalitarian community which Jesus constitutes as a circle of friendship in the Final Discourse. On the one hand, like the synoptic Jesus, he is creating a new family in which old biological, ethnic and racial ties are cut and new cords of loyalty and attachment to Jesus bind his followers to one another not only inside the group but in their interface with the world beyond. (see *inter alia* Matt 12:46–50; John 19:25b-27) On the other hand, there are political dimensions within the group as it orders itself not according to the hierarchies of the outside world, including the normative patriarchal family arrangements, but idealizes an egalitarian structure in which all have access to their chief friend (and broker) Jesus and are made equal in that access to one another.

In the Johannine epistles, the word "friend" does not appear except in the greeting of 3 John from the author, "the elder," to the recipient, "my dear friend Gaius." (1) Further in 1 John 4:7–12, cited above, the Greek words for love are not from *philein*, the root word for friend, but *agapein*. Nonetheless, the meanings I have been delineating above with regard to the gospel apply here as well. The love-language is rooted in relationality among the believers, be it the love neighbors have for one another, the affiliation of friends, or the mutual obligations among family members. As such it conveys the same call for affiliation, mutuality, reciprocity, and openness within the community as the Johannine Jesus conveyed in the Final Discourse to his followers. Further, there is an element of exclusivity to it—those who are outside the community are barred from these bonds of love. Finally, it is rooted in the love of God who initiates it and bestows it as gift to the community through Jesus the Christ.[31]

---

30. Yak-hwee Tan highlights the political dimensions of the Final Discourse through a careful analysis of the image of the vine, John 15:1–27. She says, "By drawing the disciples to himself as the new Self, Jesus is creating an alternative community in resistance to the imperial rule, defined as the world-below." "The Johannine Community," 175.

31. Rensberger, *1 John, 2 John, 3 John*, 117–18. See also Bultmann, *The Johannine Epistles*, 66.

Therefore, the ideal community that is implied in these two passages is a circle of love and friendship, brought together not by blood or social obligation and hierarchy, but by choice.[32] To be sure, it is a choice based on Jesus' initial election of his followers, "You did not choose me but I chose you." (John 15:16) However, members continue to choose whether or not to remain within the community through their primary loyalty to Jesus and the Christological affirmations about him that they share in faith and trust (*pistis*). Chief among these affirmations is a claim that he uniquely and in a fully human way places his followers into new relationship with God through his own closeness to God. In this way he is the patron-friend who raises their status before God.

Furthermore, while the members of the implied Johannine community may not be equal friends with Jesus, they are with another.[33] In fact, there is little within the Fourth Gospel or the epistles to suggest that there is much recognition of any particular distinctions, rank or otherwise, among them. As Brown says, "the gospel shows no interest in diverse charisms that distinguish Christians: it is interested in a basic, life-receiving status enjoyed by all."[34] No other structure or organizational pattern is suggested in the gospel; in the epistles we find the title "elder," but nothing to indicate the responsibilities or weight in the community that it might carry. It is comprised of persons who are fundamentally connected to Jesus and through his love with one another. Their harmony is guaranteed only by the Paraclete, the Spirit Jesus sends to protect and comfort them (John 14:16–17) as well as guard the truth of their testimony. (John 15:26; 16:7–14) And it is characterized by mutual acts of service and fidelity to one another. (see John 13:14–15; 34–35)[35] Thus at the center of Johannine ecclesiology is not a program or a structure, but a web of relationship.

Leadership in the Johannine Community of Love and Friendship

The centrality of this web of relationship in the Johannine community does not mean, however, that it did not have an understanding of leadership within that web, although it is somewhat different from leadership models present in the synoptic gospels, Acts, or the Pauline corpus. For example,

---

32. Coloe, *Dwelling in the Household of God*, 164.
33. Koester, *Symbolism in the Fourth Gospel*, 268.
34. Brown, *The Churches the Apostles Left Behind*, 90.
35. For a discussion of service in the Final Discourse, see Schneiders, *Written that You May Believe*, 188–96.

scholars often note that the word "apostle" is not used in the Johannine literature for the followers of Jesus; he himself is the one most often characterized as "sent." Only in his first resurrection appearance to the disciples as a group does Jesus say to them, "as the Father has sent me, so I send you." (20:21) At that point he also commissions them as a group when he says, "Receive the Holy Spirit. If you forgive the sins of any, they are forgiven them; if you retain the sins of any, they are retained." (20:22b–23) In this one notable instance, Jesus gives them authority to serve as unique channels for the power and activity of God, although as D. Moody Smith says, their power may be only for "inner-community discipline" and not for activity throughout the whole inhabited world.[36] Outside this resurrection scene, the disciples of Jesus as a group do not function as particular intermediaries for the faithful community or the world. There are no scenes in the Fourth Gospel in which the disciples are successful at serving as gatekeepers for access to Jesus.[37] Nor do they heal or attempt to heal anyone in the Fourth Gospel or display spirit-inspired powers like those mentioned in Paul's letters or the Acts of the Apostles. Peter's individual role is somewhat different, however, and his leadership must be considered in tandem with that of the beloved disciple, to which I will turn below.

As I mentioned above, the word "elder" is used in 2 and 3 John to designate some kind of leader within the later Johannine community. Ritva H. Williams suggests that "the Elder's letters reflect a situation in which powerful householders acting as church patrons can and do refuse hospitality to itinerant ministers and to emissaries from sister congregations. The Elder himself claims a personal authority arising from his age or seniority, his ability to recall what was from the beginning, and his possession and mediation of divine gifts."[38] While her description of the elder's leadership is provocative and may be accurate, there is little within these epistles themselves to support his conception of his "personal authority," particularly with regard to whether or not he had divine gifts.

Scholars often note the rivalry between Peter and the beloved disciple that plays out in the last chapters of the gospel as an indication of the kind of leadership that might be valued in this community. While it may be true, as Brown himself suggests, that the rivalry represents a historical struggle between followers of Peter and the apostolic traditions he taught (which eventually dominated the Great Church of the second century) and the

---

36. Smith, *John*, 380.

37. *Contra* Williams, who makes a case for the disciples as brokers based on an assumed parallel with the patron-broker-client system of the ancient world; *Stewards, Prophets, Keepers of the Word*, 51–52.

38. Williams, *Stewards, Prophets, Keepers of the Word*, 52.

followers of the beloved disciple, this characterization does not exhaust the matter.[39] For here, I would suggest, we are not simply looking at a tussle over *who* should be viewed as most authoritative in the fledgling Christian movements, but more importantly *what* aspects of leadership and authority are most significant in the faithful community and *how* they should be exercised.

The key to comprehending this distinction is in the designation of Peter's ostensible rival as the *beloved* disciple. This figure first appears in the foot washing scene of the Farewell Meal and Discourse. When Jesus mentions his betrayer, Peter gestures to the disciple leaning on the bosom of Jesus and the author adds, "the one Jesus loved." (John 13:23)[40] He is mentioned five other times: 19:25–27 at the foot of the cross at which Jesus gives his mother and the beloved to one another; 20:2–10, in the footrace to the empty tomb in which Peter and the beloved engage; 21:1–8, the appearance of the resurrected Jesus to the disciples by the Sea of Tiberias;[41] 21:20–23, in a discussion between Peter and Jesus about the beloved; and finally, 22:24, in which it is made clear that the beloved is the one who testifies to the events in the gospel. In all of these instances, except 20:2, a form of the Greek verb *agapein* for "to love," is used. In 20:2 the imperfect active form of the verb *philein* appears. As I argued above, however, the difference between these two verbs should not be overdrawn.[42] In fact, because they are practically synonymous in the Johannine literature, I would suggest that we could call this figure not only the beloved disciple but the best friend of Jesus.

This is in distinct contrast to the role Peter plays in this gospel. It would be an overstatement to suggest that Peter is only a foil to the beloved, the best friend of Jesus. Peter certainly stumbles and misunderstands in ways that the beloved, the best friend of Jesus, does not. The Fourth Gospel, after all, retains the tradition of Peter's denial of being a follower of Jesus while the best friend remains faithful throughout Jesus' suffering and death, even

---

39. Brown, *The Community of the Beloved Disciple*, 82ff. "Great Church" is Brown's shorthand designation of the second-century church that grew out of the apostolic outreach of the first century.

40. Wes Howard-Brook comments that the beloved disciple in this introduction to him is first in the bosom of Jesus, but when he asks Jesus who is to betray him he is moved to the breast—a distinction that Howard-Brook explains suggests a move from great intimacy to mere physical closeness. Howard-Brook, *Becoming Children of God*, 304.

41. For an exegesis of this text, see the essay by Stephen Plunkett in this volume.

42. Commentators often place too much weight on the alternation of the verbs in John 21 in which Jesus asks Peter three times if he loves him and commissions him to feed his sheep. I would suggest that the verbs are used interchangeably for literary interest and nothing more.

appearing at the cross.[43] And Peter, who comes in second in the footrace to the empty tomb, does not believe when he steps into the tomb and sees the linen wrappings, although the gospel makes clear that the best friend believes even if he doesn't yet understand their significance. Moreover, commentators often note that when the best friend first appears in the gospel as the one reclining closest to Jesus at the final meal, Peter has to ask him to ask Jesus who will betray him. Nonetheless, by the end of the gospel, Jesus is commissioning Peter, and not the best friend, to feed his sheep and to follow him into death.[44] As R. Alan Culpepper says, "Peter will be a *mártus* (martyr); the Beloved Disciples will give true *marturía* (testimony)."[45] It is this testimony that remains at the center of the gospel and at the center of its understanding of what leadership is. Leadership is bearing faithful witness to the truth.

However, being the best friend of Jesus who gives truest testimony does not place him in a position to Jesus that is unique to his status among the other disciples. His friendship with Jesus is still based upon the exchange system I described above in which Jesus brokers a connection between him and God as he does with his other followers. This means that the best friend also retains the same kind of relationship with the other disciples that is based upon the philosophical motifs of friendship in the Hellenistic world. He exists in harmony with them; he withholds nothing from them; he shares in their tribulations and their joys; he speaks frankly with them in open dialogue and instruction. He may be "first among equals," but he is still an equal to them. After all, it is striking to note that Jesus never overtly commissions the best friend in a singular way above or beyond the other disciples, as he does with Peter who also remains close to Jesus.

So what distinguishes the beloved from the other disciples? As best friend of Jesus he serves as the primary demonstration of the ideals of the community of friends. Derek Tidball summarizes these accordingly:

> In 'reclining' next to Jesus, he models the intimacy of a disciple with his master (13:23–25). It is out of this close relationship of love that his other qualities flow. In lingering near the cross, he models the need for faithfulness, of being a witness to the last (19:25–27). In witnessing to Jesus' death, he models the

---

43. Culpepper reminds us that Peter in this gospel does not deny that Jesus is the Messiah; only that he is a disciple of Jesus. *Anatomy of the Fourth Gospel*, 120.

44. The issue of whether or not John 21, in which this commissioning scene plays out, was written by the original audience or a later redactor is still disputed by scholars. However, because every extant manuscript of the Gospel of John contains John 21, I am treating it here as a part of the Johannine tradition. See O'Day, "John," 854.

45. Culpepper, *Anatomy of the Fourth Gospel*, 121.

courage required and the content of the testimony we should give (19:35). In approaching the empty tomb, he models the spiritual perception and faith we need (20:2–10). When fishing on the lake, he demonstrates that same spiritual perception that eludes others (21:7).[46]

Further, the best friend of Jesus serves as guarantor of the traditions that the Johannine community understood as central to their life together. The author of the Fourth Gospel states clearly that his testimony is the foundation of the gospel itself. (21:24) David Bartlett says, "The beloved disciple's role as exemplar may derive from his ability to love and follow Jesus, but his role as authority derives from his witness to the traditions about Jesus."[47]

If the beloved disciple is the primary human embodiment of the Johannine community's conception of leadership, as I have suggested here, then the following things can be said about it. First, only persons who are connected intimately with Jesus and the particular Johannine traditions about him have the capacity to serve as leaders in a community. This intimacy is made possible through the bestowal of the Paraclete who continues to inspire truth in their witness. (John 14:17) And leaders must also remain attached to all who participate in the community of friends around Jesus—practicing the norms of friendship in frank speech, open sharing, and complete loyalty. The activities of such leaders are bearing witness to what has been seen and heard about Jesus and embodying the ideals of the community. Although it might be argued that "embodying ideals" is not a leadership act, in fact, increasingly modern leadership theorists are suggesting that it is a primary function. Margaret Wheatley, author of *Leadership and the New Science*, says, "The leader's task is first to embody these principles [guiding visions, sincere values, organizational beliefs—the few self-referential ideas individuals can use to shape their own behavior] and then to help the organization become the standard it has declared for itself."[48] This is especially true in times of change and threat, externally and internally. Thus, the beloved disciple, the best friend of Jesus, models the central tenets of the Johannine community of friends in the face of enormous pressure on this early group of Christians and the conflict in which they lived.

Perhaps precisely because he is the epitome of the ideals of the community, the best friend of Jesus remains unnamed in the Fourth Gospel and unmentioned in the epistles. This in turn makes it possible for anyone who testifies to Jesus and models the norms of this community to step into the

46. Tidball, *Ministry by the Book*, 74.
47. Bartlett, *Ministry in the New Testament*, 97.
48. Wheatley, *Leadership and the New Science*, 130.

role when needed, and to step out of it when someone else is needed. The absence of a name for this person opens up the possibility that anyone can be the best friend of Jesus, at least for a little while. Of course, there is no way to prove that this notion shaped the author's portrayal of the beloved disciple or the first community's apprehension of it.

Johannine Community and Leadership Today

There is a sense in which Johannine ecclesiology, as it is describe here, sounds fairly idyllic, especially to North Americans who prize democratic, egalitarian, classless organizations. However, such an almost structure-less community is remarkably fragile and vulnerable. Indeed, according to the Brown hypothesis of the history of the Johannine community, the eaglets did tear apart the nest and all within it. Sometime in the second century the Johannine community dissolved and was assimilated into the slowly developing orthodox Christian traditions of the following centuries.[49] He writes, "[T]he very fact that a Paraclete-centered ecclesiology had offered no real protection against schismatics ultimately caused his followers to accept the authoritative presbyter-bishop teaching structure which in the second century became dominant in the Great Church but which was quite foreign to Johannine tradition."[50] I would add that this ecclesiology also offered little to help it survive in the midst of conflict within and outside the community, or to address the tremendous changes going on in the late first-century and early second-century Greco-Roman world. Furthermore, leadership defined primarily as witness to and friendship with Jesus provided very little protective structure and organization to help the community survive.

And yet, having said that, perhaps the most important goal of any Christian community or concomitant institution should never be its own survival. And it is in this recognition that I find, paradoxically, hope for the future of the traditions and practices of North American mainline churches, if not for the endurance of their institutional structures in their 20th century forms. For the most important goal should be the handing on of our teaching and wisdom about Jesus the Christ in ways that are faithful to our experiences of him and to the witness of those who have gone before us, including the best friend at the center of the Johannine community. As we face the cultural changes that are sweeping across North America and deal with the conflicts that continue to threaten our churches and denominations, friendship with one another and with Jesus may be the most significant

49. Brown, *The Community of the Beloved Disciple*, 145.
50. Ibid., 146.

expression of our faith that we can offer to those within and outside our communities. Friends can continue to be friends even when organizations undergo mutation and transformation. This friendship should continue to be marked by the same egalitarian spirit, the same mutual respect, the same honest conversation that was idealized in the Johannine community of the first century. And our leadership then, should also be exercised in a spirit of humble friendship that is rooted in relationship with the Christ who called our communities into being and with those who are also seeking to follow him faithfully.

Bibliography

Bartlett, David L. *Ministry in the New Testament*. Minneapolis: Fortress, 1993.
Black, C. Clifton. "The First, Second, and Third Letters of John." In *The New Interpreter's Bible*. Vol. XII. Nashville: Abingdon, 1998.
Brant, Jo-Ann A. *John*. Paideia Commentaries on the New Testament. Grand Rapids: Baker Academic, 2011.
Brown, Raymond E. *The Churches the Apostles Left Behind*. New York: Paulist, 1984.
———. *The Community of the Beloved Disciple: The Life, Loves, and Hates of an Individual Church in New Testament Times*. New York: Paulist, 1979.
———. *The Gospel according to John XIII-XXI*. The Anchor Bible. Vol. 29A. Garden City: Doubleday, 1970.
———. *An Introduction to the Gospel of John*. Edited by Francis J. Moloney. New Haven: Yale University Press, 2003.
Bultmann, Rudolph. *The Johannine Epistles*. Hermeneia. Philadelphia: Fortress, 1973.
Carter, Warren. *The Roman Empire and the New Testament: An Essential Guide*. Nashville: Abingdon, 2006.
Coloe, Mary L. *Dwelling in the Household of God: Johannine Ecclesiology and Spirituality*. Collegeville: Liturgical, 2007.
Crook, Zeba A. "Fictive-friendship and the Fourth Gospel." *HTS Teologiese Studies/ Theological Studies* 67 no.3 (2011) http://dx.doi.org/10/4102/hts.v67i3.997 (accessed September 28, 2013).
Culpepper, R. Alan. *Anatomy of the Fourth Gospel: A Study in Literary Design*. Philadelphia: Fortress, 1983.
Fitzgerald, John T., *Greco-Roman Perspectives on Friendship*. SBL Resources for Biblical Study 34. Atlanta: Scholars, 1997.
Howard-Brook, Wes. *Becoming Children of God: John's Gospel and Radical Discipleship*. Eugene: Wipf and Stock, 2003.
Johnson, Luke Timothy. "Making Connections: The Material Expression of Friendship in the New Testament." *Interpretation* 58 (2004) http://int.sagepub.com/content/58/2/158 (accessed September 28, 2013).
Koester, Craig R. *Symbolism in the Fourth Gospel: Meaning, Mystery, Community*. 2nd ed. Minneapolis: Fortress, 2003.
Malina, Bruce J., and Richard L. Rohrbaugh. *Social-Science Commentary on the Gospel of John*. Minneapolis: Fortress, 1998.

Martyn, J. Louis. *History and Theology in the Fourth Gospel*. 3rd ed. The New Testament Library. Louisville: Westminster John Knox, 2003.

O'Day, Gail R. "The Gospel of John." In *The New Interpreter's Bible*. Vol. IX. Nashville: Abingdon, 1995.

———. "Jesus as Friend in the Gospel of John." *Interpretation* 58 (2004). http://int.sagepub.com/content/58/2/144 (accessed September 28, 2013).

Pittman, Nancy Claire. "The Epistolary Tradition: The Letters of James, 1–2 Peter, 1–3 John, and Jude." In *Chalice Introduction to the New Testament*, edited by Dennis E. Smith, 254–280. St. Louis: Chalice, 2004.

Reinhartz, Adele. *Befriending the Beloved Disciple: A Jewish Reading of the Gospel of John*. New York: Continuum, 2001.

Rensberger, David. *1 John; 2 John; 3 John*. Abingdon New Testament Commentaries. Nashville: Abingdon, 1997.

Schnackenburg, Rudolf. *The Gospel According to St. John*. Vol. 3. New York: Crossroad, 1990.

Schneiders, Sandra M. *Written That You May Believe: Encountering Jesus in the Fourth Gospel*. Revised and expanded ed. New York: Crossroad, 2003.

Smith, D. Moody. *John*. Abingdon New Testament Commentaries. Nashville: Abingdon, 1999.

Tan, Yak-hwee. "The Johannine Community: Caught in 'Two Worlds.'" In *New Currents through John: A Global Perspective*, edited by Francisco Lozada, Jr., and Tom Thatcher, 167–82. Atlanta: Society of Biblical Literature, 2006.

Tidball, Derek. *Ministry by the Book: New Testament Patterns for Pastoral Leadership*. Downers Grove: IVP Academic, 2008.

Van der Watt, Jan. *An Introduction to the Johannine Gospel and Letters*. London: T. & T. Clark, 2007.

Wheatley, Margaret. *Leadership and the New Science: Discovering Order in a Chaotic World*. 3rd ed. San Francisco: Berrett-Koehler, 2006.

Williams, Ritva H. *Stewards, Prophets, Keepers of the Word: Leadership in the Early Church*. Peabody: Hendrickson, 2006.

5

Self-Made Eunuchs as Model Disciples
Matthew 19:12 in Narrative and Historical Context

—Jennifer Sylvan Alexander

The noun eunuchs appears three times in Matthew 19:12, the verb form "to eunuchize" (*eunouchizō*, a *hapax legomenon*) twice.[1] The verse has no parallel. Early Christians wondered what Jesus could have meant by it, especially "and there are eunuchs who have made themselves eunuchs for the sake of

---

1. I am honored to dedicate this essay to Dr. David J. Gouwens, beloved advisor, teacher, and mentor. Because Dr. Gouwens introduced me to Søren Kierkegaard and provided ongoing support as I contended with Kierkegaard's writings on Jews and Judaism, it seems apt to begin with a quote about Matthew 19 from Johannes Climacus, one of Kierkegaard's pseudonymous authors: "The whole chapter speaks of the difficulty of entering the kingdom of heaven, and the expressions are as strong as possible. Verse 12: 'There are eunuchs who have castrated themselves for the sake of the kingdom of heaven.' Verse 24: 'It is easier for a camel to go through the eye of a needle than for a rich man to enter the kingdom of God.' The disciples become so terrified that they say (verse 25) 'Who then can be saved?' After Christ has answered this, there is in turn mention in verse 29 of the reward for those who have left houses and brothers or sisters or father or mother or wife or children or lands for the sake of Christ's name—all of them terrible expressions of the collisions in which a Christian can be tested. Consequently, the entrance into the kingdom of heaven is made as difficult as possible, so difficult that even teleological suspensions of the ethical are mentioned" (Kierkegaard, *Concluding Unscientific Postscript*, 592). Climacus bluntly conveys the exceeding difficulty of entering the kingdom of heaven according to the gospel of Matthew (and also reminds readers of Kierkegaard's unforgettable treatment of another troubling text—Gen 22—in *Fear and Trembling*). Few contemporary biblical scholars connect Matthew 19:12c with this difficulty as explicitly as does Climacus; however, they should. As I will demonstrate in the following pages, Matthew's self-made eunuchs must be interpreted in context, particularly the context of chapter 19.

the kingdom of heaven. Let anyone accept this who can."[2] Was Jesus recommending castration, a practice later proscribed by a number of Roman emperors? Origen apparently thought so and castrated himself—at least, as Eusebius would lead us to believe.[3] That the First Council of Nicea banned self-castrated clerics (Canon 1) indicates that Origen (or Eusebius) was not alone in taking such an interpretation and that the practice troubled the emerging church.[4]

With few exceptions, contemporary biblical scholars interpret Matt 19:12c-d as a recommendation for voluntary celibacy. They argue that the Matthean Jesus urged unmarried disciples not to marry, divorced disciples not to remarry, or both. Several argue that Jesus instructed his disciples to eschew androcentric, patriarchal, hierarchical/kyriarchal values in favor of the egalitarian relationships represented by God's kingdom.[5] Reading Matthew's eunuchs as chaste figures of celibacy (without defining celibacy), however, obscures disparaging ancient portrayals of eunuchs as highly-sexed actors of uncertain gender and morals. A near-exclusive focus on preceding verses (Matt 19:3–11) prevents many biblical scholars from making key connections between self-castrated eunuchs and Matthew's larger narrative, particularly subsequent verses in chapter 19 that exhibit decidedly androcentric, patriarchal and hierarchical features. Most distressing, though, is

---

2. Unless otherwise stated, translations are from the NRSV.

3. *Hist. eccl.* 6.8. Origen's castration was and is disputed. See Kuefler for a helpful discussion (*Manly Eunuch*, 261). Domitian was the first to ban castration. See Guyot's discussion of Domitian, Nerva, Hadrian, Antoninus Pius, Marcus Aurelius, and Constantine (*Eunuchen als Sklaven*, 45–51). Justin Martyr wrote about a young adherent who appealed unsuccessfully to the Alexandrian governor for castration (1 *Apol.* 29).

4. This is a revised version of a term paper I wrote for a 2010 doctoral seminar. I thank my colleagues and professors, especially Dr. Ted Smith, Dr. Patout Burns, Pastor Amy Mears, and Father Dexter Brewer, as well as Ms. MAT Trotter and Reverend Elise Elrod. I am also grateful to the Matthew Section of the Society of Biblical Literature, for whom I presented a version of this thesis at the 2012 annual meeting. And although they have not yet seen this essay, Dr. Amy-Jill Levine and Dr. Jay Geller have been unflaggingly supportive of my doctoral experience.

5. The following listing is representative. Not to marry: Harrington, *Gospel of Matthew*, 274–76; Davies and Allison, *Matthew*, v. 3,21; Keener, *Matthew*, 299; Nolland, *Matthew: A Commentary*, 780–82; France, *The Gospel of Matthew*, 723–26. Not to remarry: Gundry, *Matthew: Literary and Theological*, 381–83. Quesnell, "Made Themselves Eunuchs," 346; Moloney, "Matthew 19:3–12 and Celibacy," 42–49; Barton, *Discipleship and Family Ties*, 201. Not to marry or remarry: Carter, *Matthew and the Margins*, 382–84; Luz, *Evangelium*, 111; Senior, *Matthew*, 215–16. Senior believes this might include others: Christian women who had been divorced and chose not to get remarried, missionaries, and others who wanted to imitate Jesus' lifestyle (216). Egalitarian: Carter, *Matthew and the Margins*, 383–84; Bernabé, "Of Eunuchs and Predators," 128–34; Talbott, "Kyriarchy on the Chopping Block," 21–43.

that the earthly costs of becoming a eunuch for the kingdom—not unlike the costs of becoming a disciple—are ignored at worst or minimized at best.

A defensible interpretation of Matthew's self-castrated eunuchs should attend to ancient conceptions about eunuchs and assess Matt 19:12 within its narrative context, not simply its preceding verses (19:1–11) but also within Matthew's larger narrative, particularly subsequent verses (19:13–30) This essay will do precisely this. I will argue that the Matthean Jesus offers self-made eunuchs as models of discipleship because they embody wholehearted commitment to Jesus and the kingdom of the heavens he proclaims. For their loyal service and sacrifice of earthly progeny, property, and status, they will be richly compensated in the heavenly kingdom. The essay begins with an assessment of model discipleship in Matthew, follows with an overview of eunuchs in antiquity, then proceeds to situate Matthew's self-made eunuchs within narrative and historical context.

Model Discipleship in Matthew

The Matthean Jesus has high expectations of followers. "Be perfect, therefore, as your heavenly Father is perfect," he tells disciples and crowds in the Sermon on the Mount (5:48). The Sermon (chapters 5–7) helps elucidate his expectations. Disciples follow the teachings of the Torah and prophets as Jesus does (5:17–20). They learn from Jesus. (Appropriately, the term for disciple, *mathētēs*, translates to "a learner, pupil."[6]) Discipleship in Matthew requires more than mental affirmation; it must be enacted. They must *follow* Jesus in word and deed. *Akoloutheō* (to follow) language is characteristic of discipleship for Matthew. Jesus brings the Sermon on the Mount toward its conclusion with this warning: "Not everyone who says to me, 'Lord, Lord,' will enter the kingdom of heaven, but only the one who does the will of my Father in heaven" (7:21).

There are a number of behaviors ideal disciples should display, each of which merits sustained attention. For the sake of brevity, however, this section sketches five essential characteristics. To be clear, my concern is what ideal disciples should do according to Matthew; hence the characterization of Jesus' twelve disciples is important for my purposes only insofar as their behavior models, or fails to model, desired characteristics.[7]

---

6. *LSJ* 483.

7. There has been much scholarly debate about Matthew's characterization of Jesus' disciples, especially in contrast to Mark's less flattering portrayal. See Brown's monograph for a helpful overview (*Disciples in Narrative Perspective*).

Disciples should respond to Jesus' words immediately, decisively, and faithfully. After beginning his eschatological mission with the words "Repent, for the kingdom of heaven has come near" (4:17). Jesus summons his first disciples. Two sets of brothers—Peter and Andrew, James and John—leave behind their nets and boats immediately and join Jesus when they hear his imperative "Follow me, and I will make you fish for people" (4:19). The parallel use of "immediately they left" (*hoi de eutheōs aphentes* in 4:20, 22) for the sibling pairs' identical response underscores the necessity of both hurrying and leaving. The kingdom, which has already come near, will not wait; Jesus expects, and receives, their immediate acquiescence, whatever the earthly repercussions they may face. James and John's response is especially poignant because they leave their father in the boat with the family's ongoing work of mending nets. Indeed, the three-time mention of their father heightens the pathos.[8] For these first four disciples, Jesus' authoritative call necessitates an abandonment of the existing family occupation for another that is defined by commitment to Jesus and his itinerant work.[9] Jesus does not expect all to become itinerants; some exhibit faithfulness when they obey his authoritative words immediately, without hesitation or reflection. The centurion who publicly defers to Jesus' superior authority, for example, exemplifies this faithfulness, so much so that he becomes a foil for the "sons of the kingdom" (8:12).[10]

Matthew expects model disciples to subordinate or sever their preexisting family ties. This they do upon joining Jesus' eschatological household, as occurred in dramatic fashion with James and John. Jesus' response to the man who wants to bury his father provides another example. When Jesus calls him to discipleship, the man must make an instantaneous and absolute decision about his primary family allegiance. Jack Dean Kingsbury, filling in the story's gap by reading the prospective disciple's response as an affirmative, explains the dilemma, "The problem inherent in the request of the unnamed disciple [8:21–22] is that he desires to suspend for a time his commitment to follow Jesus. Moreover, his request is exceedingly well-founded:

---

8. Carter, *Matthew and the Margins*, 122. Carter notes the three-time identification (including "son of Zebedee") that underscores family relationships. The word "pathos" reflects my interpretation.

9. Kingsbury wonders if, without Jesus' personal summons, perhaps "no one, apart from his enabling call, is capable of embarking upon this life and sustaining" such a rigorous life (*Matthew as Story*, 133).

10. Upon the centurion's demonstration of faith, Jesus marvels and says ". . . Truly I tell you, in no one in Israel have I found such faith. I tell you, many will come from east and west and will eat with Abraham and Isaac and Jacob in the kingdom of heaven, while the heirs of the kingdom will be thrown into the outer darkness, where there will be weeping and gnashing of teeth" (8:10–12).

he has a prior obligation to which he must attend, namely, the sacred trust to go and look after the burial of his father (cf. Gen. 50:5–6). Jesus' response to the disciple's request is swift and sharp. The commitment to discipleship, he declares in essence, brooks no suspension. No obligation exists that can be permitted to take precedence over it."[11]

Jesus himself models the subordination of preexisting family ties. He does this publicly in front of crowds and disciples while his natal family members, minus Joseph, wait nearby, wanting to speak with him. They might be within hearing distance. Shockingly, Jesus neither responds directly to them nor honors their wish to speak with him; instead, he tells the crowds and disciples: "'Who is my mother, and who are my brothers?' And pointing to his disciples, he said, 'Here are my mother and my brothers! For whoever does the will of my Father in heaven is my brother and sister and mother'" (12:48–50). While Matthew mentions the names of Jesus' brothers—James, Joses, Judas, and Simon—he tells us nothing more about them. They never appear on Matthew's list of twelve disciples, and among Jesus' family, only his mother *may* be present at the cross (27:56).

Disciples should share or renounce their earthly possessions in service of the kingdom. Money is a hindrance to salvation, as Jesus' warning in the parable of the sower makes clear. (13:22) Disciples' servant lifestyle entails joining Jesus in proclaiming the kingdom, healing, and feeding, not amassing earthly wealth but sharing it with the poor. Disciples will have treasure in heaven. (19:21) Jesus welcomes disciples who engage in itinerant mission with him, but those who cannot travel should support those who can with their resources and hospitality. And although it is easier for a camel to go through the eye of a needle than for a rich man to enter the heavenly kingdom (19:24) it is not impossible. Joseph of Arimathea, a wealthy man "discipled" by Jesus, demonstrates this when he diligently cares for Jesus' crucified body. Joseph requests Jesus' body from Pilate, takes it, wraps it in clean linen, and entombs it in a new tomb prepared from his own funds. (27:57–60)

Disciples must be willing to lose social status and suffer when they model Jesus' commitment to the heavenly kingdom. Discipleship has painful social consequences. Jesus sends his disciples as "sheep into the midst of wolves"

---

11. He concludes: "The resolution of this conflict is clear: the unnamed disciple boards the boat" (Kingsbury, *Matthew as Story*, 134). Matthew does not, however, provide any information about the unnamed man's decision. Also, while an initial break with kin may appear total and irrevocable, practical considerations may continue to tie the disciples to preexisting relations. Carter reminds readers of Peter's continuing relationship with his mother-in-law and his ownership of the house ("Matthean Discipleship," 70). Mother Zebedee also plays a continuing role in the narrative.

(10:16). They will be hated by all (10:22). Like their teacher, they will face persecution, humiliation, and suffering (10:17–28). In Ulrich Luz's words, because disciples accepted Jesus' "authority, his proclamation, his commission and his way of life, they were also confronted with his suffering. The gospel of the kingdom of heaven as Matthew interprets it evidently leads *eo ipso* to suffering." Since for Matthew suffering is "the inevitable consequence of taking on Jesus' commission," suffering itself becomes "a constitutive mark of discipleship."[12]

Disciples should strive for the heavenly kingdom by living righteously on earth. It is not incidental that Jesus' first words in the gospel, in response to John the Baptist's objection that he should be baptized by Jesus, are "'Let it be so now; for it is proper for us in this way to fulfill all righteousness'" (3:15). The Beatitudes (5:3–10) provide both a model and encouragement for disciples. The Sermon on the Mount clarifies that followers should seek first the kingdom of the heavens and God's righteousness (6:33) instead of worrying about food, drink, and clothing. Their actions, words and relationships will point to their lives of righteousness and display God's salvific reign and presence; their fasting, prayer, and charity will express their commitment to please God.[13] Since Jesus models righteousness, would-be disciples will not fail if they model their lives (conceding even unto death) according to his.

Eunuchs in Antiquity

Before turning to Matthew's eunuchs, we need to develop familiarity with eunuchism in Matthew's world, particularly with societal roles and popular perceptions of eunuchs. Although widely attested in antiquity, eunuchism has largely dropped out in contemporary societies, at least from the public eye.[14] Hence I begin with an overview of eunuchs and castration. A consid-

12. Luz, *Studies in Matthew*, 157–58.

13. Carter, *Storyteller, Interpreter, Evangelist*, 218. Carter lists ten traits of disciples based on his reading of Matt 4:17—11:1 (216–19). Davies and Allison argue that there is more than one interpretive possibility for righteousness. By exhibiting "moral effort or obedience to God's will: by fulfilling Scripture, John and Jesus are acting rightly, they are exhibiting 'righteousness' . . . and moral conduct in accord with God's will" (*Matthew*, v, 1, 326–27).

14. Until about fifteen years ago, few scholars devoted attention to eunuchs. The lacuna may be attributed to a lack of interest, a lack of familiarity, and a general distaste for or unease with castrated men. The recent growth in eunuch studies generally corresponds to a greater consciousness about rights of and discrimination against individuals who identify as gay, lesbian, bisexual, transgender, or queer. Eunuchs were very well-attested in the Ancient Near East, the Byzantine Empire, China, and India.

eration of key roles follows, and I conclude with perceptions about eunuchs in the Greco-Roman world.

In most cases, eunuchs were castrated boys or men. Castration typically entailed the removal of testicles only; total castration, the removal of testicles and penis. Procedures varied over time and across cultures, but total castration was never the norm. Depending on a male's age and the method employed, castration did not necessarily prevent sexual arousal. If a man was castrated after puberty, testosterone could continue to arrive through his adrenal glands and descend to his testicles if they had been crushed rather than removed. Long-term physical effects of castration on appearance and vocal chords also depended on a male's age when he was castrated.[15] Eight Greek terms for eunuchs included *spadōn* (torn) *apokopos* (cut off) *thladias* (crushed) *eunouchos* (eunuch) *ektomias* (cut out) *thlibias* (pressed) *tomias* (gelded or castrated animal) and *ithris* (eunuch). *Spadōn* was a broader category within which other terms like *thlibias* and *thladias* could be contained. Over twenty Latin equivalents existed. The range of terms underscores both the diverse types of eunuch-making and the tendency to label eunuchs by the manner in which they were castrated.[16]

The term directly relevant for Matthew's eunuchs, *eunouchos*, has uncertain etymological origins but may derive from the Greek *eunē* (bed) and *echō* (to have) with the approximate meaning "bed guard." While *eunouchos* could refer to a man who lived a sexually abstinent lifestyle, this was by no means an obvious interpretive choice for Matthew or his early auditors. Walter Stevenson makes this point humorously in reference to Matthew's use of *eunouchos*:

Even in Italy, for centuries boys were turned into castrati with the hope that they would retain their pre-pubescent voices for opera. A modern equivalent of castration might be a surgical sex change operation. Other analogues include controversial chemical and surgical castration for sex offenders and for men who have certain types of prostate or testicular cancer.

15. Bullough, "Eunuchs in History and Society," 4. For the argument that eunuchs, particularly the *sarisim* of the Old Testament, were castrated, see chapter 2 of Burke's dissertation (*Queering Acts*, 22–41) See also Everhart's discussion about etymological (and ideological) controversies surrounding the Hebrew term *saris* in the first section of chapter 3 of her dissertation (*Hidden Eunuchs*, 97–106)

16. Guyot, *Eunuchen als Sklaven*, 21–24. Guyot's footnotes for each of these terms read like lexical entries. Eunuchs did not present the only ambiguous gender form in antiquity. Ancient writers also speculated about androgyny, the union of male and female physical characteristics into one being, hermaphroditism, individuals who shared desirable characteristics of both women and men, and asexuality, a rejection to or liberation from sexual activity associated with angels and other spiritual beings as well as holy men and women who abstained from sex to help facilitate communication with the gods (Scholz, *Eunuchs and Castrati*, 13–14).

If Matthew wanted 'celibate' he could have written *agamos*, as Paul did in Corinthians 7.32, or *parthenos*, as in Apocalypse 14.4, or *apopartheneusas*, or something more specific. *Agamos* is very precise, *apopartheneusas* implies heroic ascesis, and *parthenos* would draw up images of humble, maidenly purity, while *eunouchos* certainly could not do the same for Matthew's contemporary readers. All these terms can roughly mean 'celibate,' but, as Origen's apparent misunderstanding shows, the author of Matthew's Gospel made a great mistake writing *eunouchos* if he really meant 'celibate.'[17]

What associations, then, might early auditors of Matthew's gospel have made when they heard the term *eunouchos*? Who were eunuchs? With the fivefold repetition of eunuch terms (*eunouchoi* [3x], *eunouchizō* [2x]) in just one verse, Matthew certainly expected them to pick up the referent.[18]

Most eunuchs were slaves. Matthew 19:12b ("and there are eunuchs who were eunuchized by people," my literal translation) probably denotes these eunuchs. This is a point that, regrettably, New Testament scholars neglect.[19] Slavery was well-established throughout the ancient world and is clearly presupposed by biblical texts. Slave traders castrated boys and men because castrated slaves were more profitable. Whereas a slave cost about 500 denarii in the second and first centuries B.C.E., a castrated slave cost 2000 or more. Pliny the Elder complained about the price paid for the eunuch Paezon—a staggering fifty million sesterces.[20] Writers claimed that castrated slaves were more docile and loyal. Xenophon, for instance, compared eunuchs to gelded horses, castrated bulls, and castrated dogs, all of which were more serviceable once castrated.[21] In republican and imperial Rome, castrated slaves were considered luxury items and status symbols.

---

17. Stevenson, "Eunuchs and Early Christianity," 124–25. See also Brower's dissertation ("Ambivalent Bodies") Kufeler (*Manly Eunuch*) and Hester ("Postgender Jesus," 13–40) One of Hester's explicit goals in this article is to "problematize the 'celibate' eunuch" (13).

18. I do not discount the possibility that Matthew preserved Jesus' words. It is, however, impossible to prove. This study does not seek to establish what the historical Jesus may have said.

19. I have discovered that most scholars devote scant or no attention to Matthew's first two groups. When I returned to revise this essay, I realized that I had also neglected them. I intend to rectify this by devoting a chapter to each group of Matthew's eunuchs in my dissertation.

20. Tougher, *Eunuchs in Byzantine History*, 27.

21. *Cyr.* 7.5.62–63. Bullough quotes some of these lines in "Eunuchs in History and Society," 5–6. That Xenophon compares eunuch slaves to animals suggests that eunuchs were not always perceived to be human beings.

Eunuchs helped demonstrate elites' political power. For instance, Plautianus, a prefect of Emperor Septimius Severus, reportedly had one hundred Roman boys and men forcibly castrated, some of whom were already married and all of whom were citizens. He turned them into slaves for his daughter.[22] Although castration was banned within the empire (ironically, by emperors who appreciated the services of eunuchs) slave trading of eunuchs was permissible until Justinian I, provided they were castrated outside Roman territory.

Eunuchs served in various capacities, two of which have particular relevance for this study: slaves (or servants) of elite households, and priests. Monarchical structures came to depend on eunuchs as confidants, messengers, and servants of queens and kings. Potential rivals to a throne also could be castrated, then appointed to senior positions by their subjugator(s).[23] Emperors regularly employed eunuchs in the imperial household, usually freedmen. There were numerous eunuchs in Nero's household, some of whom held high military posts and acted as trusted messengers. According to Suetonius, Claudius awarded Posides, his favorite eunuch freedman, a military prize for honor, the *Hasta Pura*, after a 44 C.E. victory in Britain.[24] Eunuchs provided not only administrative and military services, they served their masters sexually. Some were valued especially for their beauty. Domitian, the first emperor to ban castration within the empire, commissioned Statius to write a poem about his favored young eunuch Earinus.

These so-called "court eunuchs" are also well attested in the Bible.[25] The single appearance of a New Testament eunuch outside Matthew occurs in Acts 8:26–40, a remarkable narrative about Philip's encounter with and baptism of a well-educated eunuch who served the Candace, Queen of the Ethiopians, as treasurer. References to eunuchs are frequent in the Old Testament, where the Hebrew term *sry* occurs forty-five times.[26] In their

22. According to Cassius Dio 76.14, who was clearly appalled. See also Guyot, *Eunuchen als Sklaven*, 123.

23. Scholz, *Eunuchs and Castrati*, 72.

24. *Claud.* 28.1. They also served other members of Nero's household and his military commander Fabius Valens. Otho, Vitellius, Titus, and Domitian employed eunuchs in the imperial household, as did Tiberius's son. Guyot lists all known "court eunuchs" in the early empire in his chapter "*Die Hofeunuchen im Romischen Reich vom 1. Bis zum 3. Jahrhundert*" (*Eunuchen als Sklaven*, 121–29).

25. This term, though commonly used by scholars, strikes me as neutral, even innocuous. It downplays the servile or enslaved status of eunuchs. An analysis of this term, and a comparison of it with the term "court Jews," might be productive but is beyond the scope of this essay. For a useful survey of eunuchs in the Hebrew Bible, refer to chapter 3, sections 2 and 3, of Everhart's dissertation (*Hidden Eunuchs*, 106–69).

26. Burke, "Queering Acts," 29. See also page 30 for Burke's helpful table listing all

roles as servants of kings, queens, and other notables, *sarisim* performed crucial functions—even, sometimes, murder (e.g., Jezebel's eunuchs throw her from the window at Jehu's word; eunuchs actively help Esther and Mordecai arrange Haman's death)—and thereby helped facilitate the transfer of power from one ruler to another.[27] Eunuchs are most prominent in the books of Esther and Daniel, where they serve as attendants, messengers, escorts, harem supervisors and guards. Other texts exhibit concern about their non-procreative or incomplete physical status. An extraordinary passage in Isaiah 56 welcomes observant eunuchs into the eternal household of God.[28]

The role for which eunuchs gained notoriety in antiquity was that of priest. The *gallus* (plural *galli*) was a eunuch priest of Cybele (also called *Magna Mater*, Great Mother) a goddess associated from the first millennium B.C.E. with Phrygia in central Asia Minor. According to numerous Latin and Greek sources, Cybele was ushered to Rome in 204 B.C.E. with great excitement and ceremony after notables consulted the Sibylline Books and Delphic Oracle. Upon her arrival in her new home, rituals and imagery were quickly introduced to help establish her as a distinctively Roman protectress and fertility goddess. While she was a guest of the temple of the goddess Victory, her own temple was constructed on a prominent location on the Palatine Hill. Cybele was served by eunuch priests who, by Ovid's account, sought to emulate the handsome shepherd Attis, Cybele's lover whom she drove to self-castration after he committed adultery, then resurrected after his death so he could become her eternal consort.[29]

---

eunuchs in the Hebrew Masoretic text and the LXX. Parsons draws attention to Luke's repeated designation of the Ethiopian minister of the queen as *eunouchos* (8:27, 34, 36, 38, 39) as possibly the character's "dominant, defining characteristic" (Parsons, *Acts*, 120).

27. Everhart, "Jezebel Framed," 692–98.

28. Deuteronomy 23:1 proscribes admittance for those with crushed testicles (*thladias*; LXX Deut 23:2) into the "assembly of the LORD" (*ekklēsian kyriou*). Eunuchs in Isaiah evoke pity because they cannot procreate; some are freeborn nobles fated for enslavement to rival monarchs. In 39:7, Isaiah warns Hezekiah: "Some of your own sons who are born to you shall be taken away; they shall be eunuchs in the palace of the king of Babylon." Similar to Isa 56:3–5, Wis 3:14 also conveys blessing: "Blessed also is the eunuch whose hands have done no lawless deed, and who has not devised wicked things against the Lord; for special favor will be shown him for his faithfulness, and a place of great delight in the temple of the Lord."

29. Ovid *Fast.* 4. Latham, "Fabulous Clap-Trap," 86–87; Takács, *Virgins, Sibyls, Matrons*, 60–61; and Roller, *God the Mother*, 284–85. About the *Mater*'s connection with Greece (i.e., not only Phrygia) and the Delphic Oracle, see chapter 3 of Takács. The object escorted to Rome was a small, dark stone that had fallen from the sky. There were multiple accounts of her arrival. See especially chapter 9 of Roller (*God the Mother*)

Whereas Cybele was revered throughout the empire, her *galli* were despised. For centuries, writers depicted them as effeminate, wearing bright clothing, jewelry, make-up, crimped and bleached hair or wigs, and walking in an affected manner. "Mark how conspicuously they braid and adorn their hair, and how they scrub and paint their faces with cosmetics and pigments and the like," Philo complained. "In fact, the transformation of the male nature to the female is practiced by them as an art and does not raise a blush. . ."[30] Philo's disgust was shared by many. Romans, and their Greek predecessors, did not quite know what to make of eunuchs. Some, like Philo (and Aristotle centuries before him) claimed that eunuchs transformed from men into women; others, that they were neither men nor women. Eunuchs were frequently derided as licentious. Juvenal, Martial, Lucian and Philostratus all associated eunuchs with adultery.[31] Juvenal satirized their sexual capabilities in the following lines of his misogynistic *Satire VI: The Ways of Women*:

> There are girls who adore unmanly eunuchs—their kisses always delectably smooth, with no trace of a beard, and no worry about abortions! But the highest pleasure comes from one who was fully-grown, a lusty black-quilled male, before the surgeons went to work on his groin. Wait, therefore, until the testicles drop and ripen, let them fill out till they hang like two-pound weights; then what the surgeon drops will hurt no one's trade but the barber's. (Slave-dealers' boys are different: pathetically weak, ashamed of their empty bag, their lost little chickpeas.) What a specimen, everyone knows him, making his public entry to the baths, endowed in a way to challenge Priapus! And yet he's a eunuch. His mistress arranged it. So, let them sleep together—but Postumus, don't ever trust your Dionysiac boyfriend, just out of adolescence, to the—mercy of such a eunuch![32]

Juvenal's explicit lines reflect a Roman tradition that places a high value on fertility. Accordingly, men should not provide non-procreative pleasure

---

There were other eunuch priests in antiquity, but there is a paucity of evidence for these, and the Mother's priests were most famous. For a recent treatment of eunuch priests of the goddess Atargatis (also called *Dea Syria*) see Lightfoot's contribution to the volume edited by Tougher (*Eunuchs in Antiquity*, 71–86). For detail about Cybele's arrival in Rome, see especially chapter 9 of Roller (*God the Mother*, 263–85).

30. *Spec. Leg.* 3.40–42. I have taken part of a quote cited and discussed by Abush ("Philo's Exegesis," 106).

31. Stevenson, "The Rise of Eunuchs," 500–503. Stevenson claims that adultery and lechery were often synonymous in antiquity.

32. *Sat.* VI. Green, *Sixteen Satires*, 366–78.

to women. Romans (or, at least, male elite writers) were especially troubled by the *galli*'s self-emasculation. Although there is no evidence about how many actually castrated themselves, what does appear clearly in literary and material remains is that some *galli* dressed in distinctively feminine attire. A 3rd century C.E. sarcophagus of a *gallus* or *archigallus* (chief priest) in a cemetery near Ostia, for example, shows him reclining, beardless, with heavy jewelry, long robes, and a Phrygian cap.[33] Eunuchs were also derided as foreigners who engaged in debauchery and unacceptable, non-Roman practices.

Popular ancient conceptions about the father's role in the Roman family may help contemporary readers understand a key aspect of the disparagement of eunuchs. Each Roman household was thought to represent a microcosm of the empire wherein the father held exclusive power over household members, including slaves. Imperial rule was based on the importance of the *pater familias*, with the emperor serving as the *Pater Patriae*, or Father of the Fatherland. As Walter Stevenson explains, eunuchs challenged this system. "If this potency is the root of the Roman conception of power, we would expect the Romans to banish such an impossible 'pater' as a eunuch from access to power or prestige. And this is, of course, how the historical Romans reacted."[34] Roman religious practices also revered the father's procreative abilities, not only as generator of children, but as guarantor of fertility for land and crops.

Roman law reflects this esteem for the Roman father's procreative role and his place in society. The prevailing concern of elite jurists who helped formulate Roman family law in the classical period (31 B.C.E.–235 C.E.) was property and succession. An abundance of cases illustrates values about procreativity in marriage and the father as dominant authority figure of household members and property. In one ruling, jurist Ulpian made a distinction, like Matthew, between eunuchs who were born so and eunuchs who were made so. Ulpian argued that in the case of a woman who married a castrated man, no dowry was permissible. If a eunuch was not castrated, a dowry was permissible. In a different ruling, Ulpian determined that a castrated man cannot adopt a *postumus* (child in utero) as heir. If Julian's opinion reflects actual practice, eunuchs in the empire could theoretically adopt heirs and so bequeath property, provided they did not castrate themselves.

33. Hales, "Looking for Eunuchs," 93. This image, and others, are accessible on an Italian website devoted to the ancient port city of Ostia. The link at the time of this essay's submission is www.ostia-antica.org. This site includes recent, detailed bibliographies.

34. Stevenson, "The Rise of Eunuchs," 505. However, here Stevenson fails to account for the power and prestige eunuchs sometimes garnered as servants and slaves of imperial and other elite households.

However the jurists debated these issues, in Roman society at large, eunuchs were perceived as emotionally incapable of bonding long-term with a wife or children and physically incapable of procreating.[35]

Matthew's Eunuchs in Narrative and Historical Context

Jesus' saying about eunuchs makes little sense when taken out of context as a logion. Scholars uniformly interpret 19:12 within its preceding context about divorce and marriage (19:3–11).[36] While this approach provides some context, it fails to account for the verse's key position in Matthew's larger narrative. Self-made eunuchs (19:12c-d) are deeply embedded not only within Jesus' instructions on divorce and marriage but also within his teachings about children (19:13–15) earthly riches and eternal life (19:16–26) and promised rewards of the kingdom of the heavens (19:27–30). The following reading explores these connections, and while it recognizes other narrative connections in the gospel, space prevents extensive analysis.

Chapter 19 opens with Jesus leaving Galilee to enter the boundaries of Judea on the other side of the Jordan (19:1). That this entire exchange occurs on the boundaries may speak to the eunuch's liminal position. Large crowds who have followed Jesus are cured by him. Ominously, some Pharisees have also come to Jesus, but to test rather than follow him. The structurally parallel introduction of 19:2 and 19:3 highlights the contrast between the two groups—the former associated with acceptance, following, and physical wholeness granted by Jesus, the latter with hostility, testing, and judgment delivered by Jesus (*pros tēn sklē rokardian hymōn* in 19:8). That Matthew applies the same verb (*peirazō*) for the devil's temptation/testing of Jesus (4:1, 3) connects the Pharisees implicitly with the devil (cf. 16:1; 22:18; 22:35). The geographic setting of 19:1 also recalls John the Baptist's fiery encounter with Pharisees and Sadducees. When many of them came to protest John's

---

35. Frier and McGinn, citing Ulpian's thirty-third book on the edict (*Roman Family Law*, 29): They emphasize the overriding significance of property in these cases: "In truth, for every juristic ruling on child custody or parental discipline, there are a hundred or more rulings on dowry." (*Roman Family Law*, 5). Ulpian says his opinion on adoption concurs with jurists Julian and Proculus, contra Iavolenus and Cassius, who believe castrated men ought to be able to dedicate a *postumus* since they can marry and adopt heirs (Stevenson, "Rise of Eunuchs," 497).

36. There are several exceptions. Barton recognizes the importance of the preceding (17:22—18:35) and following (19:13–29) texts (*Discipleship and Family Ties*, 193). See also Nolland, *Matthew: A Commentary*, 781. Carter has made a compelling case that 19:1—20:28 may be read as Matthew's version of a household code (*Households and Discipleship*). Hester claims that it was a logion that Matthew forced into its chapter 19 context ("Rhetorical Constructions," 809–10).

baptism in Matthew 3:7, John excoriated them for their unrepentant and arrogant ways, warning them that they would be baptized shortly by Jesus himself with judgment and everlasting condemnation.[37] Hearing these two verbal cues of geographic setting and testing, Matthew's auditors would be prepared for another polemical exchange between Jesus and Pharisees. They might expect to hear Jesus speak about the heavenly kingdom and pronounce judgment.

Matthew does not disappoint them on either count. Jesus begins with judgment and ends with the kingdom (19:28–30) In 19:3–9. Matthew has the Pharisees present themselves as authorities on scripture, probably as a foil to highlight Jesus' genuine interpretive authority.[38] Jesus insults the Pharisees by asking them: "have you not read" about marriage in Genesis? The verb *anaginōskō*, to "know well, know certainly" or "to know again, recognize: to acknowledge, own" shames them by suggesting that they are not well-versed in their own scriptures (19:4; cf. 12:3,5; 21:16,42; 22:31).[39] This shaming will culminate in chapter 23, when Jesus calls them (and scribes) hypocrites seven times (23:13,14,15,23,25,27,29; cf. 6:2,16; 7:5; 15:7; 16:3; 22:18; 24:51, among other names). To their second question about Moses' divorce command, Jesus responds with a second insult by reinterpreting Moses' words as a concession, not a command, and with an accusation that their hardheartedness (not their ancestors') prompted Moses' concession.[40] Ironically perhaps, Jesus concludes the exchange with his own mandate: men must not divorce and remarry except in the case of *porneia*, or they commit adultery (19:9).[41] This would contravene the divine order established at creation.

37. In his course on Matthew, Dr. Carter once suggested that I translate *epi* as "against" in 3:7 ("Some Pharisees and Sadducees came against [i.e., to protest] John's baptism.") instead of "for" so the preposition would make better sense of John's polemics. "Against" is a legitimate translation of *epi* in BDAG. Either way, the encounter in 3:7–12 is indisputably polemical, where John harshly derides his opponents by calling them a "brood of vipers," an epithet that will be repeated twice by Jesus (12:34; 23:33).

38. Kingsbury argues that "the issue of authority underlies all the controversies Jesus has with the religious leaders and that it is therefore pivotal to his entire conflict with them." (*Matthew as Story*, 125–26)

39. LSJ, 53. Repschinski notes that the phrase "*Ouk anegōte*" occurs only in controversy stories. It is, he explains, a "much more forceful counter-accusation" than that in Mark (*Controversy Stories*, 173).

40. He does this by emphasizing the personal pronoun three times in one verse—*legei autois hoti Mōsēs pros tēn sklērokardian hymōn epetrepsen hymin apolysai tas gynaikas hymōn ap' archēs de ou gegonen houtōs*—leaving his auditors with no doubt as to whom he accuses of hardheartedness.

41. Moloney notes the typically Matthean use of *legō de hymin hoti* to express Jesus' fulfillment (six times in the so-called antitheses). "Matthew 19:3–12 and Celibacy," 44.

Matthew's gendered language in this passage is striking for its almost exclusive focus on men and its redactional differences from Mark. Jesus addresses male Pharisees directly with an audience of male disciples. Jesus, the Pharisees, and the disciples all speak of men who divorce their women. While the Greek equivalent of woman/wife occurs four times (19:5, 8–10) Matthew has replaced *anēr* (Mark 10:2) with *anthrōpos* in 19:3, which may highlight the ambiguous, non-masculine gender identity of eunuchs. Crucially, Matthew also omits Mark 10:12 ("and if she divorces her husband and marries another, she commits adultery") which keeps the predominant focus on men. Women are on the underside of this Matthean passage—they are talked about but do not speak.[42]

After Jesus verbally bests these Pharisees with his teaching on divorce, marriage, and remarriage, they drop out of the scene. The disciples, who have been listening, appear disheartened by—if not hardhearted because of—Jesus' mandate. They inquire if it is better in this case not to marry. Jesus then shares a word that not all will be able to accept (19:11). This verse has created interpretive challenges. This word (*ton logon* [*touton*]) could refer to 19:3–9, 9, 10, or 12.[43]

---

42. I find troubling a scholarly tendency to downplay androcentrism in these verses and to valorize Jesus' treatment of marriage over against Pharisees. Carter, for example, claims that Jesus allows divorce "[a]gainst the Pharisees' contemplation of unrestricted male power over a woman," that Jesus "severely curtails that power by allowing only one reason for divorce" (Matthew and the Margins, 380). Similarly, Senior claims: "In a society where the woman could be at the mercy of a husband who could write a certificate of divorce, even for seemingly insignificant offenses, Jesus' teaching also protects the rights of the woman by forbidding such divorce (and, even if the exception clause is a true exception, only in cases where there was substantial cause for a rupture)" (Senior, Matthew, 216). Not only do such readings overstate, they portray male Pharisees in a harsher light than does Matthew (at least, at this point in the narrative). This is not the only androcentric text in Matthew; throughout the gospel women are background characters, discussed by men but often voiceless. One passage that shares parallels with Matt 19:1–12 is Matt 1:18–25. Here Mary is not an active participant; Joseph is. It is Joseph who receives the angelic visitation with instructions about how to handle Mary and what to name her child. Mary is a passive vessel acted upon (or not) by Joseph, the angel of the Lord, and the Holy Spirit. The angel of the Lord instructs Joseph not to be afraid "to receive" Mary. In 19:3–11, the focus is also male-centered. The Pharisees, Jesus, and disciples talk about actions they should or should not take with respect to women ("his" woman in 19:3, 5, 9; "your" wives in 19:8; a man with a woman in 19:10, to dismiss "her" in some texts of 19:8). Mary, the Pharisees' wives and the disciples' wives or prospective wives are passive recipients of the men's actions; if they have any role in the planning and decision-making, Matthew says nothing about this. And even when we add eunuchs to the mix, although we can say that yes, eunuchs certainly challenge traditional understandings of masculinity; we cannot say that the message is or was liberating for women in that eunuchs were harshly derided for being effeminate. They were not manly enough.

43. With Quesnell ("Made Themselves Eunuchs," 341) I find unlikely a reference to

Before considering Matthew' eunuchs in the context of 19:3–11, we must address a puzzle: if the Matthean Jesus highly esteems marriage, why does he not encourage it? As 19:3–9 demonstrate, Jesus clearly links marriage with God's creation, upholds its legitimacy, and defends it from misuse. But when we consider these verses alongside other Matthean texts that rely on marital imagery, a dim view of marriage emerges. Matthew associates marriage with blood, death and end times (e.g., 22:2–14; 23–30; 24:38–39; 25:1–13).[44] Nor does Jesus promote marriage. Whereas he actively recruits male disciples to join his eschatological work, he does not encourage them to marry, have children and diligently serve earthly families. He *does* encourage them to leave everyone and everything of value and follow him (4:18–22; 19:21–29). The creative work done in an earthly marriage (e.g., according to both Genesis passages to which Matthew alludes, tilling the ground, being fruitful, having dominion) is subordinated to kingdom work. Jesus' words echo Paul's in 1 Corinthians 7 when Paul encourages Jesus-followers to emulate himself by staying single if possible and marrying only if necessary. Those who are married should remain married. Given Matthew's eschatological horizon—not terribly distant from Paul's concern about the impending crisis (1 Cor 7:26)—marriage is hardly the best plan for Jesus-followers.[45] This does not mean, however, that Jesus upends marriage. If he did, Matthew's narrative would be internally inconsistent, especially with 5:17–18 and 5:27–32 of the Sermon on the Mount. In effect, Jesus would be undercutting himself as the fulfiller of Torah and the prophets and thereby the gospel itself.

Rather than focus exclusively on marriage, divorce, adultery, and remarriage to make sense of Matthew's eunuchs as do many Matthean scholars, Matt 19:3–11 can be interpreted foremost as another polemical exchange between Jesus and the Pharisees. It is indeed one of the Matthean controversy stories and, as such, represents yet another opportunity for Matthew to highlight Jesus' superior authority as definitive interpreter of God's will over against his adversaries, whose authority he delegitimates.

19:3–9, which would suggest that Jesus relativizes his preceding instructions on divorce and marriage. A connection with 19:12 is conceivable and has patristic support with Justin (Davies and Allison note his reading in 1 *Apol.*15.4; 20) and scriptural support in that the placement of *touton* refers to later material elsewhere (Davies and Allison cite Eph 4:17). Barton, citing Moloney and Gundry, claims the word refers "almost certainly" to 19:4–9 (*Discipleship and Family Ties*, 194–95). Senior sees a reference to 19:10 (*Matthew*, 215) as does Brown (*Disciples in Narrative Perspective*, 78). These are several examples; there is no scholarly consensus on the referent.

44. See Blickenstaff, "While the Bridegroom is with Them."

45. I find generally convincing Sim's argument about the characteristics of Matthean eschatology in *Apocalyptic Eschatology in the Gospel of Matthew*.

Compared to his Markan source (Mark 10:2–12) Matthew intensifies the conflict, focuses more on the Pharisees, and frames the question to underscore the debate about Torah interpretation.[46]

A literal translation of Matt 19:12c-d reads: "and there are eunuchs who eunuchized themselves for the kingdom of the heavens. The one who is able to make room, make room."[47] Davies and Allison, with most, interpret this as Jesus' statement on celibacy. They argue that Jesus' qualifications—"not all" (19:11) "[those] to whom it is given" (19:11) and "he who is able" (19:12)—emphasize the special character of celibacy as a calling.[48] While they rightly draw attention to the qualifiers, there is insufficient evidence for the celibacy claim, particularly with respect to ancient perceptions about eunuchs (discussed in the previous section of this essay). That the scholarly majority focuses on self-made eunuchs is understandable given Matthew's rhetorical strategy of presenting groups of three (e.g., three servants in the parable of talents) where the heaviest rhetorical weight falls on the third.[49] Another point of contention concerns the proper translation of *dia* as having a causal or final sense. If *dia* acts in a final sense as an accusative of relationship, as an expression of "the idea of advantage, benefit, favorable disposition, support, or friendly relationship," Jesus conceivably recommends self-castration in 19:12c "in order to gain" the kingdom of the heavens.[50] Because prepositions in Koine are fluid, we cannot know how Matthew or early auditors may have understood this, hence any interpretation of dia must remain speculative. Just as there is no way to determine how many *galli* and *archigalli* of Cybele actually castrated themselves, there is no way to determine whether or not Matthew, or Jesus, intended self-castration. I deliberately employ the term "self-made" because it embraces both possibilities—literal castration and figurative (e.g., dedicated service to a lord or deity). Either way, in antiquity eunuchs were perceived to be castrated.

---

46. Repschinski, *Controversy Stories*, 172–183. In Matthew, the issue shifts to grounds of divorce, which allows Jesus to demonstrate his superior interpretive abilities with respect to Torah.

47. Translation mine.

48. Davies and Allison, *Matthew*, v.3, 4–5. They classify the unit 19:1–12 as "Monogamy, Divorce, Celibacy" and state plainly in their introduction to their discussion of 19:1–12 that "Vv. 10–12 have to do with celibacy." The quote is found on page 5 under the subheading (ii) Sources. Refer to Brower, Hester, and Kuefler for counter arguments.

49. Harvey, "For the Sake of the Kingdom," 7.

50. Brooks and Winbery, *Syntax of New Testament Greek*, 62. They use this verse to demonstrate the concept of "accusative of relationship" without mentioning a "final" sense. They describe "accusative of cause" separately.

The verses immediately following 19:12 indicate that others will join eunuchs in the heavenly kingdom. Disciples must allow and not hinder young children from being brought to Jesus for his prayers, "for it is to such as these that the kingdom of heaven belongs" (19:14). Jesus addresses his disciples authoritatively, with the imperative and double verbs (*aphiēmi* and *kōlyō*). This is not the first time Jesus has spoken to his disciples about young children as kingdom-bound. He responded to his disciples' question about who would be greatest in the kingdom with both a sharp warning—if they do not change and become like children, they will never enter (18:3)—and a threat—if they place a stumbling block before any believing "little ones," they would be better off drowning with a heavy millstone (18:6). Matthew 18:3, read alongside 19:12, could lend support to a reading of *dia* in its final sense.[51] The latter verse employs a graphic image of retribution: the millstone, a heavy stone (probably of basalt) often handled by donkeys and slaves, and drowning, a death made more gruesome by the millstone's weight dragging its wearer into watery depths.[52]

Like eunuchs, young children could not procreate and had low social status.[53] That Jesus applies the term *tapeinoō* (to lower; to lessen, to disparage; to humble, abase; to make lowly[54]) to these children while, at the same time, offering them as a model for whoever wishes to enter the heavenly kingdom (18:4) connects them with disparaged eunuchs. In Greco-Roman antiquity, children generally were valued not for their current position but for their anticipated future procreative role in the civic world (for boys) and the domestic world (for girls). In the meantime, children, like eunuchs, were dependent on and subject to their masters. Warren Carter explains, "Children depend on, submit to, and obey their parents. Children have no rights and are marginal to the adult, male-centered world. They are often viewed

---

51. Nolland, *Matthew: A Commentary*, 777. He also lists 18:8, 9; 19:16, 17, 23, 24, 29 as examples that favor a translation of "in order to gain" for entering the kingdom.

52. For the argument that this was a large, donkey-powered millstone, see Davies and Allison (*Matthew*, v. 2, 763). Edwards' brief summary of recent archaeological work on millstones, basalt mills, and trade in Capernaum is also helpful ("Walking the Roman Landscape," 227–30). Revelation 18:21 uses the millstone to describe the destruction of Rome: "Then a mighty angel took up a stone like a great millstone and threw it into the sea, saying, 'With such violence Babylon the great city will be thrown down, and will be found no more.'"

53. "Since such children had no social status or political significance, Jesus' symbolic action in placing the child in the disciples' midst was an appropriate way to undercut [the disciples'] speculations about status in the kingdom," (Harrington, *Gospel of Matthew*, 264). "In first-century Mediterranean cultures, children had no status within the wider community" (Senior, *Matthew*, 217).

54. *LSJ*, 792.

with suspicion, as threats to the social order, ignorant, lacking reason, unpredictable, vulnerable (so Matt 2). One way to insult an adult [male] is to call him a boy. Children, like slaves, are beaten as a means of establishing domination."[55]

Children were especially vulnerable to disease and death. One estimate of child mortality in the ancient Mediterranean suggests that one-third died before reaching age one, half before age ten.[56] For eunuchs, there were risks associated with castration, including death, as well as long-term health impacts.[57] According to ancient medical writings, infants were weak, imperfect, and physically malleable. Those who survived past forty days were hot-tempered, dominated by emotions, and were moister and hotter than adults. They had uncontrollable appetites, akin to animals.[58] Eunuchs, too, were considered dreadfully out of balance by physiognomists. They were cold, moist, and more susceptible to passion. Eunuchs fell far short of the ideal hot, dry male capable of penetration and procreation.[59]

Both children and eunuchs, though, are welcome in the divine household. Craig Keener helpfully draws attention to the children's guardian angels in 18:10. Because these angels have a high rank, they merit a special place before God. That the children draw the angels' attention underscores their worth in the eschatological kingdom, if not the earthly one. Perhaps the placement of 19:13–15 directly after 19:12 is not accidental but points to something else: children like these in the heavenly kingdom might represent Matthew's eunuchs' surrogate progeny. Jesus' promise of a hundredfold for disciples who left property and family (19:29) might lend plausibility to my speculation.[60] Janice Capel Anderson and Stephen D. Moore's suggestion

55. Carter, *Matthew and the Margins*, 384. While Carter may be correct (and he acknowledges here that there were close attachments between children and parents) it is difficult to assess Roman attitudes toward children. See also Golden for a lovely recent discussion of the difficulties of understanding ancient children ("Other People's Children").

56. Frier, "Demography," 789, citing a model scale by Coale and Demeney with numerous qualifications about the difficulty of estimating child mortality.

57. Belcastro, "Farinelli and Castration," 632. The body of famous Italian castrato Farinelli, who was castrated before puberty, was exhumed in 2006. The results of this study indicate that he shared bone thickening consistent with postmenopausal women. His skeleton showed evidence of osteoporosis and long-limbed bones.

58. Dasen, "Childbirth and Infancy."

59. Hester, "Rhetorical Constructions," 814. Recent scholarship by classicists and biblical scholars addresses issues of gender and masculinity. Although I do not have space to address this work, please see excellent analyses by Hester and Burke (in bibliography) and by Maud Gleason and Craig A. Williams, all of whom treat eunuchs.

60. Keener, *Matthew*, 286, citing Jeremias and Meier. Matt 19:29 calls to mind Job's unsettling reward of new progeny and property. I find it troubling that the Matthean

that metaphorical children supersede biological children and that actual progeny are replaced by spiritual fruit (3:8–10) offers another interpretive possibility.[61]

When a young man with many possessions approaches Jesus to ask how he may obtain eternal life, Jesus initially evades the question. Then he shifts terms, as he did with the Pharisees' question about Moses' command.[62] He tells him to keep the commandments, sell everything he owns if he wishes to be perfect (cf. 5:48) give alms, and follow him. When he gives the proceeds to the poor, he will have treasure in the heavens. Donald Senior notes the affinity of perfect (*teleios*) and goal (*telos*) in Matthew's two references. Being perfect for this young man means selling what he owns, then following Jesus.[63] In the Sermon on the Mount, Jesus already taught "You cannot serve God and wealth" (6:24). The young man does not immediately accept Jesus' instructions or his invitation to discipleship. After the young man leaves, grieving, Jesus continues instructing his disciples about the incompatibility of wealth and salvation, telling them of the exceeding difficulty for a rich person to enter the kingdom of God. Earlier, when Jesus commissioned them for itinerant ministry, he told them to acquire no gold, silver or coins for their (money)belt and bring no wallet (*pēra*) for the journey, "for laborers deserve their food" (10:10).[64] While there is no certainty about the financial status of any *gallos* or *archigallos*, they were known and harshly derided for begging alms.[65]

Jesus offers eschatological rewards for fathers (implied) who *leave* their children. Admittedly, another verse may stand in tension with my speculation: "For in the resurrection they neither marry nor are given in marriage, but are like angels in heaven" (Matt 22:30). On the other hand, perhaps eunuchs could become guardian angels for these children. This, too, is merely speculative.

61. Anderson and Moore, "Matthew and Masculinity," 75 and 91, citing Eilberg-Schwartz.

62. Here Jesus changes "have" (*echō*; 19:16) to "enter into" and "a good thing" to "one who is good."

63. Senior, *Matthew*, 218.

64. He also included two tunics (undergarments) sandals, and a walking stick on the list (10:10). In other words, they were to bring nothing with them for this traveling work.

65. This public begging for alms was a longstanding literary trope. Of the *galli*, Dionysius of Halicarnassus wrote: "but the priest and priestess of the goddess are Phrygians, and it is they who carry her image in procession through the city, begging alms in her name according to their custom, and wearing figures upon their breasts and striking their timbrels while their followers play tunes upon their flutes in honor of the Mother of the Gods. But by a law and decree of the senate no native Roman walks in procession through the city arrayed in a parti-colored robe, begging alms or escorted by flute-players, or worships the god with the Phrygian ceremonies" (*Ant. Rom.* 2.19).

At this point the disciples are not just disheartened; they are stricken. "Then who can be saved?" (19:25) they ask, exposing a sense of powerlessness. Jesus consoles them. It may not be consolation enough for Peter, who reminds Jesus that they have left everything and followed him—precisely what Jesus just told the young man to do. Peter then asks what they will get out of it. Jesus promises them fabulous eschatological rewards: thrones, a hundredfold inheritance, and eternal life. That Jesus offers his disciples shared power and glory sounds promising on the surface. That he rewards them with power to judge (*krinō*) the twelve tribes of Israel (apparently Judas still has a chance) however, is disturbing given that Matthew's vivid imagery of judgment is often tied to wrath and eternal torture (e.g., 3:7–12; 13:36–42, 48–50; 25:41). Davies and Allison demonstrate for 19:28 that judgment carries a range of meanings, including but not limited to the final judgment and condemnation. This verse, they conclude, reflects a popular vision of eschatological restoration inspired by Dan 7:9–27.[66] In any case, Matthew clearly envisions a heavenly hierarchy with God at the apex.[67] Jesus also holds an extraordinarily high position, which may be inferred by his apotheosis (Matt 28:19–20). Wendy Cotter suggests that Jesus ascended to heaven even beyond the emperors to take authority of heaven and earth.[68] Jesus' male disciples also assume authority in both realms. Jesus gave Peter the keys to the kingdom and conferred on him the power to bind and loose (16:19) then extended this to the disciples (18:18) before promising them

---

66. Davies and Allison, *Matthew*, v.3, 55–56. Yet Daniel's imagery, too, vividly conveys judgment and destruction (i.e., Dan 7:23, 26). The second part of Dan 7:11 illustrates: "And as I watched, the beast was put to death, and its body destroyed and given over to be burned with fire." The problem remains.

67. Throughout the gospel, Jesus' titles point to his kingship, even when they are on the lips of his enemies. Selected examples include Son of David (1:1; 9:27; 12:23; 15:22) King of the Jews (2:2) the anointed (1:18; 2:4; 11:2; 16:16) the Son of Man (9:6; 12:8, 32, 40; 13:37, 41) the son (11:26) "my son, the beloved" (3:17) Lord of the Sabbath (10:8) and the son of God. (4:3, 5; 8:29; 14:33; 16:16). Not just his titles but also his divinely mandated proclamation testifies to his kingship. As has already been argued at length, especially by Carter, Matthew sets Jesus over against Caesar, and God's kingdom over against Rome's, in multiple ways. Unfortunately, in the process Matthew mimics hierarchical, patriarchal, and violent imperial practices. Carter explains: "In its supreme confidence of the enforcement of God's will, its use of 'bully tactics' of 'do it—or else' to solicit compliance (see 18:35) and in its violent destruction of those who resist, God's empire resembles, rather than offers an alternative to, Rome's power. The gospel and God's empire seem co-opted by that which they resist, rather than, for example, offering an alternative model of inclusion and reconciliation" (Carter, *Matthew and the Margins*, 5). Although I do not have space to treat it here in detail, I will address the issue of power at length in my dissertation.

68. Cotter, "Greco-Roman Apotheosis," 152–53.

twelve thrones (19:28). The heavenly kingdom is distinctly tiered, masculine, and patriarchal.[69]

Verse 19:29 is consistent with Matthew's destabilization of earthly families. Earlier, Jesus disabused his disciples of the notion that he came to bring peace; rather, he came with a sword "to set a man against his father, and a daughter against her mother, and a daughter-in-law against her mother-in-law; and one's foes will be members of one's own household" (10:35–36). Peter's words' "Look, we have left everything and followed you. What then will we have?" (19:27) may at first appear petulant, but there is an unspoken violence underlying them. The disciples left family members, family occupations, and homes to follow Jesus. They suffered, but they were not the only ones. If Matt 10:35–36 and 19:27 are more than hyperbole, families were broken and factionalized. Throughout Matthew much leaving and suffering occurs for Jesus' sake (5:11; 10:18, 39; 16:25) God's sake (19:5) and the kingdom's sake (19:12). There appear to be no eschatological rewards for those family members who were left behind and no earthly rewards for anyone. Indeed, the earliest Jesus-followers who took 19:27–29 literally would have experienced costs, so too their families, if they flaunted Augustan reforms that sought to normalize marriage, remarriage, and the production of as many heirs as possible throughout the empire.[70] The voluntary sacrifice of property and progeny was not advisable in an imperial world based on patriarchal household units and succession, yet the Matthean Jesus promoted it.

With their tenuous family connections, eunuchs are perfectly suited to serve a sovereign who expected their undivided loyalty. That some castrated themselves and renounced patriarchal privilege to be derided as eunuchs expresses their decisive commitment. There is no turning back.

---

69. There is insufficient evidence to support the claim that Matthew promotes (radical) egalitarianism. Talbott, for example, reads Matt 19:12c as proof of an egalitarian kingdom and argues that Jesus' vision of the *basileia* of heaven rejected kyriarchical domination ("Kyriarchy on the Chopping Block," 40–41). I concur with Ascough, who has argued that although the Matthean community attempts to enact more egalitarian practices, "there remain in the community a structure and leadership which in themselves point to a *de facto* hierarchy." ("Matthew and Community Formation," 124, citing Stanton, Saldarini, and Duling). To be sure, the Matthean Jesus does advocate for new kinship ties that may create room for more egalitarian relationships, but there remain numerous Matthean passages that presuppose and express hierarchical and patriarchal relations. That said, I do not wish to diminish the force of such verses as Matt 23:11 ("the greatest among you will be your servant") or Matt 4:8–10, when Jesus rejects Satan's offer of the kingdoms of the world to serve God alone.

70. Augustan reforms offered financial and legal incentives for those who complied and penalties and disincentives for those who did not. See, for example, chapter 3 of Milnor, *Gender, Domesticity, and the Age of Augustus*.

Yet self-made eunuchs now have the flexibility to do precisely what Jesus has been teaching his disciples and crowds all along: listen to me, keep the commandments, give up everything and everyone that is of value to you and follow me to embrace a life of service in light of the coming kingdom. Matthew chose an apt model to capture his disciples' and auditors' imagination. As model disciples, self-made eunuchs display on their bodies (or by their clothing) the irrevocable commitment—the cut—Jesus requires of new recruits when they accept his summons to join his eschatological movement. Jesus gives his male disciples a horrifying, visceral image of self-castrated men. This image trumps even the fateful moment when the first disciples made their life-changing decision by the Sea of Galilee. This is not, of course, far from their minds, as the narrative demonstrates. As the disciples regain their voices—they were silent from 19:11 until 19:25—to express their fear, Peter quickly reminds Jesus of their sacrifice. Imitating a beneficent Roman *pater*, Jesus promises to care for them by guaranteeing an overabundant eschatological inheritance.[71]

Matthew 19 concludes with this verse: "But many who are first will be last, and the last will be first" (19:30; cf. 20:16,27). Aptly, Matthew employs "last" (*eschatos*) within his discussion of eschatological renewal (*palingenesia*; 19:28). This serves as a reminder that Matthew—and perhaps Jesus—appreciated reversals and chose unsavory characters to express those. Prostitutes, tax collectors, and sinners, too, will enter the kingdom while those originally destined for it [implied: chief priests and elders of 21:23] will watch as it is taken away and given to another nation (*ethnos*) that produces fruits (21:43). Matthew would have been hard-pressed to find a more controversial model to challenge potential followers than self-made eunuchs. Whether Matthew's auditors would have perceived these eunuchs as *galli* or as servants/slaves of nobles is not as crucial as was their familiarity with common stereotypes about eunuchs. Matthew's auditors, as well as Jesus,' would have known that eunuchs were considered despicable figures.

The benefits of the heavenly kingdom must have been compelling indeed for any would-be disciple to embrace a model associated with such dreadful earthly costs. What man in the Roman Empire would *choose* to be ridiculed as a woman, adulterer, and sexual deviant? A man who believed Jesus' compelling message and was willing to express his commitment as decisively as he could. A man who was willing to give away everything for the kingdom of heaven. A disciple. A eunuch.

---

71. Again, I am not attempting to establish whether this denoted literal or figurative castration. The graphic image probably functioned quite well rhetorically for Matthew to drive home his point about discipleship.

The book of Isaiah offers devoted eunuchs consolation and an inducement similar to (but more poetic than) that promised by Matthew in 19:29. Like Isaiah's faithful eunuchs, Matthew's may expect to receive "a monument and a name better than sons or daughters" (Isa 56:5). They, too, will have an "everlasting name that shall not be cut off" in place of their earthly losses of family, status, and future. Because they live righteously, in accordance with divine will, they will find a home in the heavenly kingdom that will never be taken away from them (Isa 56:5; Matt 19:29).

Bibliography

Abusch, Ra'anan. "Eunuchs and Gender Transformation: Philo's Exegesis of the Joseph Narrative." In *Eunuchs in Antiquity and Beyond*, edited by Shaun Tougher, 103–21. Oakville, CT: David Brown, 2002.

Ascough, Richard S. "Matthew and Community Formation." In *The Gospel of Matthew in Current Study: Essays in Memory of William G. Thompson, S.J.*, edited by David E. Aune, 96–126. Grand Rapids: Eerdmans, 2001.

Barton, Stephen C. *Discipleship and Family Ties in Mark and Matthew*. New York: Cambridge University Press, 1994.

Bauer, Walter, Frederick W. Danker, W. F. Arndt, and F. W. Gingrich. *Greek-English Lexicon of the New Testament and Other Early Christian Literature*. 3rd ed. Chicago: University of Chicago Press, 2000.

Belcastro, Maria Giovanna, et al. "Hyperostosis frontalis interna (HFI) and Castration: the Case of the Famous Singer Farinelli (1705–1782)." *Journal of Anatomy* 219 (2011) 632–37.

Bernabé, Carmen. "Of Eunuchs and Predators: Matthew 19:12 in a Cultural Context." *Biblical Theology Bulletin* 33 (2003) 128–34.

Blickenstaff, Marianne. *"While the Bridegroom is with Them": Marriage, Family, Gender and Violence in the Gospel of Matthew*. Journal for the Study of the New Testament Supplement 292. New York: T. & T. Clark, 2005.

Brooks, James A., and Carlton L. Winbery. *Syntax of New Testament Greek*. Lanham, MD: University Press of America, 1979.

Brower, Gary Robert. "Ambivalent Bodies: Making Christian Eunuchs." PhD diss., Duke University, 1996.

Brown, Jeannine K. *The Disciples in Narrative Perspective: The Portrayal and Function of the Matthean Disciples*. Leiden: Brill, 2002.

Bullough, Vern L. "Eunuchs in History and Society." In *Eunuchs in Antiquity and Beyond*, edited by Shaun Tougher, 1–17. Oakville, CT: David Brown, 2002.

Burke, Sean D. "Reading the Ethiopian Eunuch *As* a Eunuch: Queering the Book of Acts." PhD diss., Graduate Theological Union, 2009.

Cape Anderson, Janice, and Stephen D. Moore. "Matthew and Masculinity." In *New Testament Masculinities*, edited by Stephen D. Moore and Janice Capel Anderson, 67–91. Atlanta: Society of Biblical Literature, 2003.

Carter, Warren. *Households and Discipleship: A Study of Matthew 19–20*. Journal for the Study of the New Testament Supplement 103. Sheffield: Sheffield Academic, 1994.

―――. "Matthew 4:18-22 and Matthean Discipleship: An Audience-Oriented Perspective." *Catholic Biblical Quarterly* 59 (1997) 58-75.

―――. *Matthew and the Margins: A Sociopolitical and Religious Reading*. Maryknoll, NY: Orbis, 2005.

―――. *Matthew: Storyteller, Interpreter, Evangelist*. Peabody, MA: Hendrickson, 2004.

Cotter, Wendy, C.S.J. "Greco-Roman Apotheosis Traditions and the Resurrection Appearances in Matthew." In *The Gospel of Matthew in Current Study: Essays in Memory of William G. Thompson, S.J.*, edited by David E. Aune, 127-53. Grand Rapids: Eerdmans, 2001.

Dasen, Véronique. "Childbirth and Infancy in Greek and Roman Antiquity." In *A Companion to Families in the Greek and Roman World*, edited by Beryl Rawson. Blackwell Publishing, 2011. No pages. Online: http://www.blackwellreference.com.proxy.library.vanderbilt.edu/subscriber/tocnode.html?id=g9781405187671_chunk_g978140518767121.

Davies, W. D., and Dale C. Allison. *The Gospel According to Saint Matthew*. International Critical Commentary, Volume I-III. Edinburgh: T. & T. Clark, 1997.

Edwards, Douglas R. "Walking the Roman Landscape in Lower Galilee: Sepphoris, Jotapata, and Khirbet Qana." In *A Wandering Galilean: Essays in Honor of Seán Freyne*, edited by Zuleika Rodgers, et al., 219-36. Leiden: Koninklijke Brill NV, 2009.

Everhart, Janet S. "Jezebel: Framed by Eunuchs?" *The Catholic Biblical Quarterly* 72 (2010) 688-98.

―――. "The Hidden Eunuchs of the Hebrew Bible: Uncovering an Alternate Gender." PhD diss., The Iliff School of Theology and the University of Denver, 2003.

France, R.T. *The Gospel of Matthew*. Grand Rapids: Eerdmans, 2007.

Frier, Bruce W. "Demography." In *The Cambridge Ancient History, Volume XI: The High Empire, A.D. 70-192*, edited by Peter Garnsey, et al., 787-816. New York: Cambridge University Press, 2000.

Frier, Bruce W., and Thomas A.J. McGinn. *A Casebook on Roman Family Law*. New York: Oxford University Press, 2004.

Golden, Mark. "Other People's Children." In *A Companion to Families in the Greek and Roman World*, edited by Beryl Rawson. Blackwell, 2011. No pages. Online: http://www.blackwellreference.com.proxy.library.vanderbilt.edu/subscriber/tocnode.html?id=g9781405187671_chunk_g978140518767119.

Gleason, Maud W. *Making Men: Sophists and Self-Presentation in Ancient Rome*. Princeton: Princeton University Press, 1995.

Green, Peter. *Juvenal: The Sixteen Satires*. New York: Penguin, 1998.

Gundry, Robert H. *Matthew: A Commentary on His Literary and Theological Art*. Grand Rapids: Eerdmans, 1982.

Guyot, Peter. *Eunuchen als Sklaven und Freigelassene in der griechisch-römischen Antike*. Stuttgart: Klett-Cotta, 1980.

Hales, Shelley. "Looking for Eunuchs: the *galli* and Attis in Roman art." In *Eunuchs in Antiquity and Beyond*, edited by Shaun Tougher, 87-102. Oakville, CT: David Brown, 2002.

Harrington, Daniel J., S.J. *The Gospel of Matthew*. Collegeville, MN: Liturgical, 2007.

Harvey, A. E. "Eunuchs for the Sake of the Kingdom." The Ethel M. Wood Lecture 15 March 1995. London: The University of London, 1995.

Hester, J. David. "Eunuchs and the Postgender Jesus: Matthew 19:12 and Transgressive Sexualities." *Journal for the Study of the New Testament* 28 (2005) 13-40.

———. "Queers on Account of the Kingdom of Heaven: Rhetorical Constructions of the Eunuch Body." *Scriptura* 90 (2005) 809–23.

Keener, Craig. *Matthew*. Downers Grove, IL: InterVarsity, 1997.

Kierkegaard, Søren. *Concluding Unscientific Postscript to Philosophical Fragments, Volume I*. Edited and translated with introduction and notes by Howard V. Hong and Edna H. Hong. Princeton: Princeton University Press, 1992.

Kingsbury, Jack Dean. *Matthew as Story*. Philadelphia: Fortress, 1988.

Kuefler, Mathew. *The Manly Eunuch: Masculinity, Gender Ambiguity, and Christian Ideology in Late Antiquity*. Chicago: The University of Chicago Press, 2001.

Latham, Jacob. "'Fabulous Clap-Trap': Roman Masculinity, the Cult of Magna Mater, and Literary Constructions of the *galli* at Rome from the Late Republic to Late Antiquity." *The Journal of Religion* 92 (2012) 84–122.

Liddell, Henry George, Robert Scott, and Henry Stuart Jones. *A Greek-English Lexicon*. 9th ed. Oxford: Clarendon, 1996.

Luz, Ulrich. *Das Evangelium nach Matthäus*, III. Zürich; Düsseldorf; Neukirchen-Vluyn: Benziger Verlag und Neukirchener Verlag, 1997.

———. *Studies in Matthew*. Translated by Rosemary Selle. Grand Rapids: Eerdmans, 2005.

Milnor, Kristina. *Gender, Domesticity, and the Age of Augustus: Inventing Private Life*. New York: Oxford University Press, 2005.

Moloney, Francis. "Matthew 19.3–12 and Celibacy: A Redactional and Form Critical Study." *Journal for the Study of the New Testament* 2 (1979) 42–60.

Nolland, John. *The Gospel of Matthew: A Commentary on the Greek Text*. Grand Rapids: Eerdmans, 2005.

Parsons, Mikeal C. *Acts*. Grand Rapids: Baker Academic, 2008.

Quesnell, Quentin, S.J. "Made Themselves Eunuchs for the Kingdom of Heaven (Mt 19.12)." *The Catholic Biblical Quarterly* 30 (1968) 335–58.

Repschinski, Boris. *The Controversy Stories in the Gospel of Matthew: Their Redaction, Form and Relevance for the Relationship Between the Matthean Community and Formative Judaism*. Göttingen: Vandenhoeck & Ruprecht, 2000.

Roller, Lynn E. *In Search of God the Mother: The Cult of Anatolian Cybele*. Berkeley: University of California Press, 1999.

———. "The Ideology of the Eunuch Priest." *Gender & History* 9 no. 3 (1997) 542–59.

Scholz, Piotr O. *Eunuchs and Castrati: A Cultural History*. Translated by John A. Broadwin and Shelley L. Frisch. Princeton: Markus Wiener, 2001.

Senior, Donald. *Matthew*. Nashville: Abingdon, 1998.

Stevenson, Walter. "Eunuchs and Early Christianity." In *Eunuchs in Antiquity and Beyond*, edited by Shaun Tougher, 123–142. Oakville, CT: David Brown, 2002.

———. "The Rise of Eunuchs in Greco-Roman Antiquity." *Journal of the History of Sexuality* 5 (1995) 495–511.

Takács, Sarolta A. *Vestal Virgins, Sibyls, and Matrons: Women in Roman Religion*. Austin: University of Texas Press, 2008.

Talbott, Rick. "Imagining the Matthean Eunuch Community: Kyriarchy on the Chopping Block." *Journal of Feminist Studies in Religion* 22 (2006) 21–43.

Tougher, Shaun. *The Eunuch in Byzantine History and Society*. New York: Routledge, 2008.

Williams, Craig A. *Roman Homosexuality: Ideologies of Masculinity in Classical Antiquity*. New York: Oxford University Press, 1999.

Reformed Theology in Service
to the Church

6

Theological Education in a Secular Age
Challenges and Possibilities

—Nancy J. Ramsay

For more than thirty years David Gouwens has fulfilled his ministerial vocation as an exceptional teacher, faculty colleague, and university citizen. His scholarship on Søren Kierkegaard has earned him international recognition and respect. I hope the essay that follows reflects the sort of commitment David demonstrates with his students and faculty colleagues at Brite Divinity School, a readiness to anticipate and engage the challenges and possibilities of educating women and men to lead in the ministry of Christ's church, the academy, and public life as witnesses to God's reconciling and transforming love and justice.

Introduction

In this essay we will explore several of the extraordinary challenges confronting Christian theological education and educators related to Oldline Protestant denominations in the United States, and we will identify some of the prospects for responding to these challenges and the dynamic context in which they converge. As the title of this essay suggests, I am proposing that understanding our secular context is especially critical for assessing and responding to the dynamic convergence of contemporary challenges. There is a lively debate about this word, "secular" and what it in fact describes. We will engage this conversation sufficiently to understand the impact for theological educators of a context in which secularity has changed the very conditions for belief such that religious experience is described as "optional, fragile, and revisable."[1] But notice that this conversation presumes religious experience is clearly present and influential in our secular context. Nonetheless we should presume that faculty as well as students experience this fragilization of faith. How might the fragility of faith affect teaching and learning?

Within such a secular context, what form or forms does religious experience take? A recent major research project proposes that religious experience in the U.S. now appears in a pluriform range of the historic traditional forms of world religions, in various forms of spirituality and deep existential questions as personal religion, and in publicly held normative values and practices of civic engagement as public religion.[2] We will explore the implications of this pluriform character of religion for theological education in Oldline Protestant schools.

Within the category of historic forms of religion we will give particular attention to the increasingly diverse character of historic forms of religious expression found in the once normatively "Christian" United States such as Islam, Judaism, Buddhism, and Hinduism. This religious diversity is a growing influence revising Christians' understanding and experience of faith and shaping contemporary theological education. The accrediting standards of the Association of Theological Schools, for example, now require students preparing for leadership in Christian faith communities to demonstrate competency for engaging in ministry in a multifaith context.[3] Others urge religious leaders to confront and reduce violence arising from uninformed, fearful responses to religious difference.[4]

The category of personal religion poses particular challenges and opportunities for faculty in their role as mentors and in identifying a new and wider range of reference points for students whose experience includes a more diverse range of spiritualities. Unlike the more familiar historic traditional forms, personal religion references the wide range of experience that persons describe as religious. For example, it points to ways persons now use the rhetoric of spirituality to describe both experiences of

---

1. Warner, *Varieties of Secularism*, 9–10
2. Jacobsen, *No Longer Invisible*, 47
3. Graham, "Christian Hospitality," 9.
4. Jacobsen, *No Longer Invisible*, 62.

transcendence breaking into ordinary/immanent experience and utterly immanent humanistic experiences of personal empowerment and courage. For others, especially young adults, personal religion may describe moments of encounter with mystery and wonder that lead them to explore religion especially if they have access to effective mentoring. For still others, personal religion includes the popular rhetoric of "religious but not spiritual." However, a recent landmark study revises earlier confusion about these terms that understood them as a binary when in fact we now find the two most often intersect in the experience of most persons in the U.S.[5]

As the pretense of Enlightenment ideas about the superiority and objectivity of reason have yielded to postmodern insights that all knowledge is insinuated by asymmetries of power and reflects the particularity of social location, so too is the supposed neutrality of the public sphere yielding to a recognition of the multiple value laden influences including religion that inform public life.[6] Indeed in the United States our secular context includes publicly idealized values such as mutual justice, equality of opportunity, and freedom that are fraught with religious themes insinuated in the founding myths of the American colonies. Further, the multifaith religious landscape of our current national context includes diverse ideas about the relation of religion and civic engagement, and this diversity is also clearly present in contemporary Christianity. In our current secular context in the United States where a pluriform religious experience is optional, revisable, and fragile, theological educators are challenged to prepare future religious leaders for effective civic engagement that requires voicing religious commitments authentically and comprehensibly in a public sphere where they contend with neighbors who hold other value-laden points of view.

While this essay will not exhaust the challenges currently facing theological educators in the United States, this brief introduction points to how important it is to understand how our contemporary secular context shapes and is shaped by an increasingly pluriform religious experience. Given this context, what are the implications of contemporary secularity for educating religious leaders who are shaped by Oldline Protestant theological commitments? We will now explore in more depth current conversations about secularity and its impact in shaping our contemporary religious experience.

---

5. Ammerman, "Spiritual but Not Religious?"
6. Calhoun, "Secularism, Citizenship, and the Public Sphere," 81–84.

Secular Context

In addressing our context as "secular" we will give particular attention to secularity as an epistemic reality, a way of making sense of and evaluating our experience. I hope to clarify how this differs from using secular in one of its commonly held and mistaken definitions as simply the absence of religion implying a simple either/or binary with religion. Neither am I using the term as if it describes a situation of the decline or compartmentalization of religion. Either usage suggests a sort of "subtraction story"[7] by which secularization is explained as the sloughing off of the various "impediments" of religion and the recovery of a purer rational self. This binary is too simplistic and misinterprets our current context as does another current term, "post secular," which only reifies the problematic binary and implies an indefinite yet somehow rosier picture of religion than is warranted. It is true that currently in our society institutions in our public spaces such as the economy and education function apart from necessary reference to religion and fewer persons identify with a religious faith. Surely these facts matter in theological education. However, more important for theological education is the sense in which our secular context reflects a profound epistemic shift related to the above descriptive facts that Charles Taylor describes as a shift to a secular age that changes the very "conditions of belief" because we "move from a society where belief in God is unchallenged and indeed, unproblematic, to one in which it is understood to be one option among others, and frequently not the easiest to embrace."[8] Now secularity "is a matter of the whole context of understanding in which our moral spiritual or religious experience and search takes place."[9] He is calling attention to the way in which across millennia secularity and religion are always mutually constituted so that the narrative we are exploring is not one of subtraction but of transformation and differentiation.[10] Further, Taylor is describing how in this secular age religious faith is always optional, revisable, and fragile.[11] Those of us who claim a religious faith do so knowing that this is not an option that makes sense to many of our neighbors or indeed probably to some of our family and friends, and they in turn likely sometimes reflect on the possible revisability of their decision because they know of our different decision. Both they and we at times might well describe a certain sense of

---

7. Taylor, *A Secular Age*, 26–29
8. Ibid., 3.
9. Ibid.
10. Casanova, "The Secular, Secularizations, Secularisms," 54.
11. Warner, *Varieties of Secularism*, 9–10

fragility about our choice regarding faith precisely because we experience it as a choice that could be otherwise and some days it probably is different. Before we consider how it is that persons who do make this choice characterize their experience of religion, it is useful briefly to explore how this transformation in the character of secularity emerged. We will focus on secularity as a narrative about a transformation in the epistemic experience of Christians shaped by Western Christianity and the United States in particular.

Theological educators in seminaries related to Oldline Protestant denominations are surely aware that this epistemic shift in the character of secularity as the context of a fragile, optional and revisable faith is in fact a figure/ground shift from five hundred years ago as the Reformation was emerging. In Europe, Western Christianity was the norm not only religiously but as the context for human experience. In this context "secular" simply designated an aspect of experience that was worldly and temporal within this overarching religious worldview. Even 50 years ago when many current members of theological faculty were children and teenagers, religious faith was the norm and Christianity was the presumed context for most in the United States. How did Western Christianity get to this spot and what does it mean for us now?

First, a reminder of the complex way we are considering our secular context. As Michael Warner reminds us:

> Secular societies are not just mankind [sic] minus the religion. They are very specific kinds of societies, imaginable only as the outcomes of long histories. They produce not unillusioned individuals who see the facts of existence nakedly, but people constituted by a distinct set of ethical goods, temporal frameworks, and practical contexts. The secular is never just the absence of religion, or its privatization, or its waning. It is a cumulatively and dialectically achieved condition, and no one of its dimensions is the manifestation of religion as an optional axis of mobilization of belief.[12]

From what scholars[13] know of the earliest forms of religious belief and practice, it appears that such patterns of religious experience reflected an overall worldview shaped by several dyads such as social experience over individual experience; the insinuation of cosmic or transcendent spiritual realities into immanent or daily life rendering human beings vulnerable; and a focus on securing material human needs through religious practices.

12. Ibid., 24–25
13. Taylor, "Western Secularity," 31–53.

The emergence of what we now know as world religions in the first millennium B.C.E. very gradually created a shift in each of these dyads and particularly in what would become Christianity.

Consider the experience of European Christianity in the pre-Reformation period when religious practice was rife with ritualized practices that appeared to manipulate God's response and communities engaged in ritualized efforts to appease spirits that seemed immanently real and dangerous. Witchcraft was feared and diseases such as melancholy were understood as the invasion of something called black bile. Part of the rationale precipitating the Reformation was in fact to revise such ideas and ritualized practices by encouraging a less communal religious sensibility in favor of attention to the individual's faith commitment and the disciplined practice of individual Christians who did not rely on various rites to appease God but could experience God directly. Further, as the Reformation unfolded in the 16th and 17th centuries such persons were also, for a host of reasons, becoming aware of themselves as individuals who were no longer so vulnerable to the supposed enchanted cosmic spirit world but able to stand back reflectively with an emerging sense of their own agency and ability to make ethical decisions and relate to a transcendent God who intended their well-being and who invited them to aspire beyond mere human flourishing to a deeply ethical understanding and practice of love.

Clearly this narrative discloses the epistemic consequences of the concurrent transforming effects of multiple cultural forces such as modernity and emerging social institutions beyond that of religion such as education, politics, and economics alongside an important emerging sense of individual agency and a new found value for the human capacity for rationality. The naiveté of earlier enchanted millennia is lost. A reflectively rational individual is found who by the 17th century could imagine a world in which the secular or immanent seemed to be all that was. Those who embraced Deism, could imagine a God who having set the world in motion was only distantly engaged in their lives via their ethical values and behavior. Now the encompassing Christian worldview of medieval Europe that could define the secular has transformed into a privatized and suspect aspect of an overarching secularity that includes the blessing of a rather distant transcendence.

This process of secularization entwined with an unfolding modernity took different turns in the emergence of two social democracies in the American colonies and in France. The problematic role of religion, itself associated with repression in France, may account for a continuing more secularist posture in Europe. In the colonies and subsequently in the United States the constitutional provisions for the disestablishment and free practice of religion secured a more hospitable reciprocity of secularity and religion. However, the three core values constitutionally asserted in both democracies laid the groundwork for ways we may now imagine the role of religion in the sphere of contemporary public life here in the United States.[14] Liberty, equality, and fraternity (consent to exercise comity in civic engagement and mutual respect among citizens) values proudly proclaimed in the French revolution, clearly reflect their religious genealogy from an earlier stage in Europe's process of shaping the core ideas and values of a public sphere. This religious genealogy also reminds us that even as secularity was emerging as our context, religion was a critical resource for secular public reason, and that reason is certainly not neutral.[15] The political foundation for the two democracies represents an articulation of a new secular moral order that reflects an overlapping consensus among various philosophical points of view to assure the above three principles as foundational for public life. Importantly we find that together these three principles—liberty, equality, and fraternity—establish that the state will protect the full range of value-laden diversities among its citizens and privilege none of them including religious diversities.[16] Secularism is not simply a matter of separating church and state. The historical process that achieves this new secular moral order also discloses that as this new political idea took shape, religion functioned both in the private sphere and also often in progressive ways via personally and culturally and politically held values and ideas that permeated secular or public life.[17] Surely this history points to the importance of articulate, religiously informed voices in our contemporary public life, and we will return to this theme later in the essay as we consider the importance of intentional curricular and pedagogical practices for preparing religious leaders and laypersons as public theologians.

A Pluriform Religious Presence

In such a secular context where religious experience is optional, revisable, and thus fragile, how do we know religion when we see it? To pick up from our journey through the historical shifts that bring us to a secular age, the normative status of Protestantism in the public sphere in the United States shifted by the early twentieth century to a privatized position for belief that was in place for most of that century and began to shift in the tumult of

---

14. Taylor, "Why We Need a Radical Redefinition of Secularism," 34–59.
15. Calhoun, "Secularism, Citizenship, and the Public Sphere," 80–81.
16. Taylor, "Why We Need a Radical Redefinition of Secularism," 36–48.
17. Calhoun, "Secularism," 77–79.

the 1960s and 1970s. Recent research that focused on the reports of faculty and administrators attending to the religious experience of students in universities and colleges across the U.S. suggests that beginning in the late twentieth century religious experience begins to appear in a pluriform shape: the historic forms of our world religions, "personal religion" reflecting variously constructed and sometimes idiosyncratic spiritualities, and public religion especially evident as civic engagement. Further, the personal religion category includes not only familiar references to transcendence but also may include existential "big questions" about the purpose and meaning of life and deep moral concerns that may focus more on "immanent" issues of obligations that attend life in community.[18]

Personal Religion

While religion appears in these pluriform ways, each is shaped by the mark of secularity as Taylor describes it, a change in the conditions of belief from the naiveté that shaped Western Christianity in the 1500s to a reflective reliance on rationality. Religious belief is an option rather than presumed. Though each of the three aspects of a pluriform religion proves relevant for theological education, the personal religion category, which certainly intersects historic or traditional religion for many, may be especially useful for further understanding how secularity shapes the experience of students and faculty.

What the Jacobsens describe with the category "personal religion" is variously discussed within the rhetoric of "spirituality or religious" and in the developmental processes of emerging adulthood as university and professional school students develop capacities for critical systemic thinking. Personal religion is chosen in the context of what we have named earlier as the optional, revisable, and fragile character of religious belief when that context also includes the possibility if not the more plausible option of an utterly immanent embrace of the possibilities of rationality. For some, personal religion may be constructed via humanist values and goals, and be oriented by spiritually imbued ethical values that provide at least intimations of an empowering sense of courage and purpose. For believers, personal religion reflects some subjective awareness of transcendence that sometimes breaks into ordinary experience in what Charles Taylor describes as an experience of "fullness."[19] While fullness may also describe the above mentioned empowering confidence in one's own rationality, for believers it describes

---

18. Jacobsen, "No Longer Invisible." 16–17, 46–56.
19. Taylor, *A Secular Age*, 5–8.

an inbreaking sense of transcendence that arises in believers as a sense of awe and mystery and a transforming empowerment to live oriented by the love that characterizes this transcendent Being. Experiences of fullness may rise via traditional spiritual practices such as prayer, through experiences in nature, as we live in human community, and as we encounter existential questions that invite us to encounter intimations of ultimacy.

The possibility for encountering transcendence via existential questions not linked with traditional religion points us toward likely moments in seminary classrooms. Sharon Daloz Parks describes how the variegated religious landscape of contemporary secularity alters the already predictable developmental challenges for emerging young adults (20–32 years of age). She notes that the optional, revisable, and fragile conditions for belief in our secular age give an added emphasis to the task of forming and critically embracing a faith whose values provide a moral and spiritual orientation worthy of one's life and dreams.[20] Parks describes the way in which intimations of ultimacy and mystery may prompt human beings to compose and be composed by meaning that we describe with the word, faith. She reminds us that, functionally, faith is both a noun and a verb because it includes a convictional process. It points toward a sensibility of ultimacy as a trustworthy pattern of wholeness and loving relation that orients our commitments and hopes and invites us to "set our hearts" on what we come to trust as true[21] and, to borrow H. Richard Niebuhr's phrase, "to feel at home in the universe."[22] Parks, like Charles Taylor, associates faith not only with critical rationality as meaning making but also with our affections, our passions that order our lives.[23] Parks writes of these existential challenges in the context of secularity to encourage faculty and others to recognize the additional importance of mentoring young adults as intentional practice. The caution she poses for the work of "feeling at home in the universe" is broader than young adulthood.

Surely in a secular context where the conditions of belief are fragile and optional, every theological classroom and students of all ages require faculty to develop pedagogical practices and dialogical strategies that invite critical exploration and support candor in searching out ways of speaking of God and faith authentically. Information and formation intersect in seminary classrooms, and no learning environment is formationally neutral.[24] Faculty

20. Parks, *Big Questions Worthy Dreams*, x.
21. Ibid., 30–34.
22. Niebuhr, H.R., *Radical Monotheism*, 25.
23. Parks, *Big Questions Worthy Dreams*, 44.
24. Jacobsen, *No Longer Invisible*, 128.

will be more effective when their choices about texts and assignments are shaped by an appreciation of the fragilizing effects of our secular age. The complexity attending theological education because of the optional, revisable, and thus fragile character of faith in a secular age is larger than these pedagogical strategies. Whether faculty seek to keep our own views out of our teaching or are transparent about them or even advocate for them,[25] we need to acknowledge that our own faith commitments shape our course syllabi and our teaching. As Parker Palmer puts it, "As I teach, I project the condition of my soul onto my students, my subject, and our way of being together. . . . teaching holds a mirror to the soul."[26] Perhaps one of the distinctive challenges of theological education in a secular age lies in finding courage and wisdom to mentor our students in forming a lifelong posture toward convictional knowing with a readiness to be engaged again and again by difference, the other "options" all around us, and an openness to reconsider how we understand the Mystery and inbreaking love that brought us to seminary classrooms. Of course, these classroom experiences mirror the work the students are preparing to do: helping congregants imagine and trust God's transforming presence in their lives and world. This important goal of helping congregants nurture and sustain faith in a secular context is critical for religious leadership and thus an important task for effective theological education. Certainly it relates to the intersection of historic and personal faith in our pluriform religious context.

Public rhetoric and confusion about the relation of spirituality and religion poses an important quandary for seminary education. How should we interpret all the talk about "spiritual but not religious"? What do we mean by spirituality? How shall we engage its widespread diverse meanings in public and even professional education contexts such as social work and nursing?

In what will surely prove a landmark research report, Nancy Ammerman wrote, "Understanding religion requires that we take spiritualities as seriously as we have always taken belief and belonging."[27] She describes an extensive research project that includes persons who adhere to Jewish and Christian traditions, as well as persons unaffiliated with institutional religions who may embrace a range of humanist and non-traditional spiritualities as well as avowed secularists. What she describes regarding the relation of spirituality and religion unravels the popular but misguided assumption of a binary relation between religion and spirituality. Her research discloses

25. Ibid., 132–34.
26. Palmer, *The Courage to Teach*, 2
27. Ammerman, "Spiritual but Not Religious?," 276.

that this popular phrase, "spiritual but not religious," functions less as an empirical category and more as a moral and political category to describe either the priority of evangelical Christians for faith as a personal experience or the emphasis of secularists on rejecting religious belief.

Ammerman's work is important for theological education in many ways and particularly to help educators and students reflectively engage our own and cultural manifestations of the intersections rather than the binaries of religious affiliation and spiritual practices. She offers a taxonomy with eleven categories for the term spirituality such as awe, mystery, connection, practices, and God. She then describes "cultural packages" in which particular clusters of meanings and practices of spirituality occur often in relation to particular institutional settings: Theistic, Extra-Theistic, and an inclusive Ethical spirituality resonant with what we will later explore as public religion.[28] Theistic spiritualities cluster with specific institutional religious belonging. They are specifically practiced to enhance a personal relationship with God; they are most often associated with more conserving religious experience, and they focus on enhancing direct experiences of God or other specific transcendent forms. Nearly two-thirds of Americans identify with this expression of spirituality that is most often closely aligned with institutional forms of religious belonging. Extra-theistic spiritualities describe spiritual experience more akin to Taylor's description of "fullness." Extra-theistic spiritualities do not require a theistic or transcendent being. They do arise in response to persons' experience of realities that transcend themselves such as transcendence that may be experienced as mystery, awe before natural beauty, or connectedness with the human community. Importantly they do not require authorization beyond personal experience of the immanent world. However, many Christians actively participating in Oldline Protestant traditions, African American Protestants, and Catholics who do not identify as evangelicals may describe theistic and also extra-theistic spiritual practices.[29] About fifty-seven per cent of the population seems to practice or describe extra-theistic spiritual experiences.

Common to both theistic and extra-theistic spiritualities, and cutting across those affiliated with historic traditions and unaffiliated, is agreement that "real spirituality" transcends doctrinal orthodoxies and is about living a "virtuous life" by which persons mean a readiness to help others, love their neighbors, what Ammerman calls "ethical spirituality."[30] We will return to

---

28. Ibid., 265–70.
29. Ibid., 268–72.
30. Ibid., 272.

this inclusive moral or ethical discursive spirituality a bit later in this essay when we explore the significance of public religion in our secular context.

Ammerman's research discloses that while there are distinctive spiritual discourses that align with particular cultural locations, the large majority of Americans in her study are both spiritual and religious. Many who are active in religious communities see no necessary conflict between theistic and extra-theistic spirituality. This suggests that most theological students who identify with Oldline Protestant traditions and the congregants they will serve are shaped by religious and spiritual experiences that are co-constituted rather than binaries. What is different is that their spiritual experience of transcendence is at once inclusive of traditional religious experience and its familiar practices and disciplines and responsive to the immanent spiritual sensibilities and diverse practices of the larger culture.

In a context where faith is fragile and persons' spiritualities are more sensible to the possibilities of glimpsing transcendence via openings that break into the midst of immanence, perhaps the work of Barbara Brown Taylor is suggestive for listening effectively for the presence of personal religion in theological classrooms and mentoring relationships where we faculty hope to hear deeply our students' descriptions of their intimations of transcendence and to describe our own authentically. In *Altar in the World*, Brown Taylor, an Episcopal priest and educator in college and seminary classrooms, evokes what Ammerman describes as an extra-theistic sensibility by encouraging her readers to practice paying attention to God's presence in the natural world, human relationships, and ordinary daily practices so that through paying attention to the ways transcendence breaks into the immanent we experience deeply how God's presence animates our world.[31] Brown Taylor's reflections provide, for example, a highly immanent way to imagine the meaning of sacrament, a visible sign of invisible grace and connection. She references Jacob's vision of heaven as he simply slept in an open field (Gen 28:16–17) and writes, "Human beings may separate things into as many piles as we wish—separating spirit from flesh, sacred from secular, church from world. But we should not be surprised when God does not recognize the distinctions we make between the two. Earth is so thick with divine possibility that it is a wonder we can walk anywhere without cracking our shins on altars."[32] Reverence, she reminds us, arises from our capacities for humility and awe that are surely nurtured by paying attention to experiences that disclose the limits of human creativity and control. Reflections such as these are provocative for theological educators as we

---

31. Brown Taylor, *An Altar in the World*.
32. Ibid., 15.

develop strategies for helping students draw connections between their distinctive religious and spiritual experience and sacred texts and millennia of tradition as well as contemporary practices for proclamation, nurture, and care in Christian communities. Clearly, this category of personal religion must claim our attention in theological education.

Traditional Historic Religions

Historic, traditional forms of religion also require our attention differently in seminary classrooms. It is clear that that membership in traditional Christian faith communities is declining and denominational structures are evolving in ways that require innovative approaches for leadership in familiar and alternative congregational contexts. In this essay, I believe it is the increasingly diverse religious context in the United States that poses the more challenging changes for Christian theological educators. The founding of this secular nation, albeit under God, in fact assures no normative religious tradition and the opportunity for all to practice their religion. But Christianity has had an informal normative status. While it remains normative, clearly its presumptive status is evolving. Who could have imagined that at the dawn of the twenty-first century the United States would be one of the most religiously diverse countries in the world? While our focus remains on Oldline Protestant theological education, the fragility of faith that characterizes our secular context is not simply a challenge for Christians. At a time when the religious and spiritual experience and affiliation patterns of Christians in the United States are in flux, Christians and their religious leaders also find themselves daily encountering not only their familiar Jewish friends but also Muslim, Hindu, and Buddhist colleagues in business and at neighborhood events. While national holidays and civic rituals still point toward the normative role of Christianity, it is demonstrably clear to citizens that the American religious landscape is dramatically changing. We know religious freedom is promised to all Americans. Yet it is not clear to many Christian Americans how they can best live into being mutually respectful of their new "neighbors." This ambiguity is complicated by the fact that most American Christians know painfully little about their own faith traditions and are frankly illiterate about those of their religiously diverse neighbors.[33]

Unfortunately it is equally evident that some religious differences are not benign. Religious fundamentalism is embroiled in political terrorism such we have experienced with increasing numbers of white supremacist hate groups associated with Christianity in the United States and with radical Islam as the nation felt with 9/11 or more recently with the Boston Marathon bombing. This politicization of religion and especially Islam in the minds of many Christian American citizens points to an especially challenging issue for Christian religious leaders and our new religious neighbors especially when at least the Christian majority know so little about other world religions. Such ignorance foments fear that contributes to increasing vulnerability to violence against innocent persons perceived as religious others. Given their majority status, Christian religious leadership is especially important in countering such fear mongering.[34]

In a secular, religiously diverse context developing a 'dialogical heart' will be a primary goal for effective Christian theological education.[35] In 1999, *Theological Education*, the journal of the Association of Theological Schools, included an article by M. Thangaraj who noted even then that daily life in the United States included conversations across religious boundaries and that this required a response by theological educators for three reasons: 1. A Christian minister cannot have an adequate theological grounding for his or her faith without a meaningful understanding of how it relates to other faith traditions. 2. A minister cannot adequately address the everyday interfaith experience and practice of his or her laity. 3. Public ministry in today's world is increasingly interfaith.[36] Thangaraj named themes that reflect and inform the context of secularity. In a religiously diverse secular context each of the historic traditional religions finds its way in relation to the others. This is not a new "fact" but it is only in these recent years that the Christian majority is recognizing that it knows itself more fully in the reciprocity of dialogue with its religious neighbors. As Christianity in seminary classrooms moves from being "self-referential" to "cross-referential" students' understanding of sacred texts, pastoral practices, and

---

33. The Pew Forum on Religion and Public Life, "The U. S. Religious Knowledge Survey" 2010.

34. For an example, rooted in Reformed theology, of being mutually respectful while openly confessional, see the essay by Cynthia Rigby in this volume [editors' note].

35. Adeney, "The Mainline's New Moment," 41.

36. Thangaraj, "Globalization, World Religions and Theological Education," 143–53.

such foundational themes such as "hospitality" and "neighbor" deepen.[37] Interreligious dialogue strengthens members of each tradition in their own religious identities. This points to a somewhat ironic fact in this secular age: effective interreligious leadership and informed dialogical relationships with religious "others" who are our neighbors require knowledge of one's own tradition. Yet, the "clarity" about one's tradition that dialogical reciprocity requires is more than the traditional expectation reflected in accreditation standards that seminary graduates be rooted in and articulate spokespersons for Christian tradition in general and their own tradition in particular. What is now needed involves a decentering or disembedding experience in which Christian religious leaders and the congregants they serve understand Christian faith and its central claims in the context of and through conversation with the other historical religious traditions and their claims. In recognition of this decentering shift, the Association of Theological Schools (ATS) changed an accreditation standard for Master of Divinity students in 2012 to foreground the contemporary multifaith context of ministry. "M.Div. education shall engage students with the global character of the church as well as ministry in the multifaith and multicultural context of contemporary society. This should include attention to the wide diversity of religious traditions present in potential ministry settings...."[38]

Theological educators who embrace the formational and informational challenge of preparing graduates for the practice of ministry shaped by a dialogical heart will find a rich resource in the theme of hospitality so central to each of the three Abrahamic traditions. As some educators have noted, the theme of hospitality points to both the new status of Christians in this diverse context who find they too are "guests" in conversation with their religiously other neighbors and the importance of sufficient knowledge of one's tradition to contribute to a conversation.[39] Further, such formation includes a relational and ethical posture of solidarity with the marginalized religious other in expectation that God reveals Godself in such relational practices.[40]

Relational learning that is characterized by respectful and critically reflexive engagement is an important pedagogical strategy for preparing Christian religious leaders to be effective in building interfaith networks of trust and shared mission.[41] In fact, this commitment to learning in rela-

37. Rajashekar, "Theological Education for Interfaith Engagement," 167.
38. Graham, "Christian Hospitality," 9.
39. Adeney, "The Mainline's New Moment," 39, 41.
40. Ibid., 42.
41. Rose, "Pedagogical Principles for Multifaith Education," 61–63.

tion to our religiously other neighbors is what Diana Eck suggests allows us to move beyond the fact of religious diversity to achieve mutually respectful "religious pluralism."[42] Her point is that relational learning arises not in the abstract but is achieved through actively engaging one another to deepen our mutual understanding across differences through encountering and respecting our commitments in a generous and critically reflexive attentiveness.

In a secular context where religious claims stand alongside other deeply held commitments regarding public policy and communal practices such as healthcare, immigration, the economy, and education, Thangaraj was correct to note in his prescient comments in 1999 as cited above, that public ministry or witness is a third primary focus for interfaith religious leadership. As we noted earlier in this essay, in a secular context, the free practice of religion and the articulation of religious points of view are secure though not privileged above others' deeply held, value-laden viewpoints that also inform public life. In such a context Christian religious leaders will find that their commitments claim no special place in community and national debates; however, their ability to articulate those claims in conversation with their religiously other neighbors may build bridges for shared witness. Further, their relational engagement with these religiously other neighbors will allow Christians as guests to hear and consider their neighbor's witness arising from their faiths. In a secular context where religion is optional, revisable, and thus fragile, imagine, for example, the implications for the religiously plural public witness of Jewish, Christian, and Muslim leaders whose shared voices articulate the values of hospitality in current national and local debates regarding immigration or in the face of religious violence and bigotry.

Public Religion

Having explored the personal and historic dimensions of the pluriform character of contemporary religion, we turn now to the third its three-fold dimensions: public religion. This term describes the themes and values that function normatively in the public sphere of our secular context evoking citizens' commitments and public debate in civic life.[43] As we noted earlier, the evolution of our current secular context is normatively shaped by the emergence of the American and French social democracies whose constitutional claims remain the core values of civil religion in the United States:

42. Eck, http//www.pluralism.org/pluralism/what_is_pluralism.
43. Jacobsen, *No Longer Invisible*, 50–53.

liberty, equality, and justice for all. Their religious genealogy in 16th century European Christianity is transparent. Charles Taylor describes how these values emerged as a central contemporary "social imaginary" through a performative, informal, collective, evolving process and now function assumptively and normatively to project both a moral and metaphysical order in American society.[44] As we noted earlier in this essay, the three core values in this social imaginary yield a new kind of collective agency and shared political identity that authorize persons' freedom, and this political identity includes a space for religion in the political sphere and in the secular world.[45]

Of course these core values inform sharply differing interpretive frames in American political life including those who identify as secularists and those who are affiliated with historic religions. The meaning of secular and religion have evolved interactively across millennia in ways that make clear that religion has never functioned only in some private sphere but rather as a co-constitutive element in the simultaneity of our many social identities. As the current debates in the public sphere of the United States related to sexual orientation and racial justice attest, religion informs progressive and conserving points of view. It is woven throughout the evolution of public reason. Further, no one stands in a neutral epistemic location; rather, all citizens function in a "polyphonic complexity of public voices" seeking to inform political decisions about public life.[46] The secular context of social democracies presumes an ethic of inclusion among the rights of citizens that signals an expectation of effective participation.[47]

Empathic Fluency

This ethic of inclusion and effective participation in the public sphere resonates with our earlier discussion of the dialogical posture and skills that are essential for effective interfaith engagement. We need both clarity about our own points of view and a posture of readiness to learn from others as we engage in respectful dialog about our shared and differing commitments. Martha Nussbaum suggests that there are several steps involved in developing the skills we need for effectively engaging other citizens with whom we share this public sphere: a capacity for critical reflexivity; a recognition that we are essentially relational and exist within a much larger interconnected

---

44. Taylor, *Modern Social Imaginaries*, 23–30.
45. Ibid., 192–94.
46. Calhoun, "Secularism, Citizenship, and the Public Sphere," 81–84.
47. Ibid., 77.

human enterprise; and an imaginative empathic fluency she calls "narrative imagination" that allows us to build accurate empathic bridges with others that respect differences and points of overlapping consensus.[48]

Nussbaum describes the first of these skills as an intellectual commitment to examining our commitments critically rather than simply "receiving them" and with a readiness to revise them in the context of respectful dialogue. While she is unquestionably correct that this reflexive intellectual engagement is essential, it is also clear that such reflexivity is more than an intellectual enterprise. It needs to include our embodied experience which is inseparable from our intellectual life and also utterly insinuated by asymmetries of power dynamically reflected in our social identities such as sexuality, gender, race, and class.[49] In other words, this critical embodied reflexivity is also shaped by a readiness to acknowledge ways our commitments reflect our self-interests in the dynamic intersections of privilege and oppression.

This fuller reflexivity enriches her second ethical claim that to be effective citizens we need to recognize our essential interrelation with the larger human community and embrace the complex task of understanding the needs and hopes and particularity of the other rather than collapsing such differences into some more familiar but inevitably false generic humanity. This challenging second capacity points to the important third skill, developing an ability imaginatively to enter the narrative of the other, not naively, but generously in recognition that truer understanding will come from first appreciating the way the other's experience gives rise to her or his commitments. Nussbaum does not link her three proposals for ethical and effective citizenship to any historic religious tradition; rather, she presumes the normative assumptions of our civil or public religion: equality, liberty, and justice for all. The resonance of her proposals for ethical citizenship with historic religious traditions and with Christianity in particular points us toward a discussion of public theology as an effective form of Christian apologetics for a secular public sphere.[50] Or to put it another way, we can recognize the relation between ethical citizenship and good public theology.

Public theology

Christian theology and thus theological education have always recognized the relevance of public witness and the priority of pursuing God's redemptive

---

48. Nussbaum, *Cultivating Humanity*, 9–11.
49. Ramsay, "Intersectionality."
50. Stackhouse, "Public Theology and Political Economy," 191n2.

and transforming love and justice in the public sphere. Christian scripture is rife with evidences that we are called to seek the "welfare of the city" (Jer 29:7) and to "repair the breaches" (Is 58:12) in the human community with particular attention to the vulnerable. Public theological leadership is a familiar curricular goal in many Oldline Protestant Master of Divinity degree programs. Public theology draws on the resources of Christian tradition to propose responses to issues of public life that are shaped by core biblical themes such as justice, love, and compassion and shared in language that is broadly understandable and persuasive. We have already explored briefly the importance of engaging in public theological work interreligiously whenever possible. Our question here is how does the secular context we have been exploring inform effective public theology, and what are the curricular and pedagogical implications for theological education of such changes?

Elaine Graham has recently proposed that our context calls for public theology as a Christian "apologetics of presence."[51] Apologetics in Christian theology historically has referred to a persuasive presentation of the faith with the goal of conversion, but Graham shifts the focus of persuasion from conversion to demonstrating God's solidarity with the human community by shaping a public response to a recognized need in the public sphere in ways that both reflect scripture's commitments such as love, justice, and compassion and that are more widely persuasive. One immediate concern for religious leaders lies in how public theologians articulate commitments in a secular context in which they have no special authorization. As Graham would put it, the authorization for a public theology as apologetics must lie in the fact that it seeks the welfare of the city.[52] The authorization lies in the efficacy of its public witness or orthopraxis. Her concern echoes what Charles Taylor means when he uses Rawls' term, "overlapping consensus."[53] Effective public theology will support public needs in language that is authentic to Christian faith and also comprehensible and persuasive for other citizens who may rely on different normative traditions but welcome collaboration in the work of justice. A secular public theology is practiced in solidarity with others whose normative commitments may not be Christian, and whose concerns for the welfare of the city, to repair the breaches in the human community overlap with those of Christians. This practice of solidarity points to the fact that public theology in our secular context will

---

51. Graham, *Between a Rock and a Hard Place*, 212.
52. Ibid., 213.
53. Rawls, *Political Liberalism*, as cited in Taylor, *A Secular Age*, 532.

require multilingual capacities as well as the empathic accuracy and fluency Nussbaum urges us to view as an ethical obligation.

Graham also encourages us to practice public theology as an apologetics of advocacy that speaks truth to power.[54] That is, she urges religious leaders and the congregants they serve to equip themselves to be effective in analyzing the systemic and structural breaches in the fabric of the human community and to speak persuasively as advocates in weaving together an overlapping consensus among a wider public audience than simply the Christian community. Advocacy will not be effective if it does not arise from active, appreciative engagement or solidarity with the wider community. The capacity for effective advocacy will require the ethical skills for citizenship that Nussbaum proposed: critical reflexivity, respectful attention to the particular needs and experience of the other who is also our neighbor, and careful attention to that neighbor's experience and its distinctive claims on her or his life. As Eck noted in our exploration of interfaith public witness, we must engage each other through honest discussion of our commitments and look for opportunities to encourage shared commitment or overlapping consensus.

Graham concludes her discussion of public theology as apologetics by urging our attention to imagining public theology as enacting one's Christian vocation in the context of the "contested spaces" of our secular common life. It is the work not only of religious leaders but more importantly it is the daily opportunity of laypersons and as such she urges religious leaders to give more attention to equipping congregants to be articulate about their faith and its implications in their public life as citizens.[55]

The proposals of Craig Calhoun, Martha Nussbaum, and Elaine Graham are intriguingly interrelated in their attention to an ethic of inclusion and participation as citizens in a secular public sphere. They point toward several important implications for theological educators and their students that are interrelated with those that we noted earlier as important for achieving a religiously plural context and extend beyond them.

1. Christian religious leaders and laypersons need to develop a multilingual capacity to articulate our faith commitments.
2. Christian leaders and laity need to foster an embodied, critical reflexivity about our values and faith commitments in order to be effective in building an overlapping consensus with those whose beliefs, social location, and experience differ from ours and whose goals for

---

54. Graham, *Between a Rock and a Hard Place*, 213.
55. Ibid., 228.

the work of justice and love are similar. This work of solidarity will require empathic fluency and accuracy as we learn to engage the other as neighbor.

3. Christian leaders and laity need to develop skills for analysis of systems and structures and for promoting strategic change in order to be effective public theologians whose advocacy for change in the public sphere is persuasive to others who seek the welfare of the city and the repair of breaches in the human community.

In a secular context where faith is optional, revisable, and thus fragile, these three goals create a particular challenge. Theological faculty will realize that the tasks cut across particular disciplines, knowledges, and skills. They invite curricular goals, course assignments, and contextual engagements that reflect the four pedagogies of professional theological education: interpretation, formation, contextualization, and performance.[56] All of these pedagogies are impacted by taking the secular context seriously. It appears that effective public theology will require a new level of reflexivity on the part of Christian religious leaders and laity. In a secular public sphere of contested ideas about priorities in public life, Christians who hope to persuade public action that reflects the values of the Gospel will need to be able to articulate their values not only to their religiously other neighbors but also to those who do not share a religious point of view but may share the same goal of social justice. Indeed, as we engaged the implications of a pluriform religion, personal, historic, and public, we seem to have uncovered a series of decentering movements for those who identify with Christian tradition. In each case, we discovered that this capacity for understanding and dialogue require not only communication skills but call for a different and more complexly reflective way of experiencing Christian faith. Engaging the spiritual diversity that characterizes personal religion invites Christians to experience transcendence and immanence in ways that traditional practices and disciplines may not have disclosed. Engaging the religious diversity of historic traditions involves coming to understand and to experience Christian faith as one religion among other historical traditions and to value dialogical learning with religiously other neighbors knowing that through such dialogue we understand our own faith more deeply. Engaging in the work of public theology as an apologetics of presence moves Christians yet another step out of the center, and we find ourselves requiring new fluencies in order to explain the "hope that is in us" (I Pet 3:15)[57] for the human community

56. Foster, *Educating Clergy*.
57. Graham, *Between a Rock and a Hard Place*, xxiv.

with no shared religious vocabulary except the priority of love and justice especially for the most vulnerable.

Conclusion

This journey into understanding the character and impact of a secular context for mainline Protestant theological education in the United States has underscored the depth and scope of secularity as changes in the very conditions of belief rendering faith as optional, revisable, and thus fragile. It has included some surprises in revising popular binary understandings of what we mean by secular and religious and rebutted theories that presume the demise of religion. Instead it has invited us to appreciate the continuing, evolving, dynamic, complex relation of experiences of secularity and religion particularly as we find that religion in the United States now has a pluriform shape and each reflects how our secular context alters conditions of belief in personal religion, historic traditional religions, and public religion.

Bibliography

Adeney, Francis, et.al., "The Mainline's New Moment: Hospitable Christian Practice in a Multireligious World." *Theological Education* 47 (2012) 33–46.

Ammerman, Nancy. *Congregation and Community*. New Brunswick, NJ: Rutgers University Press, 1997.

———. "Spiritual But Not Religious? Beyond Binary Choices in the Study of Religion." *Journal for the Scientific Study of Religion* 52 (2013) 258–78.

Calhoun, Craig. "Secularism, Citizenship, and the Public Sphere." In *Rethinking Secularism*, edited by Craig Calhoun, et. al., 75–91. New York: Oxford University Press, 2011.

Casanova, Jose. "The Secular, Secularizations, Secularisms." In *Rethinking Secularisms*, edited by Craig Calhoun, et. al., 54–74. New York: Oxford University Press, 2011.

Eck, Diana. "What is Pluralism?" Harvard University. http://www.pluralism.org/pluralism/what_is_pluralism.

Foster, Charles, et.al. *Educating Clergy: Teaching Practices and Pastoral Imagination*. San Francisco: Jossey Bass, 2006.

Graham, Elaine. *Between a Rock and a Hard Place: Public Theology in a Post-Secular Age*. London: SCM, 2013.

Graham, Stephen. "Christian Hospitality and Pastoral Practices in a Multifaith Society." *Theological Education* (The Association of Theological Schools in the United States and Canada) 47 (2012) 1–10.

Jacobsen, Douglas & Rhonda Hustedt Jacobsen. *No Longer Invisible: Religion in University Education*. New York: Oxford University Press, 2012.

Niebuhr, H. Richard. *Radical Monotheism*. London: Faber and Faber, 1943.

Nussbaum, Martha. *Cultivating Humanity: a Classical Defense of Reform in Liberal Education*. Cambridge: Harvard University Press, 1997.

Or, Rose. "Pedagogic Principles for Multifaith Education." *Theological Education* (The Association for Theological Schools in the United States and Canada) 47 (2013) 61–66.

Palmer, Parker. *The Courage to Teach: Exploring the Inner Landscape of a Teacher's Life*. San Franscisco: Jossey Bass, 1998.

Parks, Sharon Daloz. *Big Questions Worthy Dreams*. Revised Edition. San Francisco: Jossey Bass, 2011.

Rajashekar, J. Paul. "Theological Education for Interfaith Engagement: the Philadelphia Story." In *Changing the Way Seminaries Teach: Pedagogies for Interfaith Dialogue*, edited by David Roozen and Heidi Hadsell, 157–182. Hartford: Hartford Seminary, 2009.

Ramsay, Nancy. "Intersectionality: a Model for Addressing the Complexity of Oppression and Privilege." *Pastoral Psychology* 63 (Spring 2013) 453–69.

Rawls, John. *Political Liberalism*. New York: Columbia University Press, 1993.

Roozen, David, and Heidi Hadsell. *Changing the Way Seminaries Teach: Pedagogies for Interfaith Dialogue*, Vol. II. Hartford: Hartford Seminary, 2009.

Stackhouse, Max. "Public Theology and Political Economy in a Globalizing Era." In *Public Theology for the 21st Century*, edited by William Storrar and Andrew Morton, 179–94. New York: T. & T. Clark, 2004.

Taylor, Barbara Brown. *An Altar in the World: a Geography of Faith*. New York: Harper Collins, 2009.

Taylor, Charles. "*Modern Social Imaginaries*. Durham: Duke University Press, 2004.

———. *A Secular Age*. Cambridge: Harvard University Press, 2007.

———. "Western Secularity." In *Rethinking Secularism*, edited by Craig Calhoun, et. al., 31–53. New York: Oxford University Press, 2011.

———. "Why We Need a Radical Redefinition of Secularism." In *The Power of Religion in the Public Sphere*, edited by Eduardo Mendieta and Jonathan VanAntwerpen, 34–59. New York: Columbia University Press, 2011.

Thangaraj, M. "Globalization, World Religions and Theological Education." *Theological Education* 35 (1999) 143–53.

"U.S. Religious Knowledge Survey." The Pew Forum on Religion and Public Life, 2010.

Warner, Michael, et. al. *Varieties of Secularism in a Secular Age*. Cambridge: Harvard University Press, 2010.

7

The Aesthetics of Persuasion

Rhetoric in Calvin's The Golden Book of the True Christian Life

—Warner M. Bailey

In his analysis of the current state of discord in the Presbyterian Church (U.S.A.) Thomas White Currie is guided by an observation of Dietrich Bonhoeffer in identifying the root of our unhappy state. Reflecting on his experience in America in the 1930s, Bonhoeffer described American religion as a confusion of democratic, constitutional freedom with "the freedom of the Word of God itself to gain a hearing."[1] Because of this confusion, Bonhoeffer observed, we have put self-directed freedom to choose our religion in the place of obedience to a call from God that constrains us, that is, a call that expects us to be obedient and "directs us to a life beyond self, a life whose end (*telos*) is found in Jesus Christ."[2] The question is not: What am I free to choose?, but: How will I become obedient?

Indeed, since at least the publication of Philip Rieff's, *The Triumph of the Therapeutic: Uses of Faith after Freud* in 1968,[3] pastors, lay leadership, and academics in the PCUSA, as well as other Christian groups, have been engaged in discussions probing the place of the self in Christian faith and practice.[4] I affirm Currie's putting to the church the challenge of obey-

---

1. Currie, "Stuck with Each Other," 14, quoting Dietrich Bonhoeffer in *A Testament to Freedom*, 524.

2. Currie, "Stuck with Each Other," 14.

3. Rieff's book was reissued on the fortieth anniversary of its publication with an introductory essay by Elisabeth Lasch-Quinn.

4. In the field of New Testament studies, discussions of the self commonly take

ing a directive to life beyond self. Addressing this challenge becomes an opportunity to access the theology of John Calvin on the self. This essay seeks to listen to Calvin's voice in such a way that readers can exceed and overcome our pragmatic, individualistic approach, observed by Bonhoeffer, and which continues to characterize much of religion today. Calvin scholar J. Todd Billings comments:

> Sociological studies show that most Americans see themselves as autonomous, self-made individuals. Young adults in particular. . .believe that religion is simply a matter of choosing what seems best and what pleases them personally, not a matter of truth or, even more extreme, a matter in which humans need God in order to know the truth about God. The American tendency is toward a radical libertarian view of freedom, where "freedom" assumes that we autonomously choose between this and that, in a way that is exalted above the influence of advertising, peer pressure, or culture.[5]

It is against this tidal wave of self-fascination that the Word of God means to gain a hearing.[6]

So, this essay is, broadly speaking, an example of the service Reformed theology can provide to the Church. More narrowly construed, it is an addition to the history of the reception of Calvin in the early 21st century.[7] The occasion for this essay couldn't be a happier one. It is offered in the warmest affection to David Gouwens, someone I have known as pastor, colleague, and friend throughout his tenure at Brite Divinity School. David's own generous commitment to placing his considerable theological knowledge and

---

place in the context of conversion. Stendahl launched the modern discussion with his "The Apostle Paul and the Introspective Conscience of the West" in which he argued strongly against interpreting Paul, through the lens of psychological introspection, as morally conflicted before his conversion. The nature of the self figured heavily in three studies: Moule, "Obligation," Styler, "The Basis of Obligation," and Keck, "The Accountable Self." These essays use a wide variety of theological approaches and show how the discussion is still in flux. Two substantial studies from the field of social scientific criticism introduce language fields that Paul may have used to describe the self in the context of his conversion: Martin, *Slavery as Salvation* and Crook, *Reconceptualising Conversion*. While each study brings valuable light to Paul's vocabulary, both are lacking in fully appreciating the theological importance Paul attaches to his conversion. For this see Dunn, "'A Light to the Gentiles'" and "2 Corinthians iii. 17"; and Hays, *Echoes of Scripture*, 122–37. For a recent introduction to the issues of Paul's conversion, see Gaventa, *From Darkness to Light*.

    5. Billings, *Union with Christ*, 39. For a description of a theology of retrieval see p. 2.

    6. For an example, see the essay in this volume by Stephen Plunkett.

    7. For studies in reception, see Billings and Hesselink, *Calvin's Theology*.

perception at the service of the church justly earns him a place as "doctor of the church."[8]

I

The question: How will I become obedient to "a life beyond self, a life whose end (*telos*) is found in Jesus Christ" is central to Calvin's understanding of the Christian life. Beginning with his first Catechism (1537) written for French speaking congregations, Calvin chose the term *pietas* as a symbol for his overall understanding and practice of Christian faith and life.

> True piety does not consist in a fear which willingly indeed flees God's judgment, but since it cannot escape is terrified. True piety consists rather in a sincere feeling which loves God as Father as much as it fears and reverences Him as Lord, embraces His righteousness, and dreads offending Him worse than death. And whoever have been endowed with this piety dare not fashion out of their own rashness any God for themselves. Rather, they seek from Him the knowledge of the true God, and conceive Him just as He shows and declares Himself to be.[9]

Indeed, the piety Calvin describes defines his view of the self that in all its parts and affections bends and intends to the embrace of God.[10]

Calvin considered himself a theologian and biblical scholar, and he devoted his service to the upbuilding of congregations. He put his considerable training as humanist and rhetorician to the purpose of expounding scripture and crafting theological discussions that would penetrate the lives of his audiences to nurture and deepen their piety.

In this essay we will consider one of Calvin's most influential descriptions of the Christian life, located in Book Three, chapters six through ten of the *Institutes* (3.6–10). These chapters entered the *Institutes* in its expanded

---

8. Calvin, *Institutes*, 4.3.T. Unless otherwise noted, all citations from the *Institutes* come from the Battles-McNeill edition.

9. Battles, *The Piety of John Calvin*, 13.

10. This view of the self can be seen clearly in Calvin's description of his spiritual pilgrimage which he wrote in his preface to his commentary on the Psalms. "Here is the true proof of obedience, where, bidding farewell to our own affections, we subject ourselves to God and allow our lives to be so governed by His will that things most bitter and harsh to us—because they come from Him—become sweet to us. Finally, here not only general praises of God's goodness are recounted to teach us to rest in Him alone, so that godly minds may await some help from Him in all necessity; but also freely given forgiveness of sins, which alone both reconciles us to God and obtains for us quiet repose in Him" (Battles, *The Piety of John Calvin*, 29).

version of 1542. They were probably written in the spring of 1539 from Strasbourg where Calvin was pastor to a French speaking congregation after being banished from Geneva by the town council.[11] While in Strasbourg, he also lectured on Paul's epistles to the Romans and the Corinthians, and 3.6–10 show the influence of these lectures.

These chapters have a distinct quality of self-containment. They have a three-fold structure: Motives for the Christian Life (3.6); A Rule for the Christian Life (3.7); and The Christian Life, Earthly Life and Eternal Life (3.8–10). Produced, most probably, within the context of direct pastoral leadership of a congregation, they are written in an easily accessible style. It appears that these chapters were quickly recognized as effective shapers of the Christian life. They enjoy the rare distinction of being a portion of the *Institutes* to be printed separately in Geneva in 1545 and reprinted in 1551 under the title *A Very Excellent Treatise on the Christian Life* or *The Golden Booklet of the (True) Christian Life*. The popularity of this separate treatise led it to be the first portion of the *Institutes* to be translated into English and published in 1549 under the title *The Life and Communicacion of a Christen Man*.[12]

II

Our investigation uncovers some of the rhetoric Calvin employs to persuade his audience to grant the Word of God a space to speak and thus to shape Christian identity or piety. The value of applying rhetorical analysis to Calvin's writing was brought to the attention of modern scholars in 1974 by E. David Willis[13] who provided an overview and bibliographical survey of studies in Calvin's rhetorical tradition.[14] Bouwsma's portrait of Calvin also noticed that the "deepest mark of his humanism was his recognition that the Bible is throughout a rhetorical document and a work of interpretation." The Gospels "do not simply narrate the facts of Christ's life, but at the same time they explain for what purpose he was born, died, and rose again, and what benefit thence comes to us." The Evangelists were not annalists but artists. Knowledge of biblical rhetoric explains the power of the text to penetrate more effectively into the hearts of the people. The amazing output of letters, sermons, commentaries and theological documents testifies to the

---

11. For the historical context of Calvin's Strasbourg period, see Bouwsma, *John Calvin*, 20–21.

12. Battles, *Institutes*, xlii.

13. "Rhetoric and Responsibility," 43–64.

14. Ibid.

breadth and depth of Calvin's erudition. However, *eruditio* was for Calvin always the handmaiden of *persuasio*. *Eruditio* explained the persuasiveness of the Scriptures.[15]

The rhetorical study of the *Institutes* received major impetus with the publication of Serene Jones' detailed presentation of Calvin's rhetoric.[16] Her basic analysis provides grounding for my investigation. Confining herself to the opening chapters of Book 1, Jones situates Calvin's rhetorical theology in the context of his early humanist training in the classical rhetorics of Cicero, Petrarch, and the French humanists. However, Jones concludes, "Calvin's use of rhetoric was much more creative; he refined and often stretched the rhetorical rules he was taught in law school. And the result is a style of presentation that is quite original. . ..one critic calls it a 'sober literary aesthetic.'"[17]

Calvin was deeply influenced by Cicero's model of the good rhetorician who swallows the treasure of the past so that, as the speaker fully absorbs the tradition, it can shape the speaker's rhetoric. He was impressed by Cicero's insight that language has power over people's minds and hearts. It can "transform states, overthrow governments, garner public support for policies, win wars, and destroy reputations and lives." In describing the power of language, Calvin paid attention to Cicero's use of rhythm and repetition and ornamentation of speech with words, images, metaphors, sounds and stories from a treasure-trove of the past.[18]

Petrarch alerted Calvin to the educative purpose of rhetoric. Jones explains: "Petrarch summarizes this educative view of rhetoric when he states that 'useful teachers of virtue are those whose first and last intention is to make the hearer and reader good, those who do not merely teach what virtue and vice are and hammer into our heads the brilliant name of one and the grim name of the other, but sow in our hearts love of the best and eager desire for it, and at the same time hatred of the worst and how to flee from it.'" The phrases "to make the reader good" and to "sow in the heart" point to the goal of persuading the listener or reader to adopt and live out what is being urged.[19]

---

15. Bouwsma, 121–123. The interplay between erudition and persuasiveness continues as a distinguishing factor in Reformed exegetical practice. See Bailey, "Authority to Edify."

16. Jones, *Calvin and Rhetoric of Piety*.

17. Ibid., 25 As this essay attends to Calvin's aesthetics of persuasion, it pays honor to original work David Gouwens is doing in the wider area of Reformed aesthetics.

18. Ibid., 20–21.

19. Ibid., 24, 122.

We have already seen how Calvin has sketched his notion of piety in the preface to the French Catechism (1537). This is brought forward now in the beginning of the *Institutes* (1539). "We are called to a knowledge of God: not that knowledge which, content with empty speculation, merely flits in the brain, but that which will be sound and fruitful if we duly perceive it, and if it takes root in the heart."[20] However, it is obvious to Calvin that to perceive knowledge which takes root in the heart is entirely impossible, humanly speaking, "since men were born in such a state that they are all too much inclined to self-love—and, however much they deviate from truth, they still keep self-love."[21] Consequently, to fulfill the conditions of sound and fruitful knowledge "the eloquence of scripture, the power of the Spirit, and the rhetorical finesse of the theologian must work together to persuade and move the hearts of the faithful."[22] Hence, the need for the aesthetics of persuasion.

For persuasion to achieve its goal, Calvin and subsequent rhetoricians of his era developed rhetorical strategies designed to provoke directly the disposition they were teaching. Jones perceptively lays open this process of rhetorical elicitation of disposition.

> In order to identify the "disposition–forming" or "virtue-shaping" dimensions of a literary text's rhetoric, modern interpreters have attempted to trace the "play of mind" that a text elicits. The notion of a "play of mind" is broadly understood to include the variety of mental and emotional activities through which the text leads its readers. At times, a text may require its readers to take an unprecedented conceptual leap aimed at not only opening up new intellectual possibilities but also evoking unprecedented affective reactions. At other times, the text may challenge its readers by deploying a startling metaphor or an unusual juxtaposition of images that forces them to perceive their world in a new way. The text may also reorient its readers' disposition by asking them to assume unfamiliar character roles

---

20. 1.5.9. See 1.10.2 and 1.14.4 among many examples, and Venema, *Accepted and Renewed*, 90–92.

21. 2.8.54 in a passage supporting 1 Cor 13:5 "Love does not seek its own." See also, among many examples, 2.2.25 "Is our diligence, insight, understanding, and carefulness so completely corrupted that we can devise or prepare nothing right in God's eyes?" a passage supporting 2 Cor 3:5 "not that we are sufficient of ourselves."

22. Jones, *Calvin and Rhetoric of Piety*, 27, points to his *Commentary of First Corinthians*, at 1:17, where Calvin explains that eloquence and rhetorical excellence are "noble gifts that men [should] put to good use," and when put to the service of the Word, "they come from the Holy Spirit."

in the hope that they may begin to experience previously foreign emotional states.²³

The affective states and dispositions of piety Calvin names are quite diverse. We are "to feel [God's] power and grace in ourselves and in the great benefits [God] has conferred upon us, and so bestir ourselves to trust, invoke, praise, and love him."²⁴ Jones points out that "Calvin typically identifies the disposition associated with a particular doctrine only after he has already taken the reader through a process of reading [the play of mind] which itself produces that disposition."²⁵ She sketches out a matrix of rhetorical maneuvers Calvin calls upon to move his readers to one or another disposition.

> When Calvin wants his readership to feel judged, challenged, or scolded he uses the classical form of forensic rhetoric, the rhetoric of defense and attack . . . . When Calvin wants to uplift and nurture his readers, he employs the classical panegyric or demonstrative form. In these sections his language becomes sermonic. He exploits the powers of rhythm and rhyme as he either gently rocks his readers in the comforting descriptions of God's grace or energetically takes them to rhetorical heights in his impassioned description of the glory and power of God's sovereign rule . . . . When his purposes are pedagogical, he deploys the classical rhetorical form of deliberative speech.
>
> In this manner, Calvin uses his rhetorical skills to construct doctrines that produce in his readers a certain play of mind, a play of mind that has as its final goal the inculcating of a faithful disposition.²⁶

III

We now turn to four examples of rhetoric described by Jones which are included in *The Golden Book of the True Christian Life* (3.6–10) to understand how his plays of mind are put to the service of persuasion. While each of the four examples has its distinctive character, every one is hymnic or lyrical in style. Battles alerts us to this aspect.²⁷ Hymnic fragments have the following

---

23. Ibid., 24–25.
24. 1.14.22.
25. Jones, 29.
26. Ibid., 30.
27. Jones does not treat Calvin's lyrical rhetoric, and Battles, *Piety*, 84, notes that it

rhetorical markings: "There is usually a repeated phrase running through the passage like a refrain. There is also a series of short, parallel phrases over against which a subsequent antithetic series is set. There is cumulative movement from a first statement to a final summation, symmetrical with the first. These traits, expressed in varied ways, unmistakably mark the lyrics of the theologian."[28] While it is notable that four hymnic fragments are concentrated in these three chapters of Book 3, Battles identifies several examples of this rhetorical style throughout Calvin's writings.[29]

Our plan is to examine each example for its structure and the play of mind it contains to persuade the reader toward an aspect of piety. We will be using Battle's translation from the French version of the *Institutes* (1541).[30] We have discovered that each of the hymnic citations is formed around a text from either First and Second Corinthians or Romans. Not coincidentally, these were the books on which Calvin gave public lectures during his Strasbourg sojourn as a pastor. In the accompanying tables, the left column will be the citation from the *Institutes* and the embedded biblical text will be indicated in italics. Lyrical motifs will be similarly highlighted. The right column will be Calvin's commentary on the New Testament text. In this way not only can we achieve a better grasp of the interplay between his exegesis and his rhetorics of persuasion but we also have an insight into the dynamic relationship between Calvin's criticism and his theology.[31]

---

is absent also in Veerman, *De stijl van Calvijn* .

28. Battles, *Piety*, 168.

29. Ibid., 167–71.

30. Ibid., 9.

31. For another example of the interplay between higher criticism and theology that interpreted critical study of Scripture in a 19th century orthodox Reformed context see Bailey, "The Theological Friendship," and "William Robertson Smith and the Revival of American Biblical Studies."

A

3 6.3	1 Cor 6:19
	Do you not know that your body is a temple of the Holy Spirit?
From a better fountain Scripture draws for us Its exhortations: Not only bids us refer Our whole life to God its author, But, after warning us we have Sunk down from the true origin of our creation, Adds that Christ, reconciling us to God His Father, has given us an example Of innocence to image in our life. What thing more forceful, more effective can one say? What more than this can one require? . . . . Consequently, from all God's benefits And from all parts of our salvation, Scripture takes occasion to exhort us. For example, when it says: *Since God* gave Himself as Father to us, *We prove our* gross ingratitude If we do not act as sons. *Since Christ* has cleansed us by the washing Of His blood and through baptism Has shared this cleansing, *It is not fitting for us* in new filth To soil ourselves. *Since He* has joined and grafted us Into His body, *we His members*, *Must* carefully keep ourselves Unspotted. *Since He*, our head, has risen into heaven, *We must* dismiss all earthly loves, *Must* wholeheartedly aspire to heavenly life. *Since the Holy Spirit consecrates us to be God's temples*, *We must* take care That in us God's glory be exalted; And conversely, *we must* guard ourselves Against receiving any pollution. *Since our souls and our bodies* are destined For the immortality of God's kingdom And the incorruptible crown of His glory, *We must* strive to keep them both Pure and unspotted, to the day of the Lord.	From the Commentary: For as the Spirit of God cannot take up his abode in a place that is profane, we do not give him a habitation otherwise than by consecrating ourselves to him as temples. It is a great honor that God confers upon us when he desires to dwell in us. Hence we ought so much the more to fear, lest he should depart from us, offended by our sacrilegious actings.

The passage shows its hymnic character through the repetition of the rhetorical structure "Since X, then Y." The apodosis, Y, is the urged behavior. It is the corollary to the protasis, X, the divine initiative. The over-riding disposition being persuaded is a life of purity. Calvin wants to engender the play of mind "Since X, then Y" which results in the reader's conviction that this behavior is understandable, reasonable and doable.[32] Yet, the difficulty of nurturing the disposition of purity of life is acknowledged through the six-fold repetition of the figure and the progression of the protasis from a Trinitarian (God/Christ/He/He/Spirit) formulation to a direct appeal to the reader, soul and body. The motive clauses in the protasis also intensify through the course of the hymn as more eschatological elements of the divine initiative are brought into the play of mind (heavenly life, the temple where God's glory is exalted, immortality of God's kingdom and incorruptible crown of God's glory, day of the Lord). The hymn reaches a climax with the direct appeal to the reader to affirm a selfhood which is gifted by God and destined to an end beyond self. This construction of selfhood creates an eschatological energy to keep the self pure until the "day of the Lord."[33]

As Jones points out, "first and foremost Calvin directs the reader to scripture, where faith is schooled in the knowledge of God and the discipline of true piety."[34] Here we can see his exegetical emphasis on the dispositional orientation that proper reading of the text should elicit. While the hymn gestures to several New Testament texts,[35] our study centers on the allusion to 1 Cor 6:19 "Do you not know you are God's Temple?" on which Calvin lectured in the course of writing this section. In Calvin's exegesis of this text, he lays out clearly the movement from divine gift to grateful and reverential human response. This text will make several appearances in the hymns under consideration.

32. Here we find lyrical expression of Calvin's signature use of the double grace of justification and sanctification which comes from union with Christ. "Let us sum these up: Christ was given to us by God's generosity, to be grasped and possessed by us in faith. By partaking of him, we principally receive a double grace: namely, that being reconciled to God through Christ's blamelessness, we may have in heaven instead of a Judge a gracious Father, and secondly, that sanctified by Christ's Spirit we may cultivate blamelessness and purity of life." 3.9.1. See Billings, "Union with Christ," 59; and Venema, *Accepted and Renewed*, 84–89. For a view that privileges justification over sanctification see Horton, "Calvin's Theology," 72–94.

33. The gratitude the believer shows to God for the gift of selfhood is "the fundamental theme, perhaps the most fundamental theme, of an entire system of theology . . . . The cardinal role of grace and gratitude is not surprising, since piety or godliness, as Calvin understands it, *is* grateful acknowledgement of the Father's gifts" (Gerrish, *Grace and Gratitude*, 20).

34. Jones, *Calvin and Rhetoric of Piety*, 27.

35. See Battles, *Institutes*, 687; and Pannier, *Institution*, 4, 244.

B

3.7.1	1 Cor 6:19
	You are not your own. For you were bought with a price; therefore glorify God in your body. Rom 14:8 (see 15:1) If we live, we live for the Lord and if we die, we die for the Lord. So, then, whether we live or whether we die, we are the Lord's.
If then, we are not our own *But belong to the Lord*, thence Can one see what we must do To avoid erring, and whither We must direct all actions of our life. *We are not our own*: accordingly Let not our reason and our will Lord it over our counsels and our tasks. *We are not our own*; then Let us not set ourselves this end— To seek out what is expedient According to the flesh. *We are not our own*: let us then, As much as in us lies, Forget ourselves and all that hems us in. Conversely, *we are the Lord's*: *Let us live and die to Him.* *We are the Lord's*: may His will, then, And wisdom rule all our acts. *We are the Lord's*: may every part Of our life be referred to Him As to their only goal. Oh, how much that man has profited Who, recognizing himself *not to be his own*, Has deprived his own reason of dominion and rule, Resigning it to God!	From the Commentary on 1 Corinthians: that we are not at our own disposal, that we should live according to our own pleasure. . .the Lord has purchased us for himself, by paying the price of our redemption. . . . .a dear rate as we are accustomed to say of things that have cost us much. . . . .The sum is this, that redemption must hold us bound, and with a bridle of obedience restrain the lasciviousness of our flesh. From the Commentary on Romans: ought not to please himself. . .for nothing impedes and checks acts of kindness more than when any one is too much swallowed up with himself, so that he has no care for others, and follows only his own counsels and feelings.

This example is located in Book III, chapter 7, the section of the *Little Golden Book* that lays out the rule for the Christian life. Fundamental to this rule is denial of self-ownership.[36] Using the classical rhetorical form of deliberative speech, Calvin engenders a play of mind which supports denial of self-ownership and the affirmation of being owned by God.[37] The clear

---

36. I believe this is a better definition of the disposition sought than the conventional "self-denial."

37. See, Venema, *Accepted and Renewed*, 122–24.

intent toward persuasion shows itself in the concluding exclamation "Oh, how much that man has profited." The three-fold repetition of the thesis "We are not our own" is matched by the antithesis "We are the Lord's." Each of these affirmations gives authority to a statement that grounds one's selfhood. Calvin displays his facility as rhetorician in the variety of ways he states the set of mind desired, first negatively, followed by a positive declaration. The entire complex becomes a paradoxical and memorable appeal to self-interest which motivates the reader to affirm the profit Calvin urges from denial of self-ownership.

The lyrics scan ABC/ C'A'B'.[38]

A. Let not our reason and our will Lord it over our counsels and our tasks.	C' *Let us live and die to Him*
B. Let us not set ourselves this end— To seek out what is expedient According to the flesh.	A' May His will, then, And wisdom rule all our acts.
C. Let us then, As much as in us lies, Forget ourselves and all that hems us in.	B' May every part Of our life be referred to Him As to their only goal.

The chiastic structure emphasizes the C/C' nexus in which is embedded the text from Romans on which Calvin anchors this persuasive appeal. It is in this nexus that the play of mind Calvin intends can be seen most clearly. Living and dying for God means forgetting ourselves and that with which we have surrounded ourselves. The concluding flourish "Oh, how much that man has profited who, recognizing himself not to be his own," underscores the disposition urged by repeating the dominant phrase of 1 Cor 6:19.

In the supporting commentary on 1 Corinthians, Calvin is sensitive to Paul's borrowing from the language of slave-master culture to describe how "redemption holds us bound," and he carefully sifts the various meanings of "bought with a price" to arrive at a construal that focuses on the costliness of our redemption rather than referring to payment to another master.[39] His

---

38. Battles, *Piety*, 84, cites the comment of Pannier, *Institution*, 4.349, "Here is one of those harmonious periods, with well-balanced antitheses, which make Calvin—as A. Lefranc has said—'the master of modern French style.'"

39. For a modern interpretation of paradoxical idea of slavery in the Greco-Roman world as salvation, see Martin, *Slavery as Salvation*. Martin describes some forms of slavery as driven by social-mobility, and he does not attend to the Paul's metaphorical treatment of the costly price that is paid to move one to salvation as a slave to Christ.

use of the figures of speech "bridles of obedience" and, in the Romans commentary, "too much swallowed up with himself" assists the reader to grasp quickly the disposition being advocated.

C

The next example is longer than the previous ones. It is divided into two parts, a demonstrative section followed by the lyrical climax. We will analyze each part separately before commenting on the impact of the entire extract.

3.8.7	2 Cor 5:15
	And he died for all, so that those who live might live no longer for themselves, but for him who died and was raised for them.
Let us not begrudge spending ourselves for God; Let us not think ourselves unhappy When with His own mouth He declares us happy. True it is that poverty valued for its own sake Is misery. Likewise exile, contempt, Disgrace, prison; lastly death Is the ultimate calamity. But when God breathes His favor None there are of these things That do not turn out for us To be happiness, felicity. With Christ's witness, not with the false Notion of our flesh, let us be content. From this it will come about that At the apostles' example we'll rejoice Whenever and how much He will count Us worthy to endure Dishonor for His name.	From the Commentary: To die to ourselves is to live to Christ; or if you would have it at greater length, it is to renounce ourselves, that we may live to Christ; for Christ redeemed us with this view—that he might have us under his authority, as his peculiar possession. Hence it follows that we are no longer our own masters.

This example is found in the section of *The Little Golden Book* that sets out how a Christian should be disposed to the use of earthly things in the light of hope for eternal life. Calvin takes up our struggle with the chronic problem of suffering. However, this sets the stage for another probing investigation into the meaning of the self. Calvin begins with stating the disposition on offer where he cites the text from 2 Cor 5:15, albeit, as the commentary shows, in a very free paraphrase. He rephrases the "live no longer for themselves" into "die to ourselves" which undergoes further modification to the opening words "Let us not begrudge spending ourselves for God." First Corinthians 6:19 continues to shape his thought as he states that the purpose of Christ redeeming us is to make us his possession so that we will spend ourselves for God.

After the opening declaration of the disposition on offer, Calvin provokes a counter-intuitive play of mind where, when we spend ourselves for God, God declares us happy in the face of unhappy circumstances. These circumstances are listed in order of increasing intensity: poverty, exile, contempt, disgrace, prison, death. Calvin affirms with his reader the unhappiness of these circumstances when "valued for its own sake." However, he places against that valuation the divine valuation: God's favor which he "breathes" and Christ's witness. The peroration closes with a return to the beginning statement of the disposition of joy. Here the apostles join with Christ's witness to persuade us to face all manner of privation under the counter-intuitive notion that God has honored us to bear it for the sake of God's Name. God anchors the self's worthiness precisely in circumstances that are calculated to cause shame.

The stirring summons to adopt this attitude now reaches its climax with the following lyrical passage.

> For *if, being innocent and of good conscience*
> We are deprived by the wickedness of evil men
> Of our possession,
> We are impoverished before men,
> But thereby toward God our true riches increase.
> *If we are hounded and banished from our homeland,*
> All the more are we received
> Into the family of the Lord.
> *If we are vexed and despised,*
> All the more are we strengthened in our Lord
> To take our refuge there.
> *If branded with disgrace and ignominy,*
> All the more are we exalted in God's kingdom.
> *If slain,* entrance to the blessed life
> Will open for us.

Through a chain of dependent clauses which are answered counter-intuitively, Calvin takes the reader rhetorically, and in the same order, through the list of privations he has already set out. By repeating five times this counter-intuitive play of mind, he coaches the reader's confidence to expect an eventual outcome that outstrips the privation. Of the five clauses, the internal three have the response "all the more." The five-fold chain climaxes with the final privation, death, being answered eschatologically. Thus, Calvin is passionately contending for the preservation of the self's integrity in the face of threats to its security.[40] He is demonstrating the power of the God made known in Jesus Christ to keep the self whole, and he strongly counsels his reader to trust in this power. Here we see Calvin in a particularly passionate persuasion, and one must remember that Calvin wrote these words after having himself experienced banishment from Geneva. Did he have himself as the intended object of his rhetoric?

D

The final example of rhetorical skill in *The Little Golden Book* is an obverse image of the preceding one. In the preceding example earthly privations were revalued in the light of God's superintending power so that in the face of privation Christians retain a positive sense of self. In the example on hand, heavenly benefits thoroughly devalue earthly existence. Whereas the intention of the former hymn was to convey, through counter-intuition, pastoral counsel in desperate circumstances, in the present piece the intention is to create an inversion in the mind of the reader so that the reader is inclined toward a more radical view of those same circumstances.

The disposition on offer appears in both the beginning and the end of the section with the embedded text appearing at the end of the piece.

---

40. For another treatment of the problem of security in the Christian life, see the essay by Paul Martens in this volume.

3.9.4	Rom 14:8
	If we live, we live for the Lord and if we die, we die for the Lord. So, then, whether we live or whether we die, we are the Lord's
Let God's servants then always pursue this goal In weighing this moral life. Seeing in it naught but misery, They should be more eager, ready To meditate upon the eternal life to come. When they come to compare the two, Not only will they be able to neglect The first, but also despise it And hold it of no value In comparison with the second. For *if heaven* is our homeland, *What else* is earth but an exile, banishment? *If leaving this world* is entering into life, *What else* is this world but a tomb? And *what else* to remain in it Than to be plunged into death? *If it is freedom to be* delivered from this body, *What else* is the body but a prison? And *if our highest happiness* is to enjoy The presence of God, Is it not misery not to enjoy it? St. Paul, feeling himself too long bound in the prison Of his body, laments his lot And sighs with fervent desire To be delivered from it. Nevertheless, to obey God's will, He asserts he is ready for one or other Because he knows he owes it To God to glorify His name, Whether through death or life. But it is for the Lord to determine What makes for His glory. *Therefore, it if befits us to live and die Unto Him, let us leave to His decision Our life as well as our death.* But in such a way that we ever May desire our death and continually Meditate upon it, Despising this mortal life In favor of the coming immortality, Desiring to renounce this life Whenever it please the Lord, Because it keeps us in sin's bondage.	From the Commentary: If at any time the flesh draws back in adversities, let it come to our minds, that he who is not free nor has authority over himself, perverts right and order if he depends not on the will of his lord. [Here again Calvin gestures to 1 Cor 6:19] Thus also is taught us the rule by which we are to live and to die, so that if he extends our life in continual sorrows and miseries, we are not yet to seek to depart before our time; but if he should suddenly call us hence in the flower of our age, we ought ever to be ready for our departure. [The gesture to 1 Cor 6:19 is further cemented by commentary on the next verse "For to this end Christ also died and rose and revived, that he might be the Lord both of the dead and the living."] Christ claims this power over us since he has obtained it by so great a price; for by undergoing death for our salvation, he has acquired authority over us which cannot be destroyed by death, and by rising again, he has received our whole life as his peculiar property. He has then by his death and resurrection deserved that we should, in death as well as in life, advance the glory of his name.

The lyrics are composed of a dependent clause beginning with "If" (A) which states a proposed condition. This condition is drawn from the theological tradition which Calvin assumes is understood between him and his readers. This is followed by a conclusion stated in such a way as to link up with the reader's thinking and to lead the reader to a provocative conclusion. This play of mind is facilitated by the recurring phrase "What else?" (B) The lyrics scan according to AB/AB/B/AB/AB́ (What else? replaced by Is it not?). The central half-couplet is actually an intensification of the preceding B element. This has the effect of throwing the concepts of life and death into stark contrast. The variety in the pattern insures the reader's sustained engagement in the act of persuasion.

Again, the disposition being urged is complex. We are to cede to God our destiny in life and in death. However, Calvin is not encouraging the development of a neutral attitude or ambivalent position regarding our destiny. On the contrary, when we give ourselves over to God, we are to do so with a preference for heavenly life which is so overpowering that we despise earthly life. The table below compares the two lists of privations between this example and the former.

3.8.7	3.9.4
Poverty	Exile/banishment
Exile/banishment	Tomb
Contempt/disgrace	Death
Prison	Prison
Death	God's absence

While the lists show considerable overlap, significant differences indicate that Calvin is not repeating himself, but is shaping the material to a different purpose. For example, poverty and contempt/disgrace are missing in the second list, and God's absence is the stand-out addition to the second list. Furthermore in 3.9.4, the members of the list have been loosened from their location in the vicissitudes of life and radicalized to describe life in its totality. In this set of lyrics, Calvin is coaching his reader to approach life from a profoundly altered perspective. This new perspective is stated in the line which concludes this segment of his thinking. "Because it [this life] keeps us in sin's bondage." Calvin is leading his reader to this radical re-construction of the world.

A view of the world being in bondage to sin explains Calvin's repeated recourse to 1 Cor 6:19 "you have been bought with a price." Evidence from the Romans commentary shows how Calvin could conceive of God's act in Jesus Christ as a struggle of eschatological proportions to deliver us from the trap of bondage in order to claim rightful ownership of us. "If at any time the flesh draws back in adversities, let it come to our minds, that he who is not free nor has authority over himself, perverts right and order if he depends not on the will of his lord. . . .Christ claims this power over us since he has obtained it by so great a price; for by undergoing death for our salvation, he has acquired authority over us which cannot be destroyed by death, and by rising again, he has received our whole life as his peculiar property." This act of cosmic deliverance profoundly reorients our attitude toward earthly existence.[41] Since we will only come into the fullness of ourselves when we are totally with God, we live out our earthly days in a conflicted state of mind. We are to be obedient to our Lord in this life but, at the same time, be thoroughly dissatisfied with our present. We are intensely charged upon death's approach to advance instantly into the perfection laid up for us.

This view of life in the world may seem to be in conflict with other parts of Calvin's thought. His leadership in the affairs of this earth is well known in the areas of politics, economics, and stewardship. In the section preceding this hymnic piece (3.9.3) as an example, he writes, "Yet faithful Christians must become accustomed to such a contempt of present life as does not engender hatred of it or ungratefulness toward God." God accommodates to our limited ability to appreciate our "inheritance of immortal glory" through letting us enjoy the blessings of this life. Surrounded by earth's blessings "we begin to taste the sweetness of His bounty in His benefits, in order to whet our hope and desire to seek after the full revelation."

Nevertheless, Calvin has a keen appreciation of our natural tendency to excessive desire which he expresses eloquently at the end of the first hymnic piece we examined (3.7.1) "For, as to please themselves [Rom 15:1] is the worst plague men have to ruin and destroy them—so the sole haven of safety is not be wise in oneself, to will nothing of oneself, but to follow the Lord alone." Again, calling upon 1 Cor 13:5 "Love does not seek its own," he comments, "our nature. . .draws us into self-love, not letting us lightly neglect our own advantage." (3.7.5) This natural bent toward self-desire is bondage to sin that leads to ruin and destruction.[42] Consequently, this world—as blest as it is—remains a potential trap, and because of that threat Calvin coaches its radical devaluation, even as he counsels its right use, in the light of God's deliverance in Jesus Christ.

41. Christ's role as Deliverer is underscored in the new translation of the Heidelberg Catechism produced jointly by the Presbyterian Church (U.S.A.) the Reformed Church in America, and the Christian Reformed Church of North America. See Hansen, *The Heidelberg Catechism*. For another modern translation, see also, Barrett, *The Heidelberg Catechism.*.

42. See n21 for additional citations of this position.

The following table is summary of the aesthetics of persuasion uncovered in the analysis of these four hymnic lyrics.

Example	Rhetorical Style	Disposition	Play of Mind	Concept of the Self
3.6.3	Since X, then Y 6 times, eschatological climax.	Life of purity	Deductive	Self is a gift from God, destined for life beyond self
3.7.1	ABC/ C'A'B'	Self-realization comes with ceding of self-ownership to God	Paradoxical	Appeals to self-interest to motivate denial of self-ownership
3.8.7	AB/ AB'/AB'/AB'/ AB eschatological climax	In privation, freely and happily spend selves for God	Counter-intuitive	New sense of self-worth in the face of privation
3.9.4	AB/AB/ B AB/AB' eschatological climax	Radical re-construction of the world	Inversion	Live obediently but unattached. Yearn for perfection

Each of the main sections of *The Little Golden Book* contains at least one hymnic piece which makes the theme of that section accessible, memorable, and able to be internalized. Calvin shows particular skill in constructing lyrics with varying rhythmic patterns, and these patterns become the scaffolding on which he builds his character-shaping project. Interestingly, the patterns of 3.8.7 and 3.9.4 are related adversely in keeping with their inverse content relationship. Calvin leads his reader through an increasingly complex series of plays of mind as his coaching becomes more intensive toward the conclusion of *The Little Golden Book*.

These four poetic pieces give ample illustration to Calvin's intense interest in the self. This is not all he has to say about the self, for the scope of our investigation has not taken into consideration his thoughtful and incisive development of the self in relationship to the community.[43] Yet he has laid the foundation for that relationship in how he shapes the reader to

---

43. See, for example how Haas, *The Concept of Equity*, 58–60, develops Calvin's concept of denial of self-ownership in its relationship to genuine love of neighbor.

a new way of thinking about how self-awareness is to be grounded. Through the oscillating rhetoric of the first poem and the paradoxical gymnastics of the second, the reader enters into a world founded on gift and learns the new language of self-ceding as the pathway to self-realization. Through the sharper rhetorics of counter-intuitivity and inversion, the reader receives invaluable guidance that protects the self's worth against evil threats and against perduring vulnerability to the trap of self-love.

IV

The task of living a satisfying life in the early 21st century is coming under increasing stress from economic, political, cultural, and inter-personal forces beyond our control. Someone who espouses the instrumentalist, utilitarian view of living has increasing difficulty maintaining an integrity founded on confidence in personal autonomy. Typical responses to this failure to maintain control are either a grim renewal to "try harder" or a quiet retreat into loneliness and privacy.

Too often the church at large buys into either or both of these options. Church program calendars fill up with self-help workshops, social action causes, or classes which increase knowledge of the Bible. Congregational worship becomes ever more fractured in an attempt to cater to personal styles and preferences. Churches figure out the most promising market sectors and craft strategies to exploit these consumer groups. Or, on the other hand, because privacy and personal autonomy are so intertwined, church members cannot distinguish a privacy which is a natural right from a privacy that is a symptom of a damaged self. Consequently, opportunities are missed to reach out or opportunities are ignored because one does not know what to say or how to say it.

Churches that ground their life in the Reformed tradition are challenged with how to counter the dominant spirit of our time with a fresh word from our tradition. In two major ways, I believe we can draw insight and energy from the thought of John Calvin on the meaning of the self.

First, we can emulate Calvin's insight into the genius of rhetoric, the power of language to move people to accept truths and take on dispositions they would not ordinarily have adopted. Trusting in the power of the Holy Spirit, Calvin uses the rhetorical power of inversion, counter-intuitivity, paradox, and deduction to open a wedge in the dominant self-consciousness of autonomy, or as he puts it to "[purify] the mind so as to give it a relish for divine truth."[44]

44. *Institutes*, 3.2.33. For a recent affirmation of this insight, see Brueggemann,

Because the Word of God displays its freedom in calling for a life beyond self, this call is directed more to the heart than to the brain, and more to one's disposition than to one's understanding.[45] Taking a cue from Calvin, our proclamation and teaching must become more self-consciously heart-centered, and our choice of rhetoric must advance that goal.

To our age which is so driven by self-preoccupation, Calvin has a surprisingly robust view of the self. He champions the human self and wants to see it thrive, even in the most extreme distresses and threats. He displays a confident human being, whose confidence is founded on a sober distrust of the lure of autonomy toward self-aggrandizement and a self-surrender to God in supreme trust in God as the origin and goal of the self and the fount of its energy, direction, stamina, and hope. The church must be bolder in proclaiming this God who is celebrated in this rhetoric of persuasion.

Bibliography

Bailey, Warner M. "Authority to Edify: Verification of Biblical Truth in William Robertson Smith's *Prophets of Israel*." In *Thus Says the Lord, Essays on the Former and Latter Prophets in Honor of Robert R. Wilson*, edited by John J. Ahn and Stephen L. Cook. Library of Hebrew Bible/Old Testament Studies 502, 87–98. New York and London: T. & T. Clark, 2009.

———. "The Theological Friendship of Albrecht Ritschl and William Robertson Smith." In *Theologische Samenkorner, Dietrich Ritschl dem Lehrenden, Gelehrten, und Lemenden zum 65, Geburststag*, edited by Reinhold Bernhardt, et al., Studien zur systematischen Theologie und Ethik 1, 54–59. Münster and Hamburg: LIT Verlag, 1994.

———. "William Robertson Smith and the Revival of American Biblical Studies." In *William Robertson Smith, Essays in Reassessment*, edited by William Johnstone, 252–263. Sheffield: Sheffield, 1995.

Barrett, Lee C., III. *The Heidelberg Catechism, A New Translation for the 21st Century*. Cleveland: Pilgrim, 2007.

Battles, Ford Lewis. *The Piety of John Calvin, An Anthology Illustrative of the Spirituality of the Reformer*. Translated and edited by Ford Lewis Battles. Grand Rapids: Baker, 1978.

Billings, J. Todd. *Union with Christ, Reframing Theology and Ministry for the Church*. Grand Rapids: Baker Academic, 2011.

———, and I. John Hesselink, editors. *Calvin's Theology and Its Reception, Disputes, Developments, and New Possibilities*. Louisville: Westminster John Knox, 2012.

Bonhoeffer, Dietrich. *A Testament to Freedom, The Essential Writings of Dietrich Bonhoeffer*. Edited by Geffrey B. Kelly and F. Burton Nelson. San Francisco: Harper, 1995.

"Four Proclamatory Confrontations," 405.

45. Ibid., 3.2.8

Bouwsma, William. *John Calvin, A Sixteenth Century Portrait*. New York and Oxford: Oxford University Press, 1988.

Brueggemann, Walter. "Four Proclamatory Confrontations in Scribal Refraction," *Scottish Journal of Theology*, 56 (2003) 404–26.

Calvin, John. *Commentaries on the Epistle of Paul the Apostle to the Corinthians*. Translated by John Pringle. Grand Rapids: Baker, 1981.

———. *Commentaries on the Epistle of Paul the Apostle to the Romans*. Translated and edited by John Owen. Grand Rapids: Baker, 1981.

———. *Institutes of the Christian Religion*. Translated by Ford Lewis Battles and edited by John T, McNeill. Philadelphia: Westminster, 1960.

———. *Institution de la Religion Chrestienne*. Translated by Jacques Pannier. Paris: Société les Belles Lettres, 1936.

Crook, Zeba A. *Reconceptualising Conversion: Patronage, Loyalty and Conversion in the Religions of the Ancient Mediterranean*. Beihefte zur Zeitschrift fur die neutestamentliche Wissenschaft, 130. Berlin: Walter de Gruyter, 2004.

Currie, Thomas White. "Stuck with Each Other. "*Insights* 127 (2012) 13–19.

Dunn, James D. G. "'A Light to the Gentiles,' or 'The End of the Law'? The Significance of the Damascus Road Christophany for Paul," 89–107. In *Jesus, Paul and the Law, Studies in Mark and Galatians*. Louisville: Westminster John Knox, 1990.

———. "2 Corinthians iii.17—'The Lord is the Spirit.'" *Journal of Theological Studies*, n. s. 21 (1970) 309–20.

Gaventa, Beverly Roberts. *From Darkness to Light, Aspects of Conversion in the New Testament*. Overtures to Biblical Theology 20. Philadelphia: Fortress, 1986.

Gerrish, B. A. *Grace and Gratitude, The Eucharistic Theology of John Calvin*. Minneapolis: Fortress, 1993.

Haas, Guenther H. *The Concept of Equity in Calvin's Ethics*. Editions SR 20. Waterloo, Ontario: Wilfrid Laurier University Press, 1997.

Hansen, Gary Neal. *The Heidelberg Catechism*. Louisville: Congregational Ministries, 2012.

Hays. Richard B. *Echoes of Scripture in the Letters of Paul*. New Haven: Yale University Press, 1989.

Horton, Michael S. "Calvin's Theology of Union with Christ and the Double Grace, Modern Reception and Contemporary Possibilities." In *Calvin's Theology and Its Reception, Disputes, Developments, and New Possibilities*, edited by J. Todd Billings and I. John Hesselink, 72–94. Louisville: Westminster John Knox, 2012.

Jones, Serene. *Calvin and Rhetoric of Piety*. Louisville: Westminster John Knox, 1995.

Keck, Leander E. "The Accountable Self." In *Theology and Ethics in Paul and His Interpreters, Essays in Honor of Victor Paul Furnish*, edited by Eugene H. Lovering, Jr. and Jerry L. Sumney, 1–13. Nashville: Abingdon, 1996.

Martin, Dale B. *Slavery as Salvation, The Metaphor of Slavery in Pauline Christianity*. New Haven and London: Yale University Press, 1990.

Moule, C. F. D. "Obligation in the Ethic of Paul." In *Christian History and Interpretation: Studies Presented of John Knox*, edited by W. R. Farmer, et. al., 389–406. Cambridge: Cambridge University Press, 1967.

Rieff, Philip. *The Triumph of the Therapeutic: Uses of Faith after Freud*. New York: HarperCollins, 1968.

Stendahl, Krister. "The Apostle Paul and the Introspective Conscience of the West," *Harvard Theological Review* 56 (1963) 199–215.

Styler, G. M. "The Basis of Obligation in Paul's Christology and Ethics." In *Christ and Spirit in the New Testament, In Honour of Charles Francis Digby Moule*, edited by Barnabas Lindars and Stephen S. Smalley, 175–87. Cambridge: Cambridge University Press, 1973.

Veerman, Antoon. *De stijl van Calvijn in de "Institution christianae religionies."* Utrecht: Kemink, 1943.

Venema, Cornelis P. *Accepted and Renewed in Christ, The "Twofold Grace of God" and the Interpretation of Calvin's Theology.* Göttingen: Vandenhoeck & Ruprecht, 2007.

Willis, E. David. "Rhetoric and Responsibility in Calvin's Theology." In *The Context of Contemporary Theology, Essays in Honor of Paul Lehmann*, edited by Alexander J. McKelway and E. David Willis, 43–64. Atlanta: John Knox, 1974.

8

Hearts Kindled

Reformed Theology and Glory to God: The Presbyterian Hymnal

—Michael Waschevski

It is an honor to offer this essay in celebration of David Gouwen's contribution to the theological life of the academy and the Church. As a student of David's at Brite Divinity School, my critical theological reflection skills were honed as he nurtured in me a deep love of theology. His passion for theology and theological reflection in service to the Church has shaped and informed my ministry in numerous ways. I am so deeply grateful.

My gratitude is on-going, not just in David's lasting influence on my ministry, but in the wonderful experience of serving as one David's pastors at First Presbyterian Church of Fort Worth. Gathering together in worship, education, and fellowship has deepened our friendship over the years and has been an on-going source of inspiration and encouragement.

David's love of worship is evident. Given his research interest in aesthetics and the arts, it is no surprise that music plays an important role in David's spiritual life and worship. Singing the bass line on hymns, and with Shari enjoying the organ postlude from their pew even as other worshippers are heading out the door, David is nourished by and deeply appreciative of music in worship.

In this essay I will reflect upon Reformed theology in service to the church through the recently published *Glory to God: The Presbyterian Hymnal* (2013). Having served as a member of the Presbyterian Committee on

Congregational Song which created *Glory to God*, David's influence as a theologian was ever present in my work on the committee. The essay will briefly explore (1) John Calvin's influence on the development of congregational song in the Reformed tradition by reflecting upon a passage from *The Institutes* that speaks to the power of music and the importance of texts sung, (2) the expansion of congregational song beyond Calvin's initial focus on the Psalms, (3) the importance of the theological organization of hymnals and songbooks, and (4) important considerations in the language used to speak about God and humanity. The Presbyterian Committee on Congregational Song's "Theological Vision Statement" and "A Statement on Language" will be referenced as they were instrumental in guiding our work in creating *Glory to God: The Presbyterian Hymnal*.

John Calvin and Congregational Song

John Calvin stands as a giant in the Reformed Tradition. His influence as Geneva's reformer reached far and broad in his own day and in the centuries that have followed. Certainly prolific, Calvin's writings do, in fact, touch upon a vast repertoire of topics in the life of the church. As with all major figures within a tradition, a great deal of credit is given Calvin for many things within the Reformed tradition. Whether addressing systematic theology, the doctrine of predestination, the roles and functions of ruling and teaching elders, or a myriad of other topics of theological and ecclesial interest, Calvin is invoked in almost mythic fashion. In a collection of papers of the 2009 Calvin Studies Society Colloquium edited by Amy Nelson Burnett, *John Calvin, Myth and Reality: Images and Impact of Geneva's Reformer*, Burnett rightly observes in commenting on Calvin and Calvinism that an entire set of "cultural values and practice . . . owed as much to developments after Calvin's death as they did to Calvin himself. The result of all these developments is a popular image of Calvin that has its roots in historical reality, but that has taken on a life of its own."[1]

When considering music and congregational song in worship, Calvin is both admired and discounted depending on one's view of the role(s), function, and practice of music and congregational singing in worship. Many contemporary musicians and worship leaders would not long to return to what is remembered, by comparison, to what seems a limited and austere diet of Psalm texts sung *a cappella* to rather simple tunes with limited vocal range and predictable rhythms consisting of long and short duration that align with syllables of the text. In addition, the elimination of organs and

---

1. Burnett, *John Calvin*, xiv.

instruments from the worship service leaves some musicians shaking their heads.

At the same time, the rejection, albeit not for long or universally,[2] of the organ and instruments in worship, elevated for many the proper recognition of the human voice as the best instrument for praise of God. After all, God created the human voice, they contend. Singing *a cappella* in unison united the congregation, of all ages, in a way that must have seemed revolutionary in Calvin's day. Rather than relying on the choir to sing on behalf of the congregation, the congregation offered praise in an integrated experience of body (breathing, vocal production) mind (text) and heart (the experience of music with human emotion).

In *The Institutes*, Calvin writes that singing "has the greatest value in kindling our hearts to true zeal and eagerness to pray."[3] It would seem that Calvin highlights the emotional impact of the experience of singing and music for the worshipper. For those who are quick to label descendants of Calvin the "frozen chosen," it may be an undeserved moniker. Many Reformed Christians find the singing of hymns and songs a highlight of the worship experience. Hearts are indeed kindled as congregational song mediates an experience that touches the soul and warms the heart.

Before assuming, however, that the severity often associated with Calvin and congregational song is pure myth, it may be worth noting the very next sentence he writes in the *Institutes*. "Yet we should be very careful that our ears be not more attentive to the melody than our minds to the spiritual meaning of the words."[4] Calvin understands the power of melody and rhythm in the music sung in worship. And in what seems authentically Calvin, he cautions against music for music's sake in worship. The primacy of text over melody impacts the selection of congregational song for Calvin. If the human voice is the perfect instrument for praising God, what better source of texts to praise God would there be than scripture? Within the canon of scripture, the Psalms, often referred to as the hymnal of Israel, provide a wealth of material for congregational singing in Christian worship.

The Expansion of Congregational Song

The singing of Psalms was central to Calvin. Beginning with the Strasbourg Psalter of 1539 and the Genevan Psalter of 1543, Reformed Christians have historically sung Psalms in worship. So integral were the Psalms historically

2. See Joby, *Calvinism and the Arts*, 73–74.
3. Calvin, *Institutes*, 895.
4. Ibid.

that many late 20th and early 21st century hymnals, such as *The Presbyterian Hymnal: Hymns, Psalms, and Spiritual Songs* of 1990, included Psalter sections to resource Reformed and Presbyterian American denominations. Calvin's preference for the plain meaning of the text or a more literal reading of scripture as opposed to allegorical or spiritual readings did not mean, however, the sung Psalms of the early Psalters were simply musical settings of the biblical text. Paraphrases were employed in order to match text with musical line. In fact, the cornerstone of the tradition's experience of singing Psalms are metrical settings of Psalm text paraphrases.

To paraphrase is to enter into the realm of interpretation. Additionally, to paraphrase is to engage in artistic, improvisational work. Bruce Ellis Benson comments that while both Luther and Calvin are associated with literal interpretation of Scripture, "their interpretations represent significant improvisational moments in the history of interpretation."[5] Improvisational moments in the interpretation of scripture through the paraphrasing of Psalm texts create within the Reformed tradition a space for openness and creativity in the texts sung during worship. Certainly based upon the biblical text and with great care exercised in bringing out faithfully the meaning(s) of the biblical text, the Psalm paraphrases nevertheless set a precedent of not being limited to the literal scriptural text in the singing of the Psalms. By extension, therefore, a modern Reformed/Presbyterian hymnal may very well contain several Psalm paraphrases. *Glory to God: The Presbyterian Hymnal* contains several examples of historical and contemporary Psalm paraphrases.

Three examples from *Glory to God: The Presbyterian Hymnal* illustrate the improvisational creativity that flows from the scriptural text. Example one, set to a tune from the Genevan Psalter, is a setting of Psalm 47. Example two, set to a tune found in the Scottish Psalter of 1615, is a setting of Psalm 91. Example three, set to an Israeli folk melody, is a setting of Psalm 24. Given Calvin's preference for primacy of text over tune in reflecting on music sung in worship, the following examples focus on the texts of the three Psalms.

---

5. Benson, "Improvising Texts," 314.

Example 1

Psalm 47 (NRSV)	Psalm 47 (Paraphrase)
Clap your hands, all you peoples, shout to God with loud songs of joy. For the Lord, the Most High, is awesome, a great king over all the earth. He subdued peoples under us, and nations under our feet. He chose our heritage for us, the pride of Jacob whom he loves. God has gone up with a shout, the Lord with the sound of a trumpet. Sing praises to God, sing praises, sing praises to our King, sing praises. For God is the King of all the earth, sing praises with a Psalm. God is king over the nations, God sits on his holy throne. The princes of the peoples gather as the people of the God of Abraham. For the shields of the earth belong to God; he is highly exalted.	Peoples, clap your hands! Shout to God with joy! King of all the earth is the Lord Most High; all humanity stands in awe of God. With a mighty hand God brings nations low, and beneath our feet casts every foe; Our inheritance comes from God the Lord. God ascends the throne with a joyful cry, And with trumpet sound has gone up on high;Sing your praise to God, sing with joyful voice! Rulers, peoples, now join to serve the Lord, for earth's mighty ones all belong to God, who exalted reigns; now with Psalms rejoice!A
A. Patterson, *Peoples, Clap Your Hands!*	

The contemporary paraphrase follows the biblical text closely while being faithful as a psalm of praise for God's rule over the nations and God's covenant relationship with Israel. The paraphrase also, through its omission of the literal references to pride of Jacob and the God of Abraham, coupled with the use of Lord, as opposed to LORD, encourages a broadening of this text that logically resonates with Christ the King Sunday in the Christian liturgical calendar. While the overall theological organization of *Glory to God: The Presbyterian Hymnal* will be discussed later in the essay, for purposes of this Psalm paraphrase, it is worth noting that this paraphrase of Psalm 47 is placed within a section of the hymnal containing hymns and songs of Christ's Ascension and Rule.

The placement of the Psalms in *Glory to God: The Presbyterian Hymnal* throughout the collection rather than in a dedicated Psalter section, as was the case in the prior hymnal of the Presbyterian Church (U.S.A.) *The Presbyterian Hymnal: Hymns, Psalms, and Spiritual Songs*, reflects two careful considerations and decisions by the Presbyterian Committee on Congregational Song. On one hand, research conducted by the General Assembly Research Services for the benefit of the committee as it began its work revealed that the most underutilized section of the current hymnal was the section of Psalms. While many reasons for this were discussed and considered, what became clear was our desire for the Psalms to be more integral to congregational singing than they had been in the church's recent experience. In addition to musical considerations, the decision to place the Psalms throughout *Glory to God: The Presbyterian Hymnal*, rather than in a separate Psalm section, also required the committee to make decisions on placement that shape on-going experience with and interpretation of the Psalm texts and paraphrases.

Example 2

In the second example, Psalm 91, the paraphrase does not reflect the length and detail of the full Psalm text.

Psalm 91 (NRSV)	Psalm 91 (Paraphrase)
You who live in the shelter of the Most High,	Within your shelter, loving God,
who abide in the shadow of the Almighty,	my refuge and my tower.
will say to the LORD,	I safely walk by day and night
"My refuge and fortress; my God in whom I trust."	beneath your guiding power.
For he will deliver you from the snare of the fowler	
and from the deadly pestilence;	Because I trust in you alone,
he will cover you with his pinions,	no evil shall come near.
and under his wings you will find refuge;	The strong defender of my home,
his faithfulness is a shield and buckler.	with you I have no fear.
You will not fear the terror of the night,	
or the arrow that flies by day,	Your holy angels bear me up
or the pestilence that stalks in darkness,	and keep my feet secure.
or the destruction that wastes at noonday.	Though fierce and angry foes assail,
A thousand may fall at your side,	in you my way is sure.
ten thousand at your right hand,	
but it will not come near you.	As often as I call to you,
You will only look with your eyes	you kindly hear my prayer.

and see the punishment of the wicked.	In times of trouble and distress
Because you have made the LORD your refuge,	I rest in your own care.
the Most High your dwelling place,	
no evil shall befall you,	All those who know your name on earth
no scourge come near your tent.	shall life abundant know.
For he will command his angels concerning you	On all abiding in your love
to guard you in all your ways.	your saving grace bestow.A
On their hands they will bear you up,	
so that you will not dash your foot against a stone.	
You will tread on the lion and the adder, the young	
lion and the serpent you will trample under foot.	
Those who love me, I will deliver;	
I will protect those who know my name.	
When they call to me, I will answer them;	
I will be with them in trouble.	
I will rescue them and honor them.	
With long life I will satisfy them,	
and show them my salvation.	

A. Dunn, *Within Your Shelter.*

As seen by reading the full text of Psalm 91 and the paraphrase, significant images and content are not included in the paraphrase. The rich imagery and content of this particular Psalm has given birth to many paraphrases and congregational songs other than the example selected for this essay. One might be familiar with *On Eagles Wings* by Michael Joncas as a popular example of imagery from this text that is not the primary focus of the selected paraphrase above. Such a narrowing of focus from a lengthy Psalm text is not uncommon. As a musician will draw out certain musical themes when improvising, so a paraphraser will highlight certain textual themes and images.

For Christians, the theme of the verses on which this paraphrase focuses rather naturally resonates with the temptation of Jesus in the wilderness.

This paraphrase is placed in the broad section of *Glory to God: The Presbyterian Hymnal* dedicated to Christ's life. In particular, this paraphrase is placed within the section of hymns and songs of the temptation of Jesus liturgically recalled at the beginning of the season of Lent. The paraphrase of Psalm 91 immediately follows the hymn text *Forty Days and Forty Nights* by George Hunt Smyttan.

Example 3

The third Psalm paraphrase provides an example of editing an existing paraphrase from the previous hymnal by removing a verse. The removal of a verse is an act of improvisation that engages in interpretation. Psalm 24:5–6 (NRSV) says:

> They will receive blessing from the LORD,
> and vindication from the God of their salvation.
> Such is the company of those who seek him,
> who seek the face of the God of Jacob.

The paraphrase of Psalm 24 found in *The Presbyterian Hymnal: Hymns, Psalms, and Spiritual Songs* includes a verse, which has been removed from *Glory to God: The Presbyterian Hymnal*, paraphrasing Psalm 24:5–6 in this way:

> They shall receive forgiveness, and have God's blessing if they
> will search for God, their Savior confessing.[6]

The author's introduction of the word "Savior" resonates easily with Christians. The Psalm text's use of "the God of Jacob," however, seems a less than direct step to the use of Savior. This may be due to the wide use of Psalm 24 with Palm Sunday liturgy in Christian worship. The committee placed this paraphrase in the section of *Glory to God: The Presbyterian Hymnal* associated with service music. As a likely entrance Psalm for Temple worship in Israel, this altered paraphrase's placement in the new hymnal emphasizes the broad use of this Psalm text less directly tied to the particular liturgical occasion of Palm Sunday.

These three brief examples provide a glimpse into the committee's continuation of including Psalms as central to congregational singing for the contemporary Reformed church. Nearly every Psalm in the three year lectionary is included through a variety of musical styles and genres in *Glory to God: The Presbyterian Hymnal*. Paraphrases and their placement

---

6. McKim, *Presbyterian Hymnal*, 177.

throughout the collection, rather than in a Psalter section, invite the church to sing God's praises and reflect on the life of faith with imagination while they continue to shape and form us.

Psalms and Psalm paraphrases, while the foundational material for Reformed congregations in Calvin's time, were not the exclusive content of the early Psalters. Selected biblical canticles such as the *Magnificat* and the *Nunc Dimittis*, in addition to settings of the Lord's Prayer and the Apostles' Creed, remind us that other biblical and non-biblical texts have been sung from the earliest days within the Reformed tradition. Over the centuries that practice has steadily increased. Modern Reformed hymnals contain texts that are biblical, biblically inspired, and products of the lived experience of faith by individuals and communities. Today's hymnals are a rich treasury of texts (and tunes) spanning thousands of years and a vast array of faith communities from all corners of the globe.

Theological Organization

The richness of the texts in *Glory to God: The Presbyterian Hymnal* will collectively inspire, nurture, and sustain the church in the coming decades. As is the case with all hymnals and songbooks, congregations sing only a percentage of the contents over time. Some will become favorites while others will not find wide acceptance or usage. Of the over 800 selections in *Glory to God: The Presbyterian Hymnal*, a particular congregation's regular use of around 200 hymns and songs would likely be normative.

If only about 25 percent of the contents of a hymnal will become familiar to any particular worshipping community, it becomes critical that the theological content of the texts are sufficiently strong enough to positively impact the community. The Presbyterian Committee on Congregational Song, in its "Theological Vision Statement" states that "Collections of Psalms, hymns, and spiritual songs give voice to the church's core beliefs and theological convictions. Their texts are 'compact theology,' and the selection of hymns and songs (both the themes that are emphasized and those that are overlooked) the order in which they are presented, and even the ways they are indexed shape the theological thinking and ultimately the faith and practices of the church."[7]

Taking to heart the idea that hymn and song texts are "compact theology"[8], we considered the context in which the new hymnal would be a resource to the church. In our increasingly post-modern world we under-

---

7. *Theological Vision Statement*, lines 3–8.
8. Ibid., lines 70–71.

stood the new hymnal would be offered "in a world in which trust in human progress has been undermined and eclectic spiritualities often fail to satisfy deep spiritual hungers. It will be used by a church many of whose members have not had life-long formation by Scripture and basic Christian doctrine, much less Reformed theology. It is meant for a church marked by growing diversity in liturgical practice. Moreover, it addresses a church divided by conflicts but nonetheless, we believe, longing for healing and the peace that is beyond understanding."[9]

Post-modern context and realities led to our decision to organize the new hymnal around the overarching theme of salvation history. Hymns and songs will invite singing and reflection on "God's powerful acts of creation, redemption, and final transformation"[10] as well our human response to God's gracious acts. This broad organizational approach reflects the thoroughly Reformed understanding that our sovereign God has acted and continues to act from before and in human history and that the basic human vocation is our response to God. Lifting up this broad theme will speak to those whose "faith in human efforts has been undermined."[11] Salvation history speaks to anxiety, conflict, and frustration in the church and in the world by reminding us that "love has come to earth and that the risen and ascended Christ is alive and active."[12]

The framework of salvation history makes room for the whole of the biblical witness. For those unfamiliar with the Bible, the organization of *Glory to God: The Presbyterian Hymnal* not only teaches the full extent of the biblical narrative, it provides the opportunity for worship to be shaped by it as well. The organization of *Glory to God: The Presbyterian Hymnal* also places the events of the Christian liturgical year, from Advent to Christ the King, in the "wider framework of God's covenantal acts in creation and towards Israel."[13]

Glory to God: The Presbyterian Hymnal's organization, as reflective of a basic Reformed understanding of salvation history, is centered on three primary sections: "God's Mighty Acts," "The Church at Worship," and "Our Response to God." Within each primary section the narrative of salvation history unfolds.

---

9. Ibid., lines 16–22.
10. Ibid., lines 24–25.
11. Ibid., lines 30–31.
12. Ibid., lines 33–34.
13. Ibid., line 48.

The opening section, "God's Mighty Acts," begins with praise of the triune God in the classic text of Reginald Heber's *Holy, Holy, Holy! Lord God Almighty!* Beginning before creation, with the voices of the heavenly host gathered with God in Three Persons, blessed Trinity, the text invites our entrance into and response to the mighty acts of God. The outline continues praise of the triune God with hymns and songs of God's acts in "Creation and Providence" and "God's Covenant with Israel."

Central to salvation history is Jesus Christ. Hymns and songs of Christ's advent, birth, life, passion and death, resurrection, and ascension and reign comprise a major section of the hymnal. The texts of these hymns and songs, as mentioned previously, occur in the wider context of creation, providence, and covenant with Israel. This is also true for the section immediately following Jesus Christ, "Gift of the Holy Spirit."

The hymnal then incorporates hymns and songs concerning the Church. Specifically hymns and songs that speak to the community and mission of the Church, the renewal of the Church, and the Church universal and triumphant. In these hymns and songs the community of faith, grounded in God's mighty acts from creation to the gift of the Holy Spirit, finds its vocation and its hope as an integral part of the narrative of salvation history.

The final three categories in the first primary section of God's Mighty Acts remind the church that God's salvation history is not parochial. The sections of hymns and songs "In the Life of the Nations," "Christ's Return and Judgment," and "A New Heaven and a New Earth," complete the grand re-telling of the biblical narrative and the theological focus on God's activity. Moved by what God has done, the Church is invited and challenged corporately and individually to respond in faith. The third primary section of *Glory to God: The Presbyterian Hymnal,* as mentioned is "Our Response to God." Between the first and third section, however, is the section "The Church at Worship."

For many hymnals and songbooks, music associated with various acts of worship (service music) is rather narrowly identified as *kyries, glorias,* alleluias, doxologies, amens, and Eucharistic responses such as the *Sanctus,* the Memorial Acclamation, and the *Agnus Dei.* These responses are quite often gathered together and placed at the end of a hymnal or songbook. The unintended message may be that these songs and texts are adjunct to worship, or supplemental to more important texts of the church.

This rather narrow view and placement of service music is reconsidered in *Glory to God: The Presbyterian Hymnal.* Service music in the new hymnal includes the elements listed above; however, the section of service music more fully reflects the movement of Christian worship. An organization of

Reformed worship that broadly includes Gathering Around God's Word, Listening to God's Word, and Responding to God's Word is expressed in the flow of this section of the hymnal in hymns and songs of Gathering, Confession, Forgiveness, The Word, Prayer, Baptism, Lord's Supper, and Sending. The placement of this entire section in the heart of the hymnal reminds the Church that it is in the act of worship that the people of God both hear and remember God's mighty acts as well as begin to respond to God.

The third primary section of *Glory to God: The Presbyterian Hymnal* is "Our Response to God." Human response begins with "Praising the Triune God." Hymns and songs of adoration, thanksgiving, and celebrating time (days, seasons, etc.) lead into hymns and songs of "Joining in the Spirit's Work" with hymns and songs of Dedication and Stewardship, Discipleship and Mission, and Justice and Reconciliation. The concluding portion of the hymnal focuses on "Hoping for the Lord's Return" and includes hymns and songs of Lament and Longing for Healing, Living and Dying in Christ, and Trusting in the Promises of God.

Considerations of Language

The organization of *Glory to God: The Presbyterian Hymnal* reflects a Reformed understanding of salvation history. Placement of hymns and songs within the outline, which include biblical texts, paraphrases of biblical texts, biblically inspired texts, and texts that are inspired from individual and communal faith experiences, communicate important Reformed theological themes. As decisions were made on which hymns and songs to include in the collection, a sub-group of members of the Presbyterian Committee on Congregational Song made recommendations to the full committee on the final form of each text that would be included in the collection. Researching each text and its history of use and revision in other hymnals and songbooks was fascinating work. It was also important work. As the Presbyterian Committee on Congregational Song's *A Statement on Language* says, "Language is close to the heart of Christian faith. As befits a community called into being by a God we know as the Word made flesh, we pray, proclaim, teach, comfort, admonish, serve and administer justice with words woven in and through all our actions. Language used in worship has great power. . . Worshipful words joined to worshipful music deeply share the faith and practices of the church."[14]

The theological framework of *Glory to God: The Presbyterian Hymnal*, salvation history, guided considerations of how texts in the collection would

---

14. *A Statement on Language*, lines 73–78.

be used in referring to the people of God and in language used for God. The Presbyterian Church (U.S.A.) along with many other denominations, has become increasingly committed to inclusive language when speaking of humanity. *Glory to God: The Presbyterian Hymnal* reflects that commitment by avoiding language that might stereotype persons according to categories. The committee was sensitive to language that "may have potentially denigrating implications of poetic metaphors. . .especially with respect to persons of color or with disabilities."[15] Also, the committee recognized that the "generic masculine" is "no longer generally understood to include persons of both genders and will therefore be avoided."[16] As was stated in our intention, those texts which did employ the use of the generic masculine were "evaluated individually to determine what alterations, if any, are poetically appropriate."[17]

The language used for God across Christian denominations, however, is not as settled in general as language used for humanity. Because "scripture uses an abundantly rich array of prose and poetry to tell us about God's powerful acts of creation, redemption, and final transformation,"[18] the final collection "reflects the full extent of the biblical narrative and also the full array of biblical language used for God."[19] The biblical narrative, in its fullness, offers to the church imagery that is familiar as well as imagery that will be to those not familiar with the biblical narrative "enriching in their newness."[20]

Perhaps the issue most sensitive to individuals concerning language for God is the use of masculine pronouns for God. Recent hymnals published by other traditions, such as *The New Century Hymnal*, purposefully eliminate nearly all masculine references to God. However, the biblical narrative does employ masculine pronouns and imagery for God. Recognizing that, the Presbyterian Committee on Congregational Song also affirms that "the God who meets us so graciously and intimately in salvation history is at the same time one who is wholly other and beyond gender. Therefore, texts will reflect a strong preference for avoiding the use of male pronouns for God. In evaluating each hymn or song, issues of tradition, theological integrity, poetic quality, and copyright will be considered. The goal is a collection in

---

15. Ibid., lines 115–17.
16. Ibid., lines 110–11.
17. Ibid., lines 112–13.
18. Ibid., lines 91–92.
19. Ibid., lines 99–100.
20. Ibid., line 121.

which traditional hymns and songs are balanced with others that are more gender-neutral or expansive in their reference to God."[21]

Because language issues are at heart theological issues, two specific references to God that are explicitly masculine were preserved in the collection. The first is the use of "Lord," which was used by Greek-speaking Jews who "sought to avoid pronouncing God's holy name, YHWH, by using a replacement term: Lord (*kúrios*). The practice has since been followed by virtually all Christian Bible translations. Rather than being an expression of domination or masculinity, 'Lord' now stands in for the name by which God chose to disclose Godself . . . ."[22]

The use of Lord (*kúrios*) with both Roman and Jewish backgrounds, also forms the basis of one of the oldest confessions concerning Jesus. As the Roman Emperor was called Lord, the "writers of the New Testament confess Jesus to be Lord. They thereby proclaim that not Caesar, but Christ rules the world. On the other hand, in applying the reference to the name of Israel's God to Jesus, the New Testament makes a startling identity statement: that in Jesus this very God has become present among us."[23] Retaining use of "Lord" in *Glory to God: The Presbyterian Hymnal* is a decidedly theological decision.

The final reference intentionally preserved in the collection concerns Trinitarian language. The formula used in baptism—Father, Son, and Holy Spirit—unites Christians across a variety of denominations and communities. "This three-fold name will not be eliminated."[24] The intentional retention of the classic Trinitarian language nevertheless allows for other images and metaphors drawn from the biblical narrative.

From issues of language used for humanity and for God, to the overall organization of the collection, to incorporation of Psalm paraphrases that began with early Reformed Psalters, *Glory to God: The Presbyterian Hymnal*, is a twenty first century hymnal that stands firmly within the Reformed theological tradition. Calvin's insistence on the primacy of text when reflecting on congregational songs in worship received a great deal of attention by the Presbyterian Committee on Congregational Song. As seen in examples from both the Theological Vision Statement and A Statement on Language, Reformed theological themes that arise from the intentional discipline of remembering the primacy of the biblical witness in theological reflection

---

21. Ibid., lines 122–29.
22. Ibid., lines 132–37.
23. Ibid., lines 142–46.
24. Ibid., lines 156–57.

will shape the next generation of Presbyterians in ways that, with integrity, kindle "our hearts to true zeal and eagerness to pray."[25]

Bibliography

Benson, Bruce Ellis. "Improvising Texts, Improvising Communities: Jazz, Interpretation, Heterophony, and the Ekklésia." In *Resonant Witness: Conversations Between Music and Theology*, edited by Jeremy S. Begbie and Steven R. Guthrie, 295–319. Grand Rapids: Eerdmans, 2011.

Bohlman. Philip V., et al. *Music and the American Religious Experience*. New York: Oxford University Press, Inc., 2006.

Burnett, Amy Nelson. *John Calvin, Myth and Reality: Images and Impact of Geneva's Reformer*. Papers of the 2009 Calvin Studies Society Colloquium. Eugene: Cascade, 2009.

Calvin, John. *Institutes of the Christian Religion*. Edited by John T. McNeill. Translated by Ford Lewis Battles. Philadelphia: Westminster Press, 1960.

Dunn, John G. *Within Your Shelter, Loving God*, 1983, revised 1985. Used by permission.

Eicher, David, et al. *Glory to God: The Presbyterian Hymnal*. Louisville: Westminster John Knox, 2013.

Joby, Christopher Richard. *Calvinism and the Arts: a Re-Assessment*. Leuven: Peeters, 2007.

McKim, Linda Jo, et al. *The Presbyterian Hymnal: Hymns, Psalms, and Spiritual Songs*. Louisville: Westminster John Knox, 1990.

Patterson, Joy F. *Peoples, Clap Your Hands*, 1990. Used by permission.

A Statement on Language of the Presbyterian Committee on Congregational Song. Westminster John Knox, 2009. Online: http://www.presbyterianhymnal.org/committeeStatements.html.

Theological Vision Statement of the Presbyterian Committee on Congregational Song. Westminster John Knox, 2009. Online: http://www.presbyterianhymnal.org/committeeStatements.html.

25. Calvin, *Institutes*, 895.

9

Learning to Live with and Love Our Neighbors
Setting Genesis 2 and John 21 in Conversation

—Stephen W. Plunkett

This essay is written with profound respect for David J. Gouwens and with deep gratitude for his service to the church through his teaching ministry. In teaching theology at Brite Divinity School since 1983, he has left an indelible mark on the lives of students across several generations. Dr. Gouwens also has had a positive impact on congregations through teaching theology. The congregation I served for 25 years, St. Andrew Presbyterian Church in Denton, Texas, is a case in point. Dr. Gouwens has taught classes on theology there, and he also provided leadership for a Brite Divinity School event held at our church that celebrated the 500th anniversary of John Calvin's birth. It is a joy to be associated with this Festschrift honoring him.

    The gospel is good news. It is the sheer, unmitigated grace of God given in the life, death, and resurrection of Jesus Christ. In this good news, we are called to a new way of life, a way of life in which what God wants for the world as revealed in scripture becomes our highest calling. God's purpose of love for all creation is the center of the gospel, and it is our privilege and joy to bear witness to God's love for the world by loving the neighbor as Christ has loved us. Given the hard realities of the world today, only the love of God has power enough to enable us to take up this calling. And doing so takes a tremendous courage of conviction.

    Hurt and despair fill our troubled world today. Whether it is the several crises in the Middle East, or the partisan battles endlessly waged in Washington, D. C., or our own broken hearts, the world today is hungry for hope, and this is the context for ministry in which we live. One of the greatest gifts the church can give to the world today is an alternative to despair; yet I often sense that the church itself needs a new reformation before it can make this gift to the world.

The need for reformation grows out of my experience as a pastor for more than three decades. Many people within the church choose to approach their social and political realities on the basis of something other than the gospel of Jesus Christ and God's love for all creation. Given some of the conversations I hear, for many church members, being a Republican or a Democrat comes before being a disciple of Jesus Christ. The specific political labels aren't always used, but the thrust of the conversation is clear: What really matters is whether one is conservative or liberal. Furthermore, my experience is that either (1) people see the religious and political realms as totally distinct, like two cubbyholes that are tidily separate, having little, if anything, to do with each other, or (2) people decide that they are liberal or conservative and then try to make the gospel fit into their pre-conceived ideas. In other words, Jesus may be conservative or liberal depending on one's ideological bent.

Let me make this as down-to-earth and concrete as possible, even at the risk of treading into sensitive territory. I am continually bewildered, for example, by the political posts I see on Facebook from people whom I believe to be well-meaning Christians, much of which does nothing to challenge the partisan environment that is swallowing up our nation and world, but instead furthers a partisan mindset, and even worse, exacerbates a hate-filled enmity among peoples and nations and religions.

Two concrete examples are the jubilation that arose among many Americans, Christians included, when Osama bin Laden was killed in May of 2011, and the deepening of the divide between Christians and Muslims that has occurred between then and now. I accept the fact that Osama bin Laden was responsible for a reprehensible act that was evil to the core, and to be totally honest, I can't say that I was sorry that he was dead. But there is a vast gulf between not being sorry that his death occurred and claiming the bragging rights that many Americans celebrated because of his death. On Facebook, people exclaimed with glee messages such as "We nailed him! He's dead! A wonderful accomplishment for us Americans!" In other words, bin Laden's death was celebrated in a way that made many Americans feel self-righteous. I personally find no justification in the gospel of Jesus Christ for the celebration of his death. In many ways, it was a day of mourning that reminded us of the countless other deaths that occurred because he was so adept at masterminding utter tragedy.

In Romans 12, Paul says, "Bless those who persecute you; bless and do not curse them . . . Do not repay anyone evil for evil . . . Beloved, never avenge yourselves, but leave room for the wrath of God; for it is written, 'Vengeance is mine, I will repay, says the Lord.'" (Rom 12:14, 17a, 19) What about these unavoidably disturbing words of the apostle? Do they get under our skin? Do they make a way into our hearts, our minds, our perspectives about the "other"? Are we honestly to believe that the gospel requires us to bless those who persecute us and to pray for those who malign us? And are we really to assume, as many people do, that because Muslims perpetrated this evil act, then all Muslims are evil and hate the United States and all things American?

These are but two illustrations of the hurt, anguish, and despair that engulf our nation and world in these turbulent times. They also are emblematic of the difficulty many of us have in relating to the neighbor, not to mention deciding which neighbor Jesus had in mind when he said, "You shall love your neighbor as yourself." (Matt 22:39) What I have seen as a pastor is that there are many people in the pew (and pulpit!) who are not accustomed to raising the God-question, and who are afraid to do so, because if it is a pastor, it will likely place him or her in jeopardy with the congregation, and if it is a congregation member, it will place that person at odds with other congregants. Raising the God-question is my purpose in this essay by bearing witness to the good news that God's love for the world empowers us to love others. We find the assurance of this love in 1 John: "God is love, and those who abide in love abide in God, and God abides in them . . . . We love because he first loved us." (1 John 4:16b, 19)

In light of this love, what is the will of God for human relationships? In what manner does the gospel of Jesus Christ call us to live as we deal with people who are different from us, especially those who are radically different? My observation is that, when it comes to matters like the death of bin Laden, relations between Christians and Muslims, additional taxes for the wealthy and large corporations, immigration reform, and taking care for the poor in our land, many Christians simply lay the gospel aside. There may be no more important matter before the church today than learning to live with and love the neighbor who is radically different. The church and its members are called to engage the world not on the basis of partisan politics or conventional wisdom, but *on the basis of the gospel of Jesus Christ and nothing else—on the basis of the God who loves us that we might love others.* No, we should not bury our heads in the sand and pay no attention to the troubled context in which we live, but we *are* to remember that the gospel always comes first. For most of us, this will involve a change of mindset and basic orientation to the "other." It will challenge the way we think and act, and engage us in a way of life that is completely at odds with conventional wisdom and with what many Americans, including Christians, espouse as sacred.

What I propose to do is imagine a conversation between the narrator of the second creation story in Genesis 2 and John 21:15–19 where Jesus tells Peter, if he truly loves him, he will tend his sheep, he will take care of his world. Then later in the essay, I will add another biblical voice from Mark 8 to the conversation.

The way the world is today is not the way God wants the world to be. The way people are adversaries with one another, based on things like race, ethnicity, nationalism, gender, sexual orientation, and economic disparity, is not what God wants, and this gives rise to the possibility, even the hope of a new social reality. In the gospel of Jesus Christ, we glimpse the new thing God is doing, the new world that is already breaking through human hurt and despair.

In his book, *Hope within History*, Walter Brueggemann discusses the new world into which God called the Hebrew slaves as they were being set free from 430 years of bondage in Egypt. Brueggemann speaks about the need in ancient Israel for "a social imagination of a new kind." This is what we need today in the church and world. To this end, Brueggemann speaks of "a transformed sense of reality," and he approaches this transformation by saying that "Israel . . . tells an alternative story, enacts an alternative reality, envisions a different shaping of life."[1] He continues, "In biblical faith, both Old and New Testaments, 'kingdom of God' is the core metaphor for a new social imagination."[2] What the church desperately needs today is fresh renewal in the faith of the gospel, a revitalized awareness that, as disciples of Jesus Christ, we live in a reality rooted in God's purpose to shape our lives with the neighbor. This reality challenges the narrative American culture tells of getting ahead no matter what the cost.

In my experience as a pastor, very few people acknowledge that we are *disciples first*, Americans second; *disciples first*, conservatives or liberals second; *disciples first*, Democrat or Republican second. In fact, our call to discipleship is to reshape decisively the way we understand what it means to be American, Democrat, Republican, conservative, liberal, or any of the other labels that we revel in brandishing. As Miroslav Volf has written, "Much like Jews and Muslims, Christians can never be first of all Asians or Americans, Croatians, Russians, or Tutsis, and then Christians. At the very core of Christian identity lies an all-encompassing change of loyalty, from a given culture with its gods to the God of all cultures. A response to a call

---

1. Brueggemann, *Hope within History*, 21.
2. Ibid., 22.

from that God entails rearrangement of a whole network of allegiances."[3] Yet I find little stomach in the church these days for the rearrangement of allegiances. We often fail to realize that "[t]here is a reality that is more important than the culture to which we belong. It is God and the new world that God is creating, a world in which people from every nation and every tribe, with their cultural goods, will gather around the triune God, a world in which every tear will be wiped away and 'pain will be no more' (Rev 21:3). Christians take distance from their own culture because they give the ultimate allegiance to God and God's promised future."[4]

This is what I mean about raising the God-question. Perhaps our greatest hunger these days is to be transformed by the gospel of love so broad and high and deep that it led to a cross and empty tomb. Instead of the narrow, parochial mindset that often claims us, we are called to live in relationship with our neighbors in a way that resembles the good news that the wideness of God's mercy is like the wideness of the sea. We turn now to the second creation story in Genesis 2 for important clues to the new social reality to which we are called.

Genesis 2: We Were Created for Each Other—Partnership and Vocation

Human beings have been created by God *for each other*. This is the good news that we are privileged to celebrate with joy and gratitude. In the creation story as told in Genesis 2, "the Lord God formed man from the dust of the ground, and breathed into his nostrils the breath of life; and the man became a living being." (Gen 2:7) God was intimately involved in the creation of humankind—in a sense, scooping the dust of the earth together and personally making it into the form of a human being. As Gerhard von Rad writes, "This man, however, formed from the earth, becomes a living creature only when inspired with the divine breath of life . . . . [O]nly this breath when united with the body makes man a 'living creature.'"[5] No claim can be made from the side of human prowess. The man contributes nothing to bringing himself to life. Everything depends upon God. God is the sole creator, and it is the very breath of God breathed into the man's nostrils that brings him to life. This is primarily a story about what God is doing in the world God has made.

---

3. Volf, *Exclusion and Embrace*, 40.
4. Ibid., 50–51.
5. Von Rad, *Genesis*, 77.

Immediately, however, God recognizes the potential loneliness of the man and declares, "I will make him a helper as his partner." (Gen 2:18b) Von Rad continues, "Solitude 'is not good'; man is created for sociability. God's kindliness sees that it would do man good if a helping creature were given to him 'as his opposite,' 'a helpful fit for him.'"[6] But after creating every animal of the field and bird of the air, the need for a helper and partner for the man still remains. "So the Lord God caused a deep sleep to fall upon the man, and he slept; then he took one of his ribs and closed up its place with flesh. And the rib that the Lord God had taken from the man he made into a woman and brought her to the man." (Gen 2:21–22) The sociability and resulting community that God wanted for the human race is now a reality. This is a gift of pure grace. Human community has now entered the realm of God's world; no longer must the man remain in solitude. As Brueggemann says in his commentary on Genesis: "The emergence of woman is as stunning and unpredicted as the previous surprising emergence of the man. The woman is also God's free creation. Now the two creatures of surprise belong together. The place of the garden is for this covenanted human community of solidarity, trust, and well-being. They are *one!* That is, in covenant (2:24). The garden exists as a context for the human community."[7]

Unfortunately, sometimes in the history of the church, a hierarchy has been made of the creation of man and woman—a hierarchy that persists in some quarters of the church even today. That reasoning goes something like this: The man comes first, so the man is top dog. The woman comes second, so she is man's subordinate underling. A close look at the text, however, makes clear that God intends neither hierarchy nor subordination.

When one views the text as a whole, it becomes clear that the sudden appearance of woman is the crowning touch of God's good creation. Her creation is the pinnacle of the story, and it is a moment of supreme joy for the man. When the man says, "'This at last is bone of my bones and flesh of my flesh,'" he is in essence saying, "Thank you, God, this is *perfect!*" The animals and birds were not suitable as a partner for the man, but this incredible creation called "woman" is *perfect* in every way. As Terence Fretheim has pointed out, "For the woman to be called 'helper' . . . carries no implications regarding the *status* of the one who helps; indeed, God is often called the helper of human beings (Ps 121:1–2). The NRSV's 'partner' may capture the note of correspondence more than 'suitable' or 'fitting.' The notion of Eve as 'helper' cannot be collapsed into procreation, not least because the

---

6. Ibid., 82.
7. Brueggemann, *Genesis*, 47.

immediate outcome specified in vv. 24–25 does not focus on this concern; the term does not offer evidence of a hierarchy."[8]

Both the man and the woman possess the "capacity for change and exchange, for mutuality and maturation," as W. Sibley Towner has said. The narrator "is talking about soul mates, people of equal standing, equal merit, and yes, equal pay! . . . [and] is affirming what was affirmed at a later time by the Priestly writer(s) in Gen 1:26, for whom the truest things that could be said about human beings are these things: They are made in the image and likeness of God, and they are male and female."[9] As male and female, they will be intimately linked, both sexually and in other ways of daily life, as the conclusion of chapter 2 makes clear. "The intimate bond between these two original human beings is underscored by *adam*'s last act of naming, which now is not an act of hegemony, but an acknowledgement of kinship and partnership: 'this one shall be called Woman [*ishshah*], for out of Man [*ish*] this one was taken.'"[10] Therefore, in this spirit of companionship, mutuality, and intimacy, "God lets the man's exultation over the woman fill the scene . . ."[11] Truly, she is the crowning touch of creation.

The partnership of the man and woman, however, does not exist in isolation from the world in which they live. In fact, their partnership is united in their God-given vocation. As previously noted, "The Lord God took the man and put him in the garden of Eden to till it and keep it." (Gen 2:15) With the creation of woman, there are now two people to work together in community to till and keep the garden. It was never God's intention that the woman and man sit idly by in the astonishing glory and wonderment of Eden. There is work to be done, and this work is neither a drudgery nor an onerous obligation, but is a participation in what God is doing in their midst.

It is worth noting that even before any other living creatures were created, God has already given the human vocation. This is how prominent the theme of vocation is in the story of creation. I again quote von Rad who suggests that verse 15 is parallel to verse 8; however, verse 15 "indicates man's purpose in being in the garden: he is to work it and preserve it from all damage . . . ."[12] Any ideas about reveling in the wonders of instant fertility or endless sensual enjoyment are missing. "That man was transferred to the garden to guard it indicates that he was called to a state of service and

---

8. Fretheim, *The Book of Genesis*, 352.
9. Towner, *Genesis*, 37.
10. Ibid., 39.
11. Fretheim, *The Book of Genesis*, 352.
12. Von Rad, *Genesis*, 80.

had to prove himself in a realm that was not his own possession."[13] Yes, man and woman were placed in the garden as a gift, but it was a gift with responsibility, a gift with a calling, a gift that required something concrete from the man and woman, namely, taking care of the garden, defending it against all damage, and remembering that it belonged not to themselves, but to God alone. They were to be stewards or managers of God's possession. Brueggemann suggests that "[f]rom the beginning of human destiny, God is prepared to entrust the garden to this special creature. From the beginning, the human creature is called, given a vocation, and expected to share in God's work."[14]

John 21: We Were Created for Each Other—What Does It Mean to Tend Christ's Sheep?

As we turn to the John 21, we find ourselves in the middle of a fish fry for breakfast. No doubt determined to regain some sense of normalcy, Peter announces that he is going fishing, and with one voice, the other disciples reply, "We're going with you!" This fishing expedition, however, leaves much to be desired. In fact, the disciples fish all night only to come up empty-handed. Not long after daybreak, however, Jesus comes and stands on the shore, but this is one of those post-resurrection appearances in which Jesus is not recognized, at least not at first. Nonetheless, Jesus engages his friends in conversation. Realizing that they have nothing to show for a long night's labor, he tells them to cast their net to the right side of the boat where they will surely find some fish. No doubt they had done this several times in the night, all to no good effect, but they decide to give the right side of the boat one more try, and incredibly they have so many fish that they can't haul them all in. Then suddenly it becomes clear to the disciple whom Jesus loved that the mystery person on the shore is Jesus, and he exclaims to Peter, "It is the Lord!" And, at this, Simon Peter tears out, making a beeline for Jesus, whereupon the other disciples follow behind, dragging the net full of fish. And they sit down to an unexpected fish fry where they enjoy the sheer abundance provided by the risen Lord and eat to their hearts' content.

After breakfast, however, Jesus engages Peter in conversation. With Peter's threefold denial of Jesus on the night of his arrest, there is some unfinished business between the two. "Simon son of John," asks Jesus, "do you love me more than these?" Peter says to him, "Yes, Lord; you know that I

---

13. Ibid., 80. In part, von Rad is referencing the work of Hellmut Frey and Benno Jacob.

14. Brueggemann, *Genesis*, 46.

love you." Jesus responds by saying, "Feed my lambs." Then Jesus asks the same question a second time, "Simon son of John, do you love me?" And a second time, Peter responds, "Yes, Lord; you know that I love you." Jesus says to him, "Tend my sheep." The third time Jesus asks Peter the question adds insult to injury. Wounded by Jesus' persistent questioning of his love, Peter responds, "Lord, you know everything; you know that I love you." "Then feed my sheep," replies Jesus.

It is striking—isn't it?—that Jesus doesn't reproach Peter in any way. As Lamar Williamson points out, Jesus neither demands an apology from Peter nor a confession of sin.[15] Instead, he places Peter in a conversation that rehabilitates Peter[16] by requiring him to plumb the very depths of his soul for an honest answer to the question of how deep his love for Jesus is. For those who want Peter to own up to his sin and perhaps apologize to Jesus, Raymond Brown suggests, "Peter's repentance would be implicit in his pathetic insistence on his love and in the anguish that the thrice-repeated question causes him (vs. 17). Instead of boasting that he loves Jesus more than others (15) a chastened Peter rests his case on Jesus' knowledge of what is in his heart (17)."[17]

Arising from Jesus' persistent questioning is Peter's threefold profession of his love for Jesus. And whether the three questions are a parallel to Peter's earlier threefold denial or not, the bottom line is unmistakable: *There is an indelible connection between loving Jesus and taking care of each other.* While there are some who argue that Jesus is talking primarily about the way Peter is to function within the body of believers, namely, as the shepherd of the faithful in Christ's stead, I embrace a broader meaning. In fact, I think Jesus is saying, "If you truly love me, Peter, then you'll take care of my world, you'll take care of all the people in my world, and you will treat the neighbor *as a neighbor and not as an adversary.* If your love for me is as deep as you say it is, then it will be as deep and high and wide as all creation." Williamson hears in these words of Jesus the call to discipleship. Jesus basically says to Peter, "Follow me!"[18] My own paraphrase suggests, "If you love me with all your heart, then follow me into all the hard-hitting realities of life where the redemptive power of the cross and empty tomb have power enough to make a difference for good; follow me in a world where the only thing that can quell human hatred is *my love for the neighbor alive in your*

---

15. Williamson, *Preaching the Gospel of John*, 296.

16. Cf. ibid., 296–98 and to Brown, *The Gospel According to John XIII–XXI*, 1110–1111, for additional comments on the rehabilitation of Peter.

17. Brown, *The Gospel according to John XIII–XXI*, 1111.

18. Williamson, *Preaching the Gospel of John*, 298–300.

love for the neighbor. And don't assume that authentic love for the 'other' is easy; instead, it is selfless."

In this regard, Gail R. O'Day writes that "[Jesus] is reminding Peter of his words in 13:34–35: 'Just as I have loved you, you also should love one another. By this everyone will know that you are my disciples, if you have love for one another.'" [Peter is] "to put his love for Jesus into practice by feeding/tending Jesus' sheep."[19] In other words, says Brown, "to love Jesus is to shape one's life according to Jesus' life . . . . [W]ords of love must be matched by a life of love."[20] Therefore, the entire conversation between Jesus and Peter establishes the fact that "Peter has the devoted love that is of the essence of discipleship,"[21] and he is responding anew to the call of Jesus—"Follow me!"

Learning to Live with and Love Our Neighbors

How will the church find its voice of hope in a world of hurt and despair, and how will it make this hope a gift to the world? I hear in Genesis 2 and John 21 a conversation that goes something like this: Human beings have been created to be in relationship with one another, and in this relationship, we are to take care of and love one another selflessly. We are to be responsive to each other's needs, and we are to help each other keep focused on what God is doing in the world. Furthermore, we are to care for the needs of the entire creation in which God has placed us. We are to preserve creation from damage and exploitation. We are to refrain from raping the earth and its God-given resources as though life on this planet is only about us.

Yet I also hear in this conversation between the two texts a voice that calls us to broaden our idea of who the neighbor is, and we do so by learning from Jesus that the neighbor is everyone on earth, and by coming to the fresh realization that we love and follow Jesus because he first loved us. Specifically, we are to love others the way Jesus does—with the love that will not let us go, the love that is totally unconditional and generous and universal in scope. This means that people who are different from me are still children of God who deserve to be treated with the same dignity and respect with which I want to be treated—people with different backgrounds, people with a different sexual orientation than my own, people who come from vastly different national and personal histories and who seem to be as different from me as different can be. And we are to join with everyone in the human family who is willing and able to protect the creation God has entrusted into

---

19. O'Day, *The Gospel of John*, 361.
20. Ibid., 364.
21. Brown, *The Gospel according to John XIII–XXI*, 1111.

our care as stewards and managers. This is the vocation God gave to the first woman and man, it is the vocation Jesus Christ gave to Peter, and it is *our vocation*, as we answer the call that comes in each new day—"Follow me!"

This is at least a provisional answer to what it means to raise the God-question in a world where so many people, Christians included, live for themselves and themselves alone.[22] The American Way, after all, is much more interesting than the gospel, and not nearly as embarrassing in a secular world with which we desperately want to be in sync. American culture doesn't challenge our values the way the gospel does. It doesn't call into question our vision of life, our wants, and our hopes for the future. We live in a world where the dominant voices urge us to go with the flow rather than against the grain of cultural values. As Volf writes, "Our coziness with the surrounding culture has made us so blind to many of its evils that instead of calling them into question, we offer our own versions of them—in God's name and with a good conscience."[23] But Christians are called to be different and always willing to live against the grain, because this is what it means to follow the Christ who relentlessly called into question so-called sacred truth and who lived against the grain of "religious" values by hanging out with the likes of tax collectors and prostitutes and other notorious sinners, all to the outrage of the religious experts.

There is, however, a part of the post-resurrection conversation in John 21 to which we have not yet come, and here we apprehend the substance of selfless love for the neighbor. After his final "Feed my sheep," Jesus says to Peter, "Very truly, I tell you, when you were younger, you used to fasten your own belt and to go wherever you wished. But when you grow old, you will stretch out your hands, and someone else will fasten a belt around you and take you where you do not wish to go." (He said this to indicate the kind of death by which he would glorify God.) After this he said to him, 'Follow me.'" Verse 19a is an explicit prediction of Peter's martyrdom. According to O'Day, "[M]any of the early church theologians interpreted OT references to stretching out one's arms (e.g., Exod 17:12; Isa 65:2) as a foreshadowing of the crucifixion."[24] Therefore, some scholars take the expression "stretch out your hands" in verse 18b as a reference to Peter's death by crucifixion. The Greek verb for "fasten your belt" in the NRSV literally means "to gird." While it's meaning here is unclear, "it may contain an allusion to the

---

22. For an example of Calvin's confrontation with living for oneself alone, see the essay in this volume by Warner Bailey.

23. Volf, *Exclusion and Embrace*, 36.

24. O'Day, *The Gospel of John*, 861.

binding of criminals to the cross or the fettering of criminals on their way to execution."[25]

One thing, however, is unmistakable. "The wording of the interpretive comment at v.19a is identical to the commentary on the manner of Jesus' death at 12:33 and 18:32. The link between Peter's death and Jesus' death is made even more explicit by the phrase 'by which he would glorify God.'"[26] The final "Follow me" of the text becomes an invitation for Peter to die as Jesus did. Jesus, the Good Shepherd, was willing to lay down his life for his sheep, as we see in 10:11 and 10:15, and the disciples have been commanded to enact the same love for one another. John completes this part of the conversation by pointing to Peter's ultimate fidelity to the commandment to love.[27] In the words of Augustine, "Our Lord's questioning and Peter's confession of love ends in the call for a selfless love that focuses on God and the neighbor rather than oneself. Peter was being called on to love the sheep even to the point of giving up his own life, even as his Lord had done."[28]

In this regard, there is yet another conversation between Jesus, Peter, and the other disciples that informs this discussion. In Mark 8:27–38, Jesus knows that the grapevine is abuzz with gossip about him, so he asks the disciples what the word on the street is. They reply, "Some people think you are John the Baptist, but others say you are Elijah or one of the other prophets." But then Jesus cuts right to the chase and asks, "But who do *you* say that I am?" To which Peter replies, "You are the Messiah, the Christ, God's anointed one; you are the one for whom we have been waiting." This is now what one might call a teachable moment. So Jesus tells them what it will mean *for him* that he is the Christ. He will undergo great suffering, be rejected by the religious leaders, be killed, and after three days rise again. Peter is stunned and immediately takes Jesus aside and rebukes him. Jesus, however, will hear none of it, and even goes so far as to equate Peter with the great adversary, Satan. "Get behind me, Satan!" he insists.

But then Jesus tells the disciples that his being the Christ will have concrete ramifications not only in *his* life, but also in *their* lives. He calls a crowd together with the disciples and issues the call that is before the church this very day: "If any want to become my followers, let them deny themselves and take up their cross and follow me. For those who want to save their life will lose it, and those who lose their life for my sake, and for the sake of the

---

25. Ibid., 861.
26. Ibid., 861.
27. Ibid., 862.
28. Augustine, in Elowsky and Oden, *Ancient Christian Commentary on Scripture*, New Testament IVb, 386.

gospel, will save it. For what will it profit them to gain the whole world and forfeit their life?" (Mark 8:34–36) When heard in connection with Jesus' prediction of Peter's martyrdom, we come uncomfortably close to what it means to love the neighbor selflessly.

There are living illustrations all around us, reminding us that loving the neighbor selflessly is indeed possible. Again, it is possible because Christ first loved us, and in the Spirit of the living Christ, we willingly respond to his call. There are even those in recent history who have become martyrs themselves in taking up their cross to follow Jesus. O'Day writes: "Martin Luther King, Jr., and Bishop Oscar Romero are the most obvious and well-known examples of love that knew no limits, but when one pays careful attention, one regularly notices stories of Christian disciples who give their lives in love: nuns and priests who have stayed at their ministries in Central America and war-torn Eastern Europe, knowing that it will cost their lives; doctors and nurses in hospitals and health-care facilities in impoverished and embattled countries around the world who will not leave those for whom they care; martyrs of religious persecution across the globe."[29]

Martyrs, however, are not the only ones who have borne faithful witness to the gospel. I think, for example, of André and Magda Trocmé and their sacrificial offering of their lives during World War II. André was an ordinary pastor, and Magda an ordinary pastor's wife, yet with the help of other loving people, they sheltered over 5,000 Jewish children and other refugees in and around the small French mountain village Le Chambon, saving them from certain death in the gas chambers. When the government learned of their activities, they demanded that the Trocmés disclose the whereabouts of all the Jews they were hiding. They refused, and André was jailed, because he had heard the call to take up his cross follow the Christ who said, "Those who want to save their life will lose it, and those who lose their life for my sake, and for the sake of the gospel, will save it." As it turned out, when the arresting officers arrived at the parsonage to take André to jail, it was suppertime and Magda has just prepared the evening meal. So she invited the arresting officers to sit down at the table and eat with them before they took her husband away. As the Trocmés and arresting officers ate their dinner, members of the Trocmés' congregation gathered outside the parsonage to sing "A Mighty Fortress Is Our God," bearing witness to the costly love of Jesus Christ.[30]

To be sure, André and Magda acted as they did because they loved their neighbors and understood that their relations with both Jews and

---

29. O'Day, *The Gospel of John*, 865.
30. Taken from the story told by Hallie, *Lest Innocent Blood Be Shed*.

government officials were to be faithful acts of discipleship. Upon their arrival in Le Chambon in 1934, André began preaching the God-given dignity of all human beings. Instead of accepting the collaboration of the Vichy government with the Nazis, "Trocmé encouraged the Chambonnais to refuse to 'give up their consciences, to participate in hatred, betrayal and murder.' The community responded by reaching out to their Jewish brothers and sisters."[31] When confronted with what was happening to the Jews, Trocmé "asserted that he 'did not know what a Jew was; he knew only men.' Trocmé viewed the human person as being reflective of God's generous love in creation. He attested that the main distinction among people is between those who believe that those in need are as precious as they themselves are, and those who do not believe this. Trocmé argued that 'decent' people who fail to respond to the humiliation and destruction of others around them because of indifference or cowardice pose the most dangerous threats to the world. Aware of the immediate and real suffering around him, André Trocmé regarded assisting Jews as part of God's work."[32]

I think also of Nelson Mandela and Desmond Tutu, neither of whom sought retaliation or revenge—only peace—when apartheid in South Africa was dismantled. And there are countless others today who, in their one small part of the world, live sacrificially for the neighbor in the daily choices they make.

None of this falls under the category of the conventional wisdom of our age. This is not something we hear politicians, or other public figures, or frankly, many preachers talking about. It's not what sells tickets. It isn't popular. It doesn't draw a crowd. All of which is to say that we Christians are indeed called to be different, not better than anyone else, but different. We have an alternative story, an alternative reality, an alternative vision of life to give the world. We are people whom God calls to live the story of the cross and the empty tomb, and to say with Peter, "Yes, Lord, you know that I love you." The alternative to despair that the church is called to share with the world is the love of Jesus Christ given willingly, joyously, selflessly, and even sacrificially to the neighbor—even the neighbor who is radically different—a concept rarely considered in our culture.

Inevitably, there comes a time when living with the neighbor is difficult. Are we really called by God to love the neighbor who is hard to love, the neighbor who chooses not to love us? Are we indeed supposed to love the "other" who comes from a culture of which we are suspicious, whose beliefs are entirely different from our own, and whose natural inclination is to be

---

31. Therieult, "André Trocmé and Le Chambon," lines 17–20.
32. Ibid., lines 28–37.

suspicious of us because we ourselves are alien to her or his experience? And the gospel answers: Yes, because to do so is to follow our crucified and risen Lord. To do so is to love the neighbor as Christ has loved us. And doing so grows out of the realization that every person on this planet is our neighbor.

Many people flatly reject this affirmation today. If Muslims are my neighbors, then surely they aren't neighbors I am called to love the same way I love people who are like me. It simply does not fit into the dominant worldview that God calls us to love every person on earth so indiscriminately. And why would we freely choose to be so generous with others? *Because this is how generous God is with us!*

Such ideas do not play too well in the part of the Bible belt where I once lived. Christians today crave a much more moderate faith. We want a religion that doesn't ask too much of us, but gives us everything on our wish list. We want a God that suits us, a religion in which the very love of the gospel is conceived in terms of easy charity—a hand-out here and a hand-out there, a turkey for a needy family at Thanksgiving and a nice juicy ham at Christmas—in other words, the kind of charity that doesn't cost us anything in the long run, the kind of charity that doesn't impinge on our lifestyle, and that is carefully calculated so that it doesn't keep us from doing the things we really want to do (i.e., spend money on ourselves). But the gospel has nothing to do with that kind of cheap, easy charity. The Lord of the church has no interest in or stomach for moderation in religious matters. Jesus Christ is interested in our full-bodied love for the neighbor.

There simply is no escaping the gospel's call to take care of the neighbor, and furthermore, to accept the radical notion that all God's children are our neighbors. Jesus Christ is no one's private domain, but all kinds of people have been given a place at the table. Volf writes that the notion of embracing others involves "the will to give ourselves to others and 'welcome' them, to readjust our identities to make space for them, . . . [and that we are to do this] prior to any judgment about others, except that of identifying them in their humanity. The will to embrace precedes any 'truth' about others and any construction of their 'justice.' This will is absolutely indiscriminate and strictly immutable; it transcends the moral mapping of the social world into 'good' and 'evil.'"[33]

Clearly, this all sounds rather outlandish and utterly foolish. Yet Paul once wrote that "God chose what is foolish in the world to shame the wise; God chose what is weak in the world to shame the strong; God chose what is low and despised in the world, things that are not, to reduce to nothing things that are, so that no one might boast in the presence of God." (1 Cor

---

33. Volf, *Exclusion and Embrace*, 29.

1:27–29).The gospel is outlandish and foolish indeed—outlandish and foolish enough to get Jesus Christ nailed to a cross.

Bibliography

Brown, Raymond E. *The Gospel according to John XIII-XXI*. The Anchor Bible. Garden City, New York: Doubleday, 1970.
Brueggemann, Walter. *Genesis*. Interpretation: A Bible commentary for Teaching and Preaching. Atlanta: John Knox, 1982.
———. *Hope within History*. Atlanta: John Knox, 1987.
Elowsky, Joel C., and Thomas C. Oden. *Ancient Christian Commentary on Scripture. New Testament IVb*. Downers Grove, Illinois: InterVarsity, 2007.
Fretheim, Terence R. *The Book of Genesis*. The New Interpreter's Bible. Vol. 1. Nashville: Abingdon, 1994.
Hallie, Philip P. *Lest Innocent Blood Be Shed*. New York: Harper & Row, 1979.
O'Day, Gail R. *The Gospel of John*. The New Interpreter's Bible. Vol. 9. Nashville: Abingdon, 1995.
Theriault, Anne. "André Trocmé and Le Chambon," No pages. Online: http://www.catholicpeacefellowship.org/nextpage.asp?m=2554.
Towner, W. Sibley. *Genesis*. Westminster Bible Companion. Louisville: Westminster John Knox, 2001.
Volf, Miroslav. *Exclusion and Embrace*. Nashville: Abingdon, 1996.
Von Rad, Gerhard. *Genesis*. The Old Testament Library. Philadelphia: The Westminster, 1961.
Williamson Jr., Lamar. *Preaching the Gospel of John*. Louisville: Westminster John Knox, 2004.

10

World-Filling Word

The extra Calvinisticum and Interfaith Dialogue

—Cynthia L. Rigby

As many of my colleagues in this volume note, David Gouwens is a preeminent Kierkegaard scholar. While the chapter before you plays with how a particular insight of Calvin might create a space for interfaith dialogue, its backdrop is even more Kierkegaardian than it is Calvinistic. As the leader of a marginalized Christian community in 16th century Geneva, Calvin's concern in relation to the making of faith claims was not to foster humility as much as it was to inspire confidence in and conviction about "God's benevolence toward us, founded upon the truth of the freely-given promise in Christ."[1] Kierkegaard, by contrast, was chagrined by the way members of the 19th century Danish church bandied about their self-identification as "Christian" without seeming to make any firm commitment to being active disciples of Jesus Christ. In reaction to this, Kierkegaard himself would not call himself "a Christian," but would say, instead, that he was "in the process of becoming one."[2] It is in this spirit of being humble, as well as confident, when it comes to our faith—also consistent (by the way) with the Reformed commitment to "always being reformed according to the Word of God"— that I embark on the ensuing study. What can Christians *learn* as well as *share*, I wonder, through conversation with those of other faiths?

---

1. This is an excerpt from Calvin's definition of faith, found in his *Institutes of the Christian Religion*, 3.2.7. Unless otherwise indicated, all citations from Calvin's *Institutes of the Christian Religion* are taken from the McNeill edition.

2. For more on Kierkegaard's understanding of what it looks like to "become a Christian," see Gouwens, *Kierkegaard as Religious Thinker*.

A major conundrum for confessing Christians who seek to be engaged, relevant, and influential in a global world is: How is it possible to maintain a distinctive Christian identity while at the same time listening and learning from the faith perspectives of others? Unfortunately, it is too often the case that Christian believers assume they have to choose between speaking with conviction about the specifics of their faith *or* speaking very generally about what they believe. Those who choose passionately to bear witness to the centrality of Jesus Christ are frequently seen as too rigid or judgmental; those who choose to be "open" to other spiritual paths and conflicting beliefs, on the other hand, are commonly viewed as relativistic and uncommitted.

The argument presented here rejects the assumption that embracing Jesus Christ as "the Way, the Truth, and the Life"[3] is incommensurable with engaging a range of spiritual experiences. On the contrary, it suggests that Christians can speak boldly about Jesus Christ as the Savior of the world while at the same time conversing with, learning from, and even being changed in their understandings by those who think differently. It shows how this "centered, but open" posture toward interfaith (and interpath[4]) dialogue is consistent with what Christians believe in one (but not the only) possible way: by revisiting the Reformed concept known as the *extra Calvinisticum* and drawing out its implications.[5]

The *extra Calvinisticum* is the idea (originating with John Calvin) that the Word who became flesh in the particular, historical person of Jesus Christ is at the same time also ubiquitous. That is, that the Word wholly incarnate in Jesus Christ is also "extra," or "outside" of him, filling the cosmos.[6] The *extra Calvinisticum* reminds us that nothing can exhaust the Word of God—not even the Son, Jesus Christ! The Word is known truly in him, and at the same time is yet unknowable by virtue of any creaturely capacity. The Word is "enfleshed" (*logos ensarkos*) therefore, but not completely emptied into Jesus of Nazareth's fleshly existence (*logos asarkos*).

---

3. See John 14:6. All Scripture verses come from the New Revised Standard Version unless otherwise indicated.

4. "Interpath dialogue" is a term sometimes used to emphasize that those included in the conversation may or may not associate with particular faith traditions. It might include, for example, those who self-identify as "atheists," "seekers," "spiritual, but not religious," "religiously unaffiliated," or "nones."

5. This essay joins others in this volume which explore the engagement of Christian faith with the multi-faith and secular worlds. See essays by Don Pittman, Kenneth Cracknell, and Nancy Ramsay.

6. Calvin himself notes that, in the Eucharist, "the whole Christ is present, but not in his wholeness" (*Institutes* 4.17.30).

Calvin exults that this is "something marvelous," that "the Son of God descended from heaven in such a way that, without leaving heaven, he willed to be borne in the virgin's womb, to go about the earth, and to hang upon the cross; yet he continuously filled the world even as he had done from the beginning!"[7] What is so "marvelous," here, for Calvin, is not that the Word was simply born of Mary or died on the cross, but that the Word entered fully into existence with us without "leaving heaven."[8] In Calvin's thinking, this is what made it possible to confess Jesus as "fully human" without compromising on his full divinity, enabling him to be the "one true Mediator between God and humanity."[9]

I am suggesting, here, that the *extra Calvinisticum* is marvelous for a reason Calvin could not have imagined (or at least could not have imagined in "full color") from his historical vantage point: that it invites us to conceptualize (in our now more global, multi-faith, context) how we might testify concretely to the event of Jesus Christ without presuming we have exhaustive understanding of all God is saying and doing in the world. It shows us how we can speak with conviction and listen with humility. It suggests, in fact, that this is what it looks like to be "becoming Christians"[10] as those grounded in the life of a Savior who is both "fully human and fully divine."

Before going further, let me assure the reader the technical language and arguments introduced to this point are meant only to deepen and advance the concrete concern that Christians find ways to speak with conviction about what they believe, while at the same time remaining open to the spiritual insights of others. While strong arguments for the importance of living in a creative tension between one's own positions and the perspectives of others have been made by experts in psychological and societal well-being,[11] the discussion in this chapter is doctrinal in orientation. In other words, the goal is to show how speaking with both conviction and openness is grounded in the most fundamental Christological confessions of the church, and in the way the Reformed tradition has interpreted these

---

7. *Institutes* 2.13.4.

8. This is a point the Lutherans could not quite swallow, for reasons that will be discussed further, below.

9. See 1 Tim 2:5. "Mediator" is a term Calvin commonly uses to reference Christ as "fully human and fully divine" (consistent with the statement made at Chalcedon in 451).

10. Kierkegaard's words, as referenced in the comment opening this chapter.

11. For example, cultural psychologist Richard A. Schweder argues that "the knowable world is incomplete if seen from any one point of view, incoherent if seen from all points of view at once, and empty if seen from nowhere in particular" (in *Why Do Men Barbeque?* 300).

confessions. It is my hope that Christians might find ways to speak and act in the world that are both bold and open not only because to live in such ways is more gratifying, pleasant, effective, and influential, but because to live with bold openness, or open boldness, is precisely what it "looks like" to live as a disciple of the world-filling Word made flesh. In other words, I am setting out to show why those who are disciples of Jesus Christ—those who abide in him, and he in them (John 15)—do not have the option of being *either* bold proclaimers of the truth or humble seekers in the face of what is *not* known, but rather are called simultaneously and fully to be both.

The argument is developed in three parts. First, it engages the meaning of and debate surrounding the *extra Calvinisticum*, suggesting that attending to it creates a conceptual space for Christians to engage in interfaith dialogue even as they remain faithful to their identity in Christ. Second, it reflects on what it might look like to enter that conceptual space as disciples of Jesus Christ, suggesting how our participation in the one who is fully human and fully divine allows us to be at once both faithful witnesses and humble seekers in our interfaith discourse. Third, it briefly illustrates what it might look like to confess Jesus as Lord in the context of being in open dialogue with people of multiple faiths, including those who might not even identify as people of faith.[12]

I. The Character of the Incarnate, Ubiquitous Word

In order to understand how the so-called "*extra Calvinisticum*" might clear a space for productive dialogue, it will be useful to review how it came to be developed as a concept.

First, it originated in the 16th century as a disparaging term directed by the Lutherans at the Reformed. It named something true that Calvin had insisted on in that era's debates about the Lord's Supper—namely, that the *logos* ("Word") exists "outside of" (*extra*) the historical figure Jesus of Nazareth even as it is fully incarnate in him. The Lutherans couldn't imagine how Calvin could think such a thing, since by their way of reasoning to say the *logos* is "outside" of Jesus Christ is necessarily to compromise on the fact that God is truly with us in the historical event of Jesus Christ. How *did* Calvin uphold the truth that "God is with us" in Christ while at the same time insisting on the *extra Calvinisticum*, and why did he think this was so important?

---

12. I am thinking, in particular, of the "Nones" (religiously nonaffiliated) the "spiritual but not religious," and even the "New Atheists" (to the degree they are willing to converse with people of faith).

Some scholars emphasize, by way of explanation, that Calvin's concern, following the Chalcedonian Statement of 451, was to shape an understanding of who Jesus Christ is that does not compromise in any way on the sovereignty of God. According to this line of thinking, to hold the idea that the person of Jesus Christ exhausts the preexistent divine *logos* is to compromise on the divine mystery. Who are we to imagine we know the sum of who God is, even in Jesus Christ? As the Reformers were fond of reminding us, "the finite is not capable of the infinite" (*finitum non capax infiniti*). To remember that the Word that fully indwells Jesus Christ is also ubiquitous is to respect the fact that God's greatness is unsearchable.[13]

As plausible as this way of thinking through Calvin's logic on this point might seem to be, there is another reason why he emphasizes that the *logos* is not completely exhausted in the person of Jesus Christ. While the first reason was to respect the character of God as omniscient, the second is more focused on honoring the character of humanity. As the fully human one who is fully divine, Jesus is the incarnation of the world-filling *logos* apart from which nothing was made that was made (John 1:2). As the fully divine one who is fully human, Jesus is the incarnation of the *logos* who is known not in abstraction from, but through identification with this particular person in this particular time. For Calvin, to take seriously the full humanity of Christ is to value and ponder the implications of what it means to be human.[14] In the person of Christ, it means refusing to emphasize the *communicatio idiomatum* ("the communication of properties") to such an extreme that what is essential to the nature of humanity is compromised by its association with divinity. In other words, Calvin thought it is not only the case that the limitation inherent in Jesus Christ as the "fully human" one fails to compromise his full divinity (which remains unlimited); it is also the case that the property of ubiquity associated with Jesus Christ's divine nature does not ruin, so to speak, his fully human nature. For Calvin, to say that Jesus Christ is fully human means that he is in some sense—and for all eternity—physically located in one place at a time.

Reflecting, for a moment, on the debate about the Eucharist in relation to this, Calvin insists that, though the body and blood of Christ are "really present" in the bread and the cup of the Eucharistic feast, they are not "locally" present. They are present by virtue of the "vivifying work of the Holy Spirit," who joins the bread and the cup to the body and blood of Jesus

---

13. See Ps 145:3.

14. For another instance of Calvin's embrace of humanity see the essay by Warner Bailey in this volume.

Christ,[15] who is "seated at the right hand of God the Father Almighty."[16] In arguing this way, Calvin is interested in respecting the confession that Jesus Christ is fully human and fully divine, without compromising on either of the two natures. Again, he sees the preservation of the integrity of both natures as essential to upholding Christ in his office as Mediator. Christ is, according to Calvin, a mediator who is not neutral, but who is a full-fledged member of both parties between which he mediates. Understanding that Jesus Christ's body is not locally present in the elements, therefore, is for Calvin essential to remembering that God has truly entered into our limited human condition.

Interestingly, Calvin is so keen on honoring the full humanity of the one in whom the *logos* is fully incarnate that he even goes out of his way to argue that Jesus is fully embodied post-resurrection. For example, while in the post-resurrection appearance of Jesus recounted in John 20 the text says Jesus "appears in the midst" of the disciples gathered in the Upper Room, Calvin in his commentary on John insists that Jesus did not pass through a "shut door." He is specifically interested in emphasizing that Jesus is physically located in his glorified state, dismissing the idea that Jesus is at this point a "spirit" who passes through the door as "Papist."[17] This is because, he reasons, Jesus is risen *in body* and bodies (unlike "spirits") do not pass through doors that have not been opened.

Despite the fact that Calvin goes out of his way to emphasize and even to defend Christ's eternal, bodily existence, his understanding of the *extra Calvinisticum* becomes associated, as the history of Calvinism unfolds, with attempts to minimize the implications that follow from "the humanity of God" in favor of promoting the idea that God remains inscrutable. Theologians such as Karl Barth, and then later William Placher,[18] see this as deeply problematic and antithetical to the best of Calvin's intentions. If the Word in its ubiquity is seen as in any way separate from the Word as it is incarnate in Jesus Christ, the risk is (as it was with Nestorianism in the 5th century) that

---

15. Calvin says, for example, that "the flesh of Christ is vivifying bread" and that "the bond of this sacred union" is the "secret and incomprehensible virtue of the Holy Spirit" (in Calvin's "Last Admonition to Joseph Westphal," *Tracts Containing Treatise on the Sacrament*, 346–495, 374).

16. Calvin argues, in his "Second Defense of the Sacraments," "it is not necessary for Christ to move his body from its place in order to infuse his vivifying virtue into us." (In *Tracts Containing Treatise on the Sacraments*, 245–345, 285.)

17. *Calvin's Commentary on John*, 2 vols.

18. See, for example, Placher, *Domestication of Transcendence*.

we will have a "double Christ"[19] through whom God is not known because it is not God who is truly with us.

While Barth sees value in affirming the *extra Calvinisticum*, he insists that to do so must never mean the Word may be thought of apart from the historical figure, Jesus of Nazareth. "In the act of God in time which corresponds to . . . the eternal decree that God be with us," Barth explains, "when the Son of God became this man, He ceased to all eternity to be God only, receiving and having and maintaining to all eternity human essence as well."[20] For Barth, it is essential that we understand "creatureliness . . . is placed at the side of the Creator" and that we are, therefore, "with God."[21] And the God we are with is "distinguished from all the idols imagined and fashioned . . . by the fact that they are not God in the flesh, but products of human speculation on naked deity."[22] In other words, to insist that the *extra Calvinisticum* does not separate who God is in God's being (as the ubiquitous *logos*) from who God is in God's appearing (as the Word made flesh) is to be open to knowing who God is as the one who is at once both known and unknowable.

Notice that, as Barth understands it, to claim the ubiquity of the Word inherent to the *extra Calvinisticum* is not to subtract from the Word's capacity to speak particularly, through a particular person and to particular people. In fact, the general, cosmos-filling character of the Word seems to work in tandem with its concrete, knowable character. Perhaps it is not too much of a stretch to invoke the words of the psalmist in Psalm 139 to make this point. The psalmist knows God is with him—that God knit him together in his mother's womb and in fact "knows every day of his life before one of them came to be." But this knowledge is available precisely because it comes from the outside *to* him: "If I go up to the heavens, you are there!" he testifies. "If I travel to the farthest limits of the sea, even there your hand will guide me! If I try to hide in the darkness, you will discover me!"[23] It is precisely because God is omnipresent that the particular psalmist is known and given the capacity to know. Isaiah 40:6 offers similar testimony to the relationship between God's power over all and God's claim on specific ones: "Lift up your eyes on high and see: Who created these? The One who brings out their host and numbers them, calling them all by name; because God is great in strength, mighty in power, not one is missing." While those with

19. Sumner, "The Twofold Life of the Word," 42–57, 50.
20. Barth, *Church Dogmatics* (hereafter *CD*) IV/2, 100.
21. Ibid., 100–101.
22. Ibid., 101.
23. I am here paraphrasing verses from Ps 139:8–13.

great power are often thought to be apathetic toward those who have far less, this is not the case of God. It is *because* God is "great in strength" that "not one is missing." The magnitude of God's presence and power make it possible for each particular one to be claimed.

When reading Calvin's theology, Marilynne Robinson notices that the particularity of God's self-revelation and claim on us is grounded in God's cosmic presence and inexhaustible power. Robinson describes this dynamic as the "conceptual problem" that drives all of Calvin's theological pursuits. "The Creator is, by his reckoning, utterly greater than any conception we can form of his creation," she writes, "and at the same time free, present, just, loving, and intimately attentive to fallen humankind, collectively and one by one." "It is as if we were to propose," Robinson adds, "that that great energy only exists to make possible our miraculously delicate participation in it."[24]

Robinson's "only," in the preceding sentence, is somewhat startling. We might understand the omnipotent God to self-limit in ways that "allow" our participation, but here it is not the *limiting* of the divine energy that makes possible creaturely participation, but the free exercise of it in all of its fullness. Few read Calvin, or the Reformed tradition, as carefully and benevolently as Robinson does. It is indeed the case that Calvin and Barth showcase the freedom, transcendence, and sovereignty of God not only to honor the one who is beyond all we can ask or imagine,[25] and not mainly to marvel that God would hold back to make room for us, but also because, in the person of Jesus Christ, it becomes clear that the great energy of God includes us in the divine life, work, and promise.

Where are we left in relation to inter-faith dialogue, at the close of these several pages of ruminations on the *extra Calvinisticum*? First, and by way of review thus far: I have shown that the Reformed tradition, following Calvin and Barth, has always been faithful to the truth that we cannot and do not have exhaustive knowledge of the infinite God, even in Jesus Christ. At the same time, it also insists that God's self-revelation in Christ need be embraced as true to who God is in God's own life, else it is not *God* we know in Jesus, but merely something God went out of God's way to do. Finally, the most radical hypothesis put forward is that somehow it is the magnitude of God (the divine ubiquity; transcendence; freedom; sovereignty; omnipotence) that upholds the particular character of the message as well as the corresponding claim on those who are given this message, in their particularity.

---

24. From Robinson's preface to *John Calvin: Steward of God's Covenant*, xvi.
25. See Eph 3:20.

The conceptual space for interfaith dialogue created by this is one in which we think about the Word being "bigger than we can even imagine" and "painfully particular" all at the same time. I will explore what this might look like further in the section that follows, considering how Christians might center their understanding of the Word in the explicit event of Jesus Christ while at the same time remaining open to the fact that those who do not subscribe to that event may still very well be privy to the same Word Christians believe has become flesh in him.

II. Jesus Christ, Savior of All But Especially of Some[26]

I Timothy 4:10 references Jesus Christ both as the "Savior of all people" and as the "Savior, especially, of those who believe." From the vantage point of the conceptual space created by the *extra Calvinisticum*, it seems possible that a Christian could claim to know God's Word in the particular figure, Jesus Christ, while at the same time acknowledging that, because the Word is ubiquitous, Jesus Christ might also be understood to be the Savior of those who do not believe in him in the way Christians do.[27] There are a myriad of New Testament texts that seem to open in this direction. In Acts 17, for example, Paul resonates with the spiritual quest of the Athenians, sharing the story of Christ with them as colleagues on the way. In John 10 Jesus uses the metaphor of sheep responding to the voice of their shepherd. While very clear about the fact that his (special) sheep will follow the shepherd because they "know his voice," Jesus suddenly asserts that there are those who "do not belong to the fold" that also will follow. "I must bring them also, and they will listen to my voice," Jesus explains (no doubt to the consternation of the special sheep who want him all to themselves!).[28]

The point of referencing these passages is not that we need to develop some new theory of the "anonymous Christian"[29] or to assess to what degree

---

26. See 1 Tim 4:10.

27. This would not mean those of us who are Christian have a way of secretly naming or identifying those who are not (Karl Rahner once came under fire, along these lines, for his "theory of the anonymous Christian"). Rather, it means that we who are Christian, within the limits of our Christian symbol system, might well understand another person's religious experience as an experience of the Word even if these are not the words/symbols they themselves would use to describe themselves.

28. John 10:11–16.

29. The "theory of the anonymous Christian" is the idea of Karl Rahner that there are those who are Christian who simply are not aware of it. While intending to be open and inclusive, Rahner inadvertently offended those who did not have interest in self-identifying as Christian. My proposal, by contrast to Rahner's, is not that we label those who do not confess Jesus Christ as Lord "Christian," but that we recognize the Word is

those who are not Christian conform to a Christian way of understanding. Rather, it is to imagine, in a conceptual space that is broad as well as particular—in a place where we do not know all there is to know about the Word even as we know the Word truly—how Christians might go about receiving and engaging members of other faiths in ways that honor the limits and confines of a Christ-centered Christian symbol system while at the same time remembering that the symbols participate in, but cannot impose limits on, the Word itself.

An example of what it might look like to be centered in our particular identity in Christ, as Christians, while at the same time being open to what the Word might be saying *extra* the figure of Christ is found in Calvin's exegesis of the story of Abraham's faith.

In Genesis 15, Abraham is looking up at the stars God is showing him and receiving the absurd promise God is extending. The space is large; the Word is specific. "Look toward heaven and count the stars," God says. "So shall your descendants be." And Abraham believes God, the story tells us. And his belief "is reckoned to him as righteousness."[30]

It is informative that someone as Christ-centered in his theology as Calvin acknowledges the faith of Abraham without hesitation. Notice that Calvin is not at all stumped by a question commonly asked today, namely: What happens to those who lived before Christ? With his understanding that the Word is ubiquitous even as it fully indwells Christ, Calvin has little trouble explaining that Abraham is made righteous in the same way Christians later would be. "There is no doubt that Adam, Noah, Abraham, and the rest of the patriarchs . . . penetrated to the intimate knowledge of God that in a way distinguished them from unbelievers," writes Calvin, going on to assert that Abraham et. al. "recognized God not only as Creator but also as Redeemer" by way of the "Word." In short: according to Calvin, Abraham is redeemed through the very same Word known in Jesus Christ—even though Abraham never even knew Jesus Christ's name.[31] Abraham is in relationship to God by way of *special revelation*, according to Calvin. God speaks to him—and through him, to the whole nation of Israel—in a particular way in a particular context.

Barth, similarly, understands Abraham (and Moses) to be encountered by the same Word known to Christians in Jesus Christ. "These who are called according to the biblical narratives are . . . witnesses of the God who, as God with us, Emmanuel, was, is and will be with . . . . creation, the

---

at work beyond (but never apart from) Christ.

30. See Gen 15:5–6.
31. *Institutes* I.6.1.

world, and all human beings."[32] Barth's use of the Christ-associated term "Emmanuel," here, identifies Abraham and Moses with the Word not in abstraction from, but always in relation to the figure of Jesus Christ. Barth speaks, along these lines, of Jesus Christ's "pre-temporal, supra-temporal, and post-temporal eternity"—because he is the "God of humanity in time" who is joined to the Word that is ubiquitous, Jesus Christ is the elect one not only for "this or that" person but for "each and all" people.[33] In Jesus Christ, according to Barth, all people are "justified, sanctified, and called,"[34] even before they hear the Word proclaimed. They are not merely eligible to be claimed by God, they are already fully claimed and included. For this reason, Barth thinks, we should not think in terms of a "rigid separation" between "Christians and non-Christians." Rather, "all that is possible is a genuinely unlimited openness . . . an unlimited readiness to see in the aliens of today the brothers (and sisters) of tomorrow."[35]

This idea, that all are claimed in the election of Jesus Christ, sets a table for interfaith dialogue that begins with an equalizing premise, from the perspective of the Christians who are present. In the terms of Christian understanding, all are elected in the specific, historical person of Jesus of Nazareth—whether they think in these terms or not. At the same time, whatever said "election" might look like may be expressed in other terms and other symbol systems. This is because, again, the Word is ubiquitous—it is not confined to the person of Jesus Christ. Christians are invited, in a way that does not violate their commitment to Christ, to listen and learn other ways in which the shape of God's Word is described.

This model does, however, provoke at least a couple of questions, from the vantage point of Christian identity. First: if all are included "even before they hear"[36] the Word in the person of Jesus Christ, then what difference does it make whether or not a person confesses Jesus as Lord and Savior? And second: if any person might in principle hear and receive the Word of God that cannot ever be exhausted, on what basis are we to assess the validity of what is being said, as we engage in conversation together? How are we to know what is right and what is wrong? What is just, and what is unjust? Surely, interfaith dialogue would be dangerous if appeals were made to the *extra Calvinisticum* as a means to justify any and every truth claim.

---

32. Barth, *CD* IV.3.2, 575.
33. Ibid., 484.
34. Ibid., 486.
35. Ibid., 494.
36. Barth's phrase.

Addressing the first of these concerns: from a Christian perspective, saying that even those who do not profess Christ are elect in him in no way detracts from the importance of bearing witness to Christ, as Christ's disciples. To be loved is one thing, and it is something that is itself good and wonderful. But to *know* one is loved is even better than being loved without knowing it. To *know* one is forgiven and claimed is to be overjoyed. It is to be grateful; it is to be changed. If one does not know one is loved and forgiven, one cannot really be changed by that love and forgiveness. Barth insists, along these lines, "reality which does not become truth for us obviously cannot affect us, however supreme may be its ontological dignity."[37] Reality that *is* known and *does* become truth, by contrast, necessarily changes us. The reason Christians proclaim the Gospel, the reason they should bear witness to it everywhere, including in the context of interfaith dialogue, is so people on an individual level and the world more broadly will be transformed by the truth of it.

It might be suspected that realities that have become truth for us might impede interfaith dialogue by getting in the way of open conversation. What is to stop a person who is aware of her or his election from touting some sort of spiritual superiority in the face of someone who is not? Certainly, religious "know it alls" have again and again kept us from being able to engage in authentic conversation with one another. And yet, from the perspective of what we have said about the character of the conceptual space created by the *extra Calvinisticum*, it should not be the case that awareness of the reality of our election in Jesus Christ should precipitate an increase in pride. Rather, it should fund a humility. It is when we lay claim to the Word only in abstraction that we are more likely to make general, absolutist claims and to resist making specific commitments. When we bear witness to the Word-made-flesh, by contrast, it is we ourselves who are subject to ongoing transformation.

The poet Christian Wiman powerfully reflects on how "reality that becomes truth for us," when this reality is the Word incarnate in Jesus Christ, changes us in ways that bring humility. Wiman contrasts, along these lines, the look and feel of spirituality oriented toward an abstract, generalized, "God" and the look and feel of spirituality oriented in relation to Jesus Christ. "Modern spiritual consciousness," he explains, is predicated upon the fact that God is gone, and spiritual experience, for many of us, amounts mostly to an essential, deeply felt and necessary, but ultimately inchoate and

---

37. Barth, *CD* IV/2, 296–97.

transitory feeling of oneness or unity with existence. It is mystical and valuable, but distant.[38]

In contrast to this, knowing the Word by way of its particular incarnation in Christ brings God very near—almost too much so. Writes Wiman, "Christ . . . is a shard of glass in your gut. Christ is God crying I am here, and here not only in what exalts and completes and uplifts you, but here in what appalls, offends, and degrades you, here in what activates and exacerbates all that you would call not-God. To walk through the fog of God toward the clarity of Christ is difficult because of how unlovely, how "ungodly" that clarity often turns out to be."

Reality that becomes truth for us humbles us when it conveys that everything we thought we knew about who God is and what we thought being "godly" is all about is turned inside out, as it is in the person of Christ. In the context of interfaith dialogue, the conviction-filled making of truth claims is often viewed as problematic because such claims are thought to inhibit the free sharing of ideas. But when the content of the truth claims that are being made are not leveraged against others, but rather throw the very ones making such claims into question, conversation may be advanced. As Wiman testifies, the reality of who Jesus Christ is opens those who know it to hearing and seeing God's Word where we wouldn't expect to hear and see it—in places, even, that seem "ungodly."

The second and related concern might be that, in engaging the space of the *extra Calvinisticum* as a context for interfaith dialogue, there might be little impetus for engaging in helpful, and even prophetic, mutual critique. Someone might even make the case that, if the Word is ubiquitous and in large degree ever-hidden, questioning any conviction is problematic. How could we ever be sure something that is claimed is wrong, the argument might run, if in fact we have no access to the entirety of the Word? Something that appears to be wrong might actually seem right, if we had all the information.

It is here that Barth's insistence that the Word is eternally joined to the historical figure of Jesus of Nazareth has significant weight. To argue that the Word known concretely in Christ is at the same time ubiquitous, and that this means there are other terms and means of expressing what is true, does not mean that anything and everything said need be accepted. It does not mean that it is impossible to discern truth from falsehood. On the contrary, that which contradicts what Christians know to be true in Jesus Christ must be boldly challenged.

---

38. Wiman, *My Bright Abyss*, 119.

That said, Christians for whom the reality of the incarnation has become a truth should invite the Spirit to nurture in them the cognizance that even the incarnation does not exhaust God's life-giving Word. Knowing something true about who God is in Jesus Christ, they can dialogue, study, learn, grow and change freely and without fear. What is inconsistent with what they know in Christ must be rejected, but there is so much more that God is up to in the world that may be talked about and explored. As Barth once put it, "God may speak to us through Russian communism, through a flute concerto, through a blossoming shrub or through a dead dog. We shall do well to listen . . . if God really does so."[39]

III. Bearing Christ in an Interfaith Context: An Illustration/Experiment

One of the most common statements Christians make about Jesus Christ, and one that is often seen as unhelpful to bring to the interfaith table, is that found in John 14:6. It is a response offered by Jesus to the disciple Thomas, after Thomas has complained that no, he *does not* know *where* Jesus is going.

Let me backtrack a little. In John 14, Jesus is comforting the disciples. He is comforting them because he knows he will soon die and leave them, and he knows they will be distraught. And so he reassures them that he will not forget them, that he will be "preparing a place" for them, and that he will "come again" to take them along with him, so that they can all be together once again.

This is the point where Jesus goes too far, from Thomas' point of view. "You already know the place where I'm going," says Jesus.

"We do not," says Thomas, more or less. "We don't even know where you are going, how *can* we know the way?"

And Jesus replies, "I am the way, and the truth, and the life. No one comes to the Father except through me."

This verse has been used to throw a wrench in interfaith dialogue on too many occasions. This happens when it is used to convey the unfortunate message that Christians are right, and everyone else is wrong. That the only way a person can be saved, the only path to eternity, the only and exhaustive way to truth, is the *Christian way*.

Is it possible to claim this powerful statement of Christ in the context of the conceptual space I have described in this chapter? Is there a way Christians can with conviction claim Jesus Christ as "the way, the truth, and the life" while still remaining genuinely open to conversation with those of

---

39. Barth, *CD* 1/1, 160.

other faiths? With the Nones and the New Atheists? If we can find a way to receive this claim of Jesus with humility as well as with conviction, I am thinking, we can surely find ways to do so with other, less-exclusive sounding claims of the Christian faith.

Here's how I suggest we think about Jesus' statement. First of all, as Christians for whom the reality of the Word-made-flesh is undeniably a particular truth, we are invited to embrace Christ's words with full conviction. We do, indeed, understand Jesus Christ to be "the way, the truth, and the life." Not a way among other ways, but *the* way.

Second, we would benefit from reading verse 6 in context. Jesus is not doing a lecture on world religions, but is responding to the disciple Thomas, who is honest enough to tell him he does not know what Jesus is talking about. Still, it seems to be the case that Thomas (as usual!) wants further details. "Where *are* you going, Jesus?" Thomas seems to be asking. Jesus' response to Thomas might be interpreted as a correction not to "unbelievers," but to us, disciples of Christ, who want to try to manage him, as Thomas did. "Pay attention, Thomas!" Jesus seems almost to be saying, "you do not need to know where you are going, nor do you need to know the route, because *I will pick you up. I'm your ride*. Furthermore, I am the only way you will manage to get there."

When understood in this way, Jesus' words could actually be read to disarm know-it-all attitudes on the part of his followers. What is important to bear in mind is not that *we* who are Christians know the "way" while others don't, but that we don't know the way apart from Jesus Christ, the one in whom the Word became flesh. Jesus' statement to Thomas should foster in us who identify as his disciples a spirit of humility. We are fellow travelers, assured by Jesus that we need not worry, we will have a ride.

Finally, in relation to the *extra Calvinisticum,* it is helpful to remember that the Word known in Jesus Christ is not exhausted by him, or in this definitive statement he utters, or in this passage of Scripture. This does not mean that the statement he makes is not true. Christians have, again, taken the reality to which these words bear witness as truth for themselves and for their community. But what would be useful to remember, when we take this reality-become-truth to the table of interfaith dialogue, is that whatever this statement means is bigger and broader than the words themselves. Whatever it means to say and to claim Jesus as the way, the truth and the life has to be much grander than that Jesus is some kind of "key" to getting into heaven.

I think back to Calvin's and Barth's understanding of Abraham's faith, and suggest it will help us, here. Calvin and Barth spoke in terms of Abraham hearing the Word of God and responding to it. Barth even identified

Abraham's response as an encounter with "Emmanuel." Both used Christian words Abraham couldn't possibly have known to honor who he was as a person of faith.

Believing that Jesus is "the way, the truth, and the life," it would be perfectly within bounds for me to say, about a Buddhist friend of mine, that I believe Jesus will manage to save him, too. In saying this, I am not necessarily hoping that someday my Buddhist friend will use my Christian language or make the kind of faith claims I make. I am simply stating what I believe, from my perspective as someone who has been claimed in a particular way and inherited a particular and powerful set of words and symbols. Knowing that the words I say and the symbols I cherish do not exhaust the realities to which they point but do participate truly in these realities, I use them boldly and with conviction. But I at the same time seek to step more deeply into the richer realities they draw me into, but can't possibly contain. And so along the way I listen to those with other words, traditions, and symbols, hoping we might all enter more fully together into the abundant life I know as promised in Christ—life in which each of us is changed, and all of us will contribute to the healing of the world.

Bibliography

Barth, Karl. *Church Dogmatics* (12 volumes). Edited by Geoffrey Bromiley and T. F. Torrance. Edinburgh: T. & T. Clark, 1956—1976.

Calvin, John. *Institutes of the Christian Religion* (Kindle edition). Translated by Henry Beveridge. Amazon Digital Services, 2011.

———. *Institutes of the Christian Religion*. 2 vols. Edited by John T. McNeill. Translated by Ford Lewis Battles. Philadelphia: Westminster, 1960.

———. *John Calvin: Steward of God's Covenant*. Edited by John Thornton and Susan Varenne. New York: Vintage, 2006.

———. *Tracts Containing Treatise on the Sacrament, Catechism of the Church at Geneva*, vol. 2. Translated by Henry Beveridge. BiblioBazaar, 2009.

Gouwens, David. *Kierkegaard as Religious Thinker*. Cambridge: Cambridge University Press, 1996.

McCormack, Bruce. "Grace and Being: The Role of God's Gracious Election in Karl Barth's Theological Ontology." In *The Cambridge Companion to Karl Barth*, edited by John Webster, 92–110. Cambridge: Cambridge University Press (Kindle Edition).

Peters, David G. "The 'Extra Calvinisticum' and Calvin's Eucharistic Theology" Wisconsin Lutheran Seminary Library. Online: www.wlsessays.net/node/1779.

Placher, William C., *The Domestication of Transcendence, How Modern Thinking about God Went Wrong*. Louisville: Westminster John Knox, 1996.

Schweder, Richard A. *Why Do Men Barbeque?* Boston: Harvard University Press, 2003.

Sumner, Darren O. "The Twofold Life of the Word: Karl Barth's Critical Reception of the *Extra Calvinisticum*." *International Journal of Systematic Theology* 15 (2013) 42–57.

Willis, E. David. *Calvin's Catholic Christology: The Function of the So-Called Extra Calvinisticum in Calvin's Theology*. Leiden: Brill, 1966.

Wiman, Christian. *My Bright Abyss: Meditation of a Modern Believer*. New York: Farrar, Straus and Giroux, 2013.

11

Robert Elliott Speer, Some Transatlantic and Ecumenical Considerations

—Kenneth Cracknell

By any account Robert Elliott Speer (1867–1947) was a remarkable figure in the history of American Presbyterianism. He is a supreme example of the effects of a theologically formed heart, in his case in Church leadership and administration. My interest in his life and work arises from my first encounter with his name and influence when I was researching the origin of the World Missionary Conference in Edinburgh 1910.[1] I discovered then that not only the choice of venue, but the whole conception of a missionary gathering in order to reflect on policy, strategy, resources, problems and challenges facing the Church and its mission in the twentieth century owed much to Robert Speer, a secretary of the Board of Foreign Missions of the Presbyterian Church in the USA. Along with John R. Mott and some others, he rejected the nineteenth tradition and style of missionary conferences. These had been essentially celebratory and triumphalist occasions, as for example, the "Centenary Conference on Foreign Missions" in 1888 in London or the grandiosely named "Ecumenical Missionary Conference" in New York in 1900. As sober and rational attempts to face up to the difficulties in the way of world-wide mission such gatherings were almost complete failures. A new vision was deemed necessary, namely that of "a thoroughly unhurried conference" of leaders of the Boards of Mission of North America and Europe rather than a single great popular convention. At Speer's urging a planning committee came into being in January 1907

---

1. See Cracknell, *Justice, Courtesy and Love*, 181–87.

and this initiated and oversaw preparatory work that was to take nearly three and a half years.[2]

As a result of Speer's forceful advocacy it was decided that eight commissions should be set up. Each one was to focus on a major issue confronting Christian mission. The most important for our purposes was Commission Four. This was asked to deal with "the Missionary Message in relation to Non-Christian Religions." Its Chairman was to be a Scots theologian: David Cairns, professor of Systematic Theology in Christ's College, Aberdeen. His name will recur often in this article. The preparatory committee then nominated a North American Vice Chairman: Robert Speer himself, then just forty years old.

Who was this man to have so much confidence reposed in him? Happily there are two biographical studies available to answer this question. Their titles indicate the esteem in which he was held by his contemporaries. The earlier is W. R. Wheeler, *A Man Sent from God: a biography of Robert E. Speer* (1956) which reproduces much original source material without critical assessment.[3] The second is a full academic study by John F. Piper, Jr., *Robert E. Speer: Prophet of the American Church;* this treats in some detail much of Speer's voluminous published work. My aim here is to offer a transatlantic and ecumenical perspective (I am a Methodist from the United Kingdom) on Speer's life and thought. In giving such attention to Speer's work, my hope is that a sense of both my indebtedness to, as well as my affection for, the Presbyterian tradition will be apparent. I offer this as a tribute to David Gouwens, close friend, former colleague and distinguished exemplar of the theologically formed heart.

Robert Speer's working career can be recorded in little more than thirty words: from 1889–1890 he was an itinerant recruiter for the Student Volunteer Movement (SVM) and from 1891 until his retirement in 1937, he was a secretary of the Presbyterian Board of Foreign Missions. He was never ordained. In the course of his working life he remained active (very often as an office holder) in the SVM, the American Foreign Missions Council, and the International Missionary Council (IMC). More surprising, he was extremely active in the Federal Council of Churches and the Council on Co-operation in Latin America. In 1927 he was elected Moderator of the General Assembly of the Presbyterian Church. He was also Moderator of the Board of Trustees at Princeton Theological Seminary. He played major roles not only in the Edinburgh Conference but also in the Jerusalem IMC

---

2. Cracknell *Justice, Courtesy and Love*, 182.

3. Wheeler had been Speer's colleague for eleven years at the Presbyterian Board of Foreign Missions.

Conference of 1928, and in the YWCA through his marriage to Emma Doll Bailey, a charter-member from 1906 and President of its National Board from 1915 to 1932.[4] In days long before jet propulsion (and, in the earliest part of his career, before the internal combustion engine) he made extended journeys to South America, Persia, India, China, Korea, Japan and South America. In many of these journeys he was accompanied by his wife, by then Emma Bailey Speer.

From an international and ecumenical perspective five areas of his life and thought are worthy of commentary in this essay. They are set out neither chronologically nor in any order of importance. They lie in Speer's theology of evangelism and mission, and later his contributions to what is now called the theology of religions, his crucial role in the Presbyterian controversies of twenties and thirties, and in his concerns about social justice, racism and the status of women in the church.

We begin with the topic of evangelism, Speer's dominant concern throughout his long life. His contribution in this area is of particular interest to a British Methodist aware of the core documents of Presbyterianism. The Westminster Confession of Faith (1646) and the Westminster Catechisms (1647–8) had been basic formularies of the American Presbyterians since 1729 (the "Adopting Act"). In these documents a double predestination is clearly enunciated. A portion of humankind was to be the elect and the remainder were to be reprobate. God had been pleased "according to the unsearchable counsel of his own will," to ordain the latter to dishonor and wrath for their sin. Those not elected, the Westminster Confession went on to declare, "cannot come unto Christ" and therefore "cannot be saved, even though they may be called by the ministry of the word."

That this was a serious obstacle to evangelistic and missionary effort there is ample evidence.[5] On the British side of the Atlantic the beginning of missionary societies had been hindered both in the Scots Kirk and among the Baptists: J. C. Ryland's rebuke to William Carey still resonates: "Young man, sit down; when God wants to convert the heathen, He'll do it without your help or mine." Evangelistic preaching was highly questionable as well: notice the title of a book by an English Presbyterian, *God's Operations of Grace but no Free Offers of Grace*.[6]

On this side of the Atlantic Robert Speer, perhaps the greatest missionary thinker of the twentieth century played a significant role in diminishing

---

4. Piper, *Speer*, 97–99.

5. See Cracknell, *Justice, Courtesy and Love*, 22.

6. Joseph Hussey of Cambridge, 1706, cited by Peter Toon. He quotes Hussey as writing "offers rob the Gospel of its properties, privileges and glory." Toon, *Hyper Calvinism*, 82.

the importance of the Westminster Confession. Speer had come to his office in the Board of Foreign Missions, and thereby to a leading part in Presbyterian affairs, through an unusual set of circumstances. He had been chosen for a place in Church administration because of his outstanding gifts as an evangelist. The Board had taken note of Speer's outstanding gifts for winning students to Christ and to missionary vocations. After his own conversion Speer had become a traveling secretary for the newly formed SVM and because of this had come under the immediate influence of Dwight L. Moody, until the latter's death in 1899). Moody's evangelistic preaching was plain, straightforward, and stressed the love of God. In his words: "I look upon this world as a wrecked vessel. God has given me a life-boat and said to me, 'Moody, save all you can.'" Speer worked closely alongside Moody, participating in the Northfield Conferences.[7] Through these he got to know other passionate evangelists like Robert P. Wilder (another Presbyterian) and John R Mott (a Methodist layman). In this environment his father's old style Presbyterianism and the Westminster formularies became less important.[8] The need to make Christ known in all the world (this is the high point of period for the slogan, "The evangelization of the world in this generation") trumped notions of limited atonement, of no free offers of grace and of preaching to the elect alone. Speer's willingness to lay aside the traditional Presbyterianism of his upbringing perhaps needs some reflection.

First we may note that in his Moody-like enthusiasm Speer was tapping into his Scots-Irish roots (his grandfather had come from County Antrim in 1822). Another and quite different tradition existed within Scots-Irish Presbyterianism, namely that of revivalist fervor in a preaching style that predated the influence of John Calvin and John Knox, and the divines of the Westminster Assembly.[9]

Second, as he began his work with Presbyterian Board of Foreign Missions in 1891, Speer was only too aware of events leading up in 1893 to the heresy trial of Charles A. Briggs, the great Biblical scholar at Union Theological Seminary in New York. His condemnation brought about Briggs suspension from the ministry, and the withdrawal of the Union Theological Seminary from the Presbyterian fold. Speer's thinking turned to the

---

7. Shenk, *North American Foreign Missiosns*, 261–80.

8. "on Sunday we had to read and memorize the catechisms . . . the Infant's Catechism, the Shorter Catechism and the Westminster Longer Catechism," Robert Speer describing his childhood in Wheeler, *A Man Sent from God*, 32.

9. Three centuries earlier John Knox recorded his amazement at this phenomenon in a letter in 1556: "If I had not seen it with my own eyes in my own country I could not have believed it. Yea, Mother, their fervency doth so ravish me that I cannot but accuse and condemn my slothfull coldness." MacCulloch, *Reformation*, 284.

history of the church and the study of ecumenical problems. Confessional orthodoxy ceased to enchant him if it ever had. He became a forthright ecumenicist and by 1921 could declare as President of the Federal Council of Churches: "Only the whole body of Christ is competent to know and experience the whole faith of Christ." Going further he said: "I want no label but Christian and mean to call no brother Christian by any other name."[10] As a missionary secretary he committed himself to the proposition, "I am a member of the Presbyterian Church but I have not the slightest zeal to have the Presbyterian church extended throughout the length of the world." He affirmed: "We Presbyterians and Methodists have no business being apart on questions of doctrine and polity."[11] This sounds extraordinarily like John Wesley's ecumenical attitude set out his sermon on *Catholic Spirit*, and put into verse by his brother Charles: "Love like death hath all destroyed/ Rendered all distinctions void/Names and sects and parties fall/Thou O Christ art all in all."[12]

Despite all this he was still regarded a loyal Presbyterian and a trustworthy conservative (had he not contributed two booklets in the *Fundamentals* series?). Speer developed his own position confidently assured of the support of close Presbyterian friends he had made in New York and in Scotland.

In New York he had the regular intellectual companionship of Henry Sloane Coffin, Minister of Madison Avenue Presbyterians Church and from 1926 President of Union Theological Seminary (now no longer affiliated with Presbyterian Church USA). Coffin had had his own clashes with those asking for adherence to the Westminster Catechism. "Most of its formulations are obsolete," he once wrote, "and I am not passing it on to another generation, but its purpose to supply Christians with definite convictions and to make them think for themselves is part of an inheritance worth striving to maintain."[13]

Through his visits to Scotland Speer had become closely associated with David Cairns, Professor of Systematic Theology in Christ's College, Aberdeen. The Speer family had stayed with the Cairns family when he gave the Duff Lectures in Aberdeen prior to the Edinburgh Conference. Speer was Cairn's Vice-Chairman in the work of Edinburgh Commission Four the following year. According to his *Autobiography,* Cairns had "wrestled with the old Calvinism" and its solutions to the problems of the world. "But it was

10. Piper, *Speer*, 71.
11. Longfield, *Presbyterian Controversy*, 187.
12. See Cracknell and White, *World Methodism*, 248–50.
13. Longfield, *Presbyterian Controversy*, 81.

in vain. It seemed to me to make God unjust and something in me rose up in inextinguishable protest against it. . . I broke clear of the Seceder theology and Calvinism, and even from the final authority of St. Paul."[14] Coffin and Cairns enabled Speer to formulate a statement of faith in 1923 where (writing in the third person) he affirmed: "as to the Bible he accepts the doctrine of the Westminster Confession and regards its authority as supreme, not in faith only but also in the practice, conduct and relations of men."[15]

This kind of statement was sufficient to enable Speer's colleagues to trust him as their guide through much further stress and unpleasantness in the twenties and thirties.[16]

Presbyterian controversy at that time was associated chiefly with the name of J. Gresham Machen and which centered upon biblical inerrancy and strict adherence to the Westminster formulations. One sparking-point for the fires of controversy was a sermon preached from a Presbyterian pulpit in New York in 1922 by the Baptist Preacher Harry Emerson Fosdick, entitled "Shall the fundamentalists win?" On the other side J. Gresham Machen, a professor in the Princeton Theological Seminary, published his *Christianity and Liberalism* in 1923, declaring that Liberalism was a totally different religion from Christianity. The battle lines were drawn up when at Princeton Seminary (previously a bastion of Old School Calvinism) there were moves in 1925 to make its teaching "more nearly approximate to mainstream evangelical orthodoxy," igniting strong protests from Machen and others of his colleagues.[17] A Special Commission was set up in 1925 to report to the General Assembly in 1927.

Speer was both an alumnus and a member of the board of directors of the Seminary. As such he was an obvious choice for the Special Commission and was unanimously elected Moderator of the General Assembly for 1927. His deeply-felt desire for peace and unity in the denomination together with his skills in handling large gatherings enabled the denomination to find some accord together with a fresh beginning for Princeton Theological Seminary.[18] Liefferts Loetscher called Speer's work of reconciliation at that

---

14. Cairns, *Autobiography*, 85. Seceder theology refers to the strict Calvinism of the United Secession Church which formed part of the United Presbyterian Church of Scotland in 1850.

15. Wheeler, *Man Sent from God*, 191.

16. For a detailed account see Longfield, *Presbyterian Controversy*, 162–80.

17. Loetscher, *Broadening Church*, 139.

18. How deftly Speer could handle large meetings and avert contention is shown in a story narrated by Piper. During the 1927 Assembly, a very conservative commissioner asked if a ruling just passed was to be interpreted that "the Church did not accept the doctrine of the virgin birth. Before any one realized what was happening, Speer began

time "one of the most important theological turning points in theological history of the church since 1869."[19]

In all these disputes Speer's greatest strength lay in his unswerving emphasis on the work of Christ as a lived experience and not a set of doctrines.[20] Christianity was in his words: "Christ the divine Lord moving in history and human hearts,"[21] that is, as a lived and living experience. Since for him Christianity was Jesus Christ, right doctrine was but a small element in this vision of the Christian faith.

His two close intellectual counterparts shared a similar vision. Henry Sloane Coffin's dedicated advocacy of the Social Gospel rested upon the conviction, often expressed in his writings, that the church was a community united not by doctrine but oneness of purpose: "the company of those who share the purpose of Christ and possess his Father's Spirit for its accomplishment."[22] And the purpose of Christ was to make the world the Kingdom of God: to this end the hope of the world lay "in the proclamation of the Gospel of God and the making of men disciples of His Son."[23] On the other side of the Atlantic Speer's friend and confidant David Cairns had also determined that the Kingdom of God was to be the key to his renewed understanding of Christianity. It was, he wrote, "a campaign against all the enemies of God and humankind . . . not only against sin but against disease and pain and death, and with victory lying not only beyond history in another world but also within history and this world."[24]

All that resonated with Speer, who had said to students in the 1890s: "Do not narrowly think that the Kingdom of God is national or sectional or racial, but believe that it was as Christ said it was and early Church believed it to be."[25] His theology of mission was profoundly in accord with this thought. The missionary movement, he believed, was about the building

---

to recite the Apostles' Creed and by the time he reached the phrase referring to the virgin birth the entire assembly had risen and joined him. The commissioner said: 'I am satisfied . . . The assembly has spoken.'" Piper, *Speer*, 360.

19. Loescher, *Broadening Church*, 139.

20. He once rebuked Gresham Machen for using the expression "the Gospel of the Cross" as unbiblical. On the contrary Speer thought that Bible teaches "not that Cross saves us or that or we are saved by the Cross. It teaches that Christ saves us, and that He saves us by Himself, by His death and by His life." Longfield, *Presbyterian Controversy*, 183.

21. Ibid., 184.

22. Ibid., 223.

23. Coffin, *Social Rebuilding*, 72.

24. Quoted in Cracknell, *Justice, Courtesy and Love*, 187.

25. Piper, *Speer*, 326.

the Kingdom of God here on earth. Missionaries were "agents to bring into reality here an order of human society regenerated and remade by Jesus Christ.[26] But by 1919 Speer has become also a leader of the Federal Council of Churches in North America and spoke continually in these circles of a new world in which Jesus Christ will be the head of humanity. This particular evangelist was aligned with the Social Gospel movement. At a meeting immediately after the First World War he told his audience: "That new world, held before men's eyes will be worth as many sacrifices as men were willing to make for what was held before their eyes in the four years that have gone by."[27]

In the twenties and thirties he became even more an advocate of social justice themes, often to the annoyance of conservative critics. But Speer reckoned that he had the resources of the Bible to draw upon, and he produced a study in 1924 entitled *Of One Blood*. He argued that all humanity was one body and that all races were part of the single organism of which Christ was head and savior. He concluded this book with these words: "if looking out over humanity, torn with race feuds and embittered with race hatred we ask with Paul, who can deliver us from the body of this death? The answer is simple and clear, Christ is the Savior of this body."[28] As a church administrator, and accustomed to thinking structurally, he ensured that race relations should be always on the agenda of the Federal Council of Churches by working there to establish the Commission on the Church and Race Relations.

From a transatlantic point of view there is a striking parallel here to another of his counterparts in Britain, Joseph H. Oldham (also of Presbyterian background) who also moved in the same directions as Speer. A former missionary in India, Oldham had organized the Edinburgh Conference, through which he knew Speer well. He became one of the secretaries of the IMC and editor of the *International Review of Missions*. Like Speer he gave much attention to racial issues and published *Christianity and the Race Problem* in 1924.[29]

Speer was also passionately concerned about the status of women, much encouraged by his wife Emma Bailey Speer. She was a forceful advocate of gender equality not least in missionary circles, where she spoke in her own voice and her own right as a member of the Jerusalem IMC in 1928 (though with unconscious irony she is called in pages of the report, Mrs.

26. Ibid.
27. Ibid.
28. Speer, *Of One Blood*, 189–99, cited in Piper, *Speer*, 344.
29. For other parallels of Oldham with Speer, see Clements, *Faith on the Frontier*.

Robert E. Speer. She commented that "if there was one thing to which the Church was summoned it was to face the implications of our Lord's teaching about women . . . the Church needed to be summoned to study Christ's teaching on this subject."[30]

She was but concurring with her husband's view that Jesus was the Friend and Redeemer of women and their full equality with men would come only "with his help through the wider acceptance among men [sic] of His teaching and will."[31] Nevertheless other currents were slowing swiftly in the post-world war world. Women's suffrage in the USA had come in 1919 (in the UK partially in 1918 and fully in 1928).[32] One consequence of that was the raising of Presbyterian women's voices about their lack of seating in the assembly and other church courts. As a church administrator Speer did his part to ensure the equal participation of women in determining the policy and doctrines of the Church.[33]

Because of these efforts some progress was made. In 1930 women were enabled to become ruling elders, though not to become ordained ministers or lay evangelists. Speer commented that he would not hear the sweet voice of any authorized women ministering the Presbyterian pulpit "though he did not give up hope. Someday our Church," he said, "will get into accord with the teaching of the Scriptures in this matter."[34]

As we leave this topic we may note that the conviction of the full equality of women and men was all part of his understanding of the Bible and was part of the vision message of united humanity which Speer considered the fruit of "living in the Gospels," and also as a proper hermeneutic of Gal 3:28: "There is neither Jew nor Greek, there is neither slave nor free, there is neither male nor female for you are all one in Jesus Christ." These words, he declared, were "the charter of human liberty."[35]

In our final reflections we turn to an area less noticed by previous studies of Speer. The concerns of what is now generally known as the theology of religions still perplex the churches and their theologians.[36] Most approaches

---

30. Speer, *Jerusalem Report*, 373.

31. Piper, *Speer*, 333.

32. See elsewhere in this book for Susan White's detailed account of social and political forces that raised the question in the UK of women's ordination, "The Church Militant."

33. There is succinct account of his role in Piper, *Speer*, 366–73.

34. Ibid., Ordination of women in the Presbyterian Church in the USA to the ministry of word and sacrament had to wait until 1956.

35. Piper, *Speer*, 367.

36. Cracknell, *Good and Generous Faith*, Appendix One "Ambivalent Theology and Ambivalent Policy: the World Council of Churches and Interfaith Dialogue 1938–1999,"

to understanding the theological status of other religion before the end of the nineteenth century had been either dismissive and disparaging or polemic and destructive. This was particularly so in the Reformed tradition.[37] A recent book, *Only One Way?* published in the UK in 2011 takes the form of a "trialogue" among three major exponents of the theology of religions, a conservative Roman Catholic (Gavin D'Costa) a liberal Roman Catholic (Paul Knitter) and an exponent of the Reformed tradition (Daniel Strange). In his position paper Strange spells out "our *a priori* approach, which sees all non-Christian Religions in an antithetical relationship with Christianity." This, he says, necessitates elenctics to be the basis for any Christian approach to other religions. Elenctics means the study of how to "prove wrong," "to rebuke," "to confute" and "to convict." Alas this approach has been found misguided by working missionaries. Their practical experience has indicated the need of new approaches.

An early manifestation of this abandonment of the older ways of thought is to be found in the findings of Commission Four of the World Missionary Conference in 1910. Entitled "The Missionary Message in Relation to Non-Christian religions" it reported that, in answer to a survey question, "What attitude should the Christian preacher take toward the religion of the people among whom he labors?" the responses were almost unanimous. In the words of one Commissioner: "there is perfect agreement of all missionaries who have dealt with this question as to the necessity of sympathy and understanding in relation to the old religions."[38]

Some of the American Presbyterian responses are particularly relevant to us here: There is William Harris in Chiangmai, Thailand: ". . . at all times thoughtful of feelings and prejudices of the people among whom he labors. He should frankly appreciate the good and true element in the religion of the people"; D. A. Murray, Osaka, Japan, "an attitude of respect and appreciation toward the religion of the people. . . there are many excellencies in these religions . . . "; Andrew Watson, Cairo, "The Christian preacher should be willing and ready to acknowledge all that is good in non-Christian religions whether in doctrine or precept. His attitude should always be conciliatory . . . " Other Presbyterians from the USA offered succinct comments about personal attitudes: J. H. Wherry in Peking (Beijing) advised having "a quiet, eirenic compassionate bearing," and his namesake Elwood Morris Wherry in Ludhiana, North India, noted "it is love that wins," adding, "Of course

---

gives an account of the tides of controversy over the sixty years that followed.

37. D'Costa, et.al., *Only One Way ?*, 135. In support of his views Strange cites Calvin himself, Hendrik Kraemer, J. H. Bavinck, Cornelius van Til and many others.

38. Cracknell, *Justice, Courtesy and Love*, 198–202. These pages present a sample of their views.

controversy is sure to arise, but we strive to keep it within the limits of a friendly and sympathetic conversation." One last American Presbyterian example came from William A. Shedd in Uramia, Persia. "A sympathetic attitude in religious matters implies a readiness to learn from others truths which we have not apprehended; and I fully believe that in our contact with Orientals we can find something to learn." Furthermore, he urged that this attitude implies "a readiness to put the best construction possible in honesty and truth upon the practices and doctrines of the non-Christian religions."

Robert Speer could well have been a little taken aback to find some of his most distinguished missionary personnel (many of them very close friends) talking in such terms. When those opinions were joined with similar ones from Anglicans, Methodists, Baptists, Congregationalists, as well as from other Presbyterian and Reformed churches it is clear that there was a huge repudiation of polemics and elenctics by missionaries in 1910. Certainly we can see good reason for the suspicions harbored by J. Gresham Machen and his colleagues that the Presbyterian Board of Foreign Mission has fallen away from the strict Reformed path.

For Speer there were both immediate and later consequences. The first of these was in the shaping of his final remarks at Edinburgh. As Vice Chairman of Commission Four it fell to him to close the discussion on the Missionary Message and the non-Christian religions. He made four points, all of them emphasizing the uniqueness and supremacy of Christianity. All the delegates in Edinburgh were agreed, he said, that "Christianity is the final and absolute religion." He went on to stress that the issue was not whether "we thought that Christianity was supreme," but what "we were really doing to make it supreme, and how to get it accepted as such by all the world." A third section concerned the reflexive effects of laying Christianity over against the non-Christian religions of the world. He averred that did not lie in "what we will bring back into our faith that which was not in our faith before" but in what we had not discovered in it before. His final point was a call to people in the home base to make this Gospel world-conquering. "We have in these reports," he declared, "great visions of undeveloped possibilities in our Gospel, unutilized offers and promises of God, in Christ, to the life of man."[39]

What is missing in this brief summary of Speer's address is anything akin to Cairn's astonishment caused by "the practically universal testimony," that "the missionary should seek for the nobler elements in the non Christian religions," and that "in their higher forms" these religions "plainly manifest the working of the Spirit of God."[40] To deal with this meant profound

---

39. *Missionary Message*, 324–26.
40. Ibid., 267

changes had to take place in missionary preparation and in theological revaluation and education. As a theologian and a teacher of theology Cairns laid some of them out in his General Conclusions.[41]

Perhaps we may also detect a touch of defensiveness in Speer's remarks in his final speech to the Edinburgh gathering. "It has been said," he allowed, "that with regard to our Report it has emphasized the higher aspects of the non-Christian Religions and that is true." He offered as a first defense that "it appeared to us that we should do as we would be done by. We thought it best to compare the best in each pagan religion with the best in Christianity." This is not, as we have seen exactly what had happened when the commissioners had asked missionaries about their attitudes to other religions. Instead in the responses there was a near unanimity that they wanted to focus on the best in other religions without deleterious comparisons. Speer's hesitancy to commit himself to Cairns' eager affirmations lay in his sensitivities as a Church administrator and, as we shall see, justly so.

Nevertheless Speer had become recognized in ecumenical circles as an indispensable spokesman on missionary issues. So Oldham ensured that he was invited to serve the IMC at its Jerusalem Conference in 1928. This time he was to be co-chairman with William Temple, at that time the Bishop of Manchester (he was later to be Archbishop of Canterbury). Even more of a deliberative conference than Edinburgh had been, and with a much smaller number of participants, it worked with preparatory papers dealing with the world's religious traditions Before they met in Jerusalem, representatives from Continental Europe had expressed reservations about what they saw as an underlying syncretism "an effort to merge the things which were 'good' in other religions into Christianity."[42] They felt, Speer was to write later, "that the preparatory papers were drifting on the dangerous waters of syncretism and had insufficiently worked out the essential difference and absolute uniqueness of Christianity."[43] The Statement of the Council, drafted by William Temple together with Robert Speer (Temple always insisted it was "our document") recognized that the churches have not sufficiently sought out the good and noble elements in the non-Christian beliefs" and that "when men are true to the best light they have, they are

---

41. Cracknell, *Justice Courtesy and Love*, 253–260 summarizes these conclusions. These include the urgent need for training of missionaries in skills of teaching (so different from preaching); in thorough training in comparative religion ("it is in truth impossible to teach either theology or apologetics without preparation for instruction in the nature and history of the religion of the world") and thorough treatment of the issues involved in what he called "the softening of wrong antagonisms."

42. Piper, *Speer*, 219.

43. *Christian Life and Message*, 418.

able to effect some real deliverance from many of the evils that afflict the world." Such recognition "should prompt us the more to help them find the fullness of light and power in Christ." Speer and Temple affirmed that "we do not go to the nations called non-Christian because they are the worst in the world and they alone are in need . . . we go because they are part of the world and share in us the same human need . . . the need of redemption." In this context they declared the purpose of missions to be the "production of Christian character in individuals and societies though faith in and fellowship in Christ, the living Savior. Christ is our motive and Christ is our end. We can give nothing less, and we can give nothing more."[44] There is no doubt that this affirmation was deeply felt, not only by Speer and Temple but by the whole Council, who accepted their work with profound appreciation.

But by 1928 the tides in the West had turned against the missionary movement. Marxist-Leninism, fascism, crypto religious nationalism, materialist secularism and philosophical relativism were steadily on the march. In the home churches people were becoming increasingly anxious, perturbed and frightened. For Speer two different responses to these challenges led to two very different kinds of controversy in his closing years of service with the Missionary Board (he was to retire in 1937).

The voices suggesting a different more positive relationship with other religious traditions led to a sustained attack after 1928 by J. Gresham Machen on the policies of the Board of Foreign Mission, and therefore on Speer himself. This campaign was to lead to the establishment of the break-away Independent Board for Presbyterian Foreign Missions "to promote truly Biblical and truly Presbyterian mission work" in 1933. The second was furor surrounding the publication in 1932 of *Rethinking Missions: a Layman's Enquiry after One Hundred Years.*[45]

These initiatives needed two different sets of refutations, and here we will see Speer fully in command. Machen was aware of the sharp declension in the Westminster confessional orthodoxy of leading voices in the Presbyterian missionary body (Harris, Watson, Murray, the Wherrys, and Shedd) and identified them and many others as liberals. He alleged that Speer and his board tolerated and even supported modernism. In a twelve page essay called "Can Evangelical Christians Support our Foreign Board," in 1929 Machen accused the Board of discriminating against conservative candidates, and Speer himself of using vague and ambiguous language. In a twenty-page letter Speer defended himself and his Board. "I believe," he wrote, "that my own Christian convictions are not less evangelical than yours and I believe

---

44. *Christian Life and Message*, 486.
45. Longfield, *Presbyterian Controversy*, 202–5.

that our foreign missionary work and workers are also truly evangelical." The details of this particular controversy are fully covered by Longfield and Piper and came to a climax with the founding of the Independent Presbyterian Foreign Mission Board.[46]

But a different controversy with a very different group of people may have seemed to Speer to be more threatening. *Rethinking Missions: a Layman's Enquiry after One Hundred Years* was essentially a modernist manifesto, endorsed as such by the Pulitzer Prize winning novelist Pearl S. Buck who was at that time still a Presbyterian missionary in China. She called it a "unique book; a great book . . . literally true in its every observation and right in its every conclusion."[47] Its origin lay in worries about the dwindling of enthusiasm for foreign missions stirring among some wealthy laymen. They had gained considerable financial support from John D. Rockefeller Jr. for an extensive research project. With the tentative blessings of seven mainstream denominations they set off to assess the success of missionary activity in India, Burma, China and Japan. William E. Hocking, a Congregationalist and philosophy professor at Harvard, chaired the Committee of Appraisal and wrote the "General Principles" section of the Report. He famously suggested that in the face of ever increasing secularism, Christianity should make common cause with the great world religions together searching for one single unified religious truth. In these suggestions the report signally failed to assert the uniqueness of Christianity. There was an almost instantaneous repudiation of its findings by the mission boards that had given their early backing to the project. This included the Presbyterian Board.

Speer himself was horrified and reacted immediately with a solid piece of analysis and extensive criticisms in his *"Rethinking Missions" Examined*. He drew up a different set of principles at the heart of which he wrote, "Christianity should make no compromises, but anticipate the absolute triumph of Christ as acknowledged Lord and Savior . . . It should perceive and hold fast the truth of its own uniqueness. It should welcome any contribution to fuller understanding of its own character."[48]

When he wrote these last words he was consciously or unconsciously referring to the intention of what would become his last major work, *The Finality of Jesus Christ*. In a remarkable work, replete with lengthy quotations and critical commentaries, Speer argued against all tendencies toward the "equalitarianism of religions" (his expression) and affirmed "the right

---

46. Ibid., 182 and 199.
47. Ibid., 202–5.
48. Speer, *Re-thinking Missions*, 36–37.

and duty" of the religion that bears the name of Jesus Christ to displace the other religions.⁴⁹

The book was not successful in Britain; it was never published there, nor much quoted or cited. To British eyes it now appears in many respects to be a very American book, overly optimistic and rather too triumphalist.⁵⁰ Despite his participation in the drafting of the Reports of the Edinburgh and Jerusalem Conferences it seems as if Speer had reverted to the attitudes of the Westminster Confession.

One moment in Speer's text will illustrate why people from the other side of Atlantic might have had reservations about Speer's position. Speer tells us he had been asked in 1911, by the veteran Congregationalist missionary in India, Robert A. Hume to write an Introduction to his new book *An Interpretation of the Religious History of India*.⁵¹ Speer cheerfully obliged and characteristically wrote to Hume "asking him not to hesitate to decline it if it was unsatisfactory to him.⁵² And unsatisfactory it proved to be. In an equally courteous reply, Hume noted that while they were in perfect agreement about their "absolute, eternal, loving loyalty to the Lord Jesus Christ," their differences were profound. "But you speak of Christianity and I speak of Christ. You use the word 'conquer.' I use the words 'fulfill' and 'leaven.' According to my thought, neither the Lord Jesus Christ nor a Christian brother seeks to 'conquer' even the mistakes or evil of brothers in thought or life. He tries to help by showing how the Lord Jesus has taught and saved him and his, and how that same Lord can help his brothers to an abounding life and fitness for universal service." Accordingly, Hume said, he would avail himself of Speer's "very courteous permission" not to use this draft, pointing to the fact in that in the very first page of the dedication in his book he spoke to "brothers," while on the second page would be the thought of Christianity seeking to conquer India, if your draft were used." Even more pointedly, Hume added this sentence: "My experience makes me believe that such a combination would discredit me, and our Lord, and Christianity."⁵³

Remarkably Speer's response to these comments is also fully reproduced. He emphasized one significant point of disagreement. "I meant by

---

49. Speer, *Finality*," 374.

50. Hutchison, *Errand*, 91, where Hutchison quotes Speer's words "There is a false imperialism which is abhorrent to Christianity, and there is a true imperialism which is inherent in it." *Finality*, 372 as the epigraph to his chapter on the missionary movement as a "moral equivalent for Imperialism."

51. Cracknell, *Justice*, 132–33, gives an account of Hume's thinking as it was shared with the Edinburgh commissioners.

52. Speer, *Finality*, 275. His draft introduction is printed on the pages that follow.

53. Ibid., 277.

'Christianity,'" he wrote, "'the ideal Christianity'" of the New Testament, "the Christianity which is Christ Himself." This, however, is a very misleading definition of Christianity, especially in a book about religious systems and their intrinsic shortcomings. Speer normally follows the customary usage of the term where "Christianity" refers to the prevalent religious system of the West. This has nurtured in its history slavery, the subjugation of women, forcible conversion, virulent anti-Judaism, and many other forms of bigotry. To confound Christianity with Christ, we may say, is a profound mistake.

Moreover, such a confusion eliminates from the discussion the awareness that for finite human beings to claim possession of all truth dangerous. Our knowledge is imperfect and we see in a mirror dimly, *en ainigmati*. (1 Cor 13:12) The future remains enigmatic until the eschaton. We can only say "I know in part." Only in end-times shall we have yet anything like a full and final revelation. So William Temple, as he drafted the Jerusalem statement, did use the word "final" but added immediately, "yet ever unfolding revelation of the God in whom we and move, and have our being."[54]

Part of that unfolding will be as a result of the Christian encounter with other religious traditions. Cairns also glimpsed this in his General Conclusions of Commission Four. "Rightly used," he wrote, "they will fling abounding light on the undeveloped in the Christian religion.[55] Here closer attention to his friends and colleagues from Britain might have helped Speer to avoid his rather off-putting title.

There is to be sure much more to explore in the richness of Speer's legacy but we are out of space. We hope that this brief sketch might serve to remind American Presbyterians (and many others) of a man who in his day was called "a prophet for the American church."

Bibliography

Cairns, David. *An Autobiography, Some Recollections of a Long Lif,e and Selected Letters*. London: SCM, 1950.

The Christian Life and Message in relations to Non Christian Systems: Report of the Jerusalem Meeting Report of the International Missionary Council, March 24th-April 8th 1928, Volume 1. London: Oxford University Press, 1928. (note though no name appears as that of the editor, there is a sentence at the end of the brief preface on p. vii: "A word of appreciation must be added in recognition of the thought and work contributed by Dr Robert E. Speer to the editing of this volume").

Clements, Keith. *Faith on the Frontier: A Life of J. H. Oldham*. Edinburgh: T. & T. Clark, 1999.

---

54. *Christian Life and Message*, 248.
55. *Missionary Message*, 273.

Coffin, Henry Sloane. *In a Day of Social Rebuilding. Lectures on the Ministry of the Church*. New Haven: Yale University Press, 1918.

Cracknell, Kenneth and Susan J. White. *An Introduction to World Methodism*. Cambridge: Cambridge University Press, 2005.

———. *In Good and Generous Faith: Christians and Religious Pluralism*. London: Epworth, 2006.

———. *Justice Courtesy and Love: Theologians and Missionaries Encountering Religions 1846-1914*. London: Epworth. 1995.

D'Costa, Gavin, et. al., *Only One Way? Three Christian Responses to the Uniqueness of Christ in the Modern world*. London: SCM, 2011.

Hocking William E. et al., *Rethinking Missions: a Layman's Enquiry after One Hundred Years*. New York: Harper & Brothers, 1932.

Hutchison, William R. *Errand to the World: American Protestant Thought and Foreign Missions*. Chicago: University of Chicago Press, 1987.

Loetscher, Lefferts A. *The Broadening Church: A Study of Theological Issues in the Presbyterian Church since 1869*. Philadelphia: University of Pennsylvania Press, 1954.

Longfield, Bradley J. *The Presbyterian Controversy: Fundamentalists, Modernists, and Moderates*. New York: Oxford University Press, 1991.

MacCullough, Diarmaid. *The Reformation, a History*. London and New York: Viking, 2004.

The Missionary Message in Relation to Non-Christian Religions, World Missionary Conference. 1910: Report of Commission IV. Edinburgh: Oliphant, Anderson and Ferrier; and New York: Fleming H. Revell, 1910.

Piper, John F., Jr. "The Development of the Missionary Ideas of Robert E. Speer." In *North American Foreign Missions 1800–1914 Theology Theory and Policy*, edited by Wilbert R. Shenk, 261–280. Grand Rapids: Eerdmans, 2004.

———. *Robert E. Speer: Prophet of the American Church*. Louisville: Geneva Press, 2000.

Speer, Robert E. "Christ: The Only Revelation of the Fatherhood of God." In *The Fundamentals: a Testimony to the Truth*. Edited by R. A. Torrey and A. C. Dixon, 2:224–38. Los Angeles: The Bible Institute, 1917.

———. *The Finality of Jesus Christ*. New York: Fleming H. Revell, 1933.

———. "Foreign Missions or World Wide Evangelism." In *The Fundamentals: a Testimony to the Truth*. Edited by R. A. Torrey and A. C.Dixon, 3:229–249. Los Angeles: The Bible Institute, 1917.

———. *The Gospel and the New World*. New York: Fleming H. Revell,1902.

———. *Of One Blood: A Short Study of the Race Problem*. New York: Council of Women for Home Missions and Missionary Education Movement of United States and Canada, 1924.

———. *"Rethinking Missions" Examined: An Attempt at a Just Review of the Report of the Appraisal Commission of the Laymen's Foreign Missions Inquiry*. New York: Fleming H. Revell, 1933.

Toon, Peter. *The Emergence of Hyper-Calvinism in English Nonconformity, 1689–1765*. London: The Olive Tree, 1967.

Wheeler, W. R. *A Man Sent from God: A biography of Robert E. Speer*. New York: Fleming H. Revell, 1956.

Studies in Søren Kierkegaard

12

Kierkegaard on Anxiety and Original Sin

—C. Stephen Evans

G. K. Chesterton once said that the Christian doctrine of original sin is the "only part of Christian theology that can really be proved."[1] Presumably Chesterton thought the evidence for this doctrine was empirical in nature, since the evening news on virtually any day could be offered as support. Whether Chesterton was right or not, the doctrine certainly gives rise to theoretical perplexities, perhaps as if to compensate for its undeniable empirical appeal. Chief among these perplexities is the traditional claim that sin is both something inevitable and inherited and something for which the individual is responsible and deservedly incurs punishment.

Philip Quinn, in his influential paper "Does Anxiety Explain Original Sin,"[2] describes three alternatives to the traditional account of original sin and argued convincingly that Kierkegaard's account[3] is superior in several significant ways to those of Kant and Schleiermacher. Kant gets rid of the idea that individuals inherit guilt by postulating a noumenal act of will by which each individual human corrupts his or her nature, thus eliminating a

---

1. Chesterton, *Orthodoxy*, 15.
2. Quinn, "Does Anxiety Explain Original Sin," 227–44.
3. In this paper I shall follow Quinn's example and speak, as he usually does, of Kierkegaard, when referring to the view of original sin developed in *The Concept of Anxiety*. Strictly speaking, the discussion should refer to the pseudonymous author of that book, Vigilius Haufniensis, as Quinn also recognizes. In this case I do not believe there are any significant differences in the views of Kierkegaard and his pseudonym, and in any case no harm will be done if the reader keeps in mind that the discussion is focused on the views of *The Concept of Anxiety*.

moral perplexity at the expense of seeing sin as grounded in an atemporal, unhistorical act.

Schleiermacher recognizes the ways in which humans inherit sinful dispositions and thus avoids the unhistorical character of Kant, but seems to flirt dangerously with the idea that such sinful natures give rise to sinful acts whenever individuals with such natures are placed in the right, or perhaps more accurately, the wrong circumstances, a view that seems to threaten moral responsibility.[4]

Kierkegaard's account, as seen by Quinn, is superior to both of these. Like Kant and Schleiermacher, Kierkegaard rejects the unhappy claim that sin is something the individual inherits and yet for which the individual is justly condemned. Kierkegaard retains the historical, situated character of Schleiermacher's view, but adds the dimension of freedom and moral responsibility that is part of Kant's view. Kierkegaard sees anxiety as making sin psychologically intelligible, but carefully denies that anxiety causally explains sin in a way that would preclude individual responsibility.

I am in full agreement with Quinn's contention that the Kierkegaardian account of original sin is an improvement over those offered by Kant and Schleiermacher, not to mention the traditional view. In this paper I shall attempt to extend and expand on Quinn's work: exploring more deeply the advantages of Kierkegaard's view, pointing out its affinities to some traditional philosophical claims, and arguing that what is offered is in fact recognizable as an account of original sin. I shall not, however, here defend the claim that the doctrine of original sin is true; that is a task better left to the theologian. The philosophical theologian will do well if she can give an account of the doctrine that makes it appear intelligible and coherent, and consistent with a plausible human psychology.

At its barest bones, the doctrine of original sin is a claim that human beings went wrong at the very beginning of the race, and that the consequences of this going wrong have been transmitted to all, or almost all, human beings. The first human beings sinned, and as a consequence all human beings are sinners. I agree with Quinn that these claims are indefensible if interpreted to mean, as has often been the case, that human beings are rightly condemned for actions of their ancestors, of whose consequences later humans are helpless victims. The question posed by Quinn's title is whether

---

4. Actually, a careful reading of Schleiermacher on this point suggests that there is some lack of clarity in his mind. It is not clear to me that Schleiermacher really wishes to hold the view that Quinn attributes to him, since in other passages he insists strenuously on the freedom and responsibility of the individual. Nevertheless, precisely because of this lack of clarity on Schleiermacher's part, I do not think Quinn's reading is unfair.

anxiety *explains* original sin. There are (at least) three things that seem to demand explanation. Why did the first human beings sin? Secondly, why do later individual human beings sin? Thirdly, why do all human beings sin? As we shall see, Kierkegaard holds a "principle of uniformity" that implies that the first two questions can be given the same answer, since whatever explains the sins of the first human beings will explain the sins of later ones and vice versa.

Well, does anxiety do the job? Does it explain what we want to have explained? Initially it appears that it does not give us very much help. Anxiety does not scientifically explain why any individual sins, including Adam;[5] still less does it explain why all human beings sin.

Nevertheless, I shall argue that Quinn is right in agreeing with Kierkegaard that anxiety helps "a little," at least with respect to the question of why individual humans sin. Perhaps it also helps a little with respect to the question of the universality of sin as well. Anxiety does not scientifically explain sin, according to Kierkegaard, because nothing can scientifically explain sin.

"'Sin does not belong in any science."[6] I understand Kierkegaard here to be denying that one can give a causal explanation of sin, meaning that one cannot describe prior conditions sufficient to guarantee that a sinful act will occur. Sin arises out of freedom (21) and a free act cannot be seen as the inevitable product of prior conditions. Hence sin is described as a "leap;" sin "presupposes itself;" one can only say that sin comes about by a sin (32).

However, this rejection of deterministic, causal explanations is compatible with giving a type of narrative explanation of sin. What is needed is an account that allows us to see sin as motivated without being determined, that allows us to see sin as historical, since it is connected intelligibly to previous psychological states of the individual, without seeing it as an inevitable outcome of those states.

Traditional psychological explanations of sin in terms of *concupiscentia,* or inordinate desire, or in terms of selfishness, are regarded as defective by Kierkegaard. Such desires, seen as an explanation of sin, offer both too much and too little. They offer too much, because once postulated in the individual, sin seems to follow from them as a matter of course and the freedom and responsibility of the individual seem threatened. They offer too little, since their presence in the individual already seems to indicate

---

5. In this paper I use "Adam" and "Eve" simply to designate the first humans, whoever they were and however they came to be.

6. Kierkegaard, *The Concept of Anxiety,* 16. All future references to this volume will be made in parentheses in the text, and all numbers given in parentheses are taken from this volume.

that the individual is morally qualified as guilty, and thus what is supposed to be explained is really presupposed (40–41; 77–79).

Anxiety is more helpful for the task of giving a psychological explanation in that anxiety puts the individual in a situation of genuine ambivalence. It is a "sympathetic antipathy and an antipathetic sympathy" (42) and thus the individual in the grip of anxiety is both attracted and repelled by a possibility. She both has reasons for doing and not doing something. The act performed can be fitted into a smooth narrative which makes it intelligible; the act is motivated and thus the myth of the *liberum arbitrium* (49) is avoided. At the same time the act is not seen as inevitable; more than one alternative action will fit the narrative.

Anxiety also helps make some sense of why sin is universal. Of course no causal explanation of this universality can be given; if a causal account cannot be given for the individual, it is clear that one cannot be given for the race. Nevertheless, anxiety helps a bit here too, because it ties the motivation for sin to a universal human characteristic. For Kierkegaard anxiety is an awareness of freedom; it is fundamentally rooted in the fact that alternative possibilities do indeed confront me as a responsible being. The possibility that both tempts me and repels me is the possibility of freedom itself. The fall is an attempt on the part of an individual to become the foundation of her own freedom; "freedom looks down into its own possibility, laying hold of finiteness to support itself" (61).

The thought here, I believe, is something like this. The freedom humans possess is a derivative, finite freedom. We are not totally autonomous, but possess ourselves, including our freedom, as a gift. Inherent in this gift of freedom, however, is the possibility that the individual will choose to declare her independence from the source of her identity. This possibility is the one that both attracts and repels. If freedom is a universal characteristic, then it is intelligible that such a fall could be a universal choice. It is at least a universal possibility. Since the choice is grounded in freedom itself, however, it could never be seen as inevitable, even if it is universal.

Does this account of sin as rooted in anxiety give us the explanation we seek? Well, it depends on what one is seeking. There is a strong temptation to say that if Adam (or anyone else) chose to sin, there must a reason. Either anxiety is that reason or it is not. If it is then we have an explanation, and if it is not, then we still don't know the why of sin.

The plausibility of this argument depends on the ambiguity of the term "reason." It is indeed plausible to say that there must be a reason for sin (and all other voluntary human actions) in the sense that actions have a point or purpose. In this sense Kierkegaard's account agrees that there is a reason for sin; we can understand the motivation of the sinner. The sinner wishes to become autonomous. But of course from the fact that there are reasons in this sense for all acts performed it does not follow that there are deterministic causal explanations for all acts. We have reasons to do many acts we do not do; in cases of weakness of will we fail to do what we have good reasons to do. Only someone in the grip of deterministic assumptions about human action will find the claim that a reason must be a determining cause appealing, but it seems unlikely to me that a deterministic theory of action will provide promising philosophical soil for an account of sin.

We must therefore situate Kierkegaard's account of sin in the vicinity of libertarian theories of human action. Kierkegaard is, I believe, more clear-headed than some libertarian philosophers in recognizing that a commitment to freedom entails that there will be an enigmatic, inexplicable dimension to human action. For him, an understanding of sin is linked to a recognition of "the qualitative leap." To speak of free actions as involving a leap is not to say that such actions are completely unintelligible or opaque to us. Rather, in a manner strikingly reminiscent of C. A. Campbell,[7] he argues that acts of freedom can only be understood from a first-person perspective. We understand what a free act is because we have the power to act freely; we know we have such a power because we exercise it. "How sin came into the world, each man understands solely by himself" (51).

There is a tremendous temptation to abstract from this first-person perspective and view sin as an objective condition, requiring an objective explanation, but to yield to this temptation is a mistake. Kierkegaard strenuously resists any such move. For example, he claims that one ought not to speculate about what might have happened if Adam had not sinned (60). It is not immediately apparent why this question is improper, but I believe that the first-person character of sin is what underlies the claim. The person who asks such a question about Adam "asks about sin as if it were something foreign to him" (50). Such a person is already half-way to viewing sin as something that can be attributed to his ancestors, and not himself. If the person were really innocent and sin really foreign to him, he would not understand it and would not ask about it. If the person is in fact already a sinner, then Kierkegaard says the person must already understand why Adam sinned, because "sin never enters the world differently and has never entered differently" (50). I understand Adam because I have made the same choice as he.

---

7. See Campbell, "Is Free-Will a Pseudo-Problem?," 446–66, reprinted in Berofsky, *Free Will and Determinism*, for an argument that free will, which involves creative activity, can only be understood from the viewpoint of the agent and is opaque to the standpoint of the external observer.

It is in fact probably this mistake of theorizing about sin as an objective phenomenon that lies behind the doctrine of inherited guilt which the traditional doctrine labored under. When one views the sinfulness of all human beings as an objective fact requiring an explanation, a causal theory involving biological transmission immediately suggests itself. However, if one holds firmly to the claim that sin cannot be causally explained in the individual, then it will be apparent that no such explanation can be given for the race either. Kierkegaard's account of sin here agrees with the view Donald Davidson takes of weakness of will: "What is the agent's reason for doing A when he believes it would be better, all things considered, to do another thing, . . . the answer must be: for this the agent has no reason." I think that Davidson means by this that the agent has no reason that is sufficient to explain the action. Davidson would presumably go on to give some nonrational, causal explanation of why the agent nonetheless performed the act he did, with the ultimate account being neurophysiological in character. For Kierkegaard, however, such a causal account would excuse the agent from responsibility. The best explanation that we can hope to give for sin will be a narrative account that ties sinfulness to some characteristic that is inherent in all human beings, and this is precisely what Kierkegaard has offered. We can give no "reason" in the sense of giving an explanation that explains why the act had to happen, given the circumstances.

The enigmatic character of sin is therefore no special barrier to belief in its reality to anyone who finds libertarian views of action plausible. The enigmatic character of sin is simply a special instance of the enigmatic character of human agency.

Can Sin Be Inherited?

A different type of objection may be raised at this point. Kierkegaard, in agreement with Kant and Schleiermacher, rejects the idea of inherited guilt and posits a principle of uniformity: Adam and Eve are essentially no different from me, and what explains their sin explains mine and vice versa. Is such a view still recognizable as a doctrine of original sin, or inherited sin, as the somewhat literal English translation of the Danish *Arvesynd* implies? What is inherited on Kierkegaard's view? If sinfulness is not inherited, then are we not left with a Pelagian theory of uncorrupted human nature, which makes the claim that sin is universal even more enigmatic and mysterious? Is anything left of the traditional claim that "all sinned in Adam?"

It is at this point that, in order to preserve the historical character of human freedom and human sinfulness, Schleiermacher speaks of sinfulness as inherited. Kierkegaard does not like to speak of sinfulness as inherited, with good reason, since sinfulness logically is linked to guilt, though Schleiermacher tries to disentangle them. Nevertheless, sin has real consequences for Kierkegaard as well. What gets transformed by sin and inherited is not sinfulness but sensuousness, which is something the individual in turn transforms back into sinfulness by sin.

Sensuousness for Kierkegaard is closely linked to anxiety, since anxiety is linked to our incongruous character as bodily spirits. We could not feel anxiety if we were purely spiritual, nor if we were purely physical. It is freedom combined with physical finitude that makes it possible for freedom "to attempt to lay hold of finitude" and thereby become its own foundation. Sensuousness is not sinfulness but it is the ground of sinfulness, and sensuousness is transformed into sinfulness when a person actually sins.

What Kierkegaard claims is that though sinfulness cannot be transmitted as such, sensuousness can be and is passed down from generation to generation, both biologically and environmentally. When an individual sins, sensuousness is transformed into sinfulness, and thus it is true in a way that our sinfulness (which is transformed sensuousness) is inherited. Our situation really is different from that of Adam and Eve, because of the character of the sensuousness we have inherited. However, the uniformity principle is preserved by a distinction between quantitative and qualitative change. The differences between the first humans and later humans like ourselves are purely quantitative; we are more sensuous than they were (though some of us more than others) and our anxiety is consequently greater. Nevertheless, when I sin there is a qualitative similarity to the sin of Adam and Eve.

What sense can be made of these claims? I understand Kierkegaard to be saying that human beings who are born after Adam and Eve inherit and are socialized with "raw materials" (sensuousness) that are shaped by the consequences of sin. (No real theorizing is done about the mechanisms whereby these consequences are transmitted, but one could plausibly assume that they are both biological and environmental.) Our raw physical urges, aggressive inclinations and dispositions, and so on, are greater than was the case for Adam and Eve, and the anxiety occasioned by our character as spiritual beings with such powerful, unchosen physical aspects is consequently greater.

One could say that human beings are born with everything against them; they are certainly not born as blank tablets or as possessing anything like a *liberum arbitrium*. Despite these quantitative differences, however, our situation does not really differ qualitatively from that of the first humans. Adam and Eve also had bodily-based physical urges and inclinations which occasioned anxiety. They attempted to "lay hold of their finiteness" so as to become the foundation of their own freedom. Later humans fall in the same way. We fall when we make the same choice, though when we make that choice the finitude that we attempt to lay hold of is very different, quantitatively speaking, from that of Adam and Eve.

Without sin, finitude and sensuousness are only finitude and sensuousness. However troubling and disturbed our natural endowment might be, it is not sin if it could be accepted in faith as coming from God's hand. In faith I can accept myself as I am while trusting that God will help me become the being I should be and wish to be. In declaring our independence from God (attempting to become the foundation of our own freedom) however, those natural endowments are transformed into sinfulness. So something is indeed inherited from Adam, something that becomes sinfulness when we declare our solidarity with Adam and Eve. That solidarity in sinfulness is expressed by Kierkegaard several times in the obscure claim that "every individual is both himself and the race" (28). It is because of this unity that one can say that there is a sense in which "all sinned in Adam," though one could also say that there is a sense in which Adam sinned in all others as well. How can this be true? In what sense can an individual be both himself and the race?

Making sense of this thesis as well as any claim of Kierkegaard to orthodoxy rests on the following premise: "Guilt has the dialectical character that it does not allow itself to be transferred, but whoever becomes guilty also becomes guilty of that which occasioned the guilt" (109). We do not inherit guilt from Adam, but we become guilty of Adam's sin when we appropriate its fruits in a guilty act of our own.

I shall try to make this principle plausible by offering an extended analogy. Ethical treatments of reverse discrimination and preferential hiring programs often are faced with the question of dealing with past wrongs against minority groups. Arguments are advanced that because certain groups have been discriminated against in the past or treated unfairly in other ways, they should be given preferential treatment to compensate for these inequities. Objections to such arguments often point out that the people who are likely to be adversely affected by such preferential programs are not usually the people who engaged in the past acts of discrimination. A white male may object, for example, that even if his ancestors mistreated blacks, this guilt is not transferable, and that he should not suffer for his ancestors' sins.

Suppose that the following conditions are met, however. I am a white male whose ancestors treated blacks unjustly, perhaps by enslaving them or in other ways. Suppose that these past acts of injustice have created certain inequalities that benefit me. I have access to more resources, education, and opportunities, relative to blacks, than I would otherwise have had. Am I not enjoying the fruits of injustice and is that not unjust? It is a well-established legal principle that wrong-doers are not entitled to the fruits of their wrong-doing. If I murder my parents to inherit their estate, I am not entitled to that estate. Still, someone might argue, in the case of a descendant of racists, the descendant has done no wrong, and thus it is not obvious that it is the descendant who should bear the burden of rectifying the past wrongs.

I shall assume that this argument is a strong one and that so far there is no case for any kind of inherited liability. To make such liability plausible, let's change the case. Suppose that the descendant has taken advantage of some of these inherited benefits in ways that resemble the actions of his ancestors. Suppose further that the additional educational resources, increased money, and other opportunities that were the product of past injustices, have been employed for racist ends. Of course, someone might argue that in this case the descendant would be guilty on his own and deserves to be a victim of preferential treatment apart from whatever his ancestors did, and that would be true. But is it not also true that there is substantial solidarity between ancestor and descendant in this case? In appropriating the inherited fruits of racism for racist ends, does the descendant not in a sense appropriate the guilt of the ancestor as well? A real solidarity between ancestor and descendant would exist.

In any case, I believe there is an analogy between this case and the way Kierkegaard conceives of original sin. The history of the race is not to be ignored, and the consequences of that sin are passed down from generation to generation. Nevertheless the solidarity of the race in sin is not to be explained in any objective, causal manner. "The individual is both himself and the race" means that the individual is both the product of the race, the outcome of what his ancestors have done, but also the producer of the race, the one who recapitulates the actions of his ancestors and identifies with them, thus continuing to perpetuate sin.

The analogy to original sin here would be even greater if we suppose in our example that some predisposition to racist acts has been inherited. So long as the predisposition is itself regarded as morally innocent, and guilt is incurred only when the individual in question freely chooses to affirm and appropriate the disposition, then in no objectionable sense can we say that the individual has inherited guilt. The individual has inherited something which the individual himself has transformed into guilt.

Such a reconstruction of original sin hardly removes all the theoretical perplexities. On the Kierkegaardian view I have been expounding, to make sense of original sin, one must be able to make sense of libertarian theories of action and a host of related views about the nature of freedom, the opacity of freedom from a third-person perspective, reasons which motivate without causally determining, and so on. But I hope I have shown that the perspectives Kierkegaard uses to make sense of the doctrine are not ad hoc, but recognizable views that are defended by other philosophers in their own right. Furthermore, I hope that the reconstructed view is recognizable as a doctrine of original sin; that is, that it captures the intent of earlier versions of this Christian doctrine, however different it may be from some of those versions.

Bibliography

Berofsky, Bernard. *Free Will and Determinism.* New York: Harper and Row, 1966.
Campbell, C. A. "Is Free-Will a Pseudo-Problem?" *Mind,* LX, 240, 1951, 461–65.
Chesterton, G. K. *Orthodoxy.* Garden City, New York: Doubleday and Company, 1959.
Kierkegaard, Søren. *The Concept of Anxiety,* edited and translated by Reidar Thomte. Princeton: Princeton University Press, 1980.
Quinn, Philip L. "Does Anxiety Explain Original Sin," *Noûs* 24, 1990, 227–44.

13

At The Foot of the Altar

Kierkegaard's Communion Discourses as the Resting Point of His Authorship

—Sylvia Walsh Perkins

In the Preface to *Two Discourses at the Communion on Fridays*, published on August 6, 1851, Kierkegaard writes:

> A gradually advancing author-activity that began with *Either/Or* seeks here its decisive point of rest at the foot of the altar, where the author, personally most conscious of his own imperfection and guilt, by no means calls himself a truth-witness but only a singular kind of poet and thinker who, "without authority," has had nothing new to bring but "has wanted to read through once again, if possible in a more inward way, the original text of the individual human existence-relationships, the old, familiar text handed down from the fathers...."[1]

In *On My Work as an Author*, published on the same day, he describes the movement of the authorship more specifically as proceeding "*from* 'the poet,' from the esthetic—*from* the 'philosopher,' from the speculative—*to* the indication of the most inward qualification of the essentially Christian; from the *pseudonymous Either/Or*, through *Concluding Postscript*, with *my name as editor*, to *Discourses at the Communion on Fridays*..."[2] Kierkegaard further claims that "this movement was traversed... *uno tenore*, in one

---

1. Kierkegaard, *Discourses at the Communion on Fridays*, 125. Cf. Kierkegaard, *Concluding Unscientific Postscript*, 1, 629–30.
2. Kierkegaard, *The Point of View*, 5–6.

breath ... thus the authorship, regarded as a *totality*, is religious from first to last, something anyone who can see, if he wants to see, also must see."[3]

It is not my intention in this essay to argue either pro or con regarding the religious character of Kierkegaard's authorship as a whole[4]—an issue that has already been copiously debated in the secondary literature with no consensus on the matter likely, especially since Kierkegaard himself states concerning his authorship: "In a certain sense it is a question of choice ... one must choose either to make the esthetic the total idea and interpret everything in that way, or the religious."[5] Opting for a hermeneutic of trust rather than suspicion on this question, I want instead to focus on the internal structural and thematic import of Kierkegaard's multiple claims that the communion discourses provide the resting point for his authorship as a whole. Even before 1851—that is, after the publication of seven communion discourses as Part IV of *Christian Discourses* in 1848 and three communion discourses titled *The High Priest—The Tax Collector—The Woman Who Was a Sinner* in 1849, plus one more that was delivered at a Friday communion service in the Church of Our Lady in 1848 and published in 1850 as the first of seven "Christian Expositions" in *Practice in Christianity*—Kierkegaard had already decided by 1849, the year in which the last communion discourses were written, that the communion discourses were to function "once and for all" as the resting point of his authorship.[6] That same year he states that "The authorship conceived as a whole ... points definitively to 'Discourses at the Communion on Fridays'" and that "the conception of my productivity finally gathers itself together in the Friday discourses," which "have always appealed to me as the place to end."[7] Since there is no indication that Kierkegaard ever changed his mind on this matter, we may take it as an established view on his part that the communion discourses constitute the final telos and unifying element of his authorship as a whole. As such, they can be said to occupy a crucial place in the Kierkegaardian corpus and

---

3. Ibid., 6.

4. See the essay by Paul Martens in this volume for a treatment of the religious character of at least a major portion of Kierkegaard's authorship.

5. Kierkegaard, *Journals and Papers*, 6:6520, translation modified. See, for example, Fenger, *Kierkegaard, the Myths and Their Origins*; Garff, "The Eyes of Argus," 29–54, and "*Den Søvnløse;*" Walsh, "Reading Kierkegaard With Kierkegaard Against Garff," 4–8; Westfall, *The Kierkegaardian Author*, 223–40; and *International Kierkegaard Commentary: The Point of View*, especially the essays by David Law, Mark A. Tietjen, Carl S. Hughes, Eleanor D. Helms, David Cain, John F. Whitmire Jr., and W. Glenn Kirkconnell.

6. Kierkegaard, *Journals and Papers*, 6:6519.

7. Ibid., 6:6407, 6487, 6418, translation modified.

to play a decisive role in bringing his writings to their ultimate point of concentration and culmination at the foot of the altar.

Niels Jørgen Cappelørn has rightly pointed out that the communion discourses actually constitute a new genre within the broader category of specifically Christian writings that began to appear in the authorship in 1847.[8] For that reason alone they deserve consideration in their own right as well as in comparison with other types of discourses in the authorship.[9] Moreover, they are virtually unique in modern Christian devotional literature, constituting a genre of religious discourse that has been sorely neglected in the modern age. As Cappelørn has shown, Kierkegaard's communion discourses are actually sermons, but they were not written for delivery from the pulpit on Sundays or holy days like most sermons; rather, they were intended for a specific liturgical occasion, namely the Eucharist or Holy Communion on Fridays, which was Kierkegaard's favorite time to attend communion.[10] Although communion was also offered on Sundays and holy days after the morning worship service at Our Lady's Church where Kierkegaard worshiped, Friday was to him the most intimate and solemn of all times to go to communion, as most people were at work on that day and the few who came did so out of a sense of inner need rather than duty.[11] Written for presentation during the interval between the confessional and the altar, that is, after the confession and remission of sins in the confessionary and right before receiving the elements and pledge of forgiveness at the altar in the main sanctuary, the communion discourses do not seek to instruct or to impress upon prospective communicants "the old familiar doctrines" but simply to give them "pause for a moment on the way to the altar" so that they may privately confess their sins before God and personally hear Christ's voice in the words spoken by the Lord's servant.[12] As sermons, then, the communion discourses place their focus on the altar rather than the pulpit and on the significance of Christ's death rather than his life and teachings, which are essentially witnessed to and proclaimed from the pulpit.[13]

---

8. Cappelørn, "Søren Kierkegaard at Friday Communion," 288.

9. See Walsh, "Introduction" to Kierkegaard, *Discourses*, 1–33, and "Comparing Genres," 71–90. See also Law, "Kierkegaard's Understanding of the Eucharist," 273–97; Barrett, "Christ's Efficacious Love and Human Responsibility," 251–72; Plekon, "Kierkegaard and the Eucharist," 214–36.

10. Cappelørn, "Søren Kierkegaard at Friday Communion," 279–82.

11. Ibid., 272, 276, 281; Kierkegaard, *Discourses at the Communion on Fridays*, 56. See also Kierkegaard, *Journals and Papers*, 5:6121.

12. Kierkegaard, *Discourses at the Communion on Fridays*, 57–58.

13. Ibid., 142. See also Cappelørn, "Søren Kierkegaard at Friday Communion," 281–82.

Although only three of Kierkegaard's communion discourses or sermons were actually delivered at communion, all of them are written as if they are being delivered on such an occasion. Like all of his upbuilding and Christian discourses, they are addressed to "that single individual" (*hinn Enkelte*) whom he called "*my* reader," imaginatively referred to in the context of a communion sermon as "my listener" or "attentive listener," who is invited to receive the author's words as a gift for his/her personal benefaction.[14]

While Kierkegaard's communion discourses are distinctive and worthy of consideration in their own right, the kind of writings that most closely correspond to his Christian discourses in general and the communion discourses in particular are the *Erbauungsliteratur* or upbuilding writings of late medieval Catholicism and the Protestant pietist tradition. As Christopher Barnett has recently pointed out, Kierkegaard was extremely well read in this literature, particularly in the writings of Johannes Tauler, Thomas à Kempis, and Johann Arndt, all of whom made the imitation of Christ a central theme in their devotional writings.[15] Kierkegaard's decision to make the motif of *imitatio Christi* or *Christi Efterfølgelse*, the imitation of Christ, a prominent feature of his "second authorship" or specifically Christian writings was undoubtedly influenced by these thinkers. Thomas à Kempis is cited more than any other Catholic devotional writer in Kierkegaard's journals, and all of his references to *The Imitation of Christ*, published anonymously but generally attributed to Thomas, stem from 1849, which indicates that Kierkegaard was reading this work at that time if not earlier, as a new Danish edition of it appeared in 1848 and was one of two copies owned by him, the other being a Latin edition dating from 1702.[16] Of particular importance for our consideration here is the fact that Book Four (originally Book Three) of *The Imitation of Christ* is devoted to the Eucharist, especially the earnest inward preparation needed to receive Holy Communion worthily, which indicates that it was intended to be used in a liturgical and sacramental context.[17] As scholarly studies of late medieval

---

14. Kierkegaard, *Discourses at the Communion on Fridays*, 38, 65, 74, 89–91, 99, 108, 113, 119, 122–24, 127, 129, 132–34, 143.

15. Barnett, *Kierkegaard, Pietism and Holiness*, 63–107. See also Šajda, "Tauler: A Teacher in Spiritual Dietethics," 265–87; Rasmussen, "Thomas à Kempis," 289–98; Ballan, "Johann Arndt," 21–30; Thulstrup, "Pietism," 173–222; "Studies of Pietists, Mystics, and Church Fathers," 60–80; "Søren Kierkegaard og Johann Arndt," 7–17.

16. Barnett, 73, 79. See also Habsburg, *Catholic and Protestant Translations of the "Imitatio Christi,"* 31.

17. I am grateful to Barnett, 79n108, for calling attention to this fact. The translators of *The Imitation of Christ* report that most editors have changed the order of the book in order to make it more logical (viii). The Danish translation that Kierkegaard owned also has the section on the Eucharist as Book Four of that text. See also Habsburg,

Catholic devotional writings and practices have pointed out, there was an avid interest in the Eucharist as well as the *imitatio Christi* in this period, particularly in meditations and sermons related to the celebration of the Eucharistic Feast of Corpus Christi.[18]

I cannot engage in a full scale comparison here, but it is worth noting that Book Four of *The Imitation of Christ* on the Eucharist opens with the same passage from Matt 11:28, "Come to me, all who labor and are heavy laden," that serves as the text for Kierkegaard's second communion discourse from 1848, and like the first discourse in this series, Thomas emphasizes the ardent and heartfelt longing for communion with Christ with which the devout disciple should go to communion.[19] It would be too much to say that Kierkegaard's communion discourses are modeled on Thomas's work, but there is considerable thematic overlap between them, not least of which is the deep sense of personal unworthiness, sinfulness, and nothingness with which the devout disciple receives the holy sacrament and God's gift of grace, love, mercy, and consolation in drawing him from sin and evil for the redemption, spiritual nourishment, and health of his body and soul.[20] Like Kierkegaard, Thomas calls for the cultivation of a deep interiority in the form of self-examination, contrition, humble confession, and firm resolve in preparing oneself to receive communion and forgiveness from Christ, who is "wholly present" and addresses the disciple or communicant directly.[21] Although the disciple in Thomas's meditation is either a fellow-religious in a monastic community or an ordained priest who celebrates communion, the *Imitatio* was widely adapted for and embraced by non-monastic communities such as the Brothers and Sisters of the Common Life and played "an integral role in shaping lay piety."[22] The single individual who is the intended recipient of Kierkegaard's communion discourses is likewise

---

Catholic and Protestant Translations of the "Imitatio Christi," 26, n. 80.

18. Kieckhefer, "Major Currents in Late Medieval Devotion," 75–108; Rubin, *Corpus Christi*, 164–232. See also Habsburg, *Catholic and Protestant Translations of the* "Imitatio Christi," 27.

19. Kempis, *The Imitation of Christ*, Bk. 4:1.115; 14.134–35; cf. Kierkegaard, *Discourses at the Communion on Fridays*, 39–40.

20. Ibid., Bk. 4:1.116, 2.119, 3.121, 4.122–23, 16.136; cf. Kierkegaard, *Discourses at the Communion on Fridays*, 44–45, 51–52, 76–79, 102–5, 121.

21. Ibid., Bk.4: 1.117; 4.122; 7.125–26; 9.127, 11.130; cf. Kierkegaard, *Discourses at the Communion on Fridays*, 41, 50–52, 57–58, 73–74, 77.

22. Habsburg, *Catholic and Protestant Translations of the* "Imitatio Christi," 8–9, 44, 46. See also Post, *The Modern Devotion*, 533, which argues that the *Imitatio* was written solely for monks.

a layperson, although the spiritual content of the discourses is applicable to all persons regardless of their spiritual office or lack thereof.[23]

A notable feature of Thomas's work is the disciple's desire to become "completely united to" and "absorbed by" Christ in and through Holy Communion, revealing a mystical strain in Thomas that is generally lacking in Kierkegaard, although the Magister does speak of Christ as living in his followers so as to "be and become" their life, and of identification with him in such a way as to preserve communion with him in their daily lives.[24] Thomas also admits the possibility of entering into a spiritual communion with Christ apart from receiving the sacrament, stating that "Any devout person may at any hour on any day receive Christ in spiritual communion profitably and without hindrance," and "as often as he devoutly calls to mind the mystery and passion of the Incarnate Christ, and is inflamed with love for Him, he communicates mystically, and is invisibly refreshed."[25] Regular attendance at sacramental communion is nevertheless strongly recommended by Thomas in order to ward off the assaults and temptations of Satan and to be freed from passion and vice so as to become more vigilant and strong in the love of God and devotion to Christ.[26] Kierkegaard likewise affirms the possibility of a spiritual communion with Christ but for him it is linked with sacramental communion by viewing Christ and the altar as spiritually accompanying the followers of Christ wherever they go, thereby making the Christian task paradoxically one of remaining at the altar upon leaving it and the Christian life one of engaging in "divine service every day."[27]

Thomas views the death of Christ as a complete sacrifice of himself in order to propitiate or "appease the divine wrath" for the sins of humankind, but the disciple must also sacrifice himself by making an offering to Christ at the altar in return, giving himself entirely and freely to Christ in

---

23. The Danish edition of *The Imitation of Christ* owned by Kierkegaard lacks a whole chapter as well as two paragraphs in another chapter devoted to the priestly office in Thomas's work, with the result that Book Four in Kierkegaard's copy contains only 17 chapters as opposed to 18 chapters in English translations. I am grateful to Cynthia Lund of the Kierkegaard Library at St. Olaf College for helping me to detect and explain this difference by scanning Book Four of the Danish edition in their library for my inspection.

24. Kempis, *The Imitation of Christ*, Bk. 4:13.133–34; 16.137; cf. Kierkegaard, *Discourses at the Communion on Fridays*, 48, 60, 143.

25. Ibid., Bk. 4:10.130. On the practice of spiritual communion in the late Middle Ages, see Caspers, "The Western Church during the Late Middle Ages," 83–97.

26. Kempis, *The Imitation of Christ*, Bk. 4:10.128–29; 12.133.

27. Kierkegaard, *Discourses at the Communion on Fridays*, 60.

self-renunciation in order to achieve a perfect union with him.[28] Kierkegaard likewise views Christ's death as a sacrifice that makes satisfaction for the sins of the world by suffering the punishment for sin, but for him it is not to propitiate or appease God but rather to expiate or atone for human sin.[29] Moreover, for him the atonement happens on an individual basis, not for human beings in general, and in such a way that it has to be made true in the life of each person individually by loving Christ much in and through the confession of sin.[30] While the pledge of faithfulness to Christ is renewed at the altar, the offering dearest to God and Christ, he claims, is the gift of reconciliation with one's enemy, which can be brought wherever Christ is spiritually present.[31] For Thomas the celebration of communion "should seem as great, as new, as sweet to [the disciple] as if on that very day Christ. . .suffered and died for the salvation of man."[32] For Kierkegaard too the death of Christ is not a past event that is over and done with but a present one for which the whole human race is responsible, making every individual an accomplice in bringing about his death.[33] Although it is hoped that communion will be a joy and blessing for all those who partake of the elements and receive forgiveness for their sins, Kierkegaard is aware of the difficulty and rarity of feeling entirely relieved of sin at the altar so as to depart from it "as light of heart as a newborn child," yet he finds benefit in portraying us "as imperfect as we are" so as "to be kept in a constant striving" to love Christ more in the future.[34]

There are then some important similarities as well as differences between Kierkegaard and Thomas on the Eucharist. What is most significant about Thomas's work for the present study, however, is the fact that an emphasis on the imitation of Christ in the preceding three books of the work is combined with a focus on the Eucharist in the fourth and final book, indicating not only that these two aspects of the Christian life belong together but also that partaking of holy communion is necessary for the refreshment and rest of the disciple's body and soul.[35] A great injustice was thus done

28. Kempis, *The Imitation of Christ*, Bk. 4: 8.126; 9.128; 15.136. On the distinction between sacrifice as a sin-offering by Christ and as a gift-offering by his followers in response, see Fiddes, *Past Event and Present Salvation*, 63–64.

29. Kierkegaard, *Discourses at the Communion on Fridays*, 99. On the distinction between propitiation as something human beings do to God and expiation as something God does for humankind, see Fiddes, *Past Event and Present Salvation*, 68–75.

30. Kierkegaard, *Discourses at the Communion on Fridays*, 58–59, 114.

31. Ibid., 60, 75. See also Kierkegaard, *Journals and Papers*, 2:1207, 1209.

32. Kempis, *The Imitation of Christ*, Bk. 4:2.120.

33. Kierkegaard, *Discourses at the Communion on Fridays*, 64–66.

34. Ibid., 128–29.

35. Kempis, *The Imitation of Christ*, Bk. 4:11.131.

to *The Imitation of Christ* when the book on Eucharistic piety was omitted in the first Protestant translation of it into German in 1531 by Kaspar von Schwenckfeld and in early Swiss, Latin, and English Protestant translations.[36] It was subsequently translated in this incomplete form in 1606 by Johann Arndt for use in the German Lutheran Church.[37] Fortunately, the 1848 Danish edition which Kierkegaard owned contains all four books, with the meditation on the Eucharist comprising the fourth book in this edition. Consequently, even though Kierkegaard started jotting down ideas for Friday sermons in 1847 and delivered two of them at Our Lady's Church that same year, Thomas's work could have influenced his decision to include communion sermons or discourses in his authorship and in a certain sense to conclude it with them.[38]

However that may be, the communion discourses do play a similar role both structurally and thematically in Kierkegaard's authorship, enabling him to combine the Atonement with the *Christi Efterfølgelse* theme, Christ the Redeemer and Atoner with Christ the Exemplar or Prototype, as the chief foci of his specifically Christian writings. Like Book Four of *The Imitation of Christ,* the seven communion discourses that make up Part IV of *Christian Discourses* follow upon a strong emphasis on Christ as the prototype for Christian existence in the preceding three parts of that work. In like manner, the three communion discourses of 1849 and the two communion discourses published in 1851 respectively follow upon and parallel the writing of *The Sickness unto Death* and *Practice in Christianity,* where the imitation of Christ is again emphasized. Kierkegaard envisioned writing some discourses on the Atonement as early as 1847 under the title "Work of Love" to parallel the publication of *Works of Love* that same year.[39] Toward the end of 1847 he began writing "Does a Human Being Have the Right to Let Himself Be Put to Death for the Truth?" as the first of two ethical-religious essays published pseudonymously in 1849 in which the

---

36. Habsburg, *Catholic and Protestant Translations of the "Imitatio Christi,"* 107, 127–30, 143, 145–77. Habsburg points out that earlier Catholic French and English translations also omitted Book Four and made numerous emendations to the text (129, 143). Protestant translations also removed references to monasticism, intercessory prayers, veneration of the saints, and purgatory to make the text conform to Protestant theology, and some translators appended an additional treatise in place of the fourth book.

37. Wallmann, "Johann Arndt," 30. Habsburg reports that a sermon by Luther was translated into Danish that same year by Christen Pedersen, who attached a series of chapters from the *Imitatio* to it (*Catholic and Protestant Translations of the "Imitatio Christi,"* 107n2).

38. See Kierkegaard, *Journals and Papers,* 3:3420.

39. Ibid., 5:6092.

limits of imitation are contemplated and the death of Christ is seen not only as the atonement for the sins of the human race but also retroactively for his death.[40] In 1848 Kierkegaard again contemplated writing a book on the Atonement, this time to be called "Thoughts That Cure Radically, Christian Healing," which would consist of two parts, the first to be called "The Sickness unto Death," showing that "the root of the sickness is sin," and the second "Radical Cure," focusing on "Christian Healing" or "The Atonement."[41] *The Sickness unto Death* thus was originally envisioned as preparatory to a focus on the Atonement. Having completed it in May 1848, Kierkegaard writes in his journal in July that "now the doctrine of the forgiveness of sins must come forth in earnest" in a book to be written under the title "The Radical Cure or The Forgiveness of Sins and the Atonement."[42] Prior to writing that work, however, he decided to write a smaller book on the theme of "Blessed is he who is not offended in me" as an appendix to "Come to me," which together became Numbers I and II of *Practice in Christianity*, published in 1850. Number III in this work, "From On High He Will Draw All To Himself," was originally projected to consist of seven discourses for the communion on Fridays, only one of which was actually written and delivered at a Friday communion in September 1848, then was reclassified and included as the first of seven "Christian expositions" that ultimately make up No. 3.[43] Having decided to publish *Practice in Christianity* pseudonymously and thus impersonally, Kierkegaard first thought this communion discourse would have to be omitted because it clearly belonged to him rather than his Christian pseudonym. But on further reflection, and with the addition of a note duly crediting Magister Kierkegaard as the author, he concluded that it had to be included because it "has substantially determined the whole book—thus in a way belongs with it," a statement which once again attests to the crucial role the communion discourses play in the authorship from his point of view.[44] Upon the completion of *Practice in Christianity* in 1849, Kierkegaard then states: "With this the writing stops; essentially it has already stopped (that which is wholly mine) with 'The Friday Discourses.'"[45] But since "From on High" was in his view "somewhat polemical," he decided that "some additional discourses for the Communion on Fridays should be written," one of which was "already as good as finished."[46] A second dis-

40. Ibid., 5:6050. See also Kierkegaard, *Without Authority*, 64.
41. Ibid., 5:6110.
42. Ibid., 6:6210.
43. Ibid., 6:6245.
44. Ibid., 6:6417, 6578.
45. Ibid., 6:6461.
46. Ibid., 6:6487.

course was written later that year and published along with the first in 1851, bringing the production of discourses in this genre literally to an end and prompting the prefatory statement with which this essay began.[47]

Of course, the authorship itself did not end at this point, as *For Self-Examination* (1851) *Judge for Yourself!* (written in 1851/2 and published posthumously in 1876) and the late writings that make up *The Moment* (1854/55) were yet to come. However, upon the completion of *Practice in Christianity*, in which the ethical rigorousness of Christianity and thus the price of becoming a Christian is raised to its zenith, Kierkegaard again writes in his journal: "If I now continue to be an author, the subject must be "sin" and "reconciliation" in such a way that in an upbuilding discourse I would now make use of the fact that the pseudonym has appropriately raised the price."[48] Like the Guadalquibir River, which "plunges into the earth somewhere and then comes out again," Kierkegaard sees himself as emerging from pseudonymity to write again in his own name, which he in fact does in these later writings.[49] With the exception of *The Moment*, these works are once again conceptually tied to the communion discourses by the twin themes of the imitation of Christ, now raised to the highest degree of suffering for the doctrine, and the atonement of Christ, who "as the *prototype* required *imitation*, yet by his *reconciliation* expels, if possible, all anxiety from a person's soul."[50]

Thematically, then, the imitation of Christ and the atonement of Christ clearly stand in a complementary dialectical relationship in Kierkegaard's authorship, each implying and necessitating the other. As Anti-Climacus states in *Practice in Christianity*, "Christ came to the world with the purpose of saving the world, also with the purpose—this in turn is implicit in his first purpose—of being *the prototype*."[51] Christ's role as prototype is introduced in the very first Christian discourse in "The Gospel of Sufferings" in *Upbuilding Discourses in Various Spirits*. Affirming a spiritual kinship with the divine that makes a prototype for human beings possible, Kierkegaard views Christ as having established himself "unconditionally and eternally" as the prototype in his lifetime through the heavy suffering he endured, from which he learned obedience "unto death on the cross."[52] In accordance with the principle that "As the prototype was, so also ought the follower to

---

47. Kierkegaard, *Without Authority*, 162.
48. Kierkegaard, *Journals and Papers*, 6:6445.
49. Ibid., 6:6416.
50. Kierkegaard, *Judge for Yourself!*, 209.
51. Kierkegaard, *Practice in Christianity*, 238.
52. Kierkegaard, *Upbuilding Discourses in Various Spirits*, 231–32, 250, 255, 263.

be," Christ calls for those who believe in him to take up their crosses and follow him (Matt 16:24).[53] To Kierkegaard this means that one must "deny oneself" and *"walk the same road"* Christ walked, "in the lowly form of a servant, indigent, forsaken, mocked, not loving the world and not loved by it."[54] The basis of imitation, then, is Christ in his lowliness or abasement, although in Kierkegaard's view "Christianity has never taught that literally to be a lowly person is synonymous with being a Christian, nor that there is a direct and inevitable transition from literally being a lowly person to becoming a Christian; neither has it taught that if the worldly eminent person relinquished all his power he therefore was a Christian."[55] But if one does not do that, one must at least engage in "the most rigorous self-examination" as a "precautionary measure" in order to make sure that one is at least willing to do so.[56] In his later, more rigorous writings, however, Kierkegaard emphasizes that true self-denial always involves suffering on the part of the disciple, and anyone who does not suffer incurs guilt and must admit it.[57]

Although Kierkegaard was undoubtedly deeply influenced by the late medieval emphasis on the imitation of Christ, his understanding of imitation differs significantly from that tradition. The basic error of the Middle Ages, he thought, was "childishly" or naïvely to think that one could succeed in resembling the prototype.[58] He also criticized it for making asceticism an end in itself rather than a means of witnessing to the truth, thus a matter of copying rather than following or imitating Christ.[59] Most of all, he objected to the honor, admiration, merit, and extraordinary religious status associated with the imitation of Christ in medieval asceticism and monasticism.[60] In contrast to that tradition, Kierkegaard does not see Christ as functioning either *literally* or *directly* as a prototype inasmuch as he is heterogeneous to ordinary human beings "by a full quality" by virtue of the "infinite sublimity" or ideal perfection that makes him "qualitatively different from the merely human."[61] As the prototype of humankind, therefore, he is "so far in advance" that the imitator is "demolished" and "crushed" by the infinite

53. Ibid., 221, 240.
54. Ibid., 221, 223.
55. Kierkegaard, *Practice in Christianity*, 238; *Christian Discourses*, 54–55.
56. Kierkegaard, *Christian Discourses*, 55.
57. Kierkegaard, *Judge for Yourself!* 201–8.
58. Kierkegaard, *Journals and Papers*, 2:1857.
59. Ibid., 2:1893, 1905.
60. Kierkegaard, *For Self-Examination*, 15–17; *Judge for Yourself!*, 192, 205; *Journals and Papers*, 1:1090; 2:1847, 1914; 4:4906; 6:6966.
61. Kierkegaard, *Journals and Papers*, 2:1432, 1921, 1922. See also Walsh, *Kierkegaard: Thinking Christianly*, 142.

distance between them.⁶² All direct efforts at resembling Christ thus "fall infinitely short and are reduced to nothing."⁶³ While Kierkegaard concedes that "in spite of the infinite imperfection there is nevertheless a slight advance" in striving to be like Christ, the chief function of the prototype for him, as in Lutheran theology generally, is to teach us how infinitely far away we are from fulfilling the ideal and thus how greatly we need God's grace.⁶⁴

It is at this point that Christ alternates to his other role as Redeemer and Atoner in relation to the Christian striver.⁶⁵ The opening prayer of Part II, "Christ as the Prototype," in *Judge for Yourself!* expresses this complementary dialectical relation most admirably:

> Help us all, each one of us, you who both will and can, you who are both the Prototype and the Redeemer, and in turn both the Redeemer and the Prototype, so that when the striving one droops under the prototype, crushed, almost despairing, the Redeemer raises him up again; but at the same moment you are again the Prototype so that he may be kept in the striving. O Atoner, by your holy suffering and death you have made satisfaction for everyone and everything; no eternal salvation either can or shall be earned—it has been earned. Yet you left your footprints, you, the holy Prototype for the human race and for every individual, so that by your Atonement the saved might at every moment find the confidence and boldness to want to strive to follow you.⁶⁶

As Kierkegaard sees it, Christ's role as Prototype is emphasized in the gospels, while his role as Redeemer and Atoner is stressed in the epistles of the New Testament.⁶⁷ With respect to his work as Atoner there is of course no imitation at all inasmuch the atonement is not a task for imitation.⁶⁸ Imitation aspires to be like Christ, whereas "the Atonement is the expression for the heterogeneity between him and every other human being" with respect

---

62. Kierkegaard, *Journals and Papers*, 1:349; 2:1861, 1857; Kierkegaard, *Judge for Yourself!*, 147.

63. Walsh, *Living Poetically*, 238.

64. Kierkegaard, *Journals and Papers*, 1:334, 692, 993; 2:1785, 1857, 1861, 1903, 1905, 1906. On Kierkegaard's appropriation of the second use of the law in Lutheran theology, see Barrett, "Faith, Works, and the Uses of the Law," 82–91. See also Kolb and Wingert, *The Book of Concord*, 311–12.

65. Kierkegaard, *Journals and Papers*, 1:334; 2:1863, 1877.

66. Kierkegaard, *Judge for Yourself!* 147.

67. Kierkegaard, *Journals and Papers*, 2:1877, 1911, 1920.

68. Ibid., 1:693; 2:1223; 4:4454.

to redemption, which only Christ can accomplish.[69] The Atonement is directed toward the past, while the Prototype is oriented toward the future.[70] But the Atonement also points forward to Christ as Prototype and Example inasmuch as the vicarious satisfaction with which the believer "puts on" Christ (Rom 13:14) means not only to appropriate his merit for the forgiveness of sin but also to seek to be like him, to borrow his clothes, as it were, so as to "re-present (*gengiver*) him."[71]

Imitation thus follows as well as precedes the Atonement and clearly constitutes a very important aspect of Kierkegaard's theology. But grace is still "the decisive factor" for Kierkegaard.[72] While admitting that his authorship has moved in the direction of Christ as pattern (*Exempel*) and prototype (*Forbilledet*) Kierkegaard nevertheless maintains that "the Atonement and grace are and remain definitive."[73] *Philosophical Fragments* poetically depicts the eternal resolve of God to bring about reconciliation with humankind out of love by descending into the lowly human form of a servant in order to establish equality, unity, and understanding between them, thereby annulling the absolute qualitative difference between God and human beings brought about by sin.[74] That resolve is later reiterated in "The Gospel of Sufferings," where Kierkegaard states that reconciliation, making satisfaction for guilt, and the forgiveness of sin constitute God's plan from eternity for the salvation of humankind.[75]

The place where this happens historically, of course, is in the death and atonement of Christ. Although Jesus can be said to have borne the sins of the world and declared them forgiven during his lifetime, Kierkegaard views such acts as an *anticipation* or prolepsis of Christ's death and atonement, at which time the sacrifice for the sins of humankind was actually accomplished.[76] The efficacy of this event is liturgically re-enacted at Holy Communion, which for Kierkegaard is not only a meal of remembrance of Christ's suffering and death but also and most essentially the meal of reconciliation, love, and blessing instituted by Christ as an eternal pledge of the forgiveness of sin.[77] As early as 1835 Kierkegaard wondered in his

69. Ibid., 2:1911.
70. Ibid., 2:1919.
71. Ibid., 2:1858.
72. Ibid., 2:1877.
73. Ibid., 3:2503; 2:1909.
74. Kierkegaard, *Philosophical Fragments*, 25–36.
75. Kierkegaard, *Upbuilding Discourses in Various Spirits*, 246–47, 258–59.
76. Kierkegaard, *Without Authority*, 158–60; *Journals and Papers*, 2:1223.
77. Kierkegaard, *Discourses at the Communion on Fridays*, 47, 68, 87.

journals why the Danish church reformer Grundtvig did not emphasize the Lord's Supper rather than baptism as the basis of the church since it was "something already instituted," thus making it more natural "to think of the Lord's Supper as the originally true center of the Church."[78] In another journal entry from 1839 he notes that communion is something more than a token of the brotherhood that should exist between human beings and with Christ, inasmuch as its "preeminent significance" lies in the assurance of reconciliation with God.[79]

Appropriately, then, Kierkegaard's communion discourses begin with a meditation on the heartfelt longing for communion with Christ that is required for going worthily to communion and becoming reconciled with God. Like the heartfelt longing of Christ to share a Passover meal with his disciples before his death, such longing constitutes "the true godly introduction or entrance" to the Lord's Supper.[80] This longing may be ignored, turned into a momentary impulse, resisted, prevented from deepening, or allowed to die, indicating an element of human agency and responsibility on the part of the prospective communicant, but it may also be a blessing when received with gratitude as a gift from God and assisted by earnest thoughts and holy resolutions that serve to increase the longing for communion with Christ both before and after going to the altar.[81] Portrayed as speaking in first person, the prospective communicant reminds him/herself of the vanity and uncertainty of everything except death, the frightful loneliness of every person in the world, the depth of sin and evil to which human beings have sunk in committing atrocities against one another, and above all the opposition and suffering of soul Christ endured from sinners, including the prospective communicant, who admits that he/she "certainly would have participated in the mockery."[82]

This appalling scene is placed even more vividly before the communicant's eyes in another communion discourse recalling the night Christ was betrayed and crucified, which for Kierkegaard, as noted earlier, is "not a bygone event, although it is past, not a past event over and done with, although it was eighteen hundred years ago," but a present event in which

---

78. Kierkegaard, *Journals and Papers*, 5:5089.

79. Ibid., 1:451.

80. Kierkegaard, *Discourses at the Communion on Fridays*, 39.

81. Ibid., 39–41, 48. On the role of human agency in the communion discourses of *Christian Discourses*, see Barrett, "Christ's Efficacious Love and Human Responsibility," 251–97.

82. Kierkegaard, *Discourses at the Communion on Fridays,* 39–46. For a detailed analysis of this discourse see Cappelørn, "Longing for Reconciliation with God," 318–36.

the whole human race participates, making all of us accomplices in bringing about his death.[83] The recognition of this universal complicity enables the prospective communicant to understand something about him/herself, namely that "to be a human being is to be a sinful human being."[84] For that reason every person is in need of an atoner, whose death is not only the sacrifice of atonement for the sins of the world but also for his crucifixion, which makes the need for an atoner clearer than ever before.[85]

When the invitation to come unto him is issued by Christ, therefore, Kierkegaard underscores the fact that no one is excluded inasmuch as Christ requires every person, not just the sick and troubled, to know what it is to labor and be heavy laden, and all must labor and be heavy laden in the deeper sense of having acquired a godly sorrow in the form of the consciousness of sin and repentance for "those actions, hidden or disclosed," by which they have committed an offense against God or other persons.[86] Within the "inmost recesses of every human being's heart," Kierkegaard observes, there dwells a confidant or "privy preacher" called the conscience, which is present with us wherever we go and does not allow us to hide our sins from ourselves or from God, however much we may be successful in hiding them from others.[87] Conscience speaks "simply and solely about you, to you, within you," he observes, creating a need to hide oneself even though it is impossible:

> Oh, that I knew how to flee to a deserted island where no human being ever came or comes; oh, that there were a place of refuge where I likewise could flee, far away from myself; that there were a hiding place where I am so hidden that not even the consciousness of my sin can find me; that there were a boundary, even if ever so narrow, where I could stand while the consciousness of my sin must remain on yonder side; that there were a forgiveness, a forgiveness that does not make my sense of guilt be increased but truly takes the guilt from me, also the consciousness of it; [oh] that there were an oblivion![88]

For Kierkegaard the consciousness of sin is the way, indeed the only way Christ draws a person to himself. Inasmuch as one may be led further away from faith and forgiveness by the intensification of despair and offense in

---

83. Kierkegaard, *Discourses at the Communion on Fridays*, 65.
84. Ibid., 67.
85. Ibid., See also Kierkegaard, *Without Authority*, 64.
86. Kierkegaard, *Discourses at the Communion on Fridays*, 50–51.
87. Ibid., 138.
88. Ibid., 139.

the consciousness of sin as described in *The Sickness unto Death*, however, it must be further qualified so as to become what Luther called "the anguished conscience" in a person.[89] For the individual who seeks to flee from the consciousness of sin in this form, the invitation of Christ promises rest for the soul in the only way possible for a sinner, namely in the assurance of the forgiveness of sin on the basis that satisfaction has been made by Christ.[90] The penitent communicant thus comes to the altar seeking the forgiveness of sin and reconciliation with God through Christ the Atoner.[91]

Before that can happen, however, a private confession of sin to God must be made. As Niels Jørgen Cappelørn has pointed out, the communion discourses are not confessional addresses intended for the confessional service that takes place prior to communion.[92] The need for a contrite confession of sins on the part of the communicant nevertheless constitutes a major topic in the communion discourses. Kierkegaard devotes no less than two communion discourses specifically to confession, focusing first of all on the tax collector of Luke 18:13 who stands far off in the temple and sighs, "God be merciful to me a sinner," as an example of what it means to confess, namely to stand far off and to cast one's eyes down, an even stronger expression of which is to kneel at the altar, where one is inversely lifted up to God and comes nearest to him.[93] The second discourse on this theme follows immediately after the first, focusing this time on the woman who was a sinner in Luke 7:47.[94] Hating herself with a sense of shame that, according to Kierkegaard, finds its strongest expression in woman, the female sinner (*Synderinden*) allows herself no leniency by openly confessing her sin before Christ at a feast while sitting at his feet, wetting them with her tears, and drying them with her hair.[95] By this act she expresses that she is capable of doing literally nothing at all to atone for her sins, which means inversely that she loves Christ much, for the more one thinks one is capable of doing, the less one loves and depends on Christ, who is capable of doing absolutely

---

89. Ibid., 123. See also Kierkegaard, *Works of Love*, 201; *Journals and Papers*, 3: 2461; 4: 4018. On the consciousness of sin and forgiveness in Kierkegaard's thought see also Cappelørn, "The Movements of Offense," 95–124. See also Walsh, *Living Christianly*, 95–124.

90. Kierkegaard, *Discourses at the Communion on Fridays*, 52.

91. Ibid., 76.

92. Cappelørn, "Søren Kierkegaard at Friday Communion," 278–82.

93. Kierkegaard, *Discourses at the Communion on Fridays*, 106.

94. On this biblical figure see also Walsh, "Comparing Genres," 71–90, and "Prototypes of Piety," 313–42.

95. Kierkegaard, *Discourses at the Communion on Fridays*, 109–11.

everything.[96] Totally forgetting herself in love for Christ, the woman who was a sinner thus becomes a symbol or parable of confession by loving Christ much.[97] As Kierkegaard sees it, "nothing else rests as heavy upon a person as sin's heavy secret; there is only one thing that is heavier: to have to go to confession."[98] Moreover, "no other secret is as frightful as the secret of sin: there is only one thing that is even more frightful: confession."[99] Since there is nothing one clings to more desperately than sin, to confess one's sin is precisely to love Christ much.[100] Indeed, for Kierkegaard "a perfectly honest, deep, altogether true, entirely unsparing confession of sin is the perfect love; such a confession of sin is to love much."[101]

In other communion discourses Kierkegaard points out that confession is not meant to burden us with guilt but rather to help us discard that burden by engaging in "earnest and honest self-examination" that leads to self-accusation and perhaps to self-condemnation in the confession of sin in secret before God.[102] No one is forced to confess nor does anyone accuse or condemn us if we do not do it ourselves. While self-accusation does not always lead to self-condemnation, in Kierkegaard's view all of us stand in need of the same consolation, namely of God's greatness in forgiving and showing mercy, which is infinitely greater than the heart that condemns itself.[103] Pointing out that "all our discourse about God is naturally human discourse," Kierkegaard maintains that the appropriate human measure of comparison in speaking about and forming a conception of God is not the most loving, forgiving, and merciful person but conversely the contrite heart that condemns itself.[104] This means that there is no direct resemblance between God and a human being based on the scale of "great, greater, greatest" but only an inverse relation and resemblance between them.[105] In like manner, it is not by lifting one's head up that a human being draws closer to God

---

96. Ibid., 111.
97. Ibid., 111–12.
98. Ibid., 110.
99. Ibid.
100. Ibid., 114.
101. Ibid.
102. Ibid., 74, 77.
103. Ibid., 77–78.
104. Ibid., 78–79.
105. Ibid., 79. On inverse dialectic in Kierkegaard's thought, see Walsh, *Living Christianly*, 7–15.

but inversely "by casting himself down deeper and deeper in worship."[106] As Kierkegaard puts it:

> The contrite heart that condemns itself cannot have, seeks in vain to find, an expression strong enough to describe its guilt, its wretchedness, its defilement—even greater is God in showing mercy! . . . All human purity, all human mercy is not good enough for comparison; but a penitent heart that condemns itself—with this God's greatness is compared in showing mercy, except that it is even greater: as deep as this heart can lower itself, and yet never deep enough, so infinitely exalted, or infinitely more exalted is God's greatness in showing mercy!"[107]

Having made a private accounting to God, then, the contrite communicant comes to the altar to receive the pledge of forgiveness of sin, to renew communion or fellowship with Christ and one's pledge of faithfulness to him, and to be reconciled with God.[108]

Reflecting the Lutheran doctrine of the real presence of Christ, according to which Christ is truly present "in, with, and under" the elements, which nevertheless remain bread and wine, Kierkegaard emphasizes Christ's spiritual presence at the altar not only in the elements but also orally, as it must be his voice that is heard there or else one is not really at the altar, spiritually speaking, and goes to communion in vain.[109] Those who hear his voice receive Christ himself in partaking of the bread and wine, making the communion not only a meal of reconciliation but also one of blessing.[110] While God's blessing is required for any godly undertaking by a human being, who is capable of doing nothing at all without God's consent, Kierkegaard stresses that, like the woman who was a sinner, we are capable of doing "less than nothing" at the altar with regard to making satisfaction for our guilt and sin. The satisfaction, the sacrifice, the atonement is wholly accomplished by another—the Atoner—who must do absolutely everything in

---

106. Kierkegaard, *Discourses at the Communion on Fridays*, 79.

107. Ibid., 79.

108. Ibid., 56, 63, 75, 76, 134, 143.

109. Ibid., 58. On the Lutheran view of the real presence of Christ, see Kolb and Wingert, *The Book of Concord*, 44–45, 505–6, 591–99, 610, 621.29. See also Law, "Kierkegaard's Understanding of the Eucharist," 294–95. Law maintains that Kierkegaard departs from Luther by situating the real presence of Christ in his voice rather than in the elements. But Law seemingly contradicts himself when he goes on to say: "It is the blessing of Christ, who is himself the blessing offered to the believer, which is offered in the bread and wine. But this divine blessing, which is itself Christ's presence, is present not only in the Eucharistic elements, but in the entire drama of the Lord's Supper."

110. Kierkegaard, *Discourses at the Communion on Fridays*, 86–87.

this regard. "[I]t was another who paid the debt, another who accomplished the reconciliation, another who brought you close to God, another who suffered and died in order to restore everything, another who steps forward for you. If at the altar you want to be able to do the least thing yourself, even merely to step forward yourself, then you upset everything, prevent the atonement, make the satisfaction impossible."[111]

Clearly subscribing to a substitutionary view of the Atonement, Kierkegaard portrays Christ as the High Priest in the Epistle to the Hebrews who puts himself entirely in our place in every respect except sin, which is the only way he does not and cannot put himself in our place.[112] Christ puts himself in our place first of all by becoming a human being and suffering more than any human being ever has suffered or ever can suffer by being tested in all things, including temptation and spiritual trials, in order to be able to offer true sympathy and consolation for our weaknesses, which only divine consolation can do.[113] Suffering thus reaches its highest point but also its limit in the inversion that Christ is "the Consoler" whose only consolation is to console others, inasmuch as we cannot put ourselves in his place, whereas he is the only one who can entirely put himself in our place.[114] In the Atonement Christ puts himself entirely in our place by acting as our deputy, replacing us and making satisfaction for our sin and guilt by suffering the punishment of sin and dying so that we may live.[115] Emphasizing that communion is "an eternal pledge that by his suffering and death he put himself also in your place," Kierkegaard is not interested in articulating a theory of the atonement as such but rather in stressing its personal significance for the single individual seeking communion and reconciliation with Christ and God.[116]

Another way of expressing the significance of the Atonement for the single individual is set forth in the last communion discourse, based on 1 Pet 4:8: "Love will hide a multitude of sins." Here Kierkegaard claims that Christ hides or covers our sins quite literally with his death as the ultimate expression of divine love.[117] Just as a mother hen hides her chicks under her wings and lays down her life for them when attacked, Christ covers our sins

---

111. Ibid., 86.

112. Ibid., 98. On the classical theories of atonement see Aulén, *Christus Victor*; Walsh, *Kierkegaard: Thinking Christianly*, 132–33. See also Bynum, "The Power in the Blood," 177–204.

113. Kierkegaard, *Discourses at the Communion on Fridays*, 93–98.

114. Ibid., 95.

115. Ibid., 99.

116. Ibid.

117. Ibid., 136, 140–41.

and lays down his life for us. But unlike the chicks, whose hiding place is lost when the mother hen loses her life, we are not deprived of our hiding place in Christ because he hides us precisely by his death, which cannot be taken away.[118] Christ's death is not repeated at the altar, Kierkegaard observes, "but *this* is repeated: he died also for you, you who in his body and blood receive the pledge that he has died also for you, at the altar, where he gives you *himself* as a hiding place."[119] But Kierkegaard also points out that "only by remaining in him, only by identifying yourself with him are you in hiding and there is a cover over the multitude of your sins."[120] We must therefore strive to preserve communion with Christ in our daily lives by living more and more out of ourselves and identifying with him and his love, which hides a multitude of sins.[121] In this way both Christ and the altar accompany us wherever we go and in whatever we do in following him, for where Christ is, there the altar is.[122]

The communion discourses thus unite the atonement of Christ with the imitation of Christ, Christ the Redeemer and Atoner with Christ the Exemplar and Prototype, the forgiveness of sin with the contrite consciousness and confession of sin, which stand in a continual, complementary, dialectical relationship to one another. While greater stress is placed on the imitation of Christ in Kierkegaard's specifically Christian writings, the thrust of the authorship as a whole is clearly toward reconciliation with God, which is accomplished through the death and atonement of Christ and made true in the life of each person individually by loving Christ much and remaining in communion with him in one's daily life. As the point at which this moment of reconciliation takes place in the Kierkegaardian corpus, the communion discourses can rightly be said to constitute the resting point for Kierkegaard's authorship as a whole.

Bibliography

Aulén, Gustaf. *Christus Victor: Three Main Types of the Idea of the Atonement.* London:SPCK, 1975 (1931).

Ballan, Joseph. "Johann Arndt: The Pietist Impulse in Kierkegaard and Seventeenth-Century Lutheran Devotional Literature." In *Kierkegaard and the Renaissance and Modern Traditions, Tome II: Theology*, edited by Jon Stewart, 21–30. Burlington, VT: Ashgate, 2009.

118. Ibid., 141.
119. Ibid., 142.
120. Ibid., 143.
121. Ibid..
122. Ibid., 60.

Barnett, Christopher B. *Kierkegaard, Pietism and Holiness*. Burlington, VT: Ashgate, 2011.
Barrett, Lee C., III. "Christ's Efficacious Love and Human Responsibility: The Lutheran Dialectic of 'Discourses at the Communion on Fridays.'" In *International Kierkegaard Commentary: Christian Discourses and The Crisis and a Crisis in the Life of an Actress*, edited by Robert L. Perkins. 251–72. Macon, GA: Mercer University Press, 2007.
———. "Faith, Works, and the Uses of the Law: Kierkegaard's Appropriation of Lutheran Doctrine." In *International Kierkegaard Commentary: For Self-Examination and Judge for Yourself!*, edited by Robert L. Perkins, 82–91. Macon, GA:. Mercer University Press, 2001.
Bynam, Caroline Walker. "The Power in the Blood: Sacrifice, Satisfaction, and Substitution in Late Medieval Soteriology." In *The Redemption: An Interdisciplinary Symposium on Christ as Redeemer*, edited by Stephen T. David, et al., 177–204. Oxford: Oxford University Press, 2004.
Cappelørn, Niels Jørgen. "Longing for Reconciliation with God: A Fundamental Theme in 'Friday Communion Discourses,' Fourth Part of *Christian Discourses*." In *Kierkegaard Studies Yearbook 2007*, edited by Niels Jørgen Cappelørn, et.al., 318–36. New York: Walter de Gruyter, 2007.
———. "Søren Kierkegaard at Friday Communion in the Church of Our Lady." In *International Kierkegaard Commentary: Without Authority*, edited by Robert L. Perkins, 255–94. Macon, GA: Mercer University Press, 2006.
———. "The Movements of Offense Toward, Away From, and Within Faith: 'Blessed is he who is not offended at me.'" In *International Kierkegaard Commentary: Practice in Christianity*, edited by Robert L. Perkins, 95–124. Macon, GA: Mercer University Press, 2004.
Caspers, Charles. "The Western Church during the Late Middle Ages: *Augenkommunion* or Popular Mysticism?" In *Bread of Heaven: Customs and Practices Surrounding Holy Communion / Essays in the History of Liturgy and Culture*, edited by Charles Caspers, et al., 83–97. Kampen, The Netherlands: Kok Pharos, 1995.
Fenger, Henning. *Kierkegaard, the Myths and Their Origins: Studies in Kierkegaardian Papers and Letters*. Translated by George C. Schoolfield. New Haven: Yale University Press, 1980.
Fiddes, Paul S. *Past Event and Present Salvation: The Christian Idea of Atonement*. Louisville, KY: Westminster John Knox, 1989.
Garff, Joakim. "The Eyes of Argus: *The Point of View* and Points of View with Respect to Kierkegaard's 'Activity as an Author.'" Translated by Bruce Kirmmse. *Kierkegaardiana* 15 (1991) 29–54.
———"*Den Søvnløse*": *Kierkegaard læst ætetisk/biografisk*. Copenhagen: C. A. Reitzels, 1995.
Habsburg, Maximilian von. *Catholic and Protestant Translations of the "ImitatioChristi," 1425–1650: From Late Medieval Classic to Early Modern Bestseller*. Burlington, VT: Ashgate, 2011.
Kempis, Thomas à. *The Imitation of Christ*. Translated by Aloysius Croft and Harold Bolton. 1940. Reprint, Mineola, NY: Dover, 2003.
Kieckhefer, Richard. "Major Currents in Late Medieval Devotion." In *Christian Spirituality: High Middle Ages and Reformation*, edited by Jill Raitt, et al., 75–108. New York: Crossroad, 1987.

Kierkegaard, Søren. *Christian Discourses* and *The Crisis and a Crisis in the Life of an Actress*. Edited and translated by Howard V. Hong and Edna H. Hong. Princeton: Princeton University Press, 1997.

———. *Concluding Unscientific Postscript to "Philosophical Fragments."* 2 vols. Edited and translated by Howard V. Hong and Edna H. Hong. Princeton: Princeton University Press, 1992.

———. *Discourses at the Communion on Fridays*. Translated by Sylvia Walsh. Bloomington: Indiana University Press, 2011.

———. *For Self-Examination* and *Judge for Yourself!* Edited and trans. Howard V. Hong and Edna H. Hong. Princeton: Princeton University Press, 1990.

———. *Philosophical Fragments* and *Johannes Climacus*. Edited and translated by Howard V. Hong and Edna H. Hong. Princeton: Princeton University Press, 1985.

———. *The Point of View: On My Work as an Author; The Point of View for My Work as an Author; Armed Neutrality*. Edited and translated by Howard V. Hong and Edna H. Hong. Princeton: Princeton University Press, 1998.

———. *Practice in Christianity*. Edited and translated by Howard V. Hong and Edna H. Hong. Princeton: Princeton University Press, 1991.

——— *Søren Kierkegaard's Journals and Papers*. 7 vols. Edited and translated by Howard V. Hong and Edna H. Hong. Bloomington, IN: Indiana University Press, 1967–78.

———. *Upbuilding Discourses in Various Spirits*. Edited and translated by Howard V. Hong and Edna H. Hong. Princeton: Princeton University Press, 1993.

———. *Without Authority*. Edited and translated by Howard V. Hong and Edna H. Hong. Princeton: Princeton University Press, 1997.

———. *Works of Love*. Edited and translated by Howard V. Hong and Edna H. Hong. Princeton: Princeton University Press, 1995.

Kolb, Robert and Timothy J. Wingert. *The Book of Concord: The Confession of the Evangelical Lutheran Church*. Minneapolis: Fortress Press, 2000.

Law, David. "Kierkegaard's Understanding of the Eucharist in *Christian Discourses*, Part Four." In *International Kierkegaard Commentary: Christian Discourses and The Crisis and a Crisis in the Life of an Actress*, edited by Robert L. Perkins, 273–97. Macon, GA: Mercer University Press, 2007.

Perkins, Robert L. *International Kierkegaard Commentary: The Point of View*. Macon, GA: Mercer University Press, 2010.

Plekon, Michael. "Kierkegaard and the Eucharist." *Studia Liturgica* 22 (1992) 214–36.

Post, Regnerius. *The Modern Devotion: Confrontation with Reformation and Humanism*. Leiden: Brill, 1968.

Rasmussen, Joel D. S. "Thomas à Kempis: *Devotio Moderna* and Kierkegaard's Critique of 'Bourgeois-Philistinism.'" In *Kierkegaard and the Patristic and Medieval Traditions*, edited by Jon Stewart, 289–98. Burlington, VT: Ashgate, 2008.

Rubin, Miri. *Corpus Christi: The Eucharist in Late Medieval Culture*. Cambridge: Cambridge University Press, 1991.

Šajda, Peter. "Tauler: A Teacher in Spiritual Dietethics: Kierkegaard's Reception of Johannes Tauler." In *Kierkegaard and the Patristic and Medieval Traditions*, edited by Jon Stewart, 265–87. Burlington, VT: Ashgate, 2008.

Thulstrup, Marie Mikulová. 'Pietism." In *Bibliotheca Kierkegaardiana: Kierkegaard and Great Traditions*, edited by Niels Thulstrup and Marie Mikulová Thulstrup, 173–222. Copenhagen: C. A. Reitzels Boghandel A/S, 1981.

———. "Søren Kierkegaard og Johann Arndt." *Kierkegaardiana* 4 (1962) 7–17.

———. "Studies of Pietists, Mystics, and Church Fathers." In *Bibliotheca Kierkegaardiana:Kierkegaard's View of Christianity*, edited by Niels Thulstrup and Marie Mikulová Thulstrup, 60–80. Copenhagen: C. A. Reitzels Boghandel A/S, 1978.

Wallmann, Johannes. "Johann Arndt (1555–1621)." In *The Pietist Theologians*, edited by Carter Lindberg, 21–37. Malden, MA: Blackwell, 2005.

Walsh, Sylvia. "Comparing Genres: The Woman Who Was a Sinner in Kierkegaard's *Three Discourses at the Communion on Fridays* and *An Upbuilding Discourse*." In *Kierkegaard Studies Yearbook 2012: Kierkegaard's Late Writings*, edited by Niels Jørgen Cappelørn, et al., 71–90. Berlin: Walter de Gruyter, 2010.

———. "Introduction." *Discourses at the Communion on Fridays*. Bloomington,IN: Indiana University Press, 2011.

———. *Kierkegaard: Thinking Christianly in an Existential Mode*. Oxford: Oxford University Press, 2009.

———. *Living Christianly: Kierkegaard's Dialectic of Christian Existence*. University Park: The Pennsylvania State University Press, 2005.

———. *Living Poetically: Kierkegaard's Existential Aesthetics*. University Park: The Pennsylvania State University Press, 1994.

———. "Prototypes of Piety: The Woman Who Was a Sinner and Mary Magdalene." In *International Kierkegaard Commentary: Without Authority*, edited by Robert L. Perkins, 313–42. Macon, GA: Mercer University Press, 2006.

———. "Reading Kierkegaard with Kierkegaard Against Garff." *Søren Kierkegaard Newsletter* 38 (July, 1999) 4–8.

Westfall, Joseph. *The Kierkegaardian Author: Authorship and Performance in Kierkegaard's Literary and Dramatic Criticism*. Berlin: Walter de Gruyter, 2007.

14

Kierkegaard for *This* World

Thinking with Kierkegaard about the Desire for Security as a Sickness unto Death

—Paul Martens

Against the grain of the vast majority of scholarship at the time, David Gouwens's *Kierkegaard As Religious Thinker* gave voice to a reading of Kierkegaard that methodologically sought to privilege Kierkegaard's own concerns.[1] Rather than reading Kierkegaard primarily through the lens of biography, philosophy (especially existentialism), literature, deconstruction, or dogmatics, Gouwens sought to attempt to "think with" Kierkegaard, "to enter into the concerns and issues he raises with philosophical *eros* and passion."[2] In this manner, Gouwens provided a portrait of Kierkegaard that shows—and not merely describes—what religion, "and especially the Christian religion," are.[3] In the argument that follows, I am indebted to Gouwens to the extent that it is this mode of reading that I employ with respect to Kierkegaard's discourses concerning the "birds of the air" and the "lilies of

---

1. See the essay by Lee Barrett in this volume for an account of Gouwens's approach to Kierkegaard.

2. Gouwens, *Kierkegaard as Religious Thinker*, 2. Of course, Gouwens's method of reading of Kierkegaard is not entirely unique as he is borrowing heavily from a certain reading of Wittgenstein and Cavell (and that filtered through O. K. Bouwsma). Further, Richard Bell's edited volume *The Grammar of the Heart* had already been published with the subtitle *Thinking with Kierkegaard and Wittgenstein*. That said, Gouwens is one of the first to provide a book-length treatment of Kierkegaard's corpus in this mode.

3. Gouwens, *Kierkegaard as Religious Thinker*, 3.

the field" that appear in Matt 6:25–34. There is, however, a second level of debts to Gouwens that must also be acknowledged.

As *Kierkegaard As Religious Thinker* draws to a close, Gouwens's argument culminates in the conclusion that Kierkegaard's display of Christianity is "profoundly social,"[4] that Kierkegaard believes and lives as if "the world is the arena for prophetic faithfulness, courageous hope, and reconciling love."[5] Here again, the radicalness of Gouwens's analysis may not seem obvious until it is placed against the backdrop of decades of twentieth-century caricatures in which "the melancholy Dane" was concerned solely about "solitary individuals" in an acosmic "absolute relation to the absolute." Much of the subsequent rehabilitation of Kierkegaard's sociality has focused on love of the neighbor and texts such as Kierkegaard's *Works of Love* have become central to that task.[6] Gouwens, however, recognizes that rehabilitations of Kierkegaard's sociality need not be limited to direct or one-on-one interactions with the neighbor. He recognizes that there are resources in Kierkegaard for "theologically constructive political action" in a "world-affirming spirituality." Admittedly, this is "relatively 'undeveloped'" in Kierkegaard's thought.[7] But, it is precisely this pregnant suggestion that I will begin to pursue in the pages that follow as I attempt to think with and beyond Kierkegaard about the human desire for security and its problematic entailments.

To this end, I begin with an examination of Kierkegaard's discourses on Matt 6:25–34 for the purpose of illuminating how he describes the all-too-human desire for security. On the basis of this description, I then briefly outline how the human desire for security entails problematic consequences within human relationships and in human relationships with creation.

Kierkegaard on Birds, Lilies, and Killing Others for Security

Daily, and repeatedly, we are forced to question the security of our current existence. Advertisements and commercials in all kinds of media venues ask: Do you have sufficient health insurance in the event you get sick? Is your home sufficiently secure that you can leave it unattended or, more importantly, that you can provide a safe place for your children to sleep in

4. Ibid., 229.
5. Ibid., 231.
6. See, for example, Ferreira's *Love's Grateful Striving*; and Evans's *Kierkegaard's Ethic of Love*.
7. Gouwens, *Kierkegaard as Religious Thinker*, 231.

peace? Will your retirement plan allow financial security in your final years ... preferably spending afternoons on the beach walking hand-in-hand with your gracefully aging spouse? And, behind all of these allegedly immediate concerns lie the more fundamental questions—is your community and is your nation secure?

Despite the particular twenty-first-century shape of these questions about physical, financial, home, and national security, these questions are not really new. In fact, Christians have wrestled with how to handle these sorts of concerns for nearly two thousand years. One scriptural text that has stood at the center of this wrestling is Matt 6:25–34:

> Therefore I tell you, do not worry about your life, what you will eat or what you will drink, or about your body, what you will wear. Is not life more than food, and the body more than clothing? Look at the birds of the air; they neither sow nor reap nor gather into barns, and yet your heavenly Father feeds them ... Consider the lilies of the field, how they grow; they neither toil nor spin, yet I tell you, even Solomon in all his glory was not clothed like one of these ... Therefore do not worry, saying 'What will we eat?' or 'What will we drink?' or 'What will we wear?' For it is the Gentiles who strive for all these things; and indeed your heavenly Father knows that you need all these things. But strive first for the kingdom of God and his righteousness, and all these things will be given to you as well.

In the middle of the 19th century—a time of profound revolutionary upheaval, famine, and urban poverty in northern Europe, a time of intense debates about land ownership, work, and capital, and a time of preliminary steps towards the democratization of Denmark—Søren Kierkegaard turned to the birds and the lilies of Matthew's gospel to reflect upon the seemingly pervasive human desire for security. Though the times and details of the questions have changed, I intend to illustrate that what we learn from Kierkegaard is troubling, namely, that the concern for security—as one's driving concern—leads to death. Before getting ahead of myself, however, attending to Kierkegaard's engagement with these matters in some detail is in order.

In 1847, Kierkegaard published a series of three discourses devoted to the Matthew 6 passage in *Upbuilding Discourses in Various Spirits*. Two years later, a second series appeared under the title *The Lily of the Field and the Bird of the Air*. In this context, one small section of the very first of these discourses, "To Be Contented with Being a Human Being," sufficiently serves as an initial representative sample of Kierkegaard's thinking. The section of the discourse that I would like to highlight contains Kierkegaard's imaginative non-identical repetition of the text which could rightly be referred to as "the parable of the wood-dove."

It requires very little analytic ability to discern that Matt 6:25–34 directly addresses the question of anxiety (and the frequently inserted heading entitled "Do Not Worry" ensures that the reader does not miss the obvious "moral of the story"). Specifically, one of the anxieties addressed directly by the text is that of security, especially in terms of a sufficient and steady supply of food and material possessions. In order to draw his reader into the world of the text, Kierkegaard creates a parable about a wild wood-dove. Drawing upon his debts to the Romantics, Kierkegaard begins the parable as if it is a dark fairy tale: "Once upon a time there was a wood-dove; it had its nest in the scowling forest, out there where wonder lives in apprehension among the secluded tall trees. But not far away, where smoke rises from the farmer's house, lived some of its distant relatives, some tame doves. It met a pair of them occasionally."[8]

The sharp contrasts are obvious right from the start: wild v. tame; single v. pair; apprehension v. comfort; poor v. rich. Kierkegaard then continues:

> One day, while the three doves were conversing at a distance, they stumbled upon the topic of the condition of things and "about making a living." The wood-dove said, "Up until now I have made my living by letting each day have its own troubles, and in that way I get through the world." The tame doves listened patiently and respectfully, and then acknowledged: "No, we manage differently; with us, that is, with the rich farmer with whom we live, one's future is secure. When harvest time comes, I or my mate... sits up on the roof and watches. Then the farmer drives one load of grain into the barn after another, and when he has driven in so many that I lose count I know that there is provision enough for a long time."[9]

As you can imagine, the wood-dove was greatly disturbed by this revelation. As Kierkegaard turns the phrase, "It was promptly struck by the thought that it must be very pleasant to *know* that one's living was secured for a long time, whereas it was miserable to live continually in uncertainty so that one never dares to say that one *knows* one is provided for."[10] The wood-dove's first response then is to seek to imitate the tame doves within the framework of its usual food-gathering lifestyle. To its dismay, it discov-

8. Kierkegaard, *Upbuilding Discourses in Various Spirits*, 174.
9. Ibid., 174–75.
10. Ibid., 175.

ered that with all of the time needed to locate and hoard new stores of food for the future it barely had time to eat. And, every time it managed to put together a little extra in a safe place, it was always gone when he came back to look for it. The net result of this new strategic attempt at food security was, therefore, less than satisfactory: the wood-dove worked harder and actually acquired and ate less food. And, to make matters worse, the suffering the wood-dove endured was not due, at least initially, to an actual need—actual hunger. Rather, the suffering was endured because it "had acquired an *idea* of need in the future," the very idea that destroyed its peace of mind in the present and caused it to worry about making a living.[11]

Of course, once the wood-dove started down this road, it could get no rest until it contrived a scheme that would finally provide it with the now necessary security. Therefore, one day it flew to sit with the tame doves again, this time right on the farmer's roof. And, in the evening, as they flew into their home, he followed. But, when the farmer came to shut the dovecote, the wood-dove was discovered. The farmer placed it in a secure little box by itself until the next day when he killed it, finally delivering the wood-dove from its *"acquired worry about making a living."*[12] In the end, the wood-dove was trapped in its worry—"unto death."[13]

In order to deflect the discomfort Kierkegaard introduces, we might be tempted to remind ourselves that Kierkegaard could write this way because he was not married and did not have his own children to care for . . . or because he lived on a stipend left by his father and did not have to work to earn a living. That much Kierkegaard himself would readily admit. Yet, to note that Kierkegaard's life was idiosyncratic and free from select challenges that we encounter is to already lose sight of the issue at hand: to be contented with being a human being, or, to use the familiar language of a later text, to be a self that can "rest transparently in the power that established it."[14] This is the life that the wood-dove knew and then rejected with terrible consequences. And, on this characterization of human existence—even if idiosyncratic literarily—Kierkegaard does not stand alone.

Upon further review, Kierkegaard's parable contains a moral that finds considerable affirmation within the community of saints. For example, Augustine lived nearly 1500 years before Kierkegaard yet echoes of his confession that "You have made us for yourself, and our hearts are restless

11. Ibid.
12. Ibid.
13. Ibid., 176.
14. Kierkegaard, *The Sickness Unto Death*, 14.

until they find peace in you"[15] resound clearly in Kierkegaard's thought. The superficial difference between his confession and Kierkegaard's parable is the direction of movement: Augustine's statement presumes that humans are drawn from restlessness toward God to find peace; Kierkegaard's parable presumes that humans move away from peace in God in pursuit of competing forms of peace and security (a movement that would, of course, be familiar to Augustine as well). Therefore, much of this difference may be rhetorical (and there is no way to do justice to the complexity of either of these positions in this context).[16] That said, it is not by accident that Kierkegaard assumes a disordered fixation with worldly security that can only be overcome by an external impetus—a divine prodding—which then reorients humans away from the stupefying comforts of false peace and security. To illustrate, allow me to introduce Kierkegaard's succinct description of the *metanoia* of the apostle Peter: "[Peter] left his customary occupation, a quiet and simple life that, content with a modest income, was spent in security. He left the reassuring trust in the probable, within which a person usually has his life, untried in anything other than what usually happens—*he left the certain and chose the uncertain* . . . But as soon as Christ called him, he left all this . . . and yet, no, he did not choose the uncertain."[17]

With an eye also to his late critique of Christendom, it seems clear that—as in the case of the apostle Peter—the deceptive temptation of a numbingly familiar life with a steady income is perceived to be one of the greatest temptations of Kierkegaard's day.

In this way and in addition to Augustine, perhaps Luther's *Large Catechism* captures Kierkegaard's particular concern more sharply in its explication of the first commandment, that is, the command that "Thou shall have no other gods before Me."[18] The Lutheran *Catechism* clarifies: "A god means that from which we are to expect all good and to which we are to take refuge in all distress." Walking the same path that Kierkegaard did years later, it explains: "He who has money and possessions feels secure, and is joyful and undismayed as though he were sitting in the midst of Paradise . . . Lo, such a man also has a god, Mammon by name, i.e. money and possessions, on which he sets all his heart, and which is also the most common idol on earth."[19]

15. Augustine, *Confessions*, 3.

16. For further development of this theme, see Barrett, *Eros and Self-Emptying: The Intersections of Augustine and Kierkegaard*.

17. Kierkegaard, *Christian Discourses*, 182.

18. See Exod 20:3.

19. Luther, *The Large Catechism*, 44–45 (I have inverted the order of these two statements in the final direct quotation).

Stepping back for a moment, it is entirely appropriate to ask whether Luther's highly-charged language of idolatry may be a bit overwrought, a bit 16th-century-ish. The answer, however, is a bit bracing. Will Willimon reminded us not very long ago that "Luther said that for which you would sacrifice your daughter is properly your 'god.'"[20] The allusion to Iphegenia and the overtures to *Fear and Trembling* do not seem to be intended, though they are incredibly relevant. Willimon then continues: "That we, men and now women, would so readily sacrifice our sons and daughters for [the war on terror] suggests a new idol." In short, "we are attempting to accomplish through dollars and bombs that which Christians expect of God: security."[21] Like Kierkegaard's wood-dove, we are, in fact, dying for security. Willimon's point could be drawn from Matt 6, but it could also be supplemented with material from Isaiah, Jeremiah, or any number of other biblical sources. Regardless, the demand is the same: Christian discipleship is a lifetime of training in learning to live with the destabilization and insecurity that come with following the Word made flesh.[22] Kierkegaard would wholeheartedly agree with Willimon here. And, for Kierkegaard, *the Teacher*—the prototype, the Way and Truth that Christians are called to follow—is aided in prodding and displaying this training in Christianity by "assistant teachers," namely the birds and the lilies.[23]

There is much more that could and should be said on this matter. What must be said, however, is that Kierkegaard is on the right track when he reminds us that every time we seek to absolutize the relative and the contingent we make gods for ourselves that justify our worldly comfort and security.[24] In short, we seek to control the world around us on our own terms, even if that means bringing death to others. . . and perhaps to ourselves as well. In this time and place, we name this in all kinds of mundane and less-than-mundane ways . . . and perhaps most dramatically at the level of national security when we strategically affirm the cryptic goal of "renewing American leadership so that we can more effectively advance our interests in the 21st century."[25]

In recent years, love of neighbor has been the key to the vast majority of ethical appropriations of Kierkegaard. The human desire to control the

20. Willimon, "Security," 185.
21. Ibid., 185–86.
22. See ibid., 190–91.
23. See Kierkegaard, *Christian Discourses*, 9.
24. See LaMothe, "Obsession for National Security," 42.
25. The White House, *National Security Strategy*: http://www.whitehouse.gov/sites/default/files/rss_viewer/national_security_strategy.pdf.

world for the purposes of security, however, is not limited to intra-human interaction. Increasingly, we are discovering that the desire for security is also killing creation as well. And, although Kierkegaard may not have imagined exactly what the world looks like today, his reflections on anxieties concerning security can be used to illuminate the relationship between humanity's insatiable consumption and the environmental mess we find ourselves in today. To take this step forward, I will take what may look like a step back from the focal point of contemporary Kierkegaard scholarship.

Kierkegaard on Birds, Lilies, and Killing Creation for Security

The birds of the air and the lilies of the field are, for Christians, part of God's creation. As such, they serve to illustrate that God cares and provides for creation in ways that simply cannot be replicated no matter much humans desire to do so. Therefore, at its very literal level, Matt 6:25–34 is also about the beauty and limits of creaturely existence. In the above, I have attempted to demonstrate how the generic desire for security addressed in this text can have dire consequences in human relationships. But, that conclusion is already an extrapolation from the very earthiness of the text—at root, the text names the acquisition of food and material possessions as the means to security. These are the things that "the Gentiles"—or "the nations of the world"[26]—strive after. The implicit fear suggested here is the fear that one will not have enough food, that one will not have enough clothing and other pretty stuff and, in the end, a further fear that even the acquisition and preservation of these things will not be enough to stave off the threat of both thieves and moths.[27]

In the 1847 "To Be Contented with Being a Human Being" discourse, Kierkegaard provides—alongside and thickening the parable of the woodduck—another non-identical repetition of the biblical text that could be satirically called "the parable of the flying lily." This story begins with much less foreboding than the previous: "Once upon a time there was a lily that stood in an isolated spot beside a small brook and was well known to some nettles and also to a few other small flowers nearby."[28] One day, this contented lily heard about other beautiful lilies—"Crown Imperials"—that grew in another field. The carrier of this information was a chatty and capricious bird, a bird that "talked fast and loose, truthfully and untruthfully"

26. This is the phrase used in Luke 12:30.
27. See Luke 12:33.
28. Kierkegaard, *Upbuilding Discourses in Various Spirits*, 167.

about places where there was rapture and merriment, beautiful fragrances, brilliant colors, and singing beyond description. "Then the lily became worried. The more it listened to the bird, the more worried it became."[29]

In short, the lily was not worried about its own survival; the lily was worried about its inferiority and its inferior station in life. The lily became exhausted in its worry but, rather than refusing to worry any further, it began to justify its worry: "After all, my wish is not a foolish wish," it said. "After all, I am not asking for the impossible, to become what I am not, a bird, for example. My wish is only to become a gorgeous lily, or even the most gorgeous."[30]

After several days, the lily simply had enough. It hatched a plan with the bird that would allow the lily to become all that it could be, to keep the company that it properly ought to keep and, in the process, to put an end to the worry: the next morning the bird would dig up the lily and carry it to the field of beautiful lilies where it would be replanted in the company of the most beautiful lilies. It could then, if all went well, achieve all that it was meant to be . . . and perhaps even become envied by the others. Alas, the conclusion of the story takes a different turn: during the flight to the new field, the uprooted lily withered and died.

We laugh at the ironic conclusion of this parable, but we laugh uncomfortably with the suspicion that Kierkegaard is attempting to force his readers—us—to see that we act like the lily all too often. Kierkegaard expounds the moral, a moral that has contemporary significance:

> The lily is a human being. The naughty little bird is the restless mentality of comparison, which roams far and wide, fitfully and capriciously, and gleans the morbid knowledge of diversity [and here one ought to think of aesthetic and temporal distinctions] . . . Thus when the comparison with the bird's movement to and fro has incited the passion of worry and has managed to tear the worried one loose from earthboundedness, that is, from willing to be what he is intended to be, it looks for a moment as if the comparison were coming to take the worried one to the desired goal; it certainly does come and fetch him, but only as death comes to fetch a person.[31]

Long before Annie Dillard or Wendell Berry, this short parable of the flying lily and its discontent presciently gestures toward the direction our contemporary civilization has taken. We—in order to become all that we

29. Ibid., 167–68.
30. Ibid., 168.
31. Ibid., 169–70.

can be, in order to secure ourselves against the worry of perceived need and comparative inferiority—have been willing to give up our earthboundedness (both literally and metaphorically) and we have forgotten what it means to be contented with being a human being. We continually strive to acquire material things that will quench our worry. Or, to restate, we continually strive to acquire food and material possessions that will allow us to determine our own fate, to overcome a much too simple trust in God. In fact, we frequently justify our continual acquisition and consumption by defining it as an expression of God's blessing. But the worry does not die. Instead, everything else in the world dies.

This is, of course, a rather melodramatic claim. But, perhaps a little self-examination might reveal more truth than we would like to admit. To this end, a brief anecdotal example of the kitchen in my house representatively illustrates the non-earthboundedness of our (and by this I mean North American) society's desire for food security, to name just one source of anxiety. We have a small-to-medium house by Texas standards with a decidedly average kitchen. Yet, we have a double-door refrigerator/freezer for food storage equipped with an ice-maker and water filter. Immediately to the left of the fridge stands the toaster-oven, the first kitchen appliance we acquired that was not already installed before we bought the house. Beside the toaster-oven stands the coffee-maker and its partner, the kettle (and just last week we were given a coffee grinder . . . but we have yet to take it out of the box because there is simply no more room on the counter). In turn, the kettle nestles against the "real" oven which is complete with four embedded elements on the top for cooking. And, above the stove-top sits the microwave, which just may be needed if the toaster-oven, the oven, or the stove-top are insufficient or too slow in heating the requisite nourishment. Across the counter further to the left around the corner lies the sink which is, of course, equipped with a garbage disposal unit so that food scraps can be disposed of quickly and cleanly with the flick of a switch. One step further left one finds the dishwasher which is so often "required" to clean the many dishes used by our family of six to consume the large amounts of food that have been variously heated. All that said about the kitchen, the story about our food anxieties is not yet complete—a few steps in the opposite leads into the garage which contains a medium-size freezer that contains enough food for a week or two; a few steps back in the general direction of the kitchen leads to the back patio that contains a propane grill for, again, cooking food . . . and then there is the small fire pit at the back of the yard for those rare occasions when the nostalgia for earthboundedness is expressed by cooking some of the most processed foods in the world: hot dogs and marshmallows.

By my count, then, the rather average food-consuming network in our home contains nine electrical, one propane, and one wood-burning "appliances" . . . and I have not yet said anything about the pantry area full of dry goods and pre-packaged food, about the multiple cupboards full of cooking utensils, spices, dishes, and cups, or even about the vast network of farms and ranches with their array of pesticides, herbicides, and fertilizers, the processing and storage facilities, shipping channels, trucks and highways, human capital, and political and legal arrangements that enable our kitchen to do its job. Of course, there is also the safety net of local restaurants in the area should we need a bit of Kierkegaardian diversity. And why is all of this necessary? Not because we need enough food for tomorrow. No, Kierkegaard was right: we have constructed this elaborate stultifying matrix because we need to know there will be enough food for tomorrow and because we need the preferred variety of food for tomorrow. Against this pervasive cultural presumption, Drew Christiansen rightly notes that it is simply undeniable that this gospel passage links our anxiety with "the unrestrained acquisition of material resources."[32]

When we step back to reconsider our early-twenty-first-century North American lives, there is no doubt that we have arrived in Francis Bacon's futuristic New Atlantis . . . and it appears that it is sinking just like the ancient Atlantis.[33] Because of our worries about food, we are poisoning the streams and rivers, we are stuffing our land-fills, we are paving our fields, we are cutting down forests to create new fields, we are poisoning the air, and the list could go on. This, however, is not merely an environmental problem; it is a theological problem. Or, as Michael Northcott would state it: "[T]echnical progress is substituted for divine creation/redemption as the origin and end of human life and the cosmos, and the idolatry of consumer artifacts is substituted for the worship of God."[34]

Kierkegaard viewed the result of this sort of search for a sense of security as a form of slavery: "To be dependent on one's treasure—that is dependence and hard and heavy slavery; to be dependent on God, completely dependent—that is independence."[35] Following this line of thought, the 1997 Earth Day message offered by Bartholomew I, the Ecumenical Patriarch of the Eastern Orthodox Church, attempts to defy the trajectory that dominates our society:

---

32. Christiansen, "Learn a Lesson from the Flowers," 21.
33. See Bacon, *The New Atlantis and The Great Instauration*.
34. Northcott, *The Environment and Christian Ethics*, 257–58.
35. Kierkegaard, *Upbuilding Discourses in Various Spirits*, 181.

> Our Church supports an attitude of thanksgiving toward creation, rather than an attitude of egoism that results in abuse of the natural resources and life of the world. It condemns greed, avarice, limitless acquisition, and uncritical consumerism, which sometimes reach the point of insanity. In contrast, we can look to the luminous examples of the saints, who respected life and humanity, who befriended the animals and the birds, who positively influenced their environment and community, and who lived with simplicity and self-sufficiency.
>
> Therefore, we call upon everyone. . .to work together in withstanding the captivity of overconsumption. "It is for freedom that Christ has set us free. Stand firm, then, and no longer submit to any yoke of slavery" (Gal 5:1).[36]

Unfortunately, those of us living in North America today are merely beginning to understand how enmeshed we are in a world that encourages and gratifies the unrestrained acquisition of material resources. In this sort of world, the threshold of giving in to the slavery of consumption is usually crossed long before it is recognized; we find ourselves at the altar of mammon before we recognize that we have walked into its temple. And, when we find ourselves at this altar, we find we have already participated in the sacrifice of the world around us.

May We Rest in Peace

We do not need Kierkegaard to tell us that we are participating in a society that is actively bringing death to others and itself—that more than 6,000 civilians have been killed in Afghanistan since 2001, that more than 6,000 American soldiers have been killed in Iraq and Afghanistan during that same time, or that more than 800 civilians have been killed by US drone strikes over the last four years in Pakistan alone to name just a few examples. We do not need Kierkegaard to tell us that we are participating in a society that is actively destroying the environment in which we live and breathe—that over half of America's rivers can no longer support healthy aquatic life, that the US alone released nearly 7,000 million metric tons of greenhouse gases into the atmosphere in 2011, that expanding deforestation and desertification contribute to species extinction rates, well over 1,000 times the background rate to merely scratch the surface of possible examples. What Kierkegaard does reveal, however, is that we have a sickness that is unto

---

36. Cited in Chryssavgis, *Cosmic Grace, Humble Prayer*, 380–81.

death, namely, an unreflective and unbridled desire for security on our own terms.

In *Sickness Unto Death*, Kierkegaard attempts to outline that there is a sickness unto death that is more horrifying than what we would call physical death. The sickness of which he speaks is the despair of being offended by God, the despair of refusing to rest transparently in God who created all humans. This despair is the result of giving in to our desires that are driven by our anxieties. We are the knights who see a rare bird and chase after it only to find ourselves alone and lost in the wilderness; we are the individuals who are so anxious that we are led away from ourselves to become victims of that which we are most anxious about.[37] What we also find is that physical death and this sickness unto death are not entirely unrelated. That is to say that we are beginning to find out that the sickness of our widespread refusal to "strive first for the kingdom of God" leads, in actuality, to the physical death of our friends, our enemies, the world in which we live, and even our death.

In our day, Walter Brueggemann has attempted to turn back directly to Luther and indirectly to Kierkegaard by invoking "the crucified God" as the key to addressing this sickness unto death. This invocation calls us back to the raw claim that it is the utter self-giving of God in weakness that truly exhibits holiness and eluded control of the world.[38] This trusting vulnerability, displayed by the birds and the lilies, depends on God alone and, because of this, is truly free from worry. This is where we should begin. But, as Kierkegaard rightly notes, "The beginning is not that with which one begins but that to which one comes, and one comes to it backward."[39] The task of going backward is neither easy nor accomplished quickly. Neil Darragh advocates a contemporary approach that looks remarkably Kierkegaardian: "We may not want to use the term 'ascetic' to describe a contemporary Earth spirituality. 'Voluntary simplicity' or 'living simply' might communicate more easily in the contemporary world, but such gentler terms do seem to slide off the arduous and dedicated nature of the task. In any case, attention to the old asceticism reminds us that the struggle is not all out there. It is also within us. For people living in consumer societies, that struggle is chiefly a negative one of self-restraint in opposition to accepted patterns of consumption."[40]

Of course, Kierkegaard leads his reader to this point and then disappears without giving further concrete guidance—that is what he takes to be his role as a midwife without authority. He leaves us to meet the Word

---

37. See Kierkegaard, *The Sickness Unto Death*, 37.
38. Brueggemann, "Prophetic Ministry in the National Security State," 287.
39. Kierkegaard, *Without Authority*, 11.
40. Darragh, "An Ascetic Theology, Spirituality, and Praxis," 82.

within the Word on our own.[41] And, perhaps when gender, racial, environmental, and economic exploitation are all too common (as they are today) it may be entirely appropriate that Kierkegaard does not (and that we do not) determine the required level of vulnerability that others should attain once and for all . . . which is another way of saying that until my kitchen (and the rest of my house) at least approximately displays the trust of the birds and the lilies, perhaps I am not the one who should be demanding vulnerability of others. The good news is that we have not yet killed off the birds and the lilies. And, beginning with that recognition, perhaps we still have something to learn about our fixation with security from these "assistant teachers."

Bibliography

Augustine. *Confessions*. Translated by Henry Chadwick. New York: Oxford University Press.
Bacon, Francis. *The New Atlantis and The Great Instauration*. Edited by Jerry Weinberger. London: Wylie Blackwell, 1991.
Barrett, Lee C., III. *Eros and Self-Emptying: The Intersections of Augustine and Kierkegaard*. Grand Rapids: Eerdmans, 2013.
Bell, Richard H. *The Grammar of the Heart: Thinking with Kierkegaard and Wittgenstein*. San Francisco: Harper & Row, 1988.
Brueggemann, Walter. "Prophetic Ministry in the National Security State." *Theology Today* 65 (2008) 285–311.
Christiansen, Drew, S.J. "Learn a Lesson From the Flowers: Catholic Social Teaching and Global Stewardship." In *The Challenge of Global Stewardship: Roman Catholic Responses*, edited by Maura Ryan and Todd Whitmore, 19–37. Notre Dame: University of Notre Dame Press, 1997.
Chryssavgis, John. *Cosmic Grace, Humble Prayer: The Ecological Vision of the Green Patriarch Bartholomew I*. Grand Rapids: Eerdmans, 2003.
Darragh, Neil. "An Ascetic Theology, Spirituality, and Praxis." *Concilium: International Review of Theology* 3 (2009) 82.
Evans, C. Stephen. *Kierkegaard's Ethic of Love: Divine Commands and Moral Obligations*. New York: Oxford University Press, 2006.
Ferreira, M. Jamie. *Love's Grateful Striving: A Commentary on Kierkegaard's Works of Love*. New York: Oxford University Press, 2008.
Gouwens, David J. *Kierkegaard as Religious Thinker*. Cambridge: Cambridge University Press, 1996.
Kierkegaard, Søren. *Christian Discourses*. Edited and translated by Howard V. Hong and Edna H. Hong. Princeton: Princeton University Press, 1997.
———. *For Self-Examination*. Edited and translated by Howard V. Hong and Edna H. Hong. Princeton: Princeton University Press, 1990.
———. *The Sickness Unto Death: A Christian Psychological Exposition for Upbuilding and Awakening*. Edited and translated by Howard V. Hong and Edna H. Hong. Princeton: Princeton University Press, 1980.

---

41. See Kierkegaard, *For Self-Examination*, 13–51.

———. *Upbuilding Discourses in Various Spirits*. Edited and translated by Howard V. Hong and Edna H. Hong. Princeton: Princeton University Press, 1993.

———. *Without Authority*. Edited and translated by Howard V. Hong and Edna H. Hong. Princeton: Princeton University Press, 1997.

LaMothe, Ryan. "Obsession for National Security and the Rise of the National Security State-Industry: A Pastoral-Psychological Analysis." *Pastoral Psychology* (2012) 15–29.

Luther, Martin. *The Large Catechism*. Translated by Robert H. Fischer. Minneapolis: Augsburg Fortress, 1988.

Northcott, Michael S. *The Environment and Christian Ethics*. Cambridge: Cambridge University Press, 1996.

The White House. *National Security Strategy*. No pages. Online at: http://www.whitehouse.gov/sites/default/files/rss_viewer/national_security_strategy.pdf. Accessed 10/24/2013.

Willimon, William. "Security." *Ex Auditu* 24 (2008) 185–91.

Publications of David J. Gouwens

Professor of Theology

Brite Divinity School

Books

1989: *Kierkegaard's Dialectic of the Imagination*. American University Studies Series V: Philosophy, Volume 71. New York: Peter Lang.
1996: *Kierkegaard as Religious Thinker*. Cambridge: Cambridge University Press.
2012: *The Paul L. Holmer Papers*, in three volumes, co-edited with Lee C. Barrett III. Eugene, OR: Cascade.
> Volume 1: *On Kierkegaard and the Truth*. Foreword by Stanley Hauerwas. Afterword by David Cain. January 2012.
> Volume 2: *Thinking the Faith with Passion: Selected Essays*. Foreword by Don E. Saliers. Afterword by David Cain. April 2012.
> Volume 3: *Communicating the Faith Indirectly: Selected Sermons, Addresses, and Prayers*. Foreword by William H. Willimon. Afterword by David Cain. November 2012.

Journal articles and chapters in books

1982: "Kierkegaard on the Ethical Imagination," *Journal of Religious Ethics* 10/2 (Fall) 204–20.
1985: "Theological Belief and Pastoral Vision," *Encounter* 46:2 (Spring) 117–26.
1988: "Kierkegaard's Understanding of Doctrine," *Modern Theology* 5:1 (October) 13–22.
1992: "Heresy," in Donald W. Musser and Joseph Price, eds., *New Handbook of Christian Theology* (Nashville: Abingdon) 216–19.
1993: "Understanding, Imagination, and Irony in Kierkegaard's *Repetition*," in Robert L. Perkins, ed., *International Kierkegaard Commentary: Fear and Trembling and Repetition* (Macon, Georgia: Mercer University Press) 283–308.

1995: "Kierkegaard's *Either/Or Part I*: Patterns of Interpretation," in Robert L. Perkins, ed., *International Kierkegaard Commentary: Either/Or, Part I*. (Macon, Georgia: Mercer University Press) 5–50.

1999: "Imagination" and "Introspection," in Haim Gordon, ed., *Dictionary of Existentialism* (Westport, Connecticut: Greenwood) 199–201, 213–15.

1999: "Mozart, Theology, and Worship: Some Reflections on Kierkegaard, Barth, and Küng," *Doxology* 16 (Fall 1999) 1–15.

2000: "Mozart Among the Theologians," *Modern Theology* 16, no. 4 (October 2000) 461–74.

2003: "Kierkegaard's Hermeneutics of Discipleship: Communal and Critical Uses of Scripture in the 1854–55 Attack," in Poul Houe and Gordon D. Marino, eds., *Søren Kierkegaard and the Word(s) Essays on Hermeneutics and Communication* (Copenhagen: Reitzel, 2003) 81–92.

2007: "Kierkegaard's *Christian Discourses* on Upbuilding, Mildness, and Polemic: 'A Temple-Cleansing Celebration–and Then the Quiet,'" in Robert L. Perkins, ed., *International Kierkegaard Commentary: Christian Discourses* (Macon, Georgia: Mercer University Press, 2007) 143–63.

2011: "Søren Kierkegaard: Between Skepticism and Faith's Happy Passion," in Jennifer Hockenbery Dragseth, ed., *The Devil's Whore: Reason and Philosophy in the Lutheran Tradition. Studies in Lutheran History and Theology Series* (Minneapolis: Fortress, 2011) 115–22.

2012: "Hugh Ross Mackintosh: Kierkegaard as 'A Precursor of Karl Barth,'" in Jon Stewart, ed., *Kierkegaard Research: Sources, Reception, and Resources*, 21 vols. Volume 10: *Kierkegaard's Influence on Theology*, 2 tomes, Tome II: *Anglophone and Scandinavian Protestant Theology* (Burlington, VT: Ashgate, 2012) 85–103.

2013: "Foreword" to Warner M. Bailey, *The Self-Shaming God Who Reconciles: A Pastoral Response to Abandonment Within the Christian Canon.* (Eugene, OR: Pickwick, 2013).

Proceedings

2007: "Kierkegaard on the Universally Religious and the Specifically Christian as Resources for Interreligious Conversation," in Andrew J. Burgess, ed., *Kierkegaard and Religious Pluralism: Papers of the AAR Kierkegaard, Religion, and Culture Group, and the Søren Kierkegaard Society*, 83–10y. AAR 2007 Annual Meeting, San Diego. Eugene, OR: Wipf and Stock, 2007.

Reviews

1982: Vincent A. McCarthy, *The Phenomenology of Moods in Kierkegaard. International Journal for the Philosophy of Religion* 13: 192. Reprinted in *Søren Kierkegaard Newsletter No. 17* (October 1987) 10–11

1988: George Connell, *To Be One Thing: Personal Unity in Kierkegaard's Thought. Religious Studies Review* 14/3 (July) 233.

1988: Abraham H. Khan, *Salighed as Happiness?: Kierkegaard on the Concept Salighed. Religious Studies Review* 14/3 (July) 233.

1988: Robert L. Perkins, ed., *International Kierkegaard Commentary, Volume 8: The Concept of Anxiety. Critical Review of Books in Religion 1988*, pp. 382–84. Appeared also in *Philosophy of Religion* 24 (1988) 190–91.

1992: Richard H. Bell, ed., *The Grammar of the Heart: Thinking with Kierkegaard and Wittgenstein: New Essays in Moral Philosophy and Theology. Journal of the American Academy of Religion* LX/2 (Summer) 325–27.

1999: Martin J. Matustík and Merold Westphal, eds., *Kierkegaard in Post/Modernity*. Bloomington and Indianapolis: Indiana University Press, 1995. *Christian Scholar's Review* 28, no. 4 (Summer) 625–26.

2002: Jeremy S. Begbie, *Theology, Music and Time* (Cambridge: Cambridge University Press, 2000). *Modern Theology* 18:3 (July) 407–8.

2010: Jeremy S. Begbie, *Resounding Truth: Christian Wisdom in the World of Music* (Grand Rapids, Michigan: Baker Academic, 2007). *Modern Theology* 26:1 (January) 160–62.

2010: Edward S. Mooney, ed., *Ethics, Love, and Faith in Kierkegaard: Philosophical Engagements* (Bloomington and Indianapolis, Indiana: Indiana University Press, 2008). *Modern Theology* 26:4 (October) 682–84.

www.ingramcontent.com/pod-product-compliance
Lightning Source LLC
Chambersburg PA
CBHW061434300426
44114CB00014B/1679